Bernard Häring, C.Ss.R.

The Sacrament
of Reconciliation

 St Paul Publications

ACKNOWLEDGEMENT

As for many of my previous publications, my heartfelt thanks go again to Sister Gabrielle L. Jean of the Gray Nuns and to Mrs. Josephine Ryan for their help in typing and editing this book, and for their constructive suggestions about the questions to be treated.

Bernard Häring, C.Ss.R.

St Paul Publications
Middlegreen, Slough SL3 6BT

Copyright © Bernard Häring, C.Ss.R.
Nihil obstat: M. J. Byrnes ssp stl
Imprimatur: F. Diamond vg, Northampton
                January 10, 1980.
First published in Great Britain February 1980
Printed by the Society of St Paul, Slough
ISBN 0 85439 168 1

St Paul Publications is an activity of the priests and brothers of the Society of St Paul who promote the christian message through the mass media.

Soc. of empowerment, and "break thru"
enablement   + ongoing creation

INTRODUCTION

THE Sacrament of Reconciliation — or, as it was called in past centuries, the Sacrament of Penance — is a precious pearl. Happy the person who discovers its full beauty! For too long it has been hidden in ossified traditions and prejudices.

Today, many are beginning to discover its true dimensions. It is a sacrament of liberation, of Easter joy, of praise, a sacrament for healing hurt memories and restoring healthy relationships, a sacrament of ongoing conversion, of coming closer to God and restoring the unity of his family. In it we experience the blessedness of those who praise the Lord for having taken upon himself sorrow, suffering and death to make us free again. It leads us to the Eucharist through humble gratitude. And through it we learn to praise God for his saving justice, for the gift of reconciliation and peace, by becoming instruments of peace, ministers of reconciliation, and co-workers for the cause of all-embracing justice.

The Sacrament of Reconciliation demands ongoing conversion, sorrow for our sins and a humble confession of them. However, this is gladdening news, for through sorrow the Lord renews our hearts in the praise of his mercy, and through humble confession we come back to the healing truth. The crisis of this sacrament can be overcome only through an increase in gratitude that discovers the wealth of this gift which the Lord gave to his church on the day of his resurrection.

The intention of this small book is to help priests as confessors, and penitents and the faithful as people who know that they are in need of healing and who share Christ's healing mission, to understand better the Sacrament of Penance. Concelebrating it then, with renewed awareness of a gracious God, they can enrich the world by its grace.

PART ONE

THE MAIN PERSPECTIVES

1. I SHALL PRAISE THE LORD

> "Happy the person whose fault is forgiven, whose sin
> is put away! Happy is he who knows that the
> Lord lays no guilt to his account and in his spirit
> there is no deceit. When I refused to confess my
> sin my body wasted away with moaning all day
> long. For day and night thy hand was heavy upon
> me, the sap in me dried up as in summer drought.
> Then I declared my sin. I did not conceal my guilt.
> I said, 'With sorrow I will confess my disobedience
> to the Lord'; then thou didst remit the penalty of
> my sin. So every faithful heart shall pray to thee . . .
> Rejoice in the Lord and be glad, you righteous
> people, and sing aloud, all men of upright heart"
> (*Psalm* 32).

PAGAN religions and ritualistic people of all religions
have tried to placate God by scrupulous performance of
rituals and an accurate pronunciation of magic formulas.
But the good news of Christ, already prepared in the
Old Testament, is that God himself takes the initiative
and reconciles us. The apostle of the Gentiles, speaking
of God's reconciling action and the apostolic ministry,
writes: "From first to last this has been the work of
God. He has reconciled us to himself through Christ,
and he has enlisted us in the service of reconciliation.
What I mean is that God was in Christ, reconciling
the world to himself, no longer holding men's misdeeds
against them, and that he has entrusted us with the
message of reconciliation" (2 Cor 5:18-19).

The Sacrament of Reconciliation (or Penance) is liturgy, praise. It brings to fulfilment the liturgy of Israel which was an ongoing praise of God's faithfulness that showed itself above all by mercy. In his mercy he restored the fidelity of the people who, after all their sins, had no merits of their own. Paul is particularly fitted for this ministry of reconciliation by the unique way in which he experienced the undeserved grace of being called to friendship with Christ and entrusted with the ministry.

We do not go to confess our sins because we think that God is a threatening God; we confess them praising his mercy. But this praise, this liturgy is indispensable. God, gracious as he is, is God, and he grants his gifts only to those who acknowledge them as undeserved. That is what we do when we confess our sins. We are showing our trust in God, a trust that, in itself, is praise. This trust enables us to face our shortcomings, our faults and sins, and to speak out sincerely.

It is this confession, this speaking out in public confession or before a brother in Christ (who knows as well or better than we do that he too is in need of God's mercy) that is a liberating experience. To speak of our sins can be, of itself, a frustrating, humiliating experience; but if we do it together in praise of God's mercy, assured of his healing and liberating power, then it is an event of trust and of liberation from anguish.

We come to the Father and meet there as brothers and sisters to praise him for his mercy and to confess our sins to the praise of his name, because we know of his compassionate love. "I shall go to my Father and say . . .". We go to the Father confessing that by our own merit we are not worthy to be called his children; yet we dare to say, "Father . . . dear Father". We say it united with Christ who alone can entitle us to call the all-holy God our Father. The realisation that God is in heaven, the Holy One, and we on earth, creatures and even sinners, does not diminish the joy of our

8

expression, "Abba, our Father". Rather, it brings this prayer into the truth that it is an undeserved gift to be able to honour God as our Father, the Father of our Lord Jesus Christ who has come to set us free from sin, free from anguish, free from guilt complex, free for trust and praise.

Through our trusting prayer and humble confession we honour God, confessing our faith in him who is holy and at the same time merciful. We confess our sins because we know that his saving justice means peace, healing, liberation. We are no better than other sinners, just as Israel was no better than other nations. The Israelites praised God for liberating Israel whenever she humbly and trustfully called upon his name and recognised him as Liberator. We too, confessing our sins, praise the Father for the redeeming and liberating action in the death and resurrection of Christ. Thus we give honour to God and begin to adore him "in spirit and truth".

Ernst Bloch thinks that only atheism can preserve man's dignity and honour. He refuses to acknowledge a God, an "Above". He thinks that man, with his dreams and with the power of matter, can guarantee humanity a forward thrust. Real atheism, the ultimate atheism, is the refusal to acknowledge anything as gift. When man also refuses to acknowledge what others do and are for him, he is then a totally unreconciled being who can hope for "solutions" only by hatred and struggle.

Perhaps Ernst Bloch has never really understood what God, the "Above" means: the giver of all good gifts. By granting his gifts to man, God enriches him. By offering him forgiveness and healing, he restores man's dignity and calls him to be co-actor and co-artist in the ongoing history of justice and peace, of true humanness and brotherhood.

In the communal celebration of penance and reconciliation, the priest and the whole community join in humble acknowledgement of their sinfulness and in common praise of the one God and Father. In the ancient church, the bishop who prayed for forgiveness (a sacramental prayer) praised God. During the reconciliation service of Holy Thursday, the Bishop of Rome sang the great preface on the mercy and reconciling action of God throughout history.

In the Sacrament of Reconciliation, each of us brings his or her history of grace and sinfulness into the great history of God's redeeming and healing action. The confessor and the penitent join their hearts and voices in gratitude. Until the twelfth century the absolution was given in the form of an official prayer of supplication leading to praise. It is one with the penitent's humble confession, joined by a priest who also confesses his sins. Thus absolution as proclamation of God's mercy and healing power, and confession followed by praise are one. Priest and penitent experience an absolute solidarity as sinners who accept their vocation to become saint-penitents, holy people. They are one in the praise of God.

*   *   *

Lord, I thank you,
for you do not want to see me ashamed
and rejected at the last judgement;
You want to free me from my guilt
in a very kindly way.
You do not confront me
with a ruthless or meticulous human judge
but with a brother and friend
who has the mission to help me
to know better your healing love
and to join me in the praise of your mercy.
I pray to you: help the confessors
to be, for me and for others,
a true image of your kindness and mercy,
so that we may praise you together. Amen.

10

2. STOP BLAMING YOUR TROUBLES ON ONE ANOTHER

> "Be patient, my brothers, until the Lord comes. You must be patient and stout-hearted, for the coming of the Lord is near. My brothers and sisters, do not blame your troubles on one another or you will fall under judgement and there stands the Judge at the door. But the Lord is full of pity and compassion . . . Is anyone among you in trouble? He should turn to prayer. Is anyone in good health? He should sing praises . . . Confess your sins to one another and pray for one another, and then you will be healed. A good person's prayer is powerful and effective" (James 5: 7-16).

THE story of Adam and Eve (of sinful man and woman) is our story. Adam and Eve were given by God to each other as equals, as gifts to each other. But when they refused to receive themselves and one another as gifts of God, taking from God the honour and using their freedom as a stolen freedom, they began to excuse themselves for their troubles by blaming each other. "The man said, 'The woman you have joined to me, she gave me fruit from the tree and I ate'. Then the Lord God said to the woman, 'What is this that you have done?' The woman said, 'The serpent tricked me'" (Gen 3: 12-43).

There is no super-Satan as in Zarathustra's religion, but only a miserable serpent, yet it suffices to hang one's own faults around its neck. Man, when he rebels against God, begins to despise woman, yet she suffices as scapegoat on whom to hang his own faults. Unreconciled people who do not confess their sins before God and before each other will always try to excuse and to absolve themselves by accusing others and degrading them. Thus they fall ever more into the abyss.

11

Our confession of sins before God and the priest, a brother in Christ, is truthful and earnest if we then also have the courage to accept our fault and acknowledge it before those whom we have grieved and to whom we have given a bad example. The Sacrament of Reconciliation as praise of God's mercy becomes "adoration in spirit and truth" by the courage to confess humbly and thus to stop accusing others. By acknowledging our fault we restore truthful, healthy relationships.

This is very different from mere ritualism wherein one wants to perform a kind of magic ritual by confessing in a dark confessional to an unknown priest in order to avoid taking one's own accountability for the fault. But if one wants to confess, praising God's mercy, and if the priest then has the courage sometimes to tell his penitent. "What you have confessed is also to a great extent my difficulty", the penitent will find the courage to accept his own responsibility in daily life and to ask forgiveness instead of blaming his troubles on others.

The Sacrament of Penance as we know it today is divinely instituted, but its special form arises from various beginnings and traditions. We have to distinguish thoroughly between the "Canoncal Penance" imposed for gravely scandalous sins since the first centuries and, on the other hand, the spontaneous confession of sins to the praise of God's mercy.

The Canonical Penance had a dimension of judgement and demanded reparation for the grave scandal, but confession to the praise of God's mercy is mainly the experience of Christ's healing power. This kind of confession probably began in the apostolic times through the experience of fraternal correction about which James speaks in chapter 5, quoted above. James may also have had in mind the official prayer of the elders of the community for forgiveness.

A clear text on fraternal correction is Galatians 6:2. We remember that the letter to the Galatians is Paul's great message of true liberty and liberation in

Christ. Fraternal correction is a sign of freedom in mutuality and saving solidarity.

Paul helps us to discern between the harvest of the Spirit visible in love, joy, peace, kindness, goodness, gentleness and so on, and on the other hand, the harvest of an ingrained egotism rooted in one's whole thinking and constantly increased by collective egotisms. Paul's message is that, in Christ, we are set free for that freedom which allows the Spirit to bring forth in us the harvest of goodness, justice, peace.

It is in this context that Paul proposes mutual encouragement and fraternal correction as a sign of solidarity in Christ. "We must not be conceited, challenging one another to rivalry, jealous of one another. If someone should do something wrong, my brothers and sisters, on a sudden impulse, you who are endowed with the Spirit must set him right again very gently. Look to yourself, each one of you; you may be tempted too. Help one another to carry this heavy load, and in this way you will fulfil the law of Christ" (Gal 5:26-6:2).

As long as we allow our selfish self to join with the collective selfishness around us, we will be conceited, jealous and tempted to project our troubles on one another. But if we allow the Spirit of Christ to guide us, then we confess our sins and help each other with mutual encouragement.

Fraternal correction will be neither condescending nor harsh blaming. On the contrary, healing can only be offered very gently and in full awareness that we, too, need the healing power of Christ and, time and again, encouragement and correction from our brothers and sisters. This healing event is possible only if we join in the praise of God's mercy.

The eighteenth chapter of the gospel of Matthew gives us deep insights about the Sacrament of Penance and, above all, about fraternal correction as a visible sign of the Lord's meeting us with his healing power through saving solidarity. "If your brother commits a sin, go and take the matter up with him, strictly between yourselves. If he listens to you, you have won your brother over" (Mt 18:15). Jesus speaks of the readiness to forgive our brothers not only seven times but even seventy times seven" (Mt 18:22). This means unlimited willingness to forgive and to heal. The experience of the Lord's forgiveness, and a grateful memory of all he has forgiven us enable us to offer gentle and effective mutual help, encouragement and correction.

In the same context, the Lord speaks of the power of shared prayer. "Again I tell you this: if two of you agree on earth about any request you have to make, that request will be granted by my heavenly Father. For where two or three have met together in my name, I am there among them" (Mt 18:19-20). The mutual confession and shared prayer for forgiveness is a sign of being gathered in the Lord's name. This prayer is effective, pleasing to God if it comes from humble and contrite hearts joined in the confession of sins and in the praise of God's mercy.

In the thirteenth century, Albert the Great, Thomas Aquinas and other great doctors of the church synthesised a long-standing tradition which held that confession even to a lay person has a share in the Sacrament of Reconciliation. There are certain conditions, however: that correction is offered very gently and humbly, that the one in need finally accepts it in humility, and that they join in the prayer for forgiveness and in the praise of God's mercy, recognising that forgiveness is God's gift. This is still the vision of the Oriental churches. People may go spontaneously to a holy man or woman to confess their sins and to ask for the good person's prayer. Lay people, however, were not and are not entitled to celebrate the sacrament liturgically.

There is some new dimension in confession before the authorised priest. There, the priest and the penitent pray in a very special way in union with the whole church. The priest proclaims the Lord's forgiveness officially, liturgically, in the name of the successors of the apostles and in the name of the whole church.

Since the first centuries, people have gone spontaneously to priests to confess those sins that were not submitted to Canonical Penance, for they knew that priests were chosen from those endowed by the Spirit, and that the church implored for them in a special way the power of the Holy Spirit. We remember also the words of the risen Lord, spoken in a solemn moment: "Receive the Holy Spirit. If you forgive any person's sins, they stand forgiven; if you pronounce them unforgiven they remain" (Jn 20:22-23).

We should not consider side-by-side fraternal correction and confession before the priest as exclusive. Rather, they complement each other. A genuine experience of saving solidarity and fraternal encouragement and correction gives us a better understanding of the Sacrament of Reconciliation in a liturgical setting. And conversely, in celebrating the sacrament more truthfully and vitally, we rediscover the meaning and value of fraternal correction, with its shared prayer for forgiveness and shared praise of the Lord's mercy.

Revitalising the spirit and practice of fraternal correction and encouragement can help to overcome the crisis of the Sacrament of Reconciliation. The two together — but each in its own way — are blessed means to bring us closer to that freedom for which Christ has set us free. We stop blaming our troubles on others, stop excusing ourselves by accusing others. Liberated from conceit and jealousy, we help each other to discover our inner resources and continue on our road towards holiness, in mutual trust and in shared praise of the Lord's mercy, made visible in mutual understanding and encouragement.

*   *   *

Lord Jesus,
When you met sinners, you gave them trust.
When you said, "Sin no more",
you had already told them, "Your sins are forgiven".
You corrected the faults of your apostles
but in a way that they felt your friendship even more,
and desired to become more worthy of it.
Let me receive kind and helpful correction
and encouragement through your friends,
and learn to offer it to others who need it. Amen.

3. HEALING HURT MEMORIES

"Remember me, Lord, when thou showest favour to thy people; look upon me when thou savest them, that I may see the prosperity of thy chosen, rejoice in thy nation's joy and exult with thy own people.

"We have sinned like our forefathers, we have erred and done wrong. Our fathers in Egypt took no account of thy marvels, they did not remember thy many acts of faithful love, but in spite of all, they rebelled by the Red Sea. Yet the Lord delivered them for his name's sake and so made known his mighty power . . .

"Deliver us, O Lord, our God, and gather us in from among the nations, that we may give thanks to thy holy Name and make thy praise our pride.

"Blessed be the Lord, the God of Israel from everlasting to everlasting; and let all the people say, 'Amen'.

"O praise the Lord" (Psalm 106).

THE examination of conscience before the Lord and in the context of the Sacrament of Reconciliation, where the minister of Christ solemnly proclaims God's forgiveness and praises God's healing powers, has a purifying and healing influence on our memories. People who tend to excuse themselves by accusing others tend also to develop deranged memories. They will constantly remember and remind others of the hurts these others have done them. They will be ever angry and bitter because others did not honour their majesties.

The Sacrament of Reconciliation has to be seen in the context of the Resurrection. Recalling our sins in this context of all that God has done for us restores health to our memories. The remembrance of all that he has done throughout history, and the acknowledgement

17

of all the good that we have received and are receiving from God and from others develops a healthy memory. And this healthy memory allows and promotes healthy relationships. This is an essential part of redemption, of the liberty and health that Christ wants to grant us.

To speak of sin only for the sake of sin is sinful talk. To remember sins solely in their sinfulness can only hurt more. But to remember our sins in the context of a grateful memory, praising God for all that he has done for us, and to remember them in the examination of conscience with the one purpose of praising his mercy in liturgy and life: this makes sense. It is a healing event. If our memories are healed by the praise of God's mercy and assurance of his forgiveness, then remembrance of our own sins will make us compassionate, more understanding, more ready to forgive the sins of others. Also in this context, we can remember in a more wholesome way the injustices we have suffered, for we remember them only to honour and praise the Lord by healing forgiveness. Thus our own hurts and the hurt memories of others will be healed, and all the negative things will be brought home into the constructive, redemptive power of divine healing and forgiveness.

*　　*　　*

Lord, I thank you
> for the Eucharist and all your sacraments.
> In them you remind us of all your blessings upon us,
> and create in us a grateful memory.
> When I go to confession, help me to remember,
> along with my sins, all the marvels you have done
>> for us.
> And when others offend me,
> I will never remember the offence
> without remembering also that you have forgiven me
>> all my sins
> and call me to heal hurt memories. Amen.

4. YOUR UNIQUE NAME AND THE GAME OF THE SUPEREGO

"In Christ Jesus the life-giving law of the Spirit has set you free from the law of sin-solidarity and death. What the law could never do, because our lower nature robbed it of all potency, God has done: by sending his own Son in a form like our sinful nature, and as a sacrifice for sin, he has passed judgement against sin within that very nature, so that the commandment of the law may find fulfilment in us, whose conduct, no longer under the control of our lower nature, is directed by the Spirit.

"Those who live on the level of our lower nature have their outlook formed by it, and that spells death; but those who live on the level of the Spirit have the spiritual outlook, and that is life and peace. For the outlook of the lower nature is enmity with God; it is not subject to the law of God; indeed it cannot be: those who live on such level cannot possibly please God.

"But that is not how you live. You are on the spiritual level, if only God's Spirit dwells within you; and if a man does not possess the Spirit of Christ, he is no Christian. But if Christ is dwelling within you, then although the body is a dead thing because you sinned, yet the spirit is life itself because you have been justified. Moreover, if the Spirit of him who raised Jesus from the dead dwells within you, then God who raised Christ Jesus from the dead will also give new life to your mortal bodies through his indwelling Spirit.

"It follows, my friends, that our lower nature has no claim upon us" (*Romans* 8:2-12).

IN the Sacrament of Reconciliation the Lord calls each of us by our own name, and he calls us to meet him as friend, as the Thou of our I. To receive all the peace and blessing of this sacrament it is very important to distinguish the Thou-I encounter between Christ and one's self in the community of believers from the devious game of the superego.

One of the most important contributions of humanistic psychology is the distinction between the superego on the level of the not-yet-developed conscience and to its integration as a socialising factor on the level of a true conscience and, on the other hand, the superego as an agent of impersonal powers, of collective egotism in the person who has not reached a higher level of conscience or who did not integrate at all the dynamics of the superego into the growth of a true conscience.

On the first level of development of a child's personality, the superego is strongly operative. The child learns to keep clean or to be quiet through the reaction of the parents or caretakers. His ego (up to now and still mostly superego) reacts to approval and disapproval, to praise and blame, to reward and punishment. The child is in dire need of approval. He lives by approval and is shaken and threatened by disapproval. Therefore training can appeal to this need. But if parents only *train* the child, acting like moralists and policemen, then the child's true ego — the ego that perceives unselfish, abiding love, the ego that can trust and can be sure of being loved beyond temporary disapproval — will not develop.

The superego as the agent of order and discipline can be used for the profit of the caretaker, and can be overused so that the true self has little chance to develop. However, the superego as the agent of order and discipline, of coherence and role-expectation, can be integrated as a socialising factor if the prevailing relationship is one of trust, of mutual self-bestowal, of being-with and being-for each other.

The psychological findings about the game of the superego can help us to understand at least one aspect of the present crisis of the Sacrament of Penance. I want to explain some of the dimensions of this crisis.

If a child is forced to make his first confession and

to go to regular confession at an age when his ego-strength does not yet prevail over the superego, and if the training imposes a stereotyped list of sins according to the principle of order and discipline, and especially if the priest acts as an interrogator and a controller instead of one who shares trust in the Lord and the Good News of being accepted totally by the Lord: if all these coincide, there is a great danger that later, in adolescence and in adult years, confessions will remain mainly on the level of the superego. Then confession will be seen as a duty and a meeting with a controller representing the divine judge or divine policeman. If, later, the young person or the adult person outgrows this system and does not come to a better understanding of the Sacrament of Penance, he will unconsciously or consciously abandon it.

From the very beginning it is important that the child comes to a correct understanding of the Sacrament of Penance; that it is not seen as a kind of interrogation or method of control. He should not learn to give a complete catalogue of sins but to speak with a friend who makes visible the Divine Friend, Christ, who accepts the child with all the weaknesses and the need to grow.

Lawrence Kohlberg, an authority on the psychology of the development of conscience, is convinced that many people, especially in our culture, never outgrow the level of order and discipline or the level of "nice girl", "good boy". For them, the Sacrament of Penance fulfils a need of the superego. They will confess their sins in order to be "right again" before the law. However, it will not help them to overcome their sins: the moment their thought of the controller or the judge is not present, they will fall back. Then once more the powerful superego will torture them with guilt feelings that time and again will be seemingly "relieved" by regular confession.

This is not at all what Christ meant by the Sacrament of Reconciliation. Jesus means a personal encounter, restoring to the sinner or the striving person a sense of dignity, helping the person to trust and to discover his or her true self and its strengths. Therefore, in the Sacrament of Penance, we will not confess sins just in view of law and order but will tell our life situation with its ups and downs, in view of the "law of grace", in view of our concrete capacities and the many opportunities open to us for doing good. And, having missed some of them, we ask forgiveness and ask for the grace to become more alert, more vigilant and more discerning.

We do not confess our sins just to be aligned with law and order but rather to live a graced relationship, a relationship of trust with the gracious Lord, in readiness to grow and desiring to be healed from all selfishness and to reach out for healthy relationships with fellowmen and with self.

Thus, through the Sacrament of Penance, we come gradually to know better the unique name by which the Lord calls us. We begin to realise that we are called to be partners of the Lord who wants to make each of us a wonderful masterpiece. We are becoming co-artists, discovering our own inner resources and the needs of others. We realise that the Lord wants us as co-actors in the ongoing history of redemption. And we accept with renewed courage and zest this our vocation.

If we celebrate the Sacrament of Reconciliation in this dimension, then we channel the energies of the superego in the direction of genuine co-responsibility. The prevailing concern will not be whether we are approved, praised, rewarded or punished, but whether we please the Lord and are co-actors in the wonderful work of redemption, liberation, growth towards solidarity. We are becoming more concerned to love and to affirm other than to be approved by everyone.

Then we shall no longer be like a "pillar of salt", looking backward, but will participate in the FORWARD, the God of history who gives us freedom to grow, to have trust and to cooperate creatively in the ongoing renewal for a more humane society and for healthier relationships.

*　　*　　*

Lord, I thank you
　　for the gift of faith and for your friendship.
　　You call me by my unique name,
　　just as on the Easter day you called Mary Magdalen
　　　　by her name,
　　and she recognised you.
　　You guide us by the gift of your Spirit
　　who opens our hearts to many opportunities
　　to promote the kingdom of your love, peace and
　　　　justice,
　　and to help our neighbour.
　　Lord, call me!
　　Draw me to your heart
　　so that I may no longer be a slave
　　looking for reward
　　or fearing punishment and disapproval
　　from the powerful or the crowd. Amen.

5.   THE EXODUS AND THE KINGDOM

"What Christ has done is to set us free . . . Do not turn your freedom into licence for your selfish self, but be servants to one another in love, for the whole law can be summed up in a single commandment, 'Love your neighbour as yourself'. But if you go on fighting one another, tooth and nail, all you can expect is mutual self-destruction.

"I mean this: if you are guided by the Spirit you will not fulfil the desires of your ingrained selfishness. That selfish self sets its desires against the Spirit, while the Spirit fights against it. They are in conflict with one another, so that what we will to do we cannot do. But if you are led by the Spirit you are no longer a slave of law.

"Anyone can see the kind of behaviour that belongs to the ingrained selfishness: fornication, impurity and indecency; idolatry and sorcery; quarrels, a contentious temper, envy, fits of rage, selfish ambitions, dissensions, party intrigues and jealousies; drinking bouts, orgies, and the like. I warn you as I warned you before, that those who behave in such ways will never inherit the kingdom of God.

"But the harvest of the Spirit is love, joy, peace, patience, kindness, goodness, fidelity, gentleness and self-control. No law stands against these attitudes. And those who belong to Jesus have crucified their selfish self, its passions and desires. If the Spirit is the source of our life, let the Spirit also direct our course" (*Galatians* 5).

THE Sacrament of Reconciliation is a sacrament of conversion, of turning away from the bondage of sin and turning heart and mind and conduct to God. The Bible speaks of conversion frequently, both on the individual and collective levels, under the paradigm of exodus. This means a leaving-behind, a being-set-free from the bondage of sin and setting out with a clear direction to the kingdom of God. Each time we celebrate the Sacrament of Reconciliation, we should courageously enter into the great history of exodus, becoming pilgrims on the road to the kingdom of God.

We look at Abraham, at Moses and the Israelites, and at Jesus. Abraham, called by God, leaves behind an old culture with many ideologies, a superior culture but also an arrogant one. Becoming a pilgrim, setting out for the country the Lord has promised, and accepting the risks implied in his trust in God, he gains a new freedom. New horizons of faith open up to him.

Moses and the Israelites leave behind the bondage of Egypt, leaving behind also the fleshpots and a certain security and stability granted even to slaves. They are setting out because Moses trusts in divine promises. He believes in liberation and liberty, in view of a God-given covenant that would unite his people as a people of God, and make them free in cooperative responsibility before their God.

Jesus lives the exodus anew and in its fullness. He leaves behind external security, wealth, comfort and earthly glory. He resists the prevailing messianic expectation that looked for a kingdom of success, of power, of war and victories. He disallows any abuse of religion for individual or collective aggrandisement. His whole life is an exodus, a leaving-behind. He finds the fullness of life in the word of God while living in the desert and in proclaiming the good news to all who will listen, until, driven out from Jerusalem by the rulers of his people, he completes the final exodus on Mount Calvary. His painful exodus brings the kingdom of God, a kingdom of love, of true freedom, trust and peace.

The Sacrament of Reconciliation is a call to creative detachment, a call to put to death all forms of selfishness, individual and collective, and thus to follow Christ in his exodus on the road of his cross.

In the epistle to the Galatians, Paul shows the exodus from legalism and from all kinds of ritualistic securities, into the reign of true freedom. He clearly unmasks the kind of conduct that obstructs true freedom and therefore has to be left behind. The goal of this exodus is the promised land that Paul describes as the harvest of the Spirit, a new life in the love of God, wherein we join God in his love for his people and become co-actors in his kingdom of peace and joy. It is the kingdom of the Servant Messiah who does not come to overpower others but to draw them to the Father by his gentleness, kindness, goodness.

Each of us needs an exodus from our own ingrained, accumulated selfishness. But we need also a joint exodus from all the ideologies and kinds of behaviour that enslave us or threaten to enslave us in today's world. We leave behind the many misunderstandings of freedom in an individualistic culture. There, we are always tempted to seek our freedoms to the detriment of friendship, fidelity, social justice. We leave behind the freedom that is stolen, and come into the homeland of true freedom, receiving freedom ever anew as a gift of God and using it so that we can return it to God as expression of gratitude by promoting the freedom of all.

We leave behind the stereotype slogans, superficiality, distraction. We liberate ourselves from an industry of recreation that does not allow us recollection or profound meditation. This exodus leads us to our true self and opens for us the door to salvation truth.

We leave behind a self-centred, success-oriented society that cares more for having, possessing and using than for being and for loving. We leave behind a consumerism with all its artificial needs in order to discover the higher needs of our true self and of our neighbours.

We leave behind the ideologies of violence so frequently represented in our TV programmes. In the sight of Christ, the Servant of God, we liberate ourselves from the destructive ideology that the normal solution to conflict is violence, anger, fighting, and set out for the promised land of gentleness, mutual understanding, grateful reconciliation.

We leave behind the superficial culture that looks for drugs as a means of resolving normal frustration; and we leave behind a culture of boredom which unavoidably is the share of people who think they can purchase "happiness" in the discount centres. We leave behind drunkenness and the abuse of nicotine. And it is worthwhile to leave all this behind, for we are setting out for the kingdom of true joy and freedom in the Lord.

We are leaving behind the non-culture that offers cheap sex for consumers, where persons destroy each other, hurt each other or degrade each other. We leave behind all these ideologies that now want to justify and even to glorify homosexuality, extra-marital sex, marital infidelity. We are setting out for the kingdom of goodness, fidelity, reliability, mutual respect, joint search for greater truth and surer justice.

We leave behind resentment, all feeling of hatred and enmity, and learn from Christ benevolence, kindness, true friendship.

We leave behind sloth, inertia, all kinds of security complexes, and set out for the homeland of responsibility and co-responsibility, in commitment to the great task of peace and justice. We take the risk of a true life in the light of Christ, the Redeemer of the world.

We leave behind the many bondages of embodied selfishness. However, we do NOT leave behind the world of our brothers and sisters. Rather, we seek the exodus in order to return to them as reconciled people, to join hands and hearts for building a homeland for justice, for peace, for gentleness and co-responsibility.

We have the courage to undertake this exodus because we have Christ as our leader and our strength. He grants us a share in his freedom to love, his joy and peace: he promises us his Spirit, the giver of all good gifts. Therefore, with trust in the Holy Spirit, we accept our being called to holiness, to a life that produces abundantly the harvest of the Spirit, although this calling implies a strenuous battle against everything that opposes the kingdom of God.

If we open our eyes and hearts to the promised land of a life guided by the Holy Spirit, a life with Christ, we shall not hesitate to leave behind the alien land, the land of bondage, of selfishness, and the miserable "flesh-pots" it can offer us.

* * *

Lord, I thank you for having revealed to us
 the true nature and the attractive picture
 of the kingdom of God.
 This is your wonderful way of making it easier for us
 to leave behind whatever opposes the heavenly
 kingdom.
 You let us feel the beauty of your friendship;
 therefore I have the courage to pray not only
 "Grant to me whatever leads me closer to you"
 but also, "Take from me whatever hinders me on the
 way to you". Amen.

6. BLESSED ARE THE SORROWFUL

"Lord, thou hast been gracious to thy land and turned the tide of Jacob's fortunes. Thou hast forgiven the guilt of thy people and put away all their sins.

"Wilt thou not give us new life, that thy people may rejoice in thee?

"O Lord, show us thy true love and grant us thy deliverance.

"Let me hear the words of the Lord: are they not words of peace, peace to his people and his loyal servants, peace to all who turn to him and trust in him?

"Deliverance is near to those who worship him, so that glory may dwell in our land. Love and fidelity have come together; justice and peace join hands. Fidelity springs up from earth and justice looks down from heaven" (*Psalm* 85).

AT the heart of the beatitudes is the promise, "How blest are the sorrowful; they shall find consolation" (Mt 5:4).

In the Sacrament of Reconciliation, gratefully and tearfully we remember the Lord's sorrow, his passion and death caused by our sins. It is painful to remember that we were there to cause him such great suffering. But it is consoling that the Lord suffered not with hatred and resentment but because he still loved us and did everything to draw us to his heart. So we praise the suffering and death of Christ, and praise the Father for having raised him up to new life.

Joining Christ in his sorrow and joining him in the same compassionate love for all, we open ourselves to the consolation of the Paschal Mystery. Sin causes frustrating pain. And if it is not repented of it causes distorted and destructive memories The pain it causes has no positive value, but by repenting we open ourselves to a new birth, a rebirth and a new freedom. Our sorrow, however, must be truly a participation in the sorrow of Christ. It must not be self-centred.

The sorrow blessed by the Lord is not just shame for having made a bad impression, nor is it the torture of the superego that is hurt in its constant striving for saving face. It is the sorrow of our true self standing before the Lord. Our tears are genuine because we are pained by the thought that our sins have increased the collective selfishness in the world, the solidarity of perdition. Our refusing to do the good that was at hand has decreased the wealth of peace and goodness on earth.

Our sorrow is blessed if it leads us to the truth and we confess that the Lord's law, the law of love and justice, peace and truth, is holy, good, just and spiritual, and that we were unjust, ungrateful.

It is painful to realise that we are in need of conversion, a much deeper and ongoing conversion; yet in the experience of our sorrow in the presence of the Lord, we are consoled by the realisation that conversion is possible. And we are further consoled to know that we have the Lord's promises if we are willing to be thoroughly converted, if we accept the Lord's call to a holy life as holy penitents.

Sorrow that is in union with the Lord's passion and death brings liberation and consolation to many. The remorse of conscience is transformed into purifying sorrow that detests our sins not just for the legitimate interest of our own salvation but even more for the salvation of all of humankind. The rebirth willed by the Lord and wrought by contrition is a rebirth for saving solidarity, for a renewed love of God and fellowmen.

The overflow of that rebirth in ongoing conversion

and wholesome sorrow is peace, joy, trust, and a serenity that communicates itself and helps others to believe that they, too, are called to consolation. Then, with us, they can accept the pain of sorrow and the struggle of ongoing conversion.

*   *   *

Lord, send forth your Spirit
   to cleanse us and to mould us.
   Even if I confess my sins before you
   and assure you of my contrition,
   I have to be afraid of my old selfish self.
   Self-pity or self-concern for a good image before
      others
   can hinder my reaching that blessed sorrow
   that alone can bring me closer to your blessed passion
      and death
   and to the power of your resurrection.
   Lord, grant to me and to all people a heart truly
      contrite! Amen.

7. DEEPENING OUR FUNDAMENTAL OPTION [1]

"With all the witnesses to faith around us like a cloud, we must throw off every encumbrance, every sin to which we cling, and run with resolution the race for which we are entered, our eyes fixed on Jesus, on whom faith depends from start to finish: Jesus who, for the sake of the joy that lay ahead of him, endured the cross, making light of its disgrace, and has taken his seat at the right hand of the throne of God . . .

"Aim at peace with all men, and a holy life, for without that, no one will see the Lord. Look to it that there is no one among you who forfeits the grace of God" (*Hebrews* 12).

TRADITIONAL doctrine has always emphasised the importance of the firm purpose of amendment. We have to see it as does the author of the epistle to the Hebrews: a wholehearted purpose to strive towards a holy life. We can see it also in today's reflections on the fundamental option. The individual purposes to avoid some evil, to abide by laws, are not workable and effective unless they become part of a fundamental option for the Lord.

Born into a christian community, there is already given an outline of the fundamental option for a christian life. The child, being the work of the good Creator, has more innate good than evil. However, we live in a world that is at the same time redeemed yet still under the burden of sin-solidarity. We have to make a clear fundamental option for saving solidarity in Christ.

The child who wants to love Christ and to please him has already the proper fundamental option although

[1] For a more detailed treatment of "Fundamental Option" see Fr Häring's *Free and Faithful in Christ*, vol. 1, pp. 164-222, St Paul Publications, Slough, 1978.

it has to become deeper, broader, clearer, firmer. It has to take root in the whole character and the whole style of life. Only in the course of growth and ongoing conversion will our fundamental option be consolidated. Each celebration of the Eucharist and, equally and particularly, the celebration of the Sacrament of Reconciliation, should deepen, broaden and clarify our fundamental option. It has to reach for that depth where the fundamental option has its centre, where the Holy Spirit vivifies our spirit.

Mortal sin is a fundamental option for evil, a sin and attitude that contradicts in our very depths the commitment to Christ. If one has committed a mortal sin, it will manifest itself in the whole direction of decay, alienation, growing self-centredness, arrogance and the like. But if, after a sin, the Christian very soon or almost immediately experiences great sorrow and renews his fundamental option, his profound desire to please the Lord and to strive towards holiness, he can be morally sure that his sin was not a mortal one although it might well be a serious wound, a serious sickness, a dangerous weakening of the fundamental option. If, after each fault, we turn purposefully and most consciously to Christ, the Healer, in deep sorrow and in a sacramental encounter, we can hope that the distorting influence of sin is overcome and that our fundamental option can even be more consolidated.

We should make clearcut resolutions in order to fight systematically, by a positive, constructive approach, against our evil tendencies. But these concrete resolutions should be integrated in the overall resolve, the fundamental option as expressed in the epistle to the Hebrews, "To run with resolution the race for which we are entered . . . our eyes fixed on Jesus . . . and to aim at a holy life".

Some Christians today think that it is enough to go to confession only if they are sure of having committed a mortal sin. This is as unwise as delaying a visit to the physician until we are sure that he can grant a death certificate. We go to the Divine Physician immediately after each sin, with an act of sorrow, a firm purpose and great trust. We seek him more explicitly, more gratefully, more trustfully and more to the praise of his mercy by a celebration of the Sacrament of Reconciliation.

For discerning our own condition, a look at the overall direction of our life is most important. One may have committed serious faults because of old passions, habits, the negative influence of the environment, and yet in the overall direction one may be in the line of ascent, of growth, of ongoing conversion. But we all surely also need the Divine Healer to overcome difficulties and partial failures.

Much more serious is the situation of the person who, although not committing manifestly shocking sins, finds himself or herself on the path of increasing sloth, dissipation, self-centredness, in an ever more dangerous involvement in individual or group egotism. Here there is great doubt about whether the fundamental option is still for the Lord and his kingdom. The least one can do is to turn as earnestly as possible to the Divine Healer, and normally not just with acts of personal sorrow and humble prayer before God but by also accepting gratefully the offer of the Divine Physician to meet him intimately in the sacrament of healing forgiveness.

*   *   *

Lord, your love for us knows no bounds.
　　Therefore you have the right to ask for us
　　nothing less than a goodness without limit,
　　a radical resolution to seek in all things your glory
　　and to serve the cause of your kingdom.
　　By the fire of your Spirit, O Lord,
　　make me strong, able and courageous in your service.
　　Amen.

8. BECOMING ONE FAMILY

"I as a prisoner for the Lord's sake, I entreat you: As God has called you, live up to your calling. Be humble always and gentle, and patient too. Be forebearing with one another and full of love. Spare no effort to make fast with bonds of peace the unity which the Spirit gives. There is one body and one Spirit, as there is also one hope held out in God's call to you; one Lord, one faith, one baptism; one God and Father of all, who is over all, and through all and in all. But each of us has been given his gift, his due portion of Christ's bounty.

"Let us speak the truth in love; so shall we fully grow up into Christ. He is the head, and on him the whole body depends. Bonded and knit together by every constituent joint, the whole frame goes through the due activity of each part and builds itself up in love.

"Then throw off falsehood; speak the truth to each other; for all of us are parts of one body. If you are angry, do not let anger lead you into sin; do not let sunset find you still nursing it; leave no loophole for the devil.

"The thief must give up stealing, and instead work hard and honestly with his own hands so that he may have something to share with the needy . . . Be generous to one another, tender-hearted, forgiving one another as God in Christ forgave you" (*Ephesians* 4: 1-32).

GOD brings his salvation to us through his covenant. It is a covenant with the people, brought to completion in Christ who is solidarity incarnate. Christ died for all and thus calls all to unity and solidarity, "that all may be one". Therefore, conversion to God and coming closer to God is not possible without an ongoing conversion to the people of the covenant. We cannot meet God's love without joining him in his love for all his people.

The basic fundamental option is a choice between

solidarity in Christ, solidarity of salvation, as God wills, and on the other hand, solidarity of perdition. One who wants to be saved just for himself, unconcerned for the building up of God's family, unconcerned for the common good, is implicitly opting for solidarity in collective egotism, a solidarity of perdition. Therefore, if we want to consolidate our fundamental option for Christ who died for us all, by inner necessity, we must also consolidate our fundamental option for fraternal love and co-responsibility.

In examining our conscience, therefore, we consider the first commandment to love God with all our heart in the light of the great goal commandment, "Love each other as I have loved you" (Jn 15:12). We ask ourselves about personal relationships: are they healthy? . . . . are we appreciative? . . . respectful? . . . are we loving only those who can reward us or, as the Lord bids, loving especially those who cannot reward us?

But it doesn't suffice to consider only healthy person-to-person relationships, the I-Thou-we relationships, important as they are. We must also consider our responsibility for the common good, our participation in the socio-economic, cultural, political life. Are we faithful to the great peace mission of all Christians? Are we using all the gifts God has bestowed on us for the common good? It is not only sinful to do evil deeds; it is equally evil to bury one's own talents instead of using them for the common good. The unfaithful servant in the gospel is not accused of having done anything evil with his talent; he is condemned, or rather he condemns himself, by deciding not to use the one talent he had been given.

Christ has come not to build his own little family but to build up the one great family of God, calling to this family everyone created in the image and likeness of God. Hence our confession to the praise of God's mercy must lead to an ever more fruitful and ardent commitment to the common good, to the building up of the one body of Christ. This implies our renewed responsibility in private and public life. What can we do to promote justice, peace and honesty in social communications, and discernment in our political preferences?

*   *   *

Lord, I thank you
    for allowing us to call your Father, "our Father".
    I thank you for admitting me to your worldwide
        family
    with Mary, your mother and all the saints.
    Lord, make me grateful so that I may be
    a healthy, generous and helpful member
    of your great family,
    and thus repair for all my past negligence. Amen.

9. THE TRUTH THAT SETS US FREE

"If you dwell within the revelation I have brought you are indeed my disciples; you shall know the truth, and the truth will set you free . . . In very truth I tell you that everyone who commits sin is a slave. The slave has no permanent standing in the household, but the son belongs to it forever. If then the Son sets you free, you will indeed be free" (*John* 8:31-26).

"If we confess our sins, he is just, and may be trusted to forgive our sins and cleanse us from every kind of wrong; but if we say we have committed no sin, we make him out to be a liar, and then his word has no place in us. My children, in writing thus to you my purpose is that you should not commit sin. But should anyone commit a sin, we have an advocate to plead our cause with the Father, Jesus Christ, and he is just. He is himself the remedy for the defilement of our sins, not our sins only but the sins of all the world" (*1 John* 1:8-22).

THE great liberating truth is: "God is love". But this truth can be experienced as liberating only by those who are loving people who are seeking constantly to know the truth better and to put it better into practice. A part of the full truth is that the divine love still meets obstacles in our selfishness and our pride. But it is equally true that God wants to make us fully free by making us ever more ardent sharers of his love. His love is merciful and almighty.

When I confess my sins to a priest, a brother in Christ, then I profess my faith in a God who is love, mercy, healing forgiveness, a Reconciler: the God of peace. And I commit myself anew and evermore to this God of love and saving justice. He is the saving truth. But a part of my truth is that I am a sinner. Therefore I confess my sins before the all-merciful and all-holy God. I confess to a brother in Christ in order to assure my sincerity, to humble myself and to manifest my faith in saving solidarity. The freedom to confess my sins before my brothers and sisters is a God-given freedom, a freedom for fuller truth. If I refuse this truth about myself, or refuse to speak out this truth, then I may never be able to profess by my life the full truth that God is love and mercy and saving justice.

There are several sacraments of forgiveness. Above all others, there is Christ himself, THE great sacrament of healing forgiveness and saving truth. He is the One pleading our cause with the Father whenever we come to him in humble confession. In him, the church as a whole is called to be a visible and effective sign of reconciliation and healing forgiveness. That means nothing less than that each of us is called to be a kind of sacrament, making visible Jesus Christ, the all-embracing sacrament of healing forgiveness.

Only after having said this do we speak of the various sacraments insofar as they manifest and bring home to us the church's mission to be, in Jesus Christ, a sacrament of healing forgiveness.

Adult *Baptism* is acceptance of the call to total conversion. Those who are baptised with profound sorrow for their sins and who turn totally to Christ, are freed from their sins. They do not need a particular confession, since they have not yet sinned as members of the church. But the very reception of baptism is a confession of the need of redemption, the need and the willingness to undertake a total conversion to Christ.

Then there is the *Eucharist*. Each time we celebrate the Eucharist and praise the Lord Jesus Christ for the blood of the Covenant that he shed for our forgiveness, we profess our faith and acknowledge our sins and our need of further purification and healing forgiveness.

Further, there are the various forms of sacramental celebrations. Since antiquity, there were the *night vigils* in preparation for the great feasts. They were all seen in the light of the Eucharist, leading to fuller participation in the Eucharist "for the forgiveness of sins". There were the *Lenten celebrations* that ended with a solemn communal celebration of healing forgiveness and praise of the Lord's mercy. There, the whole church prayed, through her authorised ministers, for forgiveness and for that grace of conversion that makes all our life a truthful praise and thanksgiving to God.

Today, we are familiar with the *individual confession* and the *communal celebration*. They complete each other. Therefore we should seek the sacramental experience of healing forgiveness from time to time in both forms. The individual confession should be a special encounter with Christ and should evoke a very personal dialogue with the priest whenever we feel that we are threatened by decay or regression. We should go to individual confession in order to become more gratefully aware that the Lord calls each of us by our unique name to meet him and to be reassured by him in renewed friendship. But even then we should also be fully aware that this calling is a rallying call for all to greater unity, solidarity and co-responsibility.

The communal celebrations of reconciliation and healing forgiveness make us, individually and together, aware that each sin has a distinctive social (asocial) dimension. We are converted together to togetherness, to renewed co-responsibility. The communal celebration of healing forgiveness can and should open our eyes to our sins in the social realm and to the social dimension of each sin, thus committing each of us and the community as a whole to greater co-responsibility and solidarity in a more faithful commitment to the peace mission of all Christians. It not only prepares for a more fruitful reception of the Sacrament of Penance in individual confession — although this should not be overlooked — but the individual confession becomes more real and more fruitful when we join our efforts of conversion and the praise of God in a shared re-commitment. The communal celebration has its value in itself; it can become for many a very profound experi-ence of total conversion, a conversion to the Lord and to the people of the covenant.

Under certain conditions the communal celebration is followed by an explicit absolution. In this case, its full sacramental stature is recognised. In these important matters the discipline of the church must be observed. The church encourages communal celebrations every-where, but on many occasions, for the time being, explicit absolution is not allowed.

Let us not forget that, until the twelfth to thir-teenth century, the normal way to absolution was a fervent prayer of petition followed by a prayer leading into thanksgiving that implied a life that would hence-forth truthfully praise the Lord's mercy. If a whole com-munity prays fervently, with a humble and contrite heart and with great trust, then we cannot doubt the word of the Apostle James that the holy people's prayer is "powerful and effective" (James 5:16). What matters is that God's intention to convert us and to heal us, and to make us apostles of peace, becomes visible and shines through in the whole life of those who have participated in these celebrations.

*   *   *

Lord, I thank you
   for having revealed to us
   the full truth of your merciful love
   and, in this light, making us aware of our sinfulness
   while calling us to a holy life.
   Lord, grant me the courage to live as a holy penitent
   and to accept fully the truth
   that I am in need of further conversion.
   Make me free for your truth and through your truth.
   Amen.

10. GRATITUDE IS THE REMEDY

> "That day you will say: I give thanks to you,
> Yahweh; you were angry with me but your anger
> is appeased and you have given me consolation.
> See now, he is the God of my salvation but I trust
> now and have no fear, for Yahweh is my strength,
> my song; he is my salvation. And you will draw
> water joyfully from the springs of salvation.
>
> "Cry out for joy and gladness, for great in the
> midst of you is the Holy One of Israel"
> (*Isaiah* 12: 1-6).

IN the gospel of Saint Luke who, as physician, has special insight about healing and healing forgiveness, no story of healing and forgiveness ends without thanksgiving. Where there is no gratitude the gift is lost. Where there is gratitude the gifts of God are received, and being received more abundantly will bear a rich harvest.

In the new liturgy for the communal celebration of reconciliation, the ancient tradition is taken up again, and the place of thanksgiving is very important. In the personal confession there should be the spontaneous expression of this praise and thanksgiving on the part of the confessor and then especially on the part of the penitent.

It is a long-standing tradition that the confessor offers a remedy; we normally call it the "penance". But the real remedy is not so much penance in the sense of punishment and suffering as the expression of gratitude and the deepening of gratitude that prepares us also to renounce everything that hinders us on our way to God, and to accept all the sacrifices that are necessary for our conversion to God and to his commandment of all-embracing love and justice.

No penance will be effective if gratitude is not the main motive and main focus. Our penances should be more creative. Confessor and penitent together will find the most creative penance if they join minds and hearts in the praise of God's kindness and compassionate love. Then we will find penances that repair the damage our sins have caused. We will then become more compassionate and more generously involved in the cause for peace and justice in our own small world and in the larger one.

On occasions of extraordinary conversions after many years of alienation, I have repeatedly refrained from imposing or suggesting any specific penance. Instead, I have suggested that the penitent renew daily, over a certain period of time, the intention to make each day an expression of thanksgiving for God's goodness and healing forgiveness, and to determine every evening whether all his thoughts, words and deeds were in conformity with his basic motive of gratitude. In several cases penitents have written to me later or told me personally that they had first thought, "This is an altogether too easy-going confessor"; but after several weeks they realised how demanding but also how rewarding this remedy was.

It is in this way that the Sacrament of Reconciliation leads directly to its summit and source, the Eucharistic celebration. There we experience ever more that the Lord is gracious to those who praise him and are willing to offer thanks always and everywhere. The penitential rite at the beginning of the Mass should revitalise the gratitude we have experienced in the celebration of the Sacrament of Reconciliation, and should prepare us to be more willing to receive this sacrament to the praise of the Lord's mercy. Thus we learn to live our whole life in abiding gratitude, through healing forgiveness, compassion and generous dedication to the cause of the kingdom of God.

*   *   *

I thank you, Lord, for the gift of memory
   that allows me to recall all the good
   that you have done for me and given to me.
   I thank you for the Eucharist,
   the memorial of your death and resurrection
   and the reassurance of your promises.
   You teach us there
   to experience the liberating and saving power of
      gratitude.
   Had I been always grateful,
   I would have avoided the misery of sin.
   Now I thank you
   that in the sacrament of healing forgiveness
   you remind me kindly
   that gratitude is the remedy. Amen.

11. DIVINE ASSURANCE

"Jesus repeated, 'Peace be with you!' and said, 'As the Father has sent me, so I send you'. Then he breathed on them, saying, 'Receive the Holy Spirit'. If you forgive man's sins, they stand forgiven; if you pronounce them unforgiven, unforgiven they remain" (*John* 20: 21-23).

"I assure you, whatever you declare bound on earth shall be held bound in heaven, and whatever you declare loosed on earth shall be held loosed in heaven" (*Matthew* 18: 18).

A PART of the good news brought by Jesus is the clear manifestation that he has power to forgive sins, just as he has power to heal. "Is it easier to say to this paralysed man, 'Your sins are forgiven' or to say, 'Stand up, take your bed and walk'? 'But to convince you that the Son of Man has the right on earth to forgive sins' — he turned to the paralysed man — 'I say to you, stand up, take your bed and go home' " (Mk 2: 9-10).

Jesus has sent his apostles to preach the good news and to heal. Hence an essential part of their mission is to forgive, in the name of Jesus, the sins of all those who repent and confess their sins humbly. But also in the name of Jesus the church must declare unforgiven the sins of those who are unwilling to forgive the wrongs others have done to them.

The absolution is a prayer of the church for forgiveness, a prayer that, because of the faith and trust of the church, pleases God. It is a prayer in the name of Jesus, praising the Father who, through the death and resurrection of Jesus, has reconciled the world and us to himself. It asks that God, through the power of the Holy Spirit, may cleanse us from our sins and create in us a new heart and a new spirit of holiness.

Each sacrament is, in a privileged way, an encounter with Jesus. In the absolution, through the ministry of the church, Christ himself assures us that our sins are forgiven. But this does not mean just that the guilt is pardoned; it is a new assurance of Jesus' abiding friendship.

To give absolution is a most happy action for the confessor. It is joy in his heart that communicates itself to the penitent, a joyous proclamation of good news to the praise of the almighty and all-merciful God. Thereby he remembers gratefully that he, too, just as much as the penitent, lives by divine forgiveness.

How can we ever thank God enough for not only forgiving us and healing us but also for giving us a visible sign and a solemn word of reassurance! In the sacrament we are assured of the power of the Holy Spirit to cleanse us from our sins, to heal our weaknesses and to make us holy.

*   *   *

Lord, I thank you for offering us
   this sacrament of healing and liberation
   and for making us so explicitly sure
   of your forgiveness and abiding patience.
   Lord, I want to thank you always and on all occasions,
   and to do so especially
   by assuring my forgiveness to all those who offend me.
   Help me to put this purpose into practice.
   Amen.

PART TWO

CELEBRATION OF INDIVIDUAL CONFESSION

A. *Turning to Christ:*

Dear Lord,
in my dissipation I did not pay attention to you;
I did not listen to your voice.
I acted as if I had forgotten that you are my friend
and that you call me to an ever more intimate friendship
  with you.
Therefore I was not in the truth that sets us free.

Yet you have never forgotten me.
I know that I am written into your heart
and resting in your hands.
I know that I can always come to you,
cry to you as a child cries to his mother.
I can turn to you and trust you.
Yes, Lord, I come to you and pray humbly,
"Lord, I have sinned; heal me".

Jesus, I remember how you met sinners,
how patient you were with your disciples,
Peter and all the others,
and how you asked Peter after all his failures,
"Do you love me more than anything else?"
So you ask me now, and Lord, I respond,
"Yes, I want to love you with all my heart,
more than anything else".

But sin is still in me, in many corners of my being,
and blocks me on my way to you.
So I cry to you:
"Make me free; free me for you,
so that, with you, I may be free
to love your friends, to love all those whom you love".

I remember, Lord, how you met even great sinners
and invited them to be your friends.
You restored in them the sense of dignity and trust.
You made them new persons.
In Galilee and Judea, and even among the heathen,
you preached that the time had come for God
to give his people a new heart, a new way of thinking
        and loving.
You assure me, too, that here and now you want
to give me a new heart, a heart renewed, a new spirit.

Even before I begin to pray,
you desire to grant me these great gifts.
But you are the Lord and your gifts must be honoured.
Therefore I want to honour your gift in humble
        supplication
and in gratitude for the gift of prayer,
for the desire that you have awakened in me.
Strengthen my faith and my trust in you.
Strengthen in me the desire to love you above all else
and to love my fellowmen ever better.
Renew my heart, my imagination, my fantasy, my will,
        my whole being,
so that I may desire and love nothing
that you do not wish for me and will for me.

Let your Holy Spirit come upon me and open my eyes
and my heart
so that I may know myself in the light of your love,
and may be able to recognise my ingratitude and learn
        to be grateful.

RITE OF PENANCE

RITE FOR RECONCILIATION OF INDIVIDUAL PENITENTS

Texts for the Penitent

The penitent should prepare for the celebration of the sacrament by prayer, reading of Scripture, and silent reflection. The penitent should think over and should regret all sins since the last celebration of the sacrament.

RECEPTION OF THE PENITENT

The penitent enters the confessional or other place set aside for the celebration of the sacrament of penance. After the welcoming of the priest, the penitent makes the sign of the cross saying:

In the name of the Father, and of the Son, and of the Holy Spirit. Amen.

The penitent is invited to have trust in God and replies:

Amen.

READING OF THE WORD OF GOD

The penitent then listens to a text of Scripture which tells about God's mercy and calls men to conversion.

CONFESSION OF SINS
AND ACCEPTANCE OF
SATISFACTION

The penitent speaks to the priest in a normal, conversational fashion. The penitent tells when he or she last celebrated the sacrament and then confesses his or her sins. The penitent then listens to any advice the priest may give and accepts the satisfaction from the priest. The penitent should ask any appropriate questions.

PRAYER OF THE PENITENT AND ABSOLUTION

PRAYER

Before the absolution is given, the penitent expresses sorrow for sins in these or similar words:

My God,
I am sorry for my sins with all my heart.
In choosing to do wrong
and failing to do good,
I have sinned against you
whom I should love above all things.
I firmly intend, with your help,
to do penance,
to sin no more,
and to avoid whatever leads me to sin.
Our Savior Jesus Christ
suffered and died for us.
In his name, my God, have mercy.

With the blind man of Jericho, I cry and want to continue to cry:

"Jesus, Son of David, have mercy on me
Jesus, Son of Abraham, have mercy on me
Jesus, Son of Isaac, have mercy on me
Jesus, Son of Jacob, have mercy on me
Jesus, Son of Mary, have mercy on me
Jesus, Son of man, have mercy on me
Jesus, Son of the living God, have mercy on me!
I want to recover my sight".

Not only the world around me but my own sins
have made me partially blind.
I detest my self-deceit and all the tendencies
to be a liar, to be inconsistent and incoherent.
I detest the sin of somehow having deceived others
and having shared in the deceit going on in the world.
Lord, you are powerful.
Touch my eyes, touch my heart,
and I will stop deceiving myself.
I will stop deceiving others and allowing them to deceive
    me.

Send forth the Spirit of Truth to introduce me to
all truth.
Let your Holy Spirit come upon me and cleanse me,
so that I may accept fully the saddening truth about
    my sins
but also recognise more fully
the consoling truth of your liberating love.

B. *Examination of Conscience*

"Our Father who art in Heaven"

Father, what an unheard-of privilege that, with your only begotten Son, I can call you "Father, dear Father"! What a wonderful gift that, all together as your one family, we with your beloved Son can call you, "Our

Father . . .". Forgive me, Father, for I have not always proclaimed this name with all the love and trust due to you! Forgive me my distrust, my doubts, my distractions when I should have been living constantly in your presence.

Your beloved Son has taught us to adore you, the Father of all, in spirit and truth. But when I say, "Our Father", I realise that I have not always loved your children with you and your Son Jesus Christ. I was too concerned for myself. Yet I could cry out in the Spirit, "Abba, our Father", for the Spirit prays in us. So I could also have joined you more completely in your love for all your children, in your great zeal to make humankind one family to the honour of your name.

When praying to you and remembering your name, I all too often failed to realise fully that "you are in heaven", You, the Holy One, and I your creature; You, the Holy One, and I, a sinner. Yet I should remember this and be all the more grateful for your invitation to call you "Father" and to unite with all the people on earth to honour you as the Father of all.

Father, forgive me my lack of humility. Each time I pray to you in heaven, I should have deep sorrow about my sins; I should feel humble. Compared with your holiness, I should never feel exalted over others. You alone know who has received the greater gifts from you and who is the greater sinner, those who outwardly seem to be great sinners, or I who have received so many signs of your love and yet have not given you all my heart and all my life.

"Hallowed be thy name"

All my life should sing with Mary, "Holy is his name and his mercy from generation to generation". All my life should glorify your name, as you do by your saving justice, by your concern for people, by your compassion and mercy. It is my wonderful vocation to make known your name to others, especially to those entrusted to me. But so frequently I was more concerned for my own honour, my own importance, than for my mission to make known your name and Jesus whom you have sent to manifest the full extent of your goodness, love and mercy. I have not even given enough attention to know your name, that of "Father", and to know the name of Jesus, our Saviour, the Divine Healer, the One who was, is and will come. How, then, can I truthfully pray that your name be honoured, praised and known by all people?

Father, forgive me for having dishonoured your name by seeking my own self-importance or by living a distracted life that hinders me from knowing you and finding out the unique, wonderful name by which you call me! Forgive me, Father, for not honouring and accepting some of my fellow-travellers in their uniqueness, for not trying to know the wonderful unique name by which you call them and call us all together.

"Thy kingdom come"

Father, I did pray frequently for the coming of your kingdom but I was sometimes more interested in my own little world, and I confess that I did not take enough time to listen to what your Son has said about your kingdom and how he has shown it. Therefore my prayer that "your kingdom come" was not sincere enough. I could not pray to have my share in it when I neglected my basic duty to know what your kingdom looks like.

Yes, I do know some very important aspects of it but I do not act accordingly. I know that your kingdom is like the mustard seed: it needs and demands growth, a steady effort and openness, but so many times I was unwilling to learn and to be more thoroughly converted.

Often I did not have the patience needed for either myself or others; I did not allow others to grow according to the measure of grace you had bestowed on them. I frequently requested that they take the third step before the second, and did not take for myself the step I should have taken.

I knew that your kingdom is the reign of your gracious gift; it is under the law of grace. Since I did not render thanks sufficiently nor discover all your gifts, I was neither able nor willing to meet the real needs of my neighbours. I knew that your kingdom is a kingdom of justice and peace, yet inertia or selfishness hindered me from becoming involved in the cause of peace, unity, solidarity and justice.

I know that your reign is gentleness, kindness, benevolence, and yet I dared to lack gentleness with others immediately after I had prayed, "Thy kingdom come". Lord, forgive me! Lord, have mercy!

"Thy will be done on earth as it is in heaven"

Father, you sent us Jesus, your beloved Son who, by his words, life and death, made known to us on earth how your will is done in heaven. Yet I have not taken enough time to look at Jesus, to know him better in order to know your loving will. Forgive me, Father! Your name is Love, and Jesus has made manifest the full extent of this love. Still, I did not implore fervently and unceasingly the gift of your Spirit so that I might be able to discern true love and not allow the world to deceive me with counterfeits of love.

In Jesus Christ you called me to become your true image and likeness, a kind of sacrament to help other people to know better the true countenance of redeemed and redeeming love. But I have diminished your glory on earth, for by my negligence many people do not know sufficiently how your will is done in heaven and how it could be done on earth. Father, forgive me!

Even when I prayed, "Thy will be done", I was still stubborn and wanted people to do my will instead of engaging in a common search for truthful solutions to the problems of life so that your will might be done. Father, forgive me!

I have not given enough attention to the lives of the saints. I have not listened enough to the prophets who helped us to interpret your will. I have not honoured enough the simple and humble ones who frequently have the best insight about how your will should be done on earth. I considered myself wise and was not among the humble and simple ones to whom you reveal the secrets of your will. Father, forgive!

"Give us this day our daily bread"

Father, your beloved Son Jesus taught us to rejoice in calling you intimately, "Abba, dear Father", and then in our prayers to know that you are the Holy One and to be concerned for the glory of your name, your kingdom and your holy will. But all too frequently, before rejoicing in your name in the communion with you, I prayed directly for our bread, and therefore meant just "my bread". I forgot to pray equally for the bread, the health, the honour, dignity and the justice due all people. I forgot that your talents are given me to share with others, so that we all can rejoice at the common table.

Praying for our bread, I did not recognise with sufficient gratitude that you have prepared the table, your table, the table of your Word, the table of the body and blood of Christ where we all become blood brothers and sisters, and pledge to share everything in our life insofar as we can, just as Jesus shared his life and his blood with us.

Father, forgive me for overindulging in material things for my own pleasure, unconcerned that all these things are gifts from you, the Father of all! Even if I myself did not overindulge, I did not use my talents to convince my countrymen, my colleagues, my neighbours to adopt a more simple lifestyle and not to exhaust the resources of this earth to the detriment of the poor nations and future generations. And so I must confess that my prayer, "Give *us* this day *our* bread" was not always as Jesus taught us to pray. It was not fully "adoration in spirit and truth".

It is true that I did include in my prayer the dimensions of the table of your Word, the body and blood of Christ, but I must confess that I have sinned by not always giving them priority. Thus I have proved myself ungrateful. I did a little sharing of the bread and sharing of human resources for social justice, but I was not concerned enough that all people receive, along with social justice, the goods of the Spirit, the knowledge of your Word, the share in your kingdom.

"And forgive us our sins as we forgive those who sin against us"

I would never dare to say to you, Father, "Forgive me my sins just as I forgive others who sin against me", for my forgiving is imperfect, not like yours. It sometimes costs me a hard and long struggle to free myself from resentment. But if I pray, "Forgive us", I know that I pray with Jesus who did forgive on the cross. I pray with the saints, asking that you may conform me with your healing forgiveness, with the forgiveness of Jesus, and with the way the saints forgave. And praying for your forgiveness, I express sincerely my longing, my yearning to be forgiving like Jesus, to be forgiving as you, our healing and forgiving Father. Accept this, my prayer, and grant that my longing will grow and then open up to receive this great grace.

I confess with sorrow that in the midst of the bitterness existing between social classes and groups that constantly accuse each other and thus excuse themselves, I find myself from time to time half consciously and half unconsciously in some complicity with these attitudes, although I know that I am sent by you to be a peacemaker, a reconciler. Father, forgive!

"And do not put us to the dangerous test"

Father, we sinners have built up a world that has institutionalised temptations; we have caused a polluted environment that is tempting and sometimes degrading. While we pray that you lead us not into temptation, we know that you are not tempting us. But sometimes we forget that our prayer can be sincere only if we join actively with other people of good will to create a more humane, a more just, a more fraternal world, and thus eliminate the temptations that come from our personal and collective selfishness, from suspicion, arrogance and pride. Father, forgive us for making of the paradise you have created on earth a chaos that becomes for many an all too great temptation.

Father, I know that the sincerity of my love and adoration must be tested. But if I had always responded to your grace, I would be stronger. It is my fault that I am still weak. Yet, with trust I come to you and pray that you may put me to the test only as far as my strength and your special grace will help me to stand firm and to grow through the test. In prayer and in action I must be sincere, preparing myself through greater fidelity in everyday decisions to stand the test in the great decisions of my life.

But how can I pray to withstand the temptation if I do not help others, pray for them, encourage them and unite with all people of good will to remove the dangerous temptations from our earth? Father, forgive me!

The evil one, the disturber, carries on his malicious plans through unhealthy authority structures, lust for power, greed, sexism, racism. He uses each of us when we yield to these powers, whenever we are arrogant, manipulate others or allow others to manipulate us. I know, Father, that I cannot pray sincerely without repenting for all my participations in the sins of others, and for my sloth and inertia. My prayer was not earnest enough when I did not accept my own share of responsibility. Yet I come to you, Father, with trust, and pray, "Father, heal me, for I have sinned!"

"For thine is the kingdom, the power and the glory, now and forever"

Father, so often I have cried to you in my needs, and then when you helped me, I forgot to give you the glory. Already my prayer was not right when it did not lead into praise and thanksgiving. The evil one and the evil world around us have no power over us when, in praise, we turn our attention to your kingdom and your power, and seek above all things your glory.

Forgive me for all the times I have given more attention to the evil than to your marvellous deeds and the example of holy people. Father, forgive!

C. *Prayer for the Blessed Gift of Sorrow*

Father, my sins have caused great pain
for me and for others,
and this pain was not blessed;
it was self-punishment and injustice to others
for whom I should be a source of peace.

Father, grant me the gift of blessed sorrow.
May your Holy Spirit help me
to enter into the blessed sorrow of Christ
that is a redeeming manifestation of your compassion.

Grant me, Father, a heart renewed,
so that it may be filled with sorrow
for the damage my sins have wrought
to your kingdom, to the salvation of the world.
Grant me that sorrow that brings forth a rebirth,
a new zeal, greater compassion,
greater readiness to forgive and to heal.

Give me the courage, Father, to face my sins,
even if they shame me.
Give me that sorrow that makes me humble
in confession before the priest and in life.

Father, give us all that blessed sorrow
that is filled with trust in you! Amen.

D. *Confession*

If your life is marked by clear direction and serenity,
your confession occasionally may be very short, mention-
ing just two or three matters in which you can make
progress or at least exert greater effort. More important
than individual sins is the picture of a life growing ever
more in Christ, or a saddening situation of sloth and
regression.

On certain occasions when you have to make great
decisions for your life, or when you do not see clearly
how to cope with certain problems, you may ask the
priest for a dialogue where you will be given enough
time to explain your situation to the priest, in the sight
of the Divine Physician, and thereby find proper
encouragement and advice. You may pray for the priest,
that he may be truly able to manifest the attitude of
the Divine Physician and join in your concern to praise

God both by your humble confession and the life to follow.

Prayer for a good confession:

> Lord Jesus Christ, I am aware that, confessing my sins,
> I stand not only before your minister, a brother,
> but that I meet you.
> I want so to confess my sins before you
> that I can express my trust, my gratitude and my longing
> to be liberated from all bondage of sin.
> Lord, make me so free for you that, with you,
> I shall be free to love and serve my brothers and sisters,
> to bring the good news of peace to those you have redeemed.
> Lord, give me the courage to face the truth of my sinfulness
> so that the truth of your love can make me free.
> Amen.

Sometimes the priest will choose a short reading from the Scriptures. The Word of God has a purifying power. But the penitent may himself choose a short scripture reading, meditate on it before confession, and read it at the beginning, after the priest has given his blessing. The confession may focus on a word of the Bible that has struck your heart and that gives you light.

You may also suggest to your confessor the penance that you feel would be most appropriate for helping you to make serious efforts towards reparation for your sins. Before absolution, you may say aloud before the priest, a short prayer, for instance:

"Lord God, in your goodness have mercy on me!

Do not look on my sins
but take away all my guilt.
Create in me a clean heart
and renew within me an upright spirit!"

E. *Absolution*

"God, the Father of mercy, through the death and resurrection of his Son, has reconciled the world to himself and sent the Holy Spirit among us for the forgiveness of sin; through the ministry of the Church, may God give you pardon and peace. And so I absolve you from your sins in the name of the Father and of the Son and of the Holy Spirit. Amen".

The penitent may accept these words in his heart and join the priest in a prayer of praise, for instance:

"We praise you, God, Father of mercy,
for having sent us Jesus to be our Saviour,
our Divine Physician,
and that through his death and resurrection
you have reconciled the world and us to yourself.
We thank you for having sent the Holy Spirit
and for sending him again
to cleanse our hearts, to free us from guilt,
and to lead us to a holy life".

After the absolution, priest and penitent join explicitly in the praise of God:

Priest: Give thanks to the Lord for he is good.

Penitent: His mercy endures forever.

F. *Thanksgiving:*

Father, I thank you for the gift of peace,
and I want to thank you always.

Let me become a source of peace for my brothers and
    sisters,
for all who need healing, forgiveness, patience,
kind understanding and encouragement.

Your peace is your gift to me
but also a gift to be shared with others,
for it is prepared by your Son, the Saviour of all.
Let me ever more experience the power of your Spirit,
so that your peace will always abound in my heart
and mark my life and all my relationships.

Lord God, our Father, there is so much hatred and
resentment
in the lives of so many people!
Send them peacemakers.
Help them to seek and to find you,
the source of all peace and reconciliation.
Lord, unite all of us who have experienced
your healing forgiveness and your peace,
so that we may together promote peace and justice
in the world, in our families, our neighbourhood,
in economic and political relationships.

Lord, grant me a grateful memory,
so that I may no longer be a prisoner of my selfishness
and my small worries,
but do the work of peace day by day.
Amen.

PART THREE

COMMUNAL CELEBRATION OF RECONCILIATION

The following text can serve for personal preparation of the communal celebration. It can be used for the revision of life in a family or community. Above all, it should help towards a better understanding of the dimensions and purpose of the communal celebration of penance.

A. *Entrance Song:*

Yes, I shall arise and return to my Father.

To you, O Lord, I lift up my soul. In you, O my God, I place all my trust.

Look down on me; have mercy, O Lord, forgive me my sins! Behold all my grief!

My heart and soul shall yearn for your face; be gracious to me and answer my plea!

Do not withhold your goodness from me; O Lord, may your love be deep in my soul.

To you I pray, have pity on me! My God, I have sinned against your great love.

Mercy, I cry, O Lord, wash me clean; and whiter than snow my spirit shall be.

Give me again the joy of your help; now open my lips; your praise I will sing.

Happy is he, forgiven by God; his sins blotted out, his guilt is no more.

You are my joy, my refuge and strength; let all upright hearts give praise to the Lord.

My soul will sing, my heart will rejoice; the blessing
of God will fill my days.

B.   *Greeting and Mutual Blessing*

Priest: Peace and grace from God, our Father, and from
    our Lord Jesus Christ, be with you all!
Response: And with your spirit!

C.   *Collect*

Lord, we have come to celebrate your mercy,
to receive the good news that further conversion is
    possible.

We come to manifest our faith
that we can live the Gospel and deepen our resolution.
We want to live the Gospel.

O Lord, strengthen our faith, that we may truly believe
with heart, mind and lifestyle
that you can and want to renew our hearts
and the face of the earth.

Send us your Spirit
so that we may live in a new spirit of gratitude.

We want to believe fully in your promises
of the new heaven and the new earth
foreshadowed by a divine milieu of true believers.

Send forth your Spirit to cleanse our hearts,
to free us from all deceit
and to increase our faith in your calling us to a holy life.

We ask this through Christ, our Lord. Amen.

D. *Reading* from the second letter of Paul to the Corinthians (5:14-6:2).

"The love of Christ leaves us no choice when once we have reached the conclusion that one man died for all and therefore all humankind has died to selfishness. His purpose in dying for all was that men, while still in life, should cease to live for themselves and should live for him who, for their sake, died and was raised to life. With us, therefore, worldly standards cease to count in our estimate of any man; even if once they counted in our understanding of Christ, they no longer do so. When anyone is united to Christ there is a new world; the old order has gone and the new order has already begun.

"From first to last this has been the work of God. He has reconciled us to himself through Christ and he has enlisted us in this service of reconciliation. What I mean is that God was in Christ reconciling the world to himself, no longer holding men's misdeeds against them, and that he has entrusted us with the message of reconciliation. We come, therefore, as Christ's ambassadors. It is as if God were appealing to you through us: in Christ's name we implore you, be reconciled to God! Christ was innocent of sin, and yet for our sake God made him one with the sinfulness of men, so that in him we might be made one with the goodness of God himself. Sharing in God's work, we urge this appeal upon you: you have received the grace of God; do not let it go for nothing. God's own words are:

In the hour of my favour I gave heed to you;

on the day of deliverance I came to your aid.

The hour of favour has now come;

now, I say, has the day of deliverance dawned".

E.   *Personal Reflection and Shared Prayer*

We thank you, Father, for the gift of faith.
Many generations have tried to placate you
by empty rituals.
But you have revealed to us
that Christ himself is the Reconciliation and the
　　Reconciler.
You have taken the initiative and it is all your work.
In celebrating the Sacrament of Reconciliation together,
we want to honour your initiative and give to you alone
the glory for the restoration of our peace.
All too often we have stolen this glory from you,
thinking it was our achievement.
Yet only if we are grateful can we share in your work,
in the healing of our wounds and the wounds of others,
and accept our peace mission in this world.

Father, even while knowing that Christ died for us,
we have continued, time and again,
to live selfishly for ourselves,
or have made ourselves prisoners of group egotism
and collective manipulation and deceit.
Forgive us, Father!

Father, heal us
and let us wounded people become healers for others.
Allow us, Lord, to become reconciled reconciliators
and peacemakers wherever we may be.
Amen.

F.   *Longing for the New Creation*

Grant to us, O Lord, a heart renewed. Recreate in us
your own Spirit, Lord!
Behold, the days are coming, says the Lord our God,
when I will make a new covenant with the house of
Israel.

Deep within their being, I will implant my law; I will write in in their hearts.

I will be their God and they shall be my people. And for all their faults I will grant forgiveness; never more will I remember their sins.

G. *Examination of Conscience*

The Good News that We Can Live a Life in Christ Jesus (Mt 5: 1-16).

"When his disciples had gathered around him, Jesus began to address them".

Lord, our life is wonderful, a new life, a sign of the new heaven and new earth if we are gathered in your name, listen together to your word and live together according to that word for the glory of the Father. Forgive us, Lord, that so often we came together with hostile or indifferent attitudes! Forgive us for all the times we came together driven by individual or collective selfishness! Heal us, O Lord, from our dissipations that so frequently are the chief cause of our not really coming together, not being gathered in your presence.

"How blest are those who by the Spirit know their need of God; the kingdom of heaven is theirs".

Lord Jesus, looking at you, the humble servant of God, the one who has made himself poor in order to enrich us, I know what your words mean, but I would know them so much better if I would become humble like you and put your words into practice. Lord, forgive me my lack of humility, my lack of gratitude.

Looking at you, Jesus, who come from the Father and return to him with all your brothers and sisters after having shared yourself, even your lifeblood with

E

them, I know what it means to belong to the poor who are blessed. I would know it better and experience the blessedness of your kingdom if I would use all the gifts I have received for the common good and would share not only words but all that I have, all I can do, and my very self with my brothers and sisters. Lord, forgive me my self-centredness and my participation in group selfishness. (. . . personal reflection or sharing of humble confession).

"Blessed are the sorrowful; they shall find consolation".

Looking at you, Lord Jesus, I know who are the sorrowful who will find consolation. It is you and all who follow you, all those who are free from self-pity because they share in the sorrows and sufferings of all. They are those who are willing to bear the burden of all. They put to death their selfishness, whatever pain it may cost, and are willing to fulfil the great law of love of neighbour, accepting all the difficulties and pain involved. (. . .).

"How blest are those of a gentle spirit, they shall have the earth for their possession".

Looking at you, Lord Jesus, who teaches us to be humble and of a gentle spirit like you, I know what your words mean. I praise you for wanting to draw people to yourself only by your gentle love and not by force, threats and power. Forgive me, Lord, for still having a vindictive spirit, for still trying to domineer over others, for being tempted to use religion for my own advantage or that of my group. Lord, forgive!

Israel would have been saved if your people had accepted your gentle rule, the rule of your kingdom. Jerusalem would not have been destroyed if they had learned from you the gentle but irresistible power of non-violent love. The terrible sufferings of world wars would have been spared if Christians had followed you in your non-violent love, your gentle reign, in a common commitment to justice and peace. Lord, forgive! (. . .).

"How blest are those who hunger and thirst for saving justice; they shall be satisfied".

Looking at you, Lord Jesus, again we know what your words mean. But we would know you better if we were more grateful for justification by your grace. And we would not only know you better but would find more fulfilment in our life if we followed you in your concern for all people, for social justice on all levels everywhere. (. . .).

"How blest are those who show mercy; mercy shall be shown to them".

Looking at you, Lord Jesus, we can know the meaning of your command, "Be merciful as your Father". If we are merciless in spite of your saving justice, in spite of your compassionate love manifested on the cross even to your enemies, then we deserve a merciless judgement; indeed, we punish ourselves. It is a duty of justice, Lord, to follow you in your merciful love. Lord, forgive us for being, so often, hard of heart! (. . .).

"How blest are those whose hearts are pure; they shall see God".

Looking at you, Lord Jesus, we see the Father; and if we were truly gathered around you, turning our eyes, mind, heart and will only to you and serving you with pure intentions, we would know you and your Father better and find all our salvation in this saving knowledge. Lord, forgive us our dissipation. Forgive us the mixture of our motives. Forgive us for using and even abusing others while talking about love! (. . .).

"How blest are the peacemakers: God will call them his children".

Looking at you, Lord Jesus Christ, who have brought reconciliation and peace at the cost of your precious blood, we know what it means to be peacemakers. Looking at how you honoured the Father so trustfully, even on the cross, by entrusting your spirit to him and praying for those who had scourged you, wounded you, crucified you, praying for us who, by our sins, were enemies, we know how the children of God should act. Lord, forgive us for so often failing to fulfil our great peace-mission on earth and thus making ourselves unworthy to be called children of your heavenly Father! (. . .).

"How blest are those who have suffered persecution for the cause of right; the kingdom of heaven is theirs".

Looking at you, Lord Jesus, we know what it means to share in the kingdom of God by suffering for the sake of justice. If we were grateful enough we would be ready, as you were, to suffer whatever might come in fulfilling our mission to make visible the saving justice of the Father. Lord, forgive us our unwillingness to suffer for the cause of right! Forgive us our unwillingness to give up our own privileges and those of our group to prove our faith in the one God, in the one kingdom of justice and peace! (. . .).

"You are salt for the earth".

Only by gathering around you, welcoming you as the Saviour and surrendering ourselves to you, can we share in your mission and bring savour, ultimate meaning and purpose to people's lives, to life on earth. Only if we are close to you, totallly open to your word and gifts, totally given to your kingdom, can we fulfil this great mission. Lord, forgive our self-centredness, our superficiality! Forgive us for neglecting the contemplative dimension of our life and thus being manipulated by others, mis-directed, and made a part of the deceit and manipulation of an unholy world. Lord, forgive! (. . .).

"You are the light for all the world".

Gathered around you, we know that you alone are the light, the source of all truth and love, and that we are nothing without you. Forgive us, Lord, for we did not always seek our light in you alone! Forgive us the self-importance that has concealed from ourselves and others your presence in us, when we should have been seeking with pure hearts only your glory. When we become gratefully aware that we are light only in and through your Light, then we will serve you with purity of heart, and people seeing our good deeds will praise the Father. Forgive us for so frequently concealing this truth and having been unfaithful to our mission to be "light to the world". (. . .).

"Do not suppose that I have come to abolish the law and the prophets; I did not come to abolish but to complete".

We praise you, Father! You have taught us through the prophets and have sent us THE Prophet, Jesus, to teach us the kind of freedom for which he has set us free. Yet we see already in the New Testament how the apostles had to warn the Christians not to "turn freedom into licence" for their selfish self (Gal 5:13).

As Christians after Vatican II, we have liberated ourselves from many traditions and unnecessary limitations. Yet we must confess before you, O Lord, that we did not give attention to how you have perfected "the law and the prophets" by the *goal* commandments, the clear directions you have given us through the beatitudes and your solemn words, "But I tell you

69

. . .". Now we come to examine our conscience on the extent to which we have been unfaithful to the law and the prophets, and even more to the clear directions you have given to us. (. . .).

"You have learned that our forefathers were told, 'Do not commit murder; anyone who commits murder must be brought to judgement'. But I tell you this: Anyone who nurses anger against his brother or sister calls upon himself judgement".

Through Baptism and Confirmation we share in your mission, O Lord, and in the Eucharist we share ever more in your life. Having received your Spirit, we know that we can be free from all resentment and can be sources of peace and reconciliation. Yet, time and again we have nursed anger against our brothers and sisters, sometimes even for trifles, mere nothings. Lord, forgive! When we came to your altar we were not always anxious to be fully at peace in our hearts and to do all that we could do to win over our brothers and sisters to renewed friendship.

And Lord, we have even sinned against the "Law and the Prophets". We have done little or nothing to affect public and political opinions against the armaments race, against aggressive nationalism and prejudices against other nations and races: attitudes that have so often in history led to mass-murder in wars. Nor have we done enough to alleviate or prevent alcoholism and drug addiction that cause so much misery, even such great crimes as murder and abortion.

Lord Jesus, you have praised the Father for having entrusted us to you, and you have watched over us and even given your life for our salvation. You have entrusted to us our brothers and sisters, yet because of resentments and divisions, we have not helped them as we should on the way of salvation. We have not even cared enough for their health and life. Lord, forgive! (. . .).

"You have learned that they were told, 'Do not commit adultery'. But what I tell you is this: If a man looks on a woman with a lustful eye, he has already committed adultery with her in his heart".

Among Christians it should be unthinkable that sins as grave as adultery are committed, yet there are adulterers among us, and perhaps not without some fault on our part. We have not always given that example of absolute fidelity in all our relationships that would strengthen others and prevent many temptations. Our whole life should praise you, the Lord and giver of the covenant, for your great faithfulness.

In a society of consumers, where even sex becomes a consumer article, we are strongly tempted to use others for our purposes and thus prepare for the downfall into such grave sins as fornication and adultery. Forgive us, Lord, for not having learned to admire and to honour your work, your having created men and women to your image and likeness and given them to each other to be a sign of your loving presence and your unselfish love.

Lord, you have taught us that we should rid ourselves of everything that hinders us on the way to you, even if it is as dear to us as our "right eye" or our "right hand". Yet so often we have watched movies and other outlets that glorify unfaithfulness and degrade the vision of sexuality! We do not have the courage and the generosity to break with our habits and to avoid all that could lead us or others to impurity. We have not filled our memories with good and beautiful things, and therefore left too much space for dangerous thoughts and imaginations. Forgive us, Lord! (. . .).

71

"They were told, 'A man who divorces his wife must give her a note of dismissal'. But what I tell you is this: Everyone who divorces his wife — lewd conduct is a separate case — involves her in adultery".

The suffering caused by divorce in our society is unimaginable. There is so much loneliness among abandoned spouses, so many hurt memories, so many wounded hearts, so many unreconciled words and actions; and the suffering of children is unspeakable. Yet none of us has the right to throw a stone at others. Many who have been divorced are not any worse than us, and some are far better, having struggled generously and heroically to save their marriage.

We all must implore your forgiveness, Lord, for we have not done all that we should and could have done to foster a spirit of fidelity and trustworthiness among us. Many of us, as parents, teachers or pastors, have not done all that could be done to prepare young people for chastity and for future marriage. Many times, too, we could have acted as reconcilers, but some of us would rather not bother. Instead, without consideration, we would rather say, simply, "Divorce him!" or "Divorce her!" Many of us all too easily condone divorce while others harshly judge the divorced without any discernment.

Have we really done our best to help divorced people and their children to find consolation and support in a living community of hope and love? (. . .).

"Again, you have learned that our forefathers were told, 'Do not break your oath' and 'oaths sworn to the Lord must be kept'. But what I tell you is this: You are not to swear at all . . . Plain 'Yes' or 'No' is all you need to say".

Lord, you have given us the great mission of proclaiming the truth of salvation before the whole world.

But how can the world believe us if we are not absolutely sincere and honest in all our words and actions?

We are your friends, and you are the Truth. We would all be friends among ourselves if all our communications were absolutely truthful. A "Yes" among your friends should have greater value than all the oaths of those who are alienated from you. Too often, however, we have twisted our words or, for quite insufficient reasons, have distorted their meaning. Lord, heal us, help us! Make us lovers of absolute sincerity, a sincerity through which love and discernment shine through. (. . .).

"You have learned that they were told, 'Eye for eye, tooth for tooth'. But what I tell you is this: Do not set yourself against the man who wrongs you . . . If a man wants to sue you for your shirt, let him have your coat as well".

The Old Testament warns people involved in an argument or a legal dispute not to harm the other more than the other harmed them. This should be self-evident, Lord, for your own disciples; yet there are many lawsuits where people harm each other ruthlessly and without any qualms of conscience, so hardened are their hearts. This is so because many of us have not followed your way and have not learned to resolve our conflicts creatively in a non-violent way, by the power of the greater love.

Trust between doctors and patients is being undermined by a destructive tendency to gain money dishonestly by lawsuits. Do we not all have a share of responsibility for letting such things go on? If each of us who wants to be your friend, O Lord, would learn from what you told us, we would not suffer under widespread distrust and legal quarrels. We would not need police everywhere, nor would we have to take refuge in superpowered armaments, bloody revolutions and wars. Lord, heal us and help us to be creative in promoting in our everyday life the non-violent way to a saving justice and peace. (. . .).

"Give when you are asked to give; and do not turn your back on a man who wants to borrow".

Many of us with large bank accounts are unhappy about losing money constantly through inflation. Could we not turn our hearts to those who need our money for a new beginning? Could we not be more open-minded for our own poor and for those poor nations of the third world who suffer from under-development and starvation? Lord, forgive us for our lack of generosity! (. . .).

"You have learned that they were told, 'Love your neighbour. You may hate your enemy'. But what I tell you is this: Love your enemies, bless those who curse you, be good to those who hate you, pray for your persecutors and those who treat you spitefully".

Lord Jesus, you have come to break the vicious circle of hatred and violence. You call us as your friends to continue this mission. The world today is woefully in need of goodness and healing forgiveness; we are sometimes even behind what the ancients were told. Yet the world can be saved only by those who most generously follow your example and pray for those who are still slaves of anger, resentment and hatred. Help us, Lord, never to pay back evil for evil but to use good to defeat evil. And forgive us for being so uncreative and so blind that we have overlooked many occasions when we could have overcome evil with good.

"If you love only those who love you, what reward can you expect?"

Lord, if we look only for reward or act only for fear of punishment, we are no better than any sinner and unbeliever.

You have come from heaven to bring us the fire of purifying love. You have baptised us in the Holy Spirit. We have no excuse if we do not love those who are most in need. But we are not yet free for you and do not share in your freedom if we have not the generosity and the firm resolution to show love to those who cannot reward us. There are many people who cannot yet love us and cannot at all understand your love, because they have had little or no experience of goodness and unselfish love in their lives; hence we act unjustly if we withhold love until they love us.

Lord, you have given us the experience of your saving love and the love of many of your friends, to enable us to love and to help those who need the experience of unselfish love. You have given us this capacity and this mission. If the world is still so miserable and so poor in the art of loving, is it not, then, our fault? Lord, forgive us!

"There must be no limit to your goodness, as your heavenly Father's goodness knows no bounds".

Lord Jesus Christ, your heavenly Father has sent you to make his unlimited love known to your disciples, and through them to all people. If we set out courageously to fulfil, with you, this mission, then we come to know you and the Father even better, and are truly on the road of salvation.

Lord, forgive my slavish thinking! So often I have asked myself only how close I could come to sinning and still avoid punishment or not endanger my salvation. If I were filled with gratitude, filled with enthusiasm for your kingdom, I would find each day many occasions to come closer to the wonderful goal of becoming a true image of the goodness of your heavenly Father and your goodness. Lord, forgive us our negligence, and give us courage to live gratefully as Christians, in the clear directions you have given us. Make us grateful for the Holy Spirit who, in our hearts, cries "Abba, Father", and shows us how to act as sons and daughters of the heavenly Father. Help us never to stop walking in the right direction!

H. *The Good News and Trustful Prayer*

This is the Good News coming from God: the Father is healing, merciful Love. He takes the first step. Reconciliation is his work from beginning to end. But only those who are willing to forgive and to heal will experience the full power of his healing forgiveness.

If we are willing to forgive wholeheartedly, to set aside all resentment, and to accept our peace mission, then we are assured that our prayer will be heard. The prayer of the church is a solemn, authoritative assurance that the sins of those who are merciful, who forgive and are peacemakers, stand surely forgiven — with the warning, however, that the sins of those who remain unforgiving stand unforgiven.

With this in mind, we pray:

Father of all mercy, compassionate God,
You have sent us Jesus Christ to be our Reconciler,
our Divine Physician.
In his name we pray
that the sins of all those who have confessed their sins,
all those who want to be peacemakers,
may be thoroughly forgiven;
their wounds may be healed;
they may be thoroughly freed from enmity,
free for the reign of love, of peace and justice.

Since you, O Lord, through the apostle James, have assured us that the prayer of holy people is powerful and effective,
we pray all together,
trusting that some of us are holy people:

"Almighty God, have mercy on us,
forgive us our sins, and bring us to everlasting life!
Amen".

I. *Healing Forgiveness and Praise of God's Mercy*

The following Preface is a free version of an ancient Roman Preface used at the solemn celebration of reconciliation on Holy Thursday. It was sung by the bishop while all, hand in hand, made the procession towards the altar. In and through gratitude, we open our hearts to the gift of peace, and commit ourselves to show mercy as God does with us.

The Lord be with you!
  And with your spirit!
Let us lift up our hearts!
  We have lifted them up to the Lord!
Let us give thanks to the Lord!
  This is right and just!

All holy and all merciful Father, it is our delightful duty
and the way that leads us to wholeness, peace and
    salvation,
to render thanks to you always and on all occasions,
through your beloved Son, our Saviour, Jesus Christ.
Gratefully we remember the many signs and marvels
    of your mercy:

When our ancestors refused to honour you as God,
and did not render thanks to you,
they drove themselves out from the paradise.
But you did not abandon them.

In your great mercy you promised the coming Saviour.

When Cain killed his own brother, you mercifully put a mark on him,
lest anyone should kill him; slaughter and revenge should not go on.

When the earth was flooded by sins,
You called people to repentance
and saved Noah, his whole family, and even all the species of animals.

You assured your friend Noah and his descendants
that you would never strike down all living beings.

When ruthless brothers sold Joseph into slavery,
you made him a saviour of those who had sold him,
in a wonderful image of your saving justice and forgiveness.

You inspired the harlot Rahab
to show mercy to the ambassadors of Israel,
and you, in turn, taught them
to show mercy to her and all her kindred.

When David whom you had anointed as king, and so favoured,
ruthlessly took away another man's wife and killed the good man,
in your great mercy you sent him the prophet Nathan
to shake his conscience and to call for conversion.

And when he repented, you promised forgiveness
and did not take away from him the kingship and the promises.

In all ages and everywhere,
you gave innumerable signs of your healing forgiveness and mercy.

And in the fullness of time you sent us the great sign
of your compassionate mercy and your saving justice,
Jesus Christ, the Divine Physician, the Good Shepherd,
our Reconciler and our Peace,
and you associated with him the new Eve,
Mary, the Mother of Mercy.

With all who have experienced your mercy and saving
   justice and have praised you
with a life of compassionate mercy and healing forgiveness,
with all the angels and saints,
we praise your great name, and commit ourselves to
   praise you
in all of our life by compassionate love and saving
   justice
as peacemakers and reconcilers.

   Here would be an appropriate place to give each
other a sign of peace, assurance of steadfast fidelity to
the Lord's commandment to be compassionate and to
forgive, and to fulfil the mission of peacemakers. The
commitment to gratitude and to the task of thanking
the Lord by all of our life could be expressed and confirmed by a song of praise.

J.   *Our Mission*

Let us go in peace and praise the Lord as peacemakers.

Response: Let us praise the Lord and give him thanks.

Other books by Bernard Häring CSsR
published by St Paul Publications

Medical Ethics

Sin in the secular age

Manipulation

Prayer: the integration of faith and life

The sacraments in a secular age

The Beatitudes: their personal and social implications

The Song of the Servant

The Eucharist and our everyday life

Free and Faithful in Christ

CREATING INDUSTRIAL CAPACITY

CREATING INDUSTRIAL CAPACITY

Towards Full Employment

Edited by
JONATHAN MICHIE
and
JOHN GRIEVE SMITH

OXFORD UNIVERSITY PRESS

1996

Oxford University Press, Walton Street, Oxford OX2 6DP
Oxford New York
Athens Auckland Bangkok Bombay
Calcutta Cape Town Dar es Salaam Delhi
Florence Hong Kong Istanbul Karachi
Kuala Lumpur Madras Madrid Melbourne
Mexico City Nairobi Paris Singapore
Taipei Tokyo Toronto
and associated companies in
Berlin Ibadan

Oxford is a trade mark of Oxford University Press

Published in the United States
by Oxford University Press Inc., New York

British Library Cataloguing in Publication Data
Data available

Library of Congress Cataloging in Publication Data
Creating industrial capacity : towards full employment / edited by
Jonathan Michie and John Grieve Smith.
Includes bibliographical references and index.
1. Economic policy   2. Industrial capacity.
3. Unemployment–Government policy.   4. Full employment policies.
I. Michie, Jonathan.   II. Grieve Smith, John.
HD87.C74   1996   338.9—dc20   95–41485
ISBN 0–19–829029–2
ISBN 0–19–829030–6 (Pbk.)

1 3 5 7 9 10 8 6 4 2

Typeset by Hope Services (Abingdon) Ltd.
Printed in Great Britain
on acid-free paper by
Biddles Ltd.,
Guildford & King's Lynn

PREFACE AND ACKNOWLEDGEMENTS

All the following chapters were commissioned specifically for this book and draft versions were discussed at a working conference in May 1995 at Robinson College, Cambridge. We are grateful to the authors for travelling to Cambridge to participate in these discussions, and in particular to Eileen Applebaum, Michael Best, and Bob Pollin for travelling from the US and to Hidehiro Iwaki for making the journey from Japan.

We are very grateful to Robinson College for hosting and helping to fund this event. We are also grateful to the contributors to our earlier books *Unemployment in Europe* (Academic Press, 1994) and *Managing the Global Economy* (Oxford University Press, 1995) who kindly agreed that their royalty payments would go to the Robinson College Economic Research Fund, which met the remainder of the expenses, and to the contributors to this book for similarly donating their royalties to help fund future such events. We are grateful for their participation to Mike Bosman, Dan Corry, Gary Dymski, Elizabeth Garnsey, Laurence Harris, Will Hutton, Ruth Kelly, John McCombie, Mića Panić, Andy Robinson, Bob Rowthorn, Dick Sargent, Giles Slinger, and Ryo Watabe.

Our thanks as editors go to all the authors for the speedy incorporation of points made in May 1995 on their draft chapters; Jane Humphries, Geoff Harcourt, and Kit McMahon for chairing the sessions at the May conference; David Musson, Donald Strachan, and Robert Mark Ritter of Oxford University Press for the speedy turnround of the manuscript; Lesley Haird for typing and other help; and Brian Reddaway for contributing the Foreword. Our personal thanks for putting up with weekend editing go respectively to Carolyn and 5-year old Alex, and to Jean.

Jonathan Michie
John Grieve Smith

CONTENTS

LIST OF FIGURES

LIST OF TABLES

LIST OF CONTRIBUTORS

Eileen Appelbaum	Associate Research Director, Economic Policy Institute, Washington, DC
Peter Berg	Economist, Economic Policy Institute, Washington, DC
Michael H. Best	Co-Director, Center for Industrial Competitiveness and University Professor, University of Massachusetts, Lowell
Andy Cosh	Judge Institute, ESRC Centre for Business Research and Queens College, Cambridge
Ken Coutts	Faculty of Economics and Politics, Cambridge
Keith Cowling	Professor of Economics, University of Warwick
Ciaran Driver	Reader in Economics, Management School, Imperial College, University of London
Robert Forrant	Assistant Professor, College of Management, University of Massachusetts, Lowell
John Grieve Smith	Fellow of Robinson College, Cambridge
Alan Hughes	Director, ESRC Centre for Business Research, Cambridge
Hidehiro Iwaki	Center for Policy Research, Nomura Research Institute, Tokyo
Michael Kitson	Fellow of St Catharine's College and Lecturer in Economics, Newnham College, Cambridge
Simon Lee	Lecturer in Politics, University of Hull
Jonathan Michie	Judge Institute and Robinson College, Cambridge
Robert Pollin	Professor of Economics, University of California, Riverside
Brian Reddaway	Professor of Economics Emeritus, University of Cambridge
Peter Robinson	Centre for Economic Performance, LSE
Roger Sugden	Professor of Industrial Economics, School of Business, University of Birmingham
Grahame Thompson	Senior Lecturer in Economics, Open University

FOREWORD

Brian Reddaway

The production of this book has involved a substantial amount of work, both for the chapter-writers and for the managing editors. The basic motivation for this effort has been the belief that there is no need for unemployment to be at the high levels recorded persistently since about 1980, both in the UK and in many other countries; moreover these high levels of unemployment have been accompanied by levels of production and real income well below the economy's potential, both of which should be improved by measures to reduce unemployment.

The first priority for reducing unemployment is to persuade the governments of the world that they are not helpless in the matter—that they can take measures to reduce unemployment which would bring benefits (not only to the unemployed themselves, but also to the rest of the community) which are far greater than any losses caused by unfortunate side-effects.[1] Much can be done by a single country acting on its own, but still more can be achieved through effective international co-operation.

ANALYTICAL PROBLEMS

A full analysis of how the high level of unemployment could be reduced would be too formidable a task for a book of this kind, but hopefully it brings out some important issues. The basic difficulty is that a modern economy is a very complex affair, and the various factors which determine what happens in it are *mutually interactive*: they affect one another as well as affecting output or unemployment directly. Thus the policy-maker cannot proceed on the assumption that the effect on unemployment of (say) a lowering of interest rates will be confined to the *direct* effect—it may, for example, lead to a change in the exchange rate, which will itself have an effect on unemployment. A theorist may produce a nice model which shows what the effect of a change in interest will be, *ceteris paribus*: but *ceteris paribus* is hard even to define when interactions are important. Moreover,

---

[1] This does not, of course, imply that governments are all-powerful. In particular, there are other power-centres which can act in ways which may help or hinder the campaign against unemployment—notably the Central Bank, the opposition parties, trade unions, powerful employers, and industrial organizations. The main initiative for securing an effective policy rests, however, with the governments and various international organizations, on which the UK government can exert some influence.

in practice other causal factors will change for reasons other than the change in interest rates, because the world is not static.

The policy-maker faces many other complications. Government (and the community generally) has *other* objectives besides a fall in unemployment (for example, ensuring a tolerable level of inflation, or the reduction of pollution), and policy must take heed of its probable effects on these objectives also. Worse still, different people attach different degrees of importance to the various objectives (notably the *distribution* of income, as affected by taxes and welfare payments), so that political considerations are important, and there is frequently a problem over the *timing* of the results— the immediate results of some policies may differ greatly from those to be expected in later years: we are *not* dealing with the theorist's problem of working towards a static equilibrium.

This inevitably brings up the great difficulty that many actions by both producers and consumers are influenced, at least in part, by their *expectations* of what the future will bring, as well as by what is happening now. Inevitably, the future is highly *uncertain*, especially as what matters is (say) the future demand for a particular product (of the types and qualities produced by a particular producer), rather than the aggregate demand for consumer goods and services.[2]

Finally, the policy-maker suffers from the difficulty that economists and others are not agreed, on various important issues, about how the economy works. These disagreements sometimes reflect the fact that the proponents of different views are making different *assumptions* (usually implicitly) about what happens to other factors than the ones primarily under discussion—for example, what monetary policy is being followed when one is discussing the relations between saving and investment; sometimes different definitions (for example of saving) are being used. None the less, there are many real differences, and the policy-makers' decisions will be influenced by their own views on the questions.[3]

THE ROLE OF MANUFACTURING

With all these uncertainties and problems, why should the authors of this book attach so much importance to the expansion of industrial capacity? In the main I must leave the individual chapters to speak for themselves, but it is possible to make a few general remarks, which may help the reader

[2] On the consumer's side their demand for a house is particularly sensitive to their own expectations about the security of their job, as well as general factors like the future rate of interest on mortgages and the rate of inflation.

[3] A very important case is reflected in the view that it is impossible to have sustainable growth of output unless inflation is held below a certain low level (e.g. 4%, or 2.5%). Holders of this view should read the article by W. Stanners entitled 'Is Low Inflation an Important Condition for High Growth?', in the *Cambridge Journal of Economics*, 17/1 (Mar. 1993).

to see how things fit together. I must stress, however, that the points are put in a rather over-simplified and dogmatic form, for the sake of clarity.

1. *The real capital stock is inadequate to employ the available labour force in a satisfactory way.* We may start with a simple point about the economy as a whole, rather than manufacturing by itself. It is broadly true that, over really long periods, the stock of capital in the UK has grown at about the same average rate as the gross domestic product (about 2.5 per cent per annum in real terms); moreover the growth of aggregate output has basically reflected the growth of output per head, with the number of people at work growing only slowly. Average real income per worker has grown in real terms, and so has average capital per worker.

Since about 1980, however, the average annual growth of output has been, on average, subnormal, and this has been reflected in the great growth of unemployment. Real capital has—understandably enough—also grown at a subnormal rate, since decisions to add to the capital stock are much influenced by past growth of real demand and by expectations about the future: the latter are much influenced by recent experience.

Consequently the absorption of the unemployed into useful work now requires an abnormally rapid expansion of the capital stock over the next few years, which implies a high rate of investment.

2. *'De-industrialization'.* The position in manufacturing industry, however, is far more striking than for the economy as a whole. Output in 1995 is very little higher than it was as long ago as 1973, and the number of people employed in manufacturing has fallen drastically. The capital stock in manufacturing has probably declined in real terms,[4] because (as explained in several of the chapters below) the growth of 'short-termist' outlooks on the part of industrialists and suppliers of finance has led to a cautious policy on capital expenditure, in the face of inevitable uncertainty about future demand for heterogeneous output.

In brief the stock of capital in industry is now at a level which provides little scope for raising industrial output above the miserable level at which it is now running in the mid-1990s.[5]

---

[4] The measurement is difficult because of (a) the big changes in the *composition* of industrial output and (b) the very limited information on *scrapping* of capital. 'Depreciation allocations' are largely arbitrary and of little relevance.

[5] This is, of course, a highly simplified statement of a very complex position. As industrial output is very heterogeneous, it is inevitable that capacity is not fully utilized for products which are temporarily in poor demand, and for other products output may be being kept up by postponing maintenance work. Overtime provides some scope for increasing output, and it might be possible to increase weekend production and to work more double shifts. But many of the theoretically possible devices for raising output involve increased labour costs and may be unpopular with workers except on a strictly temporary basis. As a broad generalization, *time* is needed to secure a substantial rise in industrial output: it requires a much higher level of industrial investment, designed to increase output capacity (as opposed to reducing costs); and this higher rate of investment would have to be maintained for a number of years.

This means that if the UK adopts a policy of raising aggregate demand, so as to accelerate the growth of output and reduce the number of unemployed, the proportion of the extra output which consists of manufactures is likely to be undesirably small. This in turn means that there is a serious danger that the UK will incur a substantial deficit on the current account of its balance of payments, since manufactures provide the main opportunity for expanding exports and holding down the growth of imports.[6]

3. *Complementary measures are essential.* It would, of course, be a mistake to argue that the expansion of industrial capacity would, *in itself*, 'solve the unemployment problem'. Other measures are needed on the supply side—for example, to make the long-term unemployed better able to fill jobs; measures leading to appropriate exchange rates can also help a lot. Above all, it is essential to have a good set of policies to raise the level of aggregate demand to an appropriate level—starting with a relatively rapid rate of increase whilst the level of unemployment is being reduced, and then settling to a steady upward trend, in line with a steady growth of economic potential. If there is not a good overall strategy, *specific* measures to raise industrial capacity or increase the availability of suitable labour may simply leave these extra resources underemployed.

SOME FINAL OBITER DICTA

To repeat, the first task is to persuade the governments of the world (and various international institutions) that they are *not* powerless to reduce the level of unemployment. This policy objective should be given a much higher priority in relation to other objectives, which may well be desirable, but which are not as important as reducing unemployment from present levels.

A successful strategy should include many different types of action, including the improvement of existing methods of pay-determination (needed as part of the strategy for keeping inflation down to tolerable levels).[7]

In the UK an expansion of industrial capacity is an essential ingredient of a policy to reduce unemployment. It is not a cure-all, but it is a *necessary* condition for a general strategy to be successful.

'Solving the unemployment problem now' does not mean that it will stay solved, unless an appropriate strategy is also followed in later years.

---

[6] The development of oil production in the North Sea may even be more effective for this purpose, but the scope for this is limited. Moreover, extra production of oil now reduces the reserves available to provide output in future years.

[7] I would like to draw the reader's special attention to Chapter 7 on the working of the Japanese labour market—even though it reveals that special surveys, conducted at five-year intervals, give a less rosy picture of the unemployment level than the regular published statistics.

Successful policies to deal with (say) a deficit on the balance of payments should not be condemned on the argument that the 'benefit brought by devaluation had disappeared five years later': realistic economics has no place for the simple verdict 'and so they lived happily ever after'.

INTRODUCTION

Jonathan Michie

The reliance on deflationary macroeconomic policies to combat inflation has led not only to high levels of unemployment globally since the mid-1970s, but also to a serious erosion of industrial capacity in many countries, including Britain, so that we no longer have adequate capacity to employ the labour force fully. In the 1980s, with demand well below full employment levels, capacity throughout the European Union (EU) was hit by closures and inhibitions on investment in additional capacity. The problem today is that depressing demand is more effective in reducing capacity than expanding demand is in increasing it. Indeed, the desire to avoid inflation rules out the option of increasing capacity by expanding demand to the point where there are shortages and then waiting for capacity to expand to satisfy them.

In Chapter 1 John Grieve Smith stresses the importance of demand expectations and risk in firms' decisions about expanding capacity. Firms need to be confident that demand will grow at such a rate as to validate any expansion of their capacity; but experience in recent years has made managers cautious about overestimating future sales, as the penalties for doing so tend to be much greater than for losing potential business by failing to expand.

The real problem about encouraging investment in new capacity is that of risk—not that the cost of its output is higher, as the neoclassicists continually imply when suggesting that lower wage costs are needed to make it viable: new plant is, if anything, more efficient then existing plant. The key question is how to reduce this risk and how to make firms more willing to take it. Once this is recognized as one of the central problems of economic policy today, attention will focus on the various means by which this can be effected: the government's own economic strategy, the institutional factors determining the supply of capital, interest rates, company taxation, and so on.

Michael Kitson and Jonathan Michie (Chapter 2) document the relative decline in Britain's industrial performance. Manufacturing output today is barely higher than it was twenty years ago. Although the share of employment in manufacturing has been declining generally throughout the industrial world, the UK has seen by far the largest reduction—a fall of 16 per cent, for example, in the decade between 1976 and 1986, representing more than 2 million jobs. The fall in manufacturing employment has been mirrored by a rise in unemployment of a similar magnitude. This extreme decline in manufacturing employment reflects the fact that the growth of manufacturing productivity since the mid-1970s has been almost wholly reflected in job cuts rather than output growth. And the failure of manufacturing output to expand has been matched, understandably, by a corresponding lack of expansion in capacity.

This poor performance of British manufacturing industry has also resulted in a failure to produce a sufficient volume of manufactured exports to pay for imports at a reasonable level of economic growth and employment. In Chapter 3 Andy Cosh, Ken Coutts, and Alan Hughes examine the improved contribution to the balance of payments needed from manufacturing industry if Britain is to restore full employment within the foreseeable future; and they go on to estimate the increase in capacity which will be required if that is to be achieved. They compare the possible development of the UK economy over the next ten years on two hypotheses: the first, 'slow-growth' projection, assumes the continuation of past medium-term trends in manufacturing performance, and assumes that the rate of growth of gross domestic product is limited by the need to keep the current balance of payments deficit within manageable limits. The second, 'investment in capacity' projection, assumes that higher investment in new capacity and new products will improve export performance and reduce the propensity to import. A faster rate of growth is then consistent with an elimination of the current account deficit by the year 2005. In the first case unemployment in 2005 would be 2 million; in the second case 1.5 million. Such a strategy supplemented by special employment measures, such as more young people staying on in further education and training, more public sector employment, and shorter hours, could reduce recorded unemployment to less than 1 million.

The faster growth case would imply an average growth rate of manufacturing output of 3.5 per cent between 1995 and 2005, only slightly higher than the 3.2 per cent averaged in the twenty-five years up to 1973, but considerably better than the 0.8 per cent achieved between 1973 and 1995. The investment expenditure required is substantial but the growth of investment projected over the first five years would only bring investment back up to 1989 levels. The orders of magnitude which emerge from these calculations suggest that although manufacturing firms would certainly need to increase their investment, the sums required are not impossibly large. The question is what shifts in policy and attitudes would be needed to get on to that path.

In Chapter 4 Ciaran Driver examines the statistical evidence suggesting that firms have become more cautious about investing in new capacity in recent years. He analyses the answers to the CBI Industrial Trend Surveys' questions on capacity utilization and factors limiting capital expenditure and their implications for 'capacity stance', that is, the ratio of planned capacity to expected demand. Since the 1970s the capacity stance has tightened with firms implicitly accepting higher levels of restraint on output due to insufficient capacity.

Using the required rate of return in relation to the cost of capital as a proxy for reluctance to take on risk, Driver shows that there is evidence of growing caution about the risks of installing additional capacity. Means must be found to tackle this. In particular the operation of corporate taxation needs to be reconsidered. The elimination of free depreciation and the reduction of corporate tax rates have adversely altered the balance of risk between profiting from expansion and losing from over-capacity.

'Capacity' is frequently discussed as if it were solely a question of available plant and its expansion solely a matter of additional investment. But the determinants of 'capacity' in the sense of a firm's potential output are much wider, particularly in less capital intensive industries and the service sector. A firm's ability to produce depends on its managerial structure and labour force, and decisions to expand capacity involve decisions in this field as well as investment in plant. It is frequently assumed that a limiting factor here is the supply of skilled labour, but Peter Robinson (Chapter 5) suggests that this fear tends to be exaggerated. The reported incidence of skill shortages in the mid-1990s was running at only half the level reported in the late 1980s when unemployment was last down to around 8.5 per cent. Reported skill shortages only increased sharply in the late 1980s after the economy had been going through a period of very rapid output growth and sharply falling unemployment. A slower rate of output growth and more gradual reduction in unemployment might not have caused any serious skill shortages.

Considering the effects of skill shortages on wage inflation, Robinson concludes that they made only a marginal contribution, perhaps 1 per cent, to the upward creep in wage inflation in the late 1990s. A modest but sustained recovery in the mid-1990s could be expected to have even less effect.

In Chapter 6 Simon Lee discusses the supply of finance for industry in the UK and contrasts it with the 'Rhineland Model' that appears to have supported German industry so successfully. He emphasizes German banks' concern with the long-term interests of the businesses they back as opposed to the 'short-termism' prevalent in the British system, whose major concern is to establish highly liquid markets in industrial securities. A further factor limiting investment in new capacity is the unrealistically higher target rates of return set by suppliers of capital—and by firms themselves in evaluating investment proposals.

Can the problems of the supply of capital, particularly to small and medium-sized firms, be solved by changes in the 'financial products' supplied by existing institutions or can nothing effective be done without more fundamental institutional changes? One of the most pressing fields of enquiry is the role of the major clearing banks as they play such a dominant role already in industrial finance. Are they prepared to move into the field of 'risk' (that is, performance-related) finance rather than confine themselves to loans and overdrafts? Or will they continue to leave this field to more specialized institutions? Is there scope for one or more new development banks on the 3i model? Lee, quoting Will Hutton's *The State We're In*, suggests that the necessary improvements will come about only in the context of fundamental constitutional reform.

The apparent ability of the Japanese economy to maintain capacity even in face of recession is analysed in Chapter 7 by Hidehiro Iwaki with particular regard to the lifetime—or, as he characterizes it, 'long-term'—employment practice and the wage system based on *nenko* (seniority and contribution). Recorded unemployment rates in Japan remain far lower than those in the EU or even North America. Iwaki points out that survey data suggest that unemployment in Japan is in fact considerably higher than is recorded by the official jobless count; however, this does not alter the comparative picture, since similar survey work in other countries also records higher unemployment than is reported in those countries' official statistics.[1] What emerges from such work is that the unemployment crisis is far worse globally than the reported statistics generally admit.

The European picture is surveyed in Chapter 8 by Grahame Thompson, who analyses in particular the European Commission's policy responses—those proposed and those actually implemented—and discusses the likely prospects for economic expansion in face of the various political constraints. The Commission has based its policy initiatives—or at least its advocacy of them—on macroeconomic simulations, and Thompson looks behind the reported results of these, to analyse the macroeconometric model itself and the assumptions embedded within it. The model is shown to be similar to most neoclassical-synthesis types, with all the shortcomings this implies. Nevertheless, the simulations demonstrate clear benefits from increased investment; the failure of the member states to accept even the modest Commission proposals along these lines is thus shown to be due more to a lack of political will than to any serious questioning of the benefits which would flow from such a course of action.

The US picture is analysed in Chapter 9 by Peter Berg and Eileen Appelbaum of the Washington-based Economic Policy Institute, who demonstrate how business strategy is being subjected to various constraints emanating from financial markets. In particular, the new-found enthusiasm for shareholder activism is shown to pose risks for economic performance when firms are pressured to deliver short-term results and dividend payments. Even the tying of management remuneration to corporate results through share options and the like can have perverse effects. All this is inhibiting the creation of new capacity, and preventing the adoption of high-performance work systems.

---

[1] We are grateful to Peter Robinson for making this point.

How these problems can be tackled through the implementation of appropriate industrial policy is described by Michael Best and Robert Forrant in Chapter 10. By 'appropriate' is meant not just an industrial policy which is grounded in a detailed knowledge of the region for which it is being developed, but also a recognition that the ability of industry to innovate will be constrained by the time it takes to move from concept development through to final marketing, and the need to reduce the length of this cycle is therefore a key to creating an innovative industrial sector.

The creation of new and more advanced industrial capacity requires new investment, yet the need to drive up investment rates is often diverted in policy debates onto the question of how to increase savings; this has been a particularly dominant argument in the US, and can be quite damaging when it switches attention away from the need actually to create capacity. In Chapter 11 Bob Pollin therefore refutes this argument at both theoretical and empirical levels, showing that the supposed shortage of savings is an illusory constraint to the creation of new capacity and a return to full employment. Expanding investment and output will themselves tend to generate additional saving, out of the newly created wealth.

Finally, in Chapter 12, Cowling and Sugden return to the need for an industrial strategy, and argue that this should be seen in particular within the context of the increased role in the global economy—and in the economies of most individual countries—of transnational corporations. Not only has the potentially disruptive effects of transnational corporations increased the need for a conscious industrial policy to be developed by government—at local, regional, national and transnational levels—but such strategies need to be developed and implemented as part of a conscious effort to increase the extent of democratic involvement in the workings of the economy.

CONCLUSION

The key to sustainable growth and a return to full employment, then, is to ensure both a continuous expansion of demand and for this to be matched by increased output rather than by inflation or, in the case of individual countries, trade imbalances. *Genuine* supply-side policies—that is, policies which really will lead to an increased and more efficient supply of goods and services, rather than the deflationary and deregulatory policies which are so often mis-termed 'supply-side', simply because they are being promoted in the context of a disregard for demand conditions—require an expansion of industrial capacity, and economic capacity more generally.

The growth process involves 'hysteresis'—that is, history matters, and economies can get locked into vicious cycles of decline. Thus, for example, whatever the supposed increased static efficiencies of free-market policies, if these weaken the manufacturing sector of an individual economy, such as Britain, then that risks becoming a destabilizing process that will inhibit growth. Hence the need for industrial policies, as analysed in several of the following chapters; likewise, trade policies such as explored in Chapter 2 are also central to any growth strategy, as are policies to control the operation of multinationals, as explored in Chapter 12. Trends towards increased globalization—with capital becoming ever more footloose and individual transnational corporations ever more unaccountable—risk exacerbating current inequalities, and threaten to perpetuate the present high levels of unemployment. It is in this context that the increased inequalities which have been witnessed since the early 1980s, globally and within individual countries, can best be tackled—not simply by redistribution alone, but by an egalitarian growth strategy which creates the conditions, including the necessary expansion in economic capacity, to overcome poverty and inequality. Creating additional industrial capacity will not be a simple task, but it is essential for achieving any substantial reduction in unemployment.

Part I

Demand, Capacity, and Employment

1. Rebuilding Industrial Capacity

John Grieve Smith

INTRODUCTION

The retreat from full employment in the 1980s started with the use of conventional Keynesian demand management to restrain demand in order to cut the accelerating rate of inflation. Initially it represented a change in emphasis from concern with full employment to concern with inflation, rather than a revolution in political or economic ideology. But, as time went on, the re-emergence of mass unemployment became part of a widespread reaction against the post-war consensus with its commitment to full employment and co-operation between unions, employers, and government to avoid an inflationary wage–price spiral. Monetarist and free-market thinking began to dominate economic policy. At first the intellectual advocates of monetarism maintained that inflation could be avoided by controlling the money supply without any long-term effect on unemployment, and that if unemployment did continue it was due to restrictions on the free working of the labour market. But in practice the 1980s saw the emergence of a new balance of political objectives in which unemployment became a more acceptable regulator of wage demands than the 'corporatism' of earlier post-war years when strong trade unions worked closely with government and employers. Unemployment remained high despite the deregulation of labour markets.

Today, as the political and social dangers of prolonged mass unemployment have become more apparent, opinion is turning back to the need to re-establish full employment; but the still pervasive influence of monetarist thinking means that the economic policies needed to achieve it are still out of fashion, in particular the denial of any role for demand management and the insistence that the problem is essentially one of establishing greater flexibility in the labour market. Lower wages or labour costs are not a universal remedy for unemployment, although they may help one firm or country secure jobs at the expense of another.

After a decade or more in which mass unemployment has become virtually a built-in feature of the advanced economies, there are new and unprecedented problems in restoring output and employment to the levels required to restore full employment. We start from a position where effective capacity is no longer adequate to employ the work-force fully and the

I am indebted to Ciaran Driver for helpful discussions about the capacity problem.

institutional arrangements which prevented a high demand for labour leading to a wage–price spiral have been dismantled. This is a new challenge in
the post-war world. By contrast to the earlier post-war decades, there is
now a danger that increasing demand will lead to shortages of capacity and
inflationary price increases while unemployment still remains high by historical levels. The rebuilding of lost capacity is therefore a key requirement
for restoring full employment, but one which has received very little attention. Indeed, in so far as the concept of 'structural unemployment' in
Europe has any meaning in present circumstances, it might be applied to
the level of unemployment associated with the shortfall of capacity below
full employment levels.

The thesis of this chapter is that the popular labour market solutions to
the problem of restoring full employment are misconceived, and that the
four key issues at the present time are:

1. re-establishing the role of demand management as a determinant of
   output and employment, rather than solely as a means of controlling
   inflation;
2. establishing a new international financial regime, which (like Bretton
   Woods) includes among its objectives the pursuit of full employment;
3. reforming the pay-bargaining system to obviate the use of unemployment to avoid a wage–price spiral;
4. remedying the lack of adequate capacity to employ the labour force
   fully.

Of these four, the issue of capacity is the most distinctive feature of the
problem of reducing unemployment in the 1990s as compared with earlier
post-war years and is the key theme of this book. First, however, it is necessary to deal with the fashionable view that the solution to the problem of
unemployment lies in the labour market.

LABOUR-MARKET SOLUTIONS

Reducing the Cost of Labour

The dominance of monetarist thinking has led to a revival of the classical
thesis that unemployment reflects a simple imbalance between the supply
and demand for labour that can be remedied by adjusting the price. A more
sophisticated variant, as in Keynes's *General Theory*, is that lower real
wages are a necessary, but not sufficient, condition for higher employment.
But in each case the proposition rests on the fallacious assumption that the
average productivity of labour falls as output and employment increase.

This assumption, so convenient to classical theory, is resonant with the
Ricardian theory of rent with successively less productive land being

brought into production as demand increases. But while such an approach has some validity in agriculture, it bears little relation to the facts of industrial life. In industry today the two practical issues are (*a*) how is productivity related to output within a plant?; and (*b*) how does average productivity compare in different plants which only come into (or out of) use as output rises (or falls)?

In general, average productivity rises with output in an under-used plant—not because the marginal productivity of successive new workers increases, but because additional operatives (each with more or less the same productivity) dilute the overhead costs of managers etc.

As far as successive plants are concerned, the position is not symmetrical between closing a succession of plants in the recession and opening new plants in a recovery—assuming that the closed plants are closed for good, which is almost always the case. When plants are closed, the least efficient are closed first and closure involves going backwards down a rising cost curve. But when successive new plants are brought in over a period of recovery, they should each be more efficient and lower-cost than their predecessors—hence expansion follows a falling cost curve.

It is amazing that, although these facts are widely known to those who work in industry, and were recognized by many Keynesian economists over fifty years ago,[1] so much of the current discussion of unemployment implicitly assumes that lower wages or labour costs are needed to increase employment—for example, proposals to deregulate the labour market, reduce taxes on employment, or subsidize the employment of certain types of worker. The truth is that as far as operating costs are concerned, where current output is economic, additional output at today's prices and wages will almost always be equally, or more, profitable.[2] It is lack of demand, not the need to cut the price of labour, that holds back output and employment.

Wage-cutting is not a solution to unemployment because it reduces purchasing power at the same rate as it reduces costs. It is true that keeping down real wages and other costs relative to our competitors can improve our competitive position and thus increase UK employment (at the expense of others), but this is more a matter of exchange rate policy than pay-bargaining. Moreover in a situation where virtually all industrial countries are suffering from heavy unemployment (hidden rather than apparent in the case of Japan), such beggar-my-neighbour policies do not represent an acceptable solution. Exchange rate adjustments should be limited to the needs of the balance of payments and not regarded as a means of exporting unemployment.

---

[1] Jonathan Michie reviews the literature on this in *Wages in the Business Cycle* (1987).
[2] The accounting treatment of the cost of existing as opposed to new capital equipment may, however, distort the lower real cost of new equipment.

Intensifying the Search for Jobs

There is, however, another set of labour-market proposals which do not
seem to depend on a rising cost curve for labour. The theoretical
justification for these is that, by intensifying the search for jobs, wages will
rise more slowly and unemployment can, or will, be kept lower, that is, the
Non-Accelerating Inflation Rate of Unemployment (NAIRU) will be
reduced. Such proposals concentrate on getting particular sections of the
unemployed back into work. Two groups attract attention: the long-term
unemployed and those who are alleged to prefer to remain unemployed. In
both cases there seems no reason why such action should increase the total
number of jobs available.

While there may be a minority of people who are not actively seeking
employment because they feel they are better off unemployed—because
they either are in a benefit trap, or have given up hope of a job—there is
no reason why making life on the dole more unpleasant for them (or
benefits more generous if they get work) should increase the total number
of jobs; and it seems doubtful whether such measures would have any
significant effect on wage demands. But in their popular textbook on unemployment, Layard, Nickell, and Jackman maintain that 'The unconditional
payment of benefits for an indefinite period is clearly a major cause of high
European unemployment' (Layard *et al.* 1991: 62).

Unskilled Jobs

Another fashionable labour-market theory is the 'shortage of unskilled
jobs'. But the fact that a higher proportion of the less skilled and less educated may be unemployed reflects the fact that they lose out in the battle
for jobs, rather than the nature of the jobs available. This is particularly
true in the service trades where the 'better educated' tend to get the available jobs, and may in many cases be heavily overqualified for the work in
hand. For example, university graduates are taking lower-grade jobs. This
is not to deny the merits of more and better education and training. But it
does suggest that we should not try to create more unskilled jobs by further cheapening the cost of unskilled labour or other means. If there are
enough jobs in total to go round, all the evidence of wartime and post-war
history is that few people will be excluded from work because the jobs are
too skilled or the work-force too unskilled; (see Peter Robinson, Chapter 5
below).

The re-emergence of mass unemployment has already taken a sufficient
toll in terms of increased poverty and growing inequality without our deliberately aggravating it by measures to deregulate the labour market. We
should be suspicious of any measures which could make this trend worse

under the pretext of cutting unemployment. Just as readiness to sacrifice jobs to control inflation reflects a particular set of political and social values, so too does the idea of reducing wages still further for those who are already worst paid. We should, however, on social grounds, be prepared to support measures which help particularly hard-hit categories of the unemployed, such as those who have been out of work for long periods, without falling into the trap of believing that doing so will necessarily create any more jobs in total.

DEMAND MANAGEMENT

The problem of mass unemployment will not be resolved without revising the deflationary bias of fiscal and monetary policy since the 1970s, and in particular acknowledging that fiscal policy has an active role to play. It is ironic that the monetarist approach should have become fashionable, with its almost exclusive reliance on interest rates as the instrument for macro-economic control, when interest-rate policy has become increasingly sensitive to international capital flows and exchange-rate considerations leaving individual countries increasingly less room to manoeuvre. Since—as we saw when the UK was in the European Exchange Rate Mechanism (ERM)—international pressure is virtually always to raise rates, rather than to lower them, the globalization of financial markets has given monetary policy a consistently deflationary bias. It is difficult to adapt interest-rate policy to the differing needs of countries' domestic situations, when interest rate differentials inevitably reflect markets' views of potential exchange-rate movements. Again, freedom of capital movements makes pure monetarism (in the sense of controlling inflation by controlling the money supply) in one country a logical impossibility, when industry (and in principle consumers) can borrow freely abroad. In these circumstances, national governments need to place more, rather than less, reliance on budgetary policy, as opposed to monetary policy. Changes in taxation and government expenditure can be as powerful, or more powerful, instruments for affecting spending than can interest rates. But both need to work together.

Inhibitions about the use of fiscal policy to stimulate demand have been heightened by the effect of the rise in unemployment on governments' budgetary deficits. This has reduced tax revenue and increased spending on social security benefits, thus leading to a widespread deterioration in government finances. The extent to which this deterioration is a result of higher unemployment has been understated by organizations like the OECD, whose definition of 'structural' as opposed to 'cyclical' deficits is based on trend GDP (see Blanchard et al. 1990; Chouraqui et al. 1990). This is seriously misleading because only deteriorations below a new, worsened trend with higher unemployment count as 'cyclical'.

The concern over higher levels of government borrowing in European countries with normally healthy public finances has been greatly exaggerated. First, there is frequently a failure to distinguish capital from current expenditure, or purely financial transactions from those that affect the real economy. Thus governments in those countries who borrow to finance a high level of public investment are under greater pressure than those with a smaller public sector, and there is continual pressure to sell off public assets to reduce borrowing. The economic size of the budget deficit has become hopelessly entangled with what should be arguments about the size of the state sector. Higher public debt does not make a country poorer. It merely means higher transfer payments from taxpayers to holders of debt. The case for incurring higher public debt depends on the purpose for which it is incurred. Higher public investment may well be much needed in its own right, apart from any effect it may have in stimulating demand.

While additional borrowing would increase public debt in the short term, the longer-term effects of such a stimulus on economic activity would have a beneficial effect on public finances. Nor, of course, is higher public borrowing in the depths of a recession in any way inflationary. It is important therefore to examine alternative fiscal policies and their effects on demand and employment over a period of years. These and other issues were discussed in *Unemployment in Europe* (Michie and Grieve Smith 1994).

INTERNATIONAL PAYMENTS

The architects of post-war full employment were very conscious that its achievement was as much an international as a national problem. In the inter-war period exchange-rate and international developments had been important contributors to the employment problem. The Bretton Woods system was broadly effective and remained intact until the introduction of floating exchange rates at the beginning of the 1970s. But although the period of floating rates has coincided with the erosion of full employment, it would be misleading to see a direct causal link. On the one hand, fixed exchange rates have become more difficult to maintain in the face of the growing magnitude of speculative movements in financial capital. On the other hand, a desire to 'manage' or influence variable exchange rates puts continual pressure on governments to govern macroeconomic policy by external as well as internal considerations. Under either system, there could be increasing difficulty in maintaining full employment—as can be seen in the establishment and subsequent breakdown of the ERM. The need with either fixed or floating rates is for international arrangements and institutions which will support, rather than weaken, the achievement of full employment.

The growth of speculative capital movements has made almost every country vulnerable to exchange-rate pressure and thus imparted an extra deflationary bias to the system. Countries with strong currencies are under no corresponding pressure to reduce interest rates or adopt more expansionary fiscal policies—the strength of the Deutschmark in the ERM was a classical case of this problem. To achieve this, a new and more stable exchange-rate regime is needed, capable of withstanding the vastly increased weight of speculative capital movements. Detailed consideration is needed of the possibility of establishing a system of managed 'target' rates, based on a consistent strategy for current-account balances and movements of productive capital between the main trading areas. These and other problems are discussed in *Managing the Global Economy* (Michie and Grieve Smith 1995).

THE CAPACITY PROBLEM

Capacity and Inflation

In the era of full employment little attention needed to be paid to the effects of the path of demand and output (past or forecast) on the growth of productive potential: this growth was determined primarily by the growth of productivity. But in the 1980s with demand well below full employment levels, capacity throughout the EU was eroded by closures and inhibitions on investment in additional capacity. The problem today is that depressing demand is more effective in reducing capacity than expanding demand is in increasing it. The desire to avoid inflation rules out increasing capacity by expanding demand to the point where there are shortages and then waiting for capacity to expand to satisfy them.

Although recovery from the recession is still far from complete, the Treasury and the Bank of England are already concerned (albeit to different degrees) that the economy will run into capacity limitations and price increases will accelerate. This is a legitimate concern, but the imminence of capacity shortages may be exaggerated. Output in manufacturing, the sector where the concept of capacity limitations is most meaningful, is only just returning to its pre-recession peak reached in 1989. Whether we are nearing current capacity limitations is arguable. For a concept whose supposed magnitude is having such a powerful influence on budgetary and monetary policy, there is surprisingly little hard information to go on. The CBI and chambers of commerce industrial enquiries give some indications of changes in pressure on capacity but do not purport to give any absolute measure of potential output and hence how far we are away from any capacity limits. Moreover, with the shift in emphasis away from traditional manufacturing industries, what constitutes 'capacity' needs examining much more broadly. Ciaran Driver discusses the implications of the CBI Survey results in Chapter 4.

We need to establish clearly the interrelationship between capacity, unemployment, and inflation in the 1990s. To do so we must first get away from the NAIRU concept, that there must be a given minimum level of unemployment to avoid inflation accelerating. History belies this. The more recent tendency to discuss the problem of inflation in terms of the 'output gap' is a step forward: at least it takes into account the effect of a reduction in effective capacity following long periods of relatively low demand and high unemployment. But the concept fails to distinguish two distinct factors: (a) the gap between output and effective capacity, that is, the rate of capacity utilization; and (b) the propensity to inflation at any given rate of capacity utilization. Because the second factor varies with time and circumstance, the physical output gap needed to avoid inflation may also vary considerably, as did the NAIRU. Just as there is no fixed level of unemployment at which the economy will operate to keep within a given level of inflation, neither is there any fixed gap between actual and potential output. Moreover the whole idea of an 'output gap' becomes rather strange when the gap becomes negative with the implication that output exceeds capacity (Barrell and Sefton 1995).

It may be correct to think that, in the short term, keeping demand well in check will lead to a low rate of inflation; but in the longer term limiting the growth rate of capacity by limiting expectations of the growth rate of demand accentuates the danger of inflation. Keeping down the growth of capacity perpetuates not only high unemployment, but also the vulnerability of the economy to upturns in demand even if (as in the 'Lawson boom') the economy is still operating way below full capacity. Indeed setting tighter and tighter inflation targets may ironically enough be a recipe for having to operate the economy at higher and higher levels of unemployment in order to avoid inflation. There is no convincing reason for the popular political shibboleth that it will stimulate growth. Indeed, if it is the Government's view that industry should be working at less than x per cent of capacity to keep down inflation, but industry finds it most profitable and safer to operate at over x per cent of capacity (what Ciaran Driver calls their 'capacity stance': see below, Chapter 4) then there will be continual downward pressure on capacity as industry strives for maximum profitability. This is what appears to have been happening to manufacturing industry in the 1980s.

There are thus two related approaches to solving this problem. One is to encourage the expansion of capacity. The other is to take measures to reduce the tendency to inflation at any given level of capacity utilization (such as by the reform of pay-bargaining) so that the Government is less concerned to hold down demand.

Demand Expectations

Since firms' decisions to expand capacity are based to a large extent on their assessment of their future sales, the first question is: what, if anything, can government do to reinforce confidence in future expansion? Expectations depend in part on the public understanding as to government policy and objectives and in part on an assessment of how it will turn out in practice. At present that policy is expressed entirely in terms of keeping down inflation, and there is no suggestion that in pursuing it the Government will be inhibited by the level of unemployment.

For the Government merely to have a short-term target for inflation is inadequate. It is necessary to think again about the way in which macro-economic policy is conceived and expressed. As a start it should embody objectives for the growth of output and capacity as well as rates of inflation. For example the Budget Red Book should not treat the figures for output and unemployment as forecasts on some unstated policy assumptions about the relation between demand and inflation, but as an inherent part of a longer-term strategy.

Any government that is serious about achieving a long-term reduction in unemployment will have to find means of convincing industry that demand will increase enough to justify the extra capacity needed for higher employment. There are bound, of course, still to be periodic fluctuations in demand and output, but the need is to establish a longer-term trend consistent with a gradual reduction in the level of unemployment. The 1994 Budget Red Book (HM Treasury 1994) made it clear that this was not the Treasury's present intention. It assumed that in the next five years output would only increase fast enough to get back onto its previous trend—which would leave unemployment at the high average levels of the last decade.

Firms need to be confident that demand will grow at such a rate as to validate any expansion of their capacity. But in so far as experience is the greatest determinant of expectations, we start from a very difficult point. Experience in recent years had made managers naturally cautious about overestimating future sales—as the penalties for doing so tend to be much greater than for losing potential business by failing to expand. To re-establish such confidence will be difficult, and will require a major change in the whole tenor of economic policy.

Expansion and Risk

Bound up with the question of demand expectations is firms' perception of risk. The characteristic of marginal additions to capacity is not that the real cost of their output is higher as the classicists suggest—on the contrary (as argued above) it is lower. Labour costs should be lower; so too should capital costs—save to the extent that lower returns are acceptable on existing or sunk capital than new capital (see below). The critical problem is the extra *risk* involved, because demand may not expand sufficiently to validate such expansion. A key question therefore is: how can this risk be reduced and made less frightening? There are two problems: to reduce the actual risk and to make firms more willing to take it. The latter point may turn out to be a crucial one in the next decade. The generation now reaching top management posts have lived through a period in which their more adventurous and expansionist contemporaries have often had their judgement faulted and lost their jobs—or if they ran their own businesses lost their livelihood and their home. This is bound to have an inhibiting effect on decision-making—just as the generation who lived through the 1930s often seemed over-cautious in the post-war years in the face of the buoyant level of demand then prevailing.

The risks of investing in capacity which is in the event not fully utilized depends on two main factors: the magnitude of the losses, or shortfall in profits, and the ability of the company to absorb them. In so far as the costs of expanding capacity are capital costs, the key factors are first the cost of capital, and then the ability to cut dividends temporarily, or pay them out of reserves, where the capital is in the form of equity. Whatever the opportunity cost of capital, the use of a company's own reserves, rather than raising new capital, makes a temporary failure to achieve the expected returns less dangerous. In either case, however, the attitude of financial institutions and commentators are of crucial importance. Willingness to take a long-term view is vital.

In the UK a number of institutional factors militate against risk-taking. In the case of smaller firms, their dependence on bank loans and the shortage of risk capital makes them particularly vulnerable when profits are squeezed. With larger firms, their access to our highly developed stock market is a mixed blessing. The stock market is inherently short-term. Fund managers are constantly being judged on their monthly, quarterly, or annual performance. If a firm keeps on plant or labour which is temporarily underemployed in a recession, financial analysts criticize it and implicitly assume that capacity should automatically be trimmed in line with any fall in demand. As Will Hutton (1995) has argued very persuasively, the whole British financial system operates in a way which aggravates this problem.

With the development of service industries, the concept of 'capacity' is increasingly less dependent on physical capacity and more dependent on people—managerial organization, trained and experienced staff, sales agents, etc. The dilemma here is that the easier it is to hire and fire people, the less the apparent risk of taking on more staff either to work new plant or in service industries as additional 'capacity' in themselves. On the other hand, in the longer term the efficiency and competitive power of firms is greater, the more stable and committed their work-force—as the success of

German and Japanese industry testifies. Their willingness to keep on staff in a recession and cut dividends to shareholders (as opposed to vice versa in the UK) helps to preserve capacity. We have got into the perverse and damaging situation where the roles of the suppliers of risk capital and the members of the company (its work-force) have become reversed. If profits are hit, dividends are maintained and employees sacked, rather than dividends being cut and workers being kept on. Employees bear a much greater risk than the suppliers of capital.

Even with a less deflationary bias to macroeconomic policy, there are bound to be some cyclical movements, with temporary recessions from time to time. It is important to develop policies which encourage firms to keep open capacity which is temporarily under-utilized, and to hold together their labour force so that they can respond to the following upturn in demand. This is where the Japanese have hitherto been markedly successful—although, as Hidehiro Iwaki argues in Chapter 7, their system of lifetime employment may also have some adverse effects. With more spare capacity in hand, the inevitable short-term upward blips in demand are less likely to be inflationary.

Cost of Capital

As well as being dependent on sales prospects, decisions to invest in new capacity are also influenced by the cost and availability of capital and the target rates of return sought by firms and financial institutions. The increasing use of interest rates both to combat inflation and to bolster weak currencies creates a bias towards higher real interest rates. The one point where higher inflation can inhibit investment is that high *money*, as opposed to real, rates of interest can increase the real interest burden on a project in its early years relative to later years. This may inhibit start-up projects; but on the other hand investment in new products characteristically secures higher prices and better returns in early rather than later years.

In inhibiting expansion the availability of capital may be as, or more, important than its cost. As every borrower knows, the market for institutional credit is unlike any other market, in that willingness to pay the going price is no guarantee of getting a loan! Banks' losses on commercial lending during the recession seems to have led to a stiffening of their lending criteria in the recent upturn. The periods for which banks are prepared to lend is also crucial, particularly for small businesses in the UK, with their traditional reliance on bank overdrafts—although the Bank of England reports that the ratio of term loans to overdrafts rose from 2 : 3 to 3 : 2 in the period 1992–5.

The dependence of so many businesses on bank loans rather than risk-related capital is an important factor limiting expansion, particularly in high-technology or riskier sectors. In recent years the supply of venture capital has been redirected to the greener pastures of management buy-outs. The supply of equity or mezzanine finance for run-of-the-mill small or medium-sized businesses remains unsatisfactory. Most institutions are looking for a five-year exit and an internal rate of return of at least 20 per cent a year, which is unrealistically high in relation to the general run of results.

With larger businesses, the problem is not so much the supply of equity, but the pressure of the market for short-term results in terms of share prices rather than the long-term profitability of the business.

As other contributors to this volume point out, the supply of industrial capital is clearly not a market where the needs of the customer have been matched by the development of the appropriate products. Banks' 'new products' have mostly been directed at personal customers where, in the case of mortgages at any rate, the supply of capital was already adequate. Save for the establishment of venture capital subsidiaries, which are merely replicas of ordinary venture capital companies, the clearing banks have done little to widen the range of methods of company financing, particularly by developing performance-related loans.

Another area which deserves further investigation is the criteria for evaluating investment projects, particularly those which will expand capacity, adopted by firms and financial institutions. A recent survey by the Bank of England of 250 (mainly large and medium-sized) companies found that the average post-tax 'threshold' or 'hurdle' rate for the internal rate of return was 20 per cent in money terms (Wardlow 1994). Only 26 per cent of firms had reduced the threshold as inflation abated. Were it not for the arithmetical ingenuity of the project champions putting forward investment proposals, not many projects would be approved!

Once the need to reduce the risk of expanding capacity is recognized as one of the central problems of economic policy today, attention will focus on how this can be assisted by changes in the system of company taxation, the use of grants, or the establishment of new financial institutions (such as an Industrial Bank) to provide capital in a sympathetic manner. In so far as the objective is to stimulate the creation of additional capacity rather than investment *per se*, the last two essentially discretionary approaches may be more practical than changes in tax law, because of the difficulties of defining in any watertight legal sense expenditure on 'additional' capacity.

PAY-BARGAINING

To create industrial confidence in continued expansion, governments need to carry the conviction that they can restrain inflation without slamming on the brakes. If the growth of capacity and employment is not to be continually sacrificed in the effort to curb inflation, we have to tackle the wage–price spiral by other means. Experience suggests that leaving employers and unions entirely to their own devices will not (in the UK at any rate) solve the problem. The fact that in 1995 wage increases are still relatively low does not mean that the problem has been solved. Unless the economy is to be condemned to a prolonged period of depression with unemployment continuing at over 2 million, it seems more than likely that inflation would accelerate again, if any more substantial recovery were to take place. The proposition that inflation is now beaten seems extremely doubtful— unless the corollary is that we are prepared to endure an indefinite period of massive unemployment and relive the 1930s. The sooner we do try to do something about the pay-bargaining system before the rate of pay increases rises sharply again, the better.

The objective is clear enough: to establish a pay-bargaining system in which the average rate of increase in money wages is equal to, or does not greatly exceed, the rate of increase in productivity across the economy as a whole. It is frequently suggested that the appropriate criterion is that pay in any particular firm, or sector of the economy, should rise in line with productivity there. This is not a tenable proposition. Productivity inevitably rises much faster in some sectors than others: the most glaring example is the comparison between inherently labour-intensive services, such as education and health care, and manufacturing industry with its endless possibilities for replacing labour with new and more advanced machinery. To gear pay increases to the growth rate of productivity in each of these sectors would mean a growing and intolerable difference in absolute pay levels—an outcome which is not practical in a market economy where pay for similar skills tends to equalize between sectors. It would also imply that overall price stability must mean that all prices remain stable, instead of the continuous adjustment of relative prices that is natural in a dynamic market economy.

In practice the firm-by-firm, or sector-by-sector, productivity approach is a recipe for inflation, because it means that the motor industry or some other leading industry with a high rate of productivity growth, becomes the pay setter and everyone else follows suit. Similar drawbacks apply to the idea that the solution is to make pay more sensitive to market conditions. That may be all right in a recession; but once activity picks up it is a good recipe for a speedy renewal of the wage–price spiral. The fragmentation of wage-bargaining in recent years has accentuated the problem.

One of the factors behind the rate of increase in pay is the adherence to annual pay rounds. If employers and unions could be persuaded to adopt longer contracts while inflation is still low, this could be a useful advance.

The most fundamental imperative, however, is to inject into the bargaining process a recognition of the overall needs of the economy, in particular the common interest in avoiding inflation. Discussion of the precise machinery for achieving this is less fundamental than achieving recognition that it needs to be done. The idea of 'co-ordinated bargaining' was beginning to be the topic of a good deal of discussion until the recession led to the present temporary easing of the problem.

It is sometimes suggested that any national discussions about the general level of pay increases should be limited to representatives of employers and unions without the Government. But given the Government's ultimate responsibility for economic policy and intense interest in the prospects for inflation, this seems unrealistic. The abolition of the National Economic Development Council has removed the most obvious forum in which to commence any tripartite discussions in a low-key way. But there is no reason why any new initiative should not start with *ad hoc* meetings rather than any formal framework. The aim of such discussions should be to produce guidelines which both sides will adhere to in detailed negotiations within particular industries or firms. The form of such guidelines will need to vary from time to time with circumstances; but the objective should be that the agreed guidelines effectively establish the 'going rate', rather than key negotiations in leading parts of the private sector or government statements of pay policy for the public sector. This does not, of course, mean that workers in all industries or firms should get identical increases, but that the common element, or the normal expectation, that always exists in any particular wage round should be in tune with the needs of the economy as a whole.

There is obviously scope for considerable debate as to whether there should be any more formal machinery involved in such a solution. I have made some proposals for such machinery (Grieve Smith 1990), but until the need for some more co-ordinated approach re-enters the realm of public discussion any such detailed proposals seem out of place.

The object of such reform in pay-bargaining arrangements is to make it *possible* to achieve full employment without inflation by appropriate demand policies. It is not a solution in itself and should not be confused with proposals to reduce unemployment by cutting labour costs—which is in my view a fallacious approach to the problem.

CONCLUSION

There is no simple policy solution to the capacity dilemma, but the first essential is to appreciate correctly the nature of the problem, which has so far received little public recognition. It is essential to adopt two complementary approaches to solving it. On the supply side the aim must be to facilitate the expansion of capacity by improving the availability of and cost of capital and reducing or making more acceptable the risks involved. The key factor is not that marginal capacity is inherently more expensive, but that it is riskier.

Just as the whole drift of policy in recent years has been to elevate short-term financial results above long-term industrial growth, so too the need now is to re-examine our financial institutions, the provision of risk capital to industry, company taxation, take-over regulations, together with company law and corporate governance, to give a higher priority to the maintenance of industrial capacity.

On the demand side the need is to reinstate the growth of output, employment, and capacity, as well as the control of inflation, as basic objectives: none of these can be achieved in isolation for the reasons discussed above. But any strategy for expanding demand and output over a period of years sufficient to reduce unemployment, without unacceptable levels of inflation, must include a credible policy for pay-bargaining. Without it, industry will not believe that any higher level of demand is practicable and will not invest in the additional capacity required.

The problem of the interrelated intentions and expectations of government and industry can only be solved in a climate of mutual discussion and co-operation. No major impact can be made on the unemployment problem without renewed discussion between the Government, the CBI, and the TUC. The dropping of full employment as an objective and the retreat from 'corporatism' were interrelated. A return to full employment must correspondingly involve a return to a more co-operative approach to economic and industrial problems.

REFERENCES

Barrell, R., and Sefton, J., (1995), 'Output Gaps: Some Evidence from the UK, France and Germany', *NIESR Review*, 1.

Blanchard, O., Chouraqui J. C., Hagemann, R. P., and Sartor, N. (1990), 'The Sustainability of Fiscal Policy: New Answers to an Old Question', *OECD Economic Studies*, 15 (Autumn).

Chouraqui, J. C., Hagemann, R. P., and Sartor, N. (1990), *Indicators of Fiscal Policy: A Re-examination*, OECD Working Paper 78 (April).

Grieve Smith, J. (1990), *Pay Strategy for the 1990s* (London: IPPR).

HM Treasury (1994), *Financial Statement and Budget Report, 1995–6*.

Hutton, W. (1995), *The State We're In* (London: Jonathan Cape).

Layard, R., Nickell, S., and Jackman, J. (1991), *Unemployment* (Oxford: Oxford University Press).

Michie, J. (1987), *Wages in the Business Cycle: An Empirical and Methodological Analysis* (London: Frances Pinter).

—— and Grieve Smith, J. (1994) (eds.), *Unemployment in Europe* (London: Academic Press).

—— (1995) (eds.), *Managing the Global Economy* (Oxford: Oxford University Press).

Wardlow, A. (1994), 'Investment Appraisal Criteria and the Impact of Low Inflation', *Bank of England Bulletin*, 34/3.

2. Manufacturing Capacity, Investment, and Employment

Michael Kitson and Jonathan Michie

INTRODUCTION

Britain's manufacturing base is too small and uncompetitive. These problems are interconnected—increasing demand for British products can only come from improving the competitiveness of the manufacturing sector. Yet currently there is no active macroeconomic policy to expand demand for manufactures. Nor is there an effective industrial policy to improve competitiveness. These problems will remain as long as the Government sticks to its free-market approach to policy and to its belief that competitiveness can be achieved by cost-cutting measures pursued via product and labour-market deregulation.

Appropriate economic policy must be based on relevant economic theory. Starting from an economist's textbook world of Walrasian General Equilibrium, any imperfections such as the existence of trade unions, or of wage levels which are not instantaneously and costlessly adjustable, are inevitably viewed as being impediments to economic growth. But if we want to analyse actual economies we should not start from there; research within that framework tends simply to rediscover as problems that which had been theorized as such, whether explicitly or implicitly, from the start. All we get from empirical work based on such misleading assumptions is, to paraphrase Bertrand Russell, confusion at a higher level.[1]

This chapter argues, first, that deindustrialization can be a serious problem for the whole economy—not just for the industrial sector itself; secondly, that Britain's industrial performance over the past thirty years has been poor; thirdly, that neither the specific problem of deindustrialization nor the consequent general problem of continued relative economic decline were solved in the 1980s; and fourthly, that the key reason for the relatively poor performance of British industry has been underinvestment in manufacturing. This underinvestment has been allowed to persist owing to the

We are extremely grateful to John Wells for supplying us with unpublished data and for pointing out to us errors in the published data of the CSO. We are also grateful for comments from Gary Dymski, John Grieve Smith, Geoff Harcourt, Laurence Harris, Jane Humphries, and Brian Reddaway.

[1] What Russell actually said was: 'Education is a process of becoming confused at a higher level.'

lack of any strong modernizing force within British society, with the trade union movement having been too weak to force through any such modernization, and with government policy having been at best rather ineffectual and at worst positively harmful. The reasons for this policy failure lie in Britain's economic history and in the consequent distorted nature of both the economy and society. This fundamental problem, then, of a lack of any strong modernizing force, has if anything been exacerbated since 1979.[2]

DOES MANUFACTURING MATTER?

Does it *matter* that the 1980s growth was so skewed towards services, particularly financial services, and the construction of shopping malls for the sale of what were increasingly becoming imported manufactured goods? We would argue that yes, it does. The UK economy requires a large and competitive manufacturing sector in order to generate sufficient exports to pay for necessary imports and because of the symbiotic relationship between the manufacturing and service sectors.

There has been considerable debate over the causes of 'deindustrialization'.[3] The relative decline of manufacturing, and particularly manufacturing employment, and the corresponding relative growth of services, is prevalent in both slow- and fast-growing countries (see Petit 1986). This has led some to see the process as being some sort of an inevitable historical evolution; the argument that there are definable stages of economic development as advanced by Fisher (1935), Rostow (1960), Kuznets (1966), and Chenery (1960) have as a common feature that the final stages are characterised by a modern tertiary sector with growing preferences for service products.

A first explanation of this phenomenon is based on the proposition that there is a faster relative growth of labour productivity in manufacturing than in services. This will result in the costs of manufactures falling relative to services. Assuming that the demand for manufactures and services is relatively price inelastic, the share of manufacturing employment in total employment will decrease. Many studies including those by Fuchs (1968), Baumol (1967), Saxonhouse (1985) and Summers (1985) have presented evidence that productivity differences are the main source of the decline in

---

[2] It would be impossible to do justice in this chapter to all these claims, although all four points are of course discussed in detail elsewhere. A small selection of the relevant literature is, on the first point, Singh (1977), Rowthorn and Wells (1987), Singh (1987), Cosh, Hughes, and Rowthorn (1993, 1994), and Wells (1993); on the second, Eatwell (1982) and Coates (1994); on the third, the various contributors to Michie (ed.)(1992); and on the fourth, Fine and Harris (1985), Costello *et al.* (1989), Deakin, Michie, and Wilkinson (1992), Sawyer (1994), Kitson and Michie (1994), Nolan (1994), and Michie and Wilkinson (1995).

[3] See e.g. Singh (1977; 1987) and Rowthorn and Wells (1987).

manufacturing employment, although others such as Marquand (1979) dispute that services have low productivity.

Like much of the analysis of the service sector, the lagging productivity thesis is limited by the data problems. In particular there are substantial difficulties in measuring productivity in services, as in most cases no physical output is produced. In the UK, however, the evidence on relative price movements (assuming similar wage rates in manufacturing and services for the same occupation), and the suggestion that non-marketed service output may be overestimated (as such output is measured, in part, simply via wage bills)—so that service productivity may actually be lower than the official figures would suggest—does add support to the idea that differential productivity growth between the two sectors plays an important role (Gershuny and Miles, 1983).

A second explanation for the relative decline of manufacturing and the relative growth of services stems from the changing structure of demand as incomes increase. This explanation is relevant to the growth of personal or consumer services as opposed to intermediate or producer services, although the distinction is often arbitrary. It has been argued that, as their income elasticity of demand is greater than one, the growth in demand for services will exceed the growth of income. Gershuny (1978), for example, pointed out that in Britain wealthier households spent a greater proportion of their income on services; such relationships, however, seem to be unstable over time and suffer from definitional problems, as much of this service expenditure is on associated goods. Fuchs (1968) argued that the income elasticity of demand for services was only slightly greater than that for other products and was not a major explanation of the growth of the service sector. Similarly, Baumol et al. (1989) reject the demand explanation for the USA, as during the past few decades manufacturing output has risen as fast as the output of services.

A third explanation for the relative 'decline' of manufacturing is the changing source of service provision, with activities which were previously undertaken by firms becoming increasingly contracted out (to the service sector). Fuchs (1968) found that changes in intermediate service production in the USA accounted for 10 per cent of the total expansion of service sector employment.[4]

Contracting out can also take place with consumer services, such as the increased use of restaurants and housekeepers, with such service sector activity replacing work which was previously done within the household but which did not appear in the national accounts. The evidence here, however, is mixed. Rising incomes may encourage the replacement of domestic activities with commercial equivalents, but conversely the opposite may

---

[4] Gary Dymski pointed out to us that with the emergence of new industries, some of these, such as software development, may have been classified as services when they perhaps belong more naturally to manufacturing (at least in part).

happen owing to increased leisure time and the relatively high cost of services. Also, manufactured products may replace or reduce the need for some services (the television replaces the theatre). Such a substitution effect has led Gershuny and Miles (1983) to argue that we are moving towards a 'self-service' economy.

The impact of 'contracting out' is complicated not just by the usual measurement problems but also because observing the net changes for the sector may reveal little about the significant changes within the sector. Some services may be internalized within firms and households while other services are contracted out. What is required is an understanding of both processes.

The mode of service provision needs also to be considered in the context of changing economic, technological, and institutional conditions. The recessionary and uncertain environment since 1979 has led many firms in the UK to concentrate on 'core' or central activities, contracting out peripheral activities ranging from catering and cleaning to design. The impetus for this change, however, seems to differ between firms. Some responded to the contraction of markets by attempting to restructure their production processes in order to become more competitive in the long term; others by attempting simply to cut costs in the short term.

Kaldor (1966) argued that employment in services may restrict the labour supply for manufacturing; hence his advocacy of the Selective Employment Tax. Although he later retracted this argument in favour of a demand constraint one, he retained the idea that services were not as dynamic as manufacturing. This echoed the views of Lewis (1954), Cornwall (1977), and others, that manufacturing is an engine of growth. The extension of the market for manufactured products would lead through the benefits of economies of scale to increased competitive advantage and hence to increased economic growth. The implication of this argument is that the service sector may expand in terms of both output and employment; but, if full employment is to be achieved, there must be sufficient demand for manufactured products. And, as noted by Godley (1986), Britain was the only advanced industrial nation since 1960 where the growth of manufacturing output was less than the growth of output of other goods and services. Thus the relative decline in manufacturing output was a unique British phenomenon.

In neoclassical economics, divergences from 'equilibrium' can be rectified through price adjustment and/or the correction of market failures. In reality, economies do not behave like this. First, history is important (as recognized in recent path-dependent models), such that the quantity and quality of factors of production accumulated from the past determine what can be produced in the immediate future. This is inconsistent with conventional equilibrium theory, which asserts that an economy is constrained by exogenous variables which remain stable over time (Kaldor 1985).

Additionally, it implies that it is difficult and expensive to reverse many economic decisions. If a factory is closed or if a market is lost, it is difficult to regain the status quo ante. Secondly, the impact of economic shocks may not only have a once and for all impact on long-run capacity but may lead to cumulative changes. Thus, as Allyn Young stated, forces of economic change are endogenous:

They are engendered from within the economic system. No analysis, of the forces making for economic equilibrium, forces that we might say are tangential at any moment of time, will serve to illumine this field, for movements away from equilibrium, departures from previous trends are characteristic of it. (quoted in Kaldor 1985: 64)

The factor generating economic change for Young (1928) was increasing returns.[5] This led to Myrdal (1957), Kaldor (1972), and others identifying the twin processes of virtuous cycles of growth and vicious cycles of decline. For Kaldor, manufacturing acts as an engine of growth as it exhibits increasing returns while services are characterized by constant returns. This proposition may be too simplistic as increasing returns are likely to exist in services (despite problems of measurement). This does not, however, diminish the importance of the cumulative causation analysis for understanding the diverging economic performance and prospects of different countries. First, divergences in countries' growth paths can develop as a result of differences—due to the size of the market—in the ability of competing countries to exploit increasing returns in their *tradable* output sectors; and the tradable goods sector remains dominated by manufacturing. Secondly, the cumulative processes will not only lead to differences in cost competitiveness but also to other non-price factors, such as product quality, customer service, and technological development.

Growing economies, for instance, will be able to invest in capital and skills enabling them to improve processes and products. Conversely, in economies suffering relative decline, a lack of investment and a dwindling skill base are likely to constrain future growth. For the latter this may take the form of a reduction of in-house training and/or a decline in support for external provision by training agencies, so that the local infrastructure for skill generation is weakened. This, and the migration from the trade of workers in a position to do so, creates a skill shortage. The response to this, in the face of the decline in formal training, is the substitution of on-the-job instruction with a focus on a narrow range of specific skills to meet the firms' immediate needs, often accompanied by the exclusion of worker

---

[5] New models of economic growth also stress endogeneity due to externalities in the production of innovations. Endogenous technical progress, within a neoclassical framework, was developed by Romer (1986; 1990) and Lucas (1988) amongst others. Unlike the traditional neoclassical model of growth (Solow 1970), the new models may allow for divergences in growth (as in Kaldorian models) depending on the extent to which there are international spillovers of knowledge and technology.

representatives from the training design and implementation processes. Consequently, the skill content of jobs is diluted and this interacts with the deterioration of the terms and conditions of employment and the increasing pessimism about future prospects of the industry to discourage new entrants from traditional areas of recruitment. And any subsequent relaxation of hiring standards to meet the labour shortage serves to further reinforce the social downgrading of the job, the dissipation of skills, the loss of competitiveness, and industrial decline.[6]

BRITAIN'S INDUSTRIAL PERFORMANCE

As indicated in Table 2.1, which gives output, employment, and productivity for the manufacturing sector, manufacturing output in Britain was barely higher in the mid-1990s than it was twenty years before. The picture is one of rising output up to 1973, followed by a sharp fall to 1975 and subsequent recovery in the second half of the 1970s (generally taken as peaking again in 1979 although the annual index averages to a lower overall figure over 1979 than for 1978). The deep recession of the early 1980s was followed by a weak recovery, leading straight into the Lawson boom, taking manufacturing output to a new peak in 1989 before falling again in the early 1990s recession. Meanwhile productivity grew in every year apart from 1975 and 1980, even when output fell. There has been an almost continual decline in manufacturing employment from its peak level in 1966.

Table 2.2 compares, in summary form, this experience with that of the UK's main competitors. The UK is the only one of the six with a lower average level of manufacturing output over the years 1979–89 than over the years 1973–9, and was also the only country to experience a fall in output between the years 1973 and 1979; (between 1979 and 1989 this average growth returned to a positive figure, albeit lower than in any of the other countries apart from France). A similar picture emerges for manufacturing employment, with the UK being the only one to experience a fall between 1964 and 1973; while others saw employment fall between 1979 and 1989, none did so at the rate experienced in the UK, while during 1973–9 only Germany and Japan experienced a faster rate of job losses and, as indicated above, in both cases this was due to strong productivity growth rather than simply output loss as was the case for the UK. In the three peak-to-peak periods, Britain was at the bottom of the league table of the six countries in two of the periods, and second bottom in the third.[7] This poor record on manufacturing output resulted in declining manufacturing employment.

---

[6] These points are argued in more detail in Wilkinson (1992) and Michie and Wilkinson (1995).

[7] The reasons for France's particularly bad performance during 1979–89 are analysed in detail in Halimi *et al.* 1994.

Table 2.1. UK manufacturing industry, 1962–1993: output, employment, and productivity

	Output (1985 = 100)	Employment (millions)	Output per person-hour (1985 = 100)
1962	74.0	8.456	43.7
1963	77.2	8.322	46.4
1964	83.9	8.450	49.3
1965	86.8	8.561	51.0
1966	88.2	8.584	52.5
1967	88.2	8.319	54.6
1968	95.7	8.240	59.3
1969	99.2	8.353	60.6
1970	99.6	8.339	63.2
1971	98.5	8.065	65.9
1972	100.6	7.790	70.0
1973	110.0	7.842	74.7
1974	108.6	7.893	75.3
1975	101.1	7.511	74.5
1976	103.0	7.269	78.2
1977	105.0	7.317	78.4
1978	105.7	7.281	79.5
1979	103.8	7.252	78.7
1980	96.4	6.936	76.9
1981	90.6	6.220	81.7
1982	90.8	5.860	85.3
1983	93.8	5.520	92.6
1984	97.4	5.403	97.1
1985	100.0	5.362	100.0
1986	101.1	5.267	103.2
1987	106.5	5.152	110.4
1988	114.3	5.195	116.7
1989	119.0	5.187	121.8
1990	118.2	5.144	122.7
1991	112.1	4.793	126.5
1992	111.2	4.497	133.5
1993	112.8	4.289	143.3

Source: OECD, *Main Economic Indicators*, Dec. 1994, and previous issues (and own calculations).

Table 2.3 gives the average annual growth of manufacturing output for the six countries between the peak years 1964 and 1989, with the UK firmly at the foot of the performance league. Table 2.3 also reports the overall growth between 1964 and 1989, as well as for the more recent period of 1973 to 1989. The overall growth figure from 1973 to 1992 shows that,

Table 2.2. Manufacturing output and employment: international comparisons for average output and employment, and for average annual % growth

		1964–73	1973–9	1979–89
UK:	Output (1985 = 100)	95.1	105.3	101.2
	Average annual growth	*3.1%*	*–1.0%*	*1.4%*
	Employment (millions)	8.254	7.481	5.759
	Average annual growth	*–0.8%*	*–1.3%*	*–3.4%*
Italy:	Output (1985 = 100)	66.4	88.7	103.4
	Average annual growth	*6.1%*	*2.6%*	*1.8%*
	Employment (millions)	6.203	6.525	6.606
	Average annual growth	*4.3%*	*0.2%*	*–1.5%*
France:	Output (1985 = 100)	72.4	97.8	103.7
	Average annual growth	*5.9%*	*1.5%*	*0.7%*
	Employment (millions)	5.670	5.825	5.140
	Average annual growth	*2.1%*	*–0.9%*	*–1.7%*
Germany:	Output (1985 = 100)	73.4	90.2	99.5
	Average annual growth	*4.8%*	*1.2%*	*1.5%*
	Employment (millions)	8.060	7.684	6.972
	Average annual growth	*0.8%*	*–2.2%*	*–0.5%*
USA:	Output (1985 = 100)	61.1	77.5	98.0
	Average annual growth	*5.2%*	*2.7%*	*3.0%*
	Employment (millions)	19.123	19.824	19.465
	Average annual growth	*1.7%*	*0.7%*	*–0.8%*
Japan:	Output (1985 = 100)	45.7	70.3	95.8
	Average annual growth	*11.9%*	*2.0%*	*4.1%*
	Employment (1985 = 100)	97.3	96.8	97.3
	Average annual growth	*1.8%*	*–1.9%*	*1.0%*

Notes: For employment, the figures for Italy include construction; there are definition changes in the data for West Germany from 1970; the first period average for France is for 1968–73 (with the average annual growth also calculated between these years); note that the employment figures for Japan are index numbers with 1985 = 100.

Source: OECD, *Main Economic indicators*, and own calculations.

while the level of manufacturing output was more than 30 per cent higher by the end of the twenty-year period in Germany, and almost 70 per cent higher in Japan, in Britain the overall growth was barely 1 per cent; that is, the absolute level of manufacturing output in 1992 was hardly different from that achieved in 1973. Between the peak years of 1964 and 1989, the average annual growth of manufacturing output was 6.6 per cent in Japan, 3.9 per cent in the USA, 3.7 per cent in Italy, 2.9 per cent in France, 2.7 per cent in Germany, and only 1.5 per cent in the UK. Over the ten-year peak-to-peak period 1979–89, manufacturing output grew by a total of only 15 per cent, an average cumulative growth rate of barely 1 per cent a year

Table 2.3. Growth of manufacturing output, 1964–1989

	Average annual growth (%)	Total % growth from 1st to last year		
		1964–89	1973–89	1973–92
UK	1.5	41.8	8.2	1.3
Italy	3.7	138.3	39.7	68.6
France	2.9	97.2	17.5	16.5
Germany	2.7	89.4	24.0	32.1
USA	3.9	150.3	58.1	55.2
Japan	6.6	363.7	69.2	68.9

Source: OECD, *Main Economic Indicators*, and own calculations.

(before dropping back in 1992 to around the same level as it had been in 1973).

Table 2.4 reports the summary statistics, for each of the three peak-to-peak periods, for employment and productivity, both for the whole economy and for the manufacturing sector alone. Labour productivity growth in the whole economy, and in manufacturing in particular, collapsed during the 1970s. The period 1979–89, however, saw a return to similar productivity growth rates achieved during the 1964–73 period. International comparisons of productivity levels and growth rates in manufacturing are reported in Tables 2.5 and 2.6 respectively. Table 2.5 illustrates the relative decline of UK manufacturing productivity from 1960 to 1980. There was a relative recovery from 1980 although, compared to the UK's major industrial competitors, a major productivity gap still remains. A similar picture is painted by the total factor productivity growth rates reported in Table 2.6, with the UK at or near the foot of the performance table for the first two of the three periods, but showing a relative recovery in the most recent.

The relative productivity improvement has not been reflected in

Table 2.4. UK employment and productivity growth, 1964–1989 (annual average % growth, peak-to-peak years)

	Employed labour force		Output per person employed	
	Whole economy	Manufacturing	Whole economy	Manufacturing
1964–73	0.0	0.8	3.1	3.8
1973–9	0.2	–1.3	1.2	0.6
1979–89	0.3	–2.9	2.1	4.1

Source: CSO, *Economic Trends Annual Supplement* (1994).

Table 2.5. Value added per hour worked in manufacturing, 1960–1990 (UK = 100)

Year	UK	Netherlands	France	Germany	USA
1960	100.0	121.2	86.8	112.7	226.2
1961	100.0	120.9	90.3	115.7	228.3
1962	100.0	117.1	92.1	118.4	227.3
1963	100.0	113.0	90.7	114.5	227.8
1964	100.0	118.9	91.3	118.0	224.7
1965	100.0	126.5	94.8	122.0	225.2
1966	100.0	125.8	103.3	123.0	221.2
1967	100.0	131.3	104.6	123.5	210.5
1968	100.0	131.0	107.1	124.0	203.3
1969	100.0	137.2	110.4	129.0	199.2
1970	100.0	138.7	113.8	129.1	195.3
1971	100.0	141.3	113.9	126.7	195.7
1972	100.0	142.4	112.0	126.6	192.7
1973	100.0	147.8	113.3	126.8	190.8
1974	100.0	154.5	116.1	131.5	183.8
1975	100.0	142.1	119.0	137.0	186.6
1976	100.0	150.8	121.5	141.4	188.0
1977	100.0	148.6	128.1	146.0	193.8
1978	100.0	153.7	131.0	147.8	190.1
1979	100.0	157.0	134.1	151.0	186.2
1980	100.0	156.8	134.1	149.1	181.2
1981	100.0	154.4	130.9	142.4	173.3
1982	100.0	149.7	132.1	134.5	166.7
1983	100.0	150.5	128.2	132.7	166.7
1984	100.0	155.5	126.2	132.0	169.2
1985	100.0	163.6	128.8	133.8	173.3
1986	100.0	147.7	125.1	127.8	173.0
1987	100.0	139.0	121.5	121.8	172.4
1988	100.0	137.3	121.2	119.5	171.5
1989	100.0	134.6	120.4	117.4	165.3
1990	100.0	137.5	NA	121.1	171.5

Source: Van Ark (1993), appendix table IV.5 and own calculations for US series from appendix table IV.4.

improved employment performance. Continuing high levels of unemployment in Europe since the mid-1970s have been accompanied by declines in manufacturing employment, and in this process it can be seen that Britain has shown the lead. The share of employment in manufacturing fell in the decade 1976–86 from 22.8 per cent to 19.1 per cent in the USA, from 25.5 per cent to 24.7 per cent in Japan, and from 28.9 per cent to 24.4 per cent for the EU. This relative decline represented an absolute fall for Europe, of

Table 2.6. Total factor productivity growth in manufacturing (average annual % change)

	Pre-1973	1973–9	1979–89
United States	2.6	0.4	0.7
Japan	6.9	2.4	1.1
France	5.4	3.0	1.0
Germany	3.6	2.8	0.5
United Kingdom	3.3	0.0	1.3

Source: OECD, *Economic Outlook* (June 1992).

almost 5.5 million jobs. Of the twelve member states, only Portugal and Greece avoided a fall in manufacturing employment, with the UK experiencing the most extreme cut (of 16 per cent, representing more than 2 million jobs).

Figure 2.1 shows employment in manufacturing since 1960 for five of the leading industrialized nations. The timing and extent of the decline in UK manufacturing employment contrasts with the experience of the other

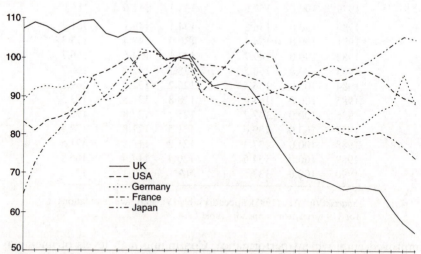

Fig. 2.1. Employment in manufacturing, 1960–1993 (1973 = 100 for each country)

Note: The French series is industrial employment and is only available from 1968.

Source: Authors' calculations from data in OECD, *Main Economic Indicators* (various editions).

countries. The decline in UK manufacturing employment dates from the mid-1960s and accelerates during the early 1980s, whereas for the other countries the decline starts much later (USA, Germany, and France) or not at all (Japan); manufacturing employment in the UK in 1993 was less than half that of 1966.

Two important points are clear: first, the decline in manufacturing employment in the UK can *not* be explained solely by shifts in consumption patterns, nor by other sectors' requirements for labour. The loss of manufacturing jobs has been accompanied by a deteriorating performance in manufacturing trade and by a rise in unemployment. And manufacturing has not experienced rapidly rising output as a result of productivity growth, but on the contrary a stagnant trend in output, with the productivity growth hence translating not into output growth but instead into job losses.

Our interpretation of this performance by UK manufacturing is first that it is one of relative failure and secondly that such failure has been caused, at least in part, by underinvestment. Table 2.7 reports manufacturing investment as a share of manufacturing output for the UK, France, and Germany. The UK series has been reasonably stable and has shown levels which are similar to those of the other two countries. A less rosy picture, however, is painted by the figures for net (as opposed to gross) investment. Table 2.8 shows that manufacturing net investment (as a share of manufacturing output) has been declining since the early 1960s, with negative figures for the early 1980s and 1990s.

A 1980s RENAISSANCE?

Some have argued that the Thatcher years transformed the supply side of the British economy, creating conditions for future prosperity. Crafts, for example, has argued that Thatcher's 'get tough' approach to trade unions had yielded significant benefits for the economy and that these might endure 'if the bargaining power of workers over manning levels remains weak' (Crafts, 1991).[8] And Metcalf (1989) argues not only that there was a decisive improvement in productivity in the 1980s but also that this was due in part to a weakening of trade unions. The 'Unions were the main reason' thesis often forms part of a wider view, that unemployment is at heart a labour-market problem. This includes the more recent line of argument, that the key to the problem lies in education and training (on which, see Chapter 5 below, by Robinson).

[8] Indeed, Crafts (1988a) claims that the industrial missions organized by the Anglo-American Council on Productivity between 1948 and 1952 had identified restrictive labour practices as posing the major obstacle to the 'Americanization' of British industry, while in fact these reports pointed rather to the shortcomings of management (see Coates, 1994; Nolan and O'Donnell 1995; and Tiratsoo and Tomlinson 1994).

Table 2.7. Manufacturing gross investment ratios at current prices (manufacturing gross investment as % of manufacturing value added)

	UK	France	Germany		UK	France	Germany
1960	12.4	NA	14.2	1980	13.3	14.2	12.5
1961	14.8	NA	14.9	1981	11.2	13.6	12.0
1962	13.8	NA	14.4	1982	10.8	13.0	11.1
1963	11.8	NA	13.7	1983	10.7	12.4	11.1
1964	12.3	NA	13.7	1984	12.7	12.7	10.7
1965	13.3	NA	14.1	1985	13.8	13.6	11.6
1966	13.4	NA	14.0	1986	12.3	13.8	12.0
1967	12.6	NA	11.9	1987	12.9	14.6	12.7
1968	13.1	NA	11.8	1988	13.2	15.4	12.5
1969	13.5	NA	13.8	1989	14.2	15.8	13.4
1970	14.1	NA	15.8	1990	13.4	17.2	14.2
1971	13.5	NA	15.7				
1972	11.0	NA	13.5				
1973	11.3	NA	11.5				
1974	13.7	NA	10.6				
1975	12.6	NA	10.5				
1976	12.4	NA	10.5	*Averages for peak-to-peak periods*			
1977	12.4	13.2	10.7	1964–73	12.8	NA	13.6
1978	13.8	12.7	10.5	1973–9	12.9	NA	10.8
1979	14.1	12.6	11.2	1979–89	12.7	13.8	11.9

Note: Data for France include mining and quarrying (not coal).

Sources: OECD, *National Accounts, Volume 2* (value added figures are market prices rather than factor cost); and CSO, *National Accounts*.

The key evidence presented in support of the Thatcher Shock is the improvement in productivity—see Crafts (1996) and Eltis (1996), and for an opposing view, Kitson and Michie (1996). Yet, we would argue, there was no productivity miracle during the 1980s—any such picture is a mirage. Certainly, labour productivity in manufacturing grew in the 1980s, but this was due largely to job cuts rather than increased output, and these jobs were not being lost in a period of full employment when the labour would be taken up productively elsewhere.

Additionally, the official productivity figures reported in Table 2.1 are constructed using a single price deflator for both output and input prices; Stoneman and Francis (1992) have shown that when the appropriate deflators are used, productivity growth is lower, at only a 34 per cent rise between 1979 and 1989 rather than the 51 per cent increase shown in the official figures. The figures for total factor productivity (TFP), which is intended to capture the increase in output above that resulting from

Table 2.8. UK manufacturing net investment, 1960–1993

	£ million (1990 prices)	Share of manufacturing output (%)		£ million (1990 prices)	Share of manufacturing output (%)
1960	4,000	5.5	1980	1,671	1.8
1961	5,451	7.5	1981	−993	−1.1
1962	4,446	6.1	1982	−1,561	−1.8
1963	2,846	3.8	1983	−1,746	−1.9
1964	3,729	4.5	1984	−279	−0.3
1965	3,896	4.6	1985	1,317	1.4
1966	3,931	4.6	1986	531	0.5
1967	3,430	4.0	1987	888	0.9
1968	3,936	4.2	1988	1,881	1.7
1969	4,378	4.5	1989	2,749	2.4
1970	4,967	5.1	1990	1,712	1.5
1971	3,817	4.0	1991	89	0.1
1972	1,947	2.0	1992	−1,229	−1.2
1973	2,106	2.0	1993	−1,881	−1.7
1974	2,985	2.8			
1975	1,790	1.8			
1976	1,004	1.0	*Averages for peak–to–peak periods*		
1977	1,216	1.2	1964–73	3,614	4.0
1978	2,747	2.7	1973–9	2,146	2.1
1979	3,174	3.1	1979–89	694	0.6

Note: The net investment series has been calculated by subtracting capital consumption from gross investment. The capital consumption series was constructed by linking the various series published in *United Kingdom National Accounts* and *National Income and Expenditure*. These series vary in their coverage as they use different definitions of manufacturing due to changes in the SIC classification system. The linked series adjusts for this by using the ratio between new and old definitions in overlapping years. This constructed series was preferred to that published in *United Kingdom National Accounts*, as the latter is deficient due to the variable inclusion of leased items and some other apparent anomalies in the series.

Sources: CSO, *Economic Trends Annual Supplement* (1994); CSO, *United Kingdom National Accounts* (various editions); CSO, *National Income and Expenditure* (various editions); and CSO, *Economic Trends* (Nov. 1994).

increased quantities of capital and labour, are also questionable: first, the growth-accounting approach which forms the basis for the construction of TFP measures usually assumes that factors of production are homogeneous, that markets are perfectly competitive (ensuring marginal productivity factor-pricing), and that there are constant returns to scale. Secondly, there are significant differences in TFP measures depending on the approach adopted and the data used. For instance, whereas the OECD results (Table 2.6) suggest a 1.3 per cent increase in TFP during the period

1979–89, Oulton and O'Mahony (1994) find only a 0.2 per cent increase for the period 1979–86 which, if the industries in their analysis are regarded as a random sample, is not significantly different from zero growth. Oulton and O'Mahony conclude that during this period the growth of output is primarily determined by the growth of inputs. This suggests that the studies which claim that the Thatcher shock generated a productivity miracle (due to changes in industrial relations and increased competitive pressures in product markets) are based on questionable data.

Furthermore, the productivity record must be considered in the context of the increased intensification of labour.[9] Nolan (1989) and Nolan and Marginson (1990) have argued that an increase in output per head as a result of increased labour input through the intensification of labour should not be defined as an increase in productivity unless the growth of output is greater than the increased input; Nolan (1989) and Nolan and O'Donnell (1995) have also gone on to argue, in our view persuasively, that, far from paving the way for genuine productivity improvements, the Government's policies of deregulation and anti-trade union legislation impaired effective labour utilization and competitiveness in product markets.[10]

Lastly, the productivity gains that have been made went disproportionately into increased profits rather than reduced output prices (which would have allowed increased market share, with higher output and employment than was in fact experienced, along with a healthier balance of payments and lower inflation), and the increased profits went disproportionately into dividend payments rather than investment.[11]

So while labour productivity growth in the 1980s returned perhaps to the rates experienced in the 1960s, these rates of growth were never satisfactory; UK productivity levels still lag behind those of other leading industrialized countries (Table 2.5); and in the 1980s the benefits of this productivity growth went overwhelmingly into cutting costs and employment rather than into developing new products and expanding output.

THE CAUSES AND THE CURES

Manufacturing employment has fallen fastest in Britain because output has failed to grow. Output has failed to grow because manufacturing capacity is too small and what capacity there is lacks competitiveness. These prob-

---

[9] For a discussion of which, see Deakin, Michie, and Wilkinson (1992).

[10] See also the discussion of these issues by Deakin (1992) and Brown (1992).

[11] See Glyn (1992) and Cosh, Hughes, and Rowthorn (1993), where these last, distributional points are analysed in depth. The following report is typical: 'Among appropriations, dividend payments rose by 17% in 1990, a lower growth rate than in the preceding two years (27% in 1989 and 33% in 1988), but one that was still surprisingly rapid. The dividend payout ratio, defined as the ratio of dividend payments to total income after deducting tax and interest payments, rose to 56% in the fourth quarter of 1990 and 64% in the first quarter of this year.' (Bank of England, *Quarterly Bulletin* (Aug. 1991), 364).

lems stem from a lack of investment, particularly in capital equipment but also in skills.

Under-Investment

It might be thought that there has been no problem of underinvestment in UK manufacturing as the ratio of gross manufacturing investment to output has remained stable (as indicated in Table 2.7). This stable ratio, however, is the result of inadequate investment matched only by stagnant output. The impact of the poor and erratic investment record has been to leave UK manufacturing with an inadequate capital stock.

Figures 2.2 and 2.3 show an increase in the gross capital stock during the 1960s and 1970s followed by stagnation in the 1980s.

Table 2.9 indicates that during all three peak-to-peak periods since the

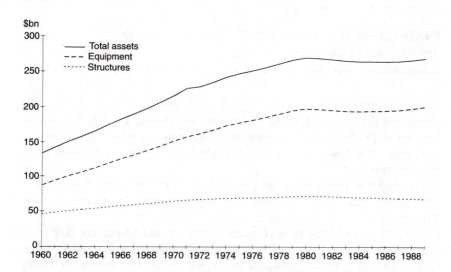

Fig. 2.2. Gross capital stock in UK manufacturing, 1960–1989 ($billion, 1985 prices)

Note: 'Equipment' includes all types of machinery, furniture, fixtures and vehicles. 'Structures' includes all types of buildings and other forms of infrastructure.

Source: Authors' calculations from data in O'Mahony (1993*b*).

mid-1960s the growth of the UK's manufacturing gross capital stock has been inferior to that of the other major industrial nations.[12] This is most evident during the 1979–89 period when, although there was a world-wide

[12] The gross capital stock series is from O'Mahony (1993*b*) which constructs estimates using an internationally consistent methodology using standard US service lives.

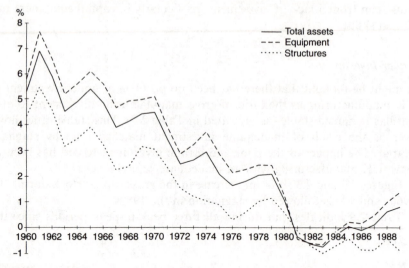

Fig. 2.3.   Gross capital stock, 1960–1989 (annual % change)

Note: See note to Figure 2.2.

Source: Authors' calculations from data in O'Mahony (1993*b*).

slowdown in the growth of manufacturing investment, the UK was the only country of the five not to experience any growth in the manufacturing capital stock. This has left a legacy of a relatively low level of capital in UK manufacturing.[13]

Figure 2.4 shows that capital per worker in the UK is significantly below that of the USA and Germany; the gap with these two countries (and France) has been widening since the mid-1960s.

In addition to a lack of investment, much of that which has taken place has been cost-cutting rather than capacity-enhancing. Thus while for the vast majority of OECD countries the growth rates of both total and industrial R&D were much higher in the 1980s than in the 1970s, the most notable exception to this was the UK (see Archibugi and Michie, 1995, table 1).

The dismal investment record of the UK economy since the 1960s has been a major cause of Britain's indifferent growth performance.[14] The lack of investment has constrained technological progress and the expansion of

[13] The estimate of the UK capital stock level may be an overestimate as the collapse of manufacturing in the early 1980s led to substantial capital scrapping which was not incorporated into official figures (see Oulton and O'Mahony 1994).

[14] Rowthorn (1995) shows that low investment since the mid-1970s, especially in manufacturing, has been a significant factor in the rise of unemployment throughout Western Europe; as indicated above, this has been a particular problem in the UK.

Table 2.9. Growth of the manufacturing gross capital stock: international comparisons (annual % growth rates)

	1964–73	1973–79	1979–89
United Kingdom			
Equipment	4.6	2.6	0.2
Structures	2.5	0.8	–0.5
Total Assets	3.9	2.1	0.0
USA			
Equipment	4.2	5.0	2.4
Structures	4.9	2.6	1.4
Total Assets	4.4	4.1	2.0
Germany			
Equipment	7.6	2.9	1.7
Structures	4.1	1.8	0.4
Total Assets	6.1	2.5	1.2
France			
Equipment	7.8	3.5	1.7
Structures	8.4	6.6	3.4
Total Assets	8.0	4.2	2.1
Japan			
Equipment	14.0	5.5	5.0
Structures	13.9	7.3	5.7
Total Assets	14.0	6.0	5.2

Note: See note to Figure 2.1.

Source: Authors' calculations from data in O'Mahony (1993*b*).

demand.[15] Furthermore, the cumulative effect of this record has resulted in British workers lacking the volume of capital equipment used by their main competitors. This capital stock gap is likely to widen as, through cumulative causation processes, the expectations that the manufacturing sector is not investing become self-fulfilling.

---

[15] Scott (1989; 1992) emphasizes, in contrast to much of new growth theory, that all types of investment, not just certain kinds (R&D expenditure, investment in education, etc.) create and reveal new investment opportunities. Additionally he stresses, in the spirit of Keynes, that investment responds to demand and the expectations of the growth of demand. The important two-way relationship between investment and demand is overlooked in many recent discussions of economic growth which ignore demand constraints on the level of economic activity. Investment can increase, as well as respond to, the level of demand, affecting the scale of production as well as its organization and technological efficiency. And through Verdoorn effects, increased scale can itself boost productivity.

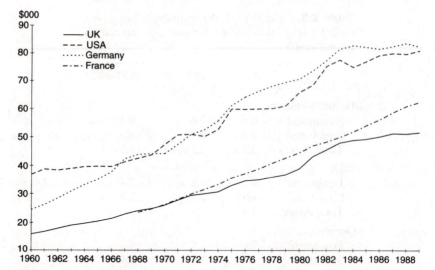

Fig. 2.4.   Gross capital stock per worker in manufacturing, 1960–1989 ($000, 1985 prices)

Note: See notes to Figures 2.1 and 2.2.

Source: Authors' calculations from data in O'Mahony (1993*b*) and OECD *Main Economic Indicators* (various editions).

A Lack of Skills

The importance of education and training has recently been emphasized by endogenous growth models where the growth rate of productivity is associated with the level of education. An educated and motivated work-force is able to facilitate the development of, adapt more easily to, and exploit more fully new processes and techniques of production. In the models of Romer (1986; 1990) increased education generates new technologies whereas for Lucas (1988) there will be positive externalities from education as a high level of human capital will encourage increased learning from others. A number of studies have illustrated the inadequacies in the provision of education and training in the UK. For instance, the OECD (1994) reports the relatively low rate of enrolment of 17- and 18-year-olds in formal education and training programmes, and Marsden and Ryan (1991) and the Small Business Research Centre (1992) indicate significant dissatisfaction with the availability and quality of training provision. While lack of skills is therefore a problem for the UK economy, it must be stressed that training programmes alone are not enough; the lack of job opportunities itself stifles skill attainment and development. The stagnation of the manufacturing sector creates conditions for social deskilling which add to the spiral of decline, since a common response by firms to their declining fortunes is to cut back on training.

The Balance of Payments

The historical legacy with which UK manufacturing has had to contend over the past thirty years has included a continued overseas orientation not only of the financial sector but also of Britain's multinational corporations; a disproportionate burden of military spending and the distorting effect this has had on R&D; and the continued inability of successive UK governments to modernize the economy.[16] One manifestation of this legacy has been a failure to produce a sufficient volume of manufactured exports to pay for imports (at a reasonable level of economic growth). Despite assertions to the contrary by Chancellor Lawson (Lawson 1992) and others, the balance of payments does matter, and the loss of Britain's manufacturing trading surplus in 1983 and the subsequent annual trading deficit in manufactured goods does pose problems for the wider economy (on which, see Coutts and Godley 1992; McCombie and Thirlwall, 1992; and Cosh, Coutts, and Hughes, Ch. 3 this volume). While Britain's balance of payments did benefit from the post-ERM devaluation,[17] for the country's long-term trading position to be resolved, particularly at anything like full employment, will require a continual improvement in industrial performance. The practically zero trend growth over the past twenty years will not do it. Neither could the service sector do it alone, as has been demonstrated for example by Cosh, Hughes, and Rowthorn (1993). Indeed, Crafts (1993) implicitly acknowledges that something is amiss, when he notes that the exchange rate needed to achieve full employment and trade balance at the same time has been falling since the early 1980s.[18]

UK macroeconomic and industrial policy: 'Care and Maintenance'

UK macroeconomic policy over the past thirty years has resulted repeatedly in an overvalued exchange rate and high interest rates, both of which are particularly damaging to manufacturing, while industrial policy has

[16] On Britain's long-run relative economic decline, see Kitson and Michie (1995a).

[17] Britain has had a deficit on trade in manufactured goods since 1983, reaching £12.9bn. in 1989 before falling in the slump to £2.4bn. in 1991, rising to £8.1bn. in 1993 and then declining slightly in 1994 to £7.5bn. with the improvement in British exports. In the three months to Jan. 1995, the deficit in trade in goods was £3.5bn. compared with £1.9bn. in the previous three months (CSO, 13 Apr. 1995).

[18] This point is made by Wells (1993b: 56). Crafts (1993) cites the estimates of Church (1992) which suggest that the Fundamental Equilibrium Exchange Rate (FEER) has been falling at a trend rate of 1.5% per annum. This implies an annual terms-of-trade induced reduction of GDP growth of 0.4% per cent—a significant proportion of the UK trend growth rate.

been ineffectual, with little attempt to use the public sector as a modernizing force.[19]

The most obvious cases of sterling being overvalued as a result of macroeconomic policy were firstly, the effects of the Thatcher Government's initial monetarist policies in 1979–1980 and secondly, membership of the Exchange Rate Mechanism at an overvalued rate.[20] But the industrial policies of the 1964 Wilson Government were also sacrificed on the altar of defending the currency, as were those of the Callaghan Government in 1975; the former was a case of defending an existing parity, while the latter was a fear that the currency would float downwards (although whether our trading partners would have really allowed us to gain the competitive advantage which would have accrued to British industry from this is doubtful).

Additionally, the high levels and volatility of interest rates have discouraged investment and business confidence. This was particularly apparent during the early 1980s when high interest rates created cash-flow problems for many companies leading to bankruptcies and plant closures as well as contributing to the appreciation of sterling and the squeeze on exports. Interest rate policy during the 1980s has been identified as the main government policy which has impeded the growth of firms. The 1991 Cambridge survey (Small Business Research Centre 1992) into business performance,[21] the most extensive since the 1971 Bolton study, indicated that a third of all firms surveyed identified interest rate policy as the most important negative government policy and half placed it in their top three policy concerns.[22]

The resulting instability to which the UK economy has been prone, particularly since 1979, has been worse than that experienced in other

[19] As Postmaster-General from Oct. 1964 to July 1965, Tony Benn concluded the following: 'This highlights in my mind one of the great difficulties of being a socialist in the sort of society in which we live. The real drive for improvement comes from those concerned to make private profit. If, therefore, you deny these people the right of extending private enterprise into new fields, you have to have some sort of alternative. You have to have some body which wants to develop public enterprise but our present Civil Service is not interested in growth. It is geared to care and maintenance' (Benn 1987: 264, diary entry for 28 May 1965).

[20] See e.g. the arguments of the Cambridge Economic Policy Group published in the Observer on 19 Apr. 1992 and denounced the following week (26 Apr.) by the Observer's own Adam Raphael in a piece entitled 'Beware the Siren Devaluers who Lure us to Ruin'; see also the reply from Coutts, Godley, Michie, and Rowthorn in the Observer of 3 May 1992.

[21] The Cambridge survey was undertaken during the spring and summer of 1991 and provides a national stock-take of approximately 2,000 enterprises. The sampling framework, and the respondents, were split equally between manufacturing and the rapidly expanding business service sector (for further details see Kitson 1994; and Small Business Research Centre 1992).

[22] In the Cambridge survey firms were asked to identify which government policies hindered or helped their business in the previous ten years. Overall, firms believed that government policy had hindered their performance. What was noticeable was the high proportion of firms which considered that they had received no help from government policy during the past decade. Nearly a third of the firms surveyed did not identify any significant help from government policy during the past ten years.

industrial nations, reflecting the UK Government's desire since 1979 to target nominal variables (inflation and interest rates) rather than real variables (jobs and output). Additionally, they have harmed the long-term growth potential of the economy. This is due to two factors. First, the depth of the recessions—they were much deeper than previous (at least pre-1974) postwar recessions—which led to large-scale scrapping of capital and the laying-off of workers. This contrasts with previous recessions where, as the long-term costs of abandonment were high (the cost of restoring capital equipment, severance payments, and search and training costs), the moderate extent of the downturns encouraged firms to maintain capacity while waiting for the cyclical upturn. Conversely, during the post-1979 recessions, the depth of the recessions encouraged firms to reduce capacity in order to minimise short-term costs and maximize the possibility of survival.[23]

Secondly, as the domestic economy has, albeit falteringly, developed, the industrial structure has shifted to more segmented and niche-product markets. These sectors require specialist capital equipment and sector-specific skills. The loss of such factors due to a recession may be more difficult to replace in a period of recovery. Furthermore, it is not possible to rely on future investment to make good the position; the existence of sunk costs means that restarting operations will be expensive requiring a higher yield (in excess of the required or 'hurdle' rate) to encourage the replacement investment (Dixit 1992). This alone indicates that governments should adopt suitable expansionary policies to ameliorate the potential impact of external shocks and certainly should not use severe contractionary policies to counter inflation. The long-term costs of recessions place an increasing premium on achieving stable economic growth.

We have stressed the negative impact of the economic shocks of the 1980s on the UK's long-run growth potential. Others have argued that the reduced bargaining power of workers and the creation of a more flexible labour market have had beneficial effects. This notion is based on a neo-classical view of the competitive process, where producers face a large number of competitors and price is the key indicator of competitiveness. In reality many firms have few effective competitors and the key factors which contribute to competitive advantage are product quality and the characteristics of the customer–client relationship.[24] Thus, in order to create and sustain a competitive economy, firms require stable economic growth to foster

[23] The contrasting impacts of mild versus deep recession can also lead to contrasting productivity changes. With mild recessions we tend to observe 'Okun's Law', with a *short-term* productivity loss associated with a fall in output. With deep recession we observe a 'shock effect', with a short-term gain in productivity due to the shedding of labour and capacity.

[24] The 1991 Cambridge survey (Small Business Research Centre, 1992) indicated that 40% of manufacturing firms had fewer than five competitors and 70% had fewer than ten competitors. The survey also showed that personal attention to client needs, product quality, and an established reputation were the most important factors which contributed to the competitiveness of manufacturing firms. Price was ranked sixth out of eleven identified factors.

inter-firm co-operation and encourage innovation and product development and the upgrading of the skill base of the economy.

To return to a position of full employment on a sustainable basis will require a dramatically better industrial performance than that witnessed since 1979—or since 1960 for that matter. Indeed, in many ways the situation has deteriorated since 1979; net manufacturing investment, which had averaged £3,514m. a year over the 1964–73 peak-to-peak period, and £2,146m. a year over the 1973–9 period, plummeted to a mere £694m. a year between 1979 and 1989 (Table 2.8).

CONCLUSION: POLICIES FOR RENEWAL AND REVIVAL

Future economic growth requires an investment strategy that will enable the UK to close the capital stock gap with the other major industrialized countries. The alternative is to accept that the UK cannot compete with these countries and that its comparable competitors are the newly industrialized countries, with all that this entails for domestic living standards and employment opportunities. An investment strategy—increasing the quantity and quality of equipment and structures—must be accompanied by adequate training. Given the present tendency for politicians to stress the importance of education and training without being prepared to recognize the need for accompanying expansionary macroeconomic policies and interventionist industrial ones, it has to be stressed that giving the unemployed skills when they have little opportunity to use them is insufficient.

The two major prerequisites for investment-led growth are, first, a sufficiently rapid growth in demand and, secondly, reform of the financial system. Fiscal, monetary, and exchange rate policies should aim to ensure a continuous and sustainable expansion of aggregate demand. Additionally, in the presence of shocks such instruments should be deployed to ameliorate adverse impacts on investment, output, and employment.

Reform of the financial system is required to eradicate the biases against industrial investment and the short-termism embedded in UK capital markets (Hutton 1995).[25] Increased profits in Britain all too often simply feed dividend payments rather than increased investment (Glyn 1992). Thus policies that seek to raise profits—through controls on wages or changes in the tax regime—will not be sufficient to increase investment and may have adverse impacts on aggregate demand and the distribution of income. The institutional reforms required are substantial. First, a national investment bank to channel funds towards long-term investments and projects—espe-

---

[25] As President of the Board of Trade, Heseltine recognized the problem of short-termism but failed to see through any serious industrial policies to alter this state of affairs (see Kitson and Michie 1996).

cially in high-tech activities—which would promote major positive externalities for the whole economy. Secondly, a regional investment banking structure to respond to the investment needs of regional and local economies. Thirdly, an investment bank for small and medium-sized enterprises, not only to help start-ups, but to facilitate the growth of small firms and the creation of a competitive *Mittelstand* sector. Fourthly, the regulation of dividends, possibly through the tax system, to encourage the use of retained earnings for investment. Fifthly, the increased regulation of takeovers, to prevent the breakup of firms for short-term asset-stripping. And sixthly, measures to encourage the banks and other financial institutions to provide finance in return for equity, to encourage investors to seek the long-term survival of firms suffering short-term difficulties rather than resorting to the calling in of loans which may precipitate corporate collapse.

Deindustrialization can seriously damage your wealth, first because much of the service sector itself will depend on the size and rate of growth of the manufacturing sector; certainly, some service sector jobs are created in the process of liquidating manufacturing enterprises, but this cannot be a long-term solution. Secondly, and as argued persuasively by Kaldor, processes of cumulative causation can lead to a spiral of decline which can spread out from manufacturing to other sectors, so that, for example, if deindustrialization creates a depressing environment for training, this will obstruct one of the very processes necessary for any successful shift into new sectors. And thirdly, a deteriorating position in manufacturing trade creates a number of dangers, not least the deflationary macroeconomic policies which tend to follow any resulting balance of payments deficit or pressure on the currency. To reverse Britain's deindustrialization will require a sustained increase in manufacturing investment. Piecemeal policies—manipulating tax rates and allowances—will not be sufficient. What is needed is the implementation of a macroeconomic and industrial strategy directed towards achieving sustainable economic growth and the root-and-branch reform of a financial system that has been failing British industry since Victorian times.

REFERENCES

Archibugi, D., and Michie, J. (1995), 'The Globalisation of Technology: A New Taxonomy', *Cambridge Journal of Economics*, 19/1 (Feb.): 121–40.

Baumol, W. (1967), 'Macroeconomics of Unbalanced Growth', *American Economic Review*, 57: 415–26.

——, Blackman, S., and Wolff, E. (1989), *Productivity and American Leadership: The Long View* (Cambridge, Mass.: MIT Press).

Benn, T. (1987), *Out of the Wilderness: Diaries 1963–1967* (London: Hutchinson).

Brown, W. (1992), 'Collective Rights', in J. Michie (ed.), *The Economic Legacy, 1979–1992* (London: Academic Press).

Cambridge Economic Policy Group (1992), 'Hands-off Economics Equals Stagnation', *Observer*, 19 Apr.

Chenery, H. B. (1960), 'Patterns of Industrial Growth', *American Economic Review*, 50.

Church, K. (1992), 'Properties of the Fundamental Equilibrium Exchange Rate in Models of the UK Economy', *National Institute Economic Review*, 141: 62–70.

Coates, D. (1994), *The Question of UK Decline: The Economy, State and Society* (London: Harvester Wheatsheaf).

Cornwall, J. (1977), *Modern Capitalism: Its Growth and Transformation* (Oxford: Martin Robertson).

Cosh, A. D., Hughes, A., and Rowthorn, R. E. (1993), 'The Competitive Role of UK Manufacturing Industry: 1979–2003', ch 2 of K. Hughes (ed.), *The Future of UK Competitiveness and the Role of Industrial Policy* (London: Policy Studies Institute).

—— —— —— (1994), *The Competitive Role of UK Manufacturing Industry: 1950–2003—A Case Analysis*, mimeo, University of Cambridge.

Costello, N., Michie, J. and Milne, S. (1989), *Beyond the Casino Economy* (London: Verso).

Cousins, J. (1993), 'Labour's Policies for the Revival of British Competitiveness', ch. 11 of K. Hughes (ed.), *The Future of UK Competitiveness and the Role of Industrial Policy* (London: Policy Studies Institute).

Coutts, K., and Godley, W. (1992), 'Does Britain's Balance of Payments Matter Any More?', in J. Michie (ed.), *The Economic Legacy, 1979–1992* (London: Academic Press).

—— —— Michie, J., and Rowthorn, B. (1992), 'Devaluation of Sterling is no "Quick Fix"', *Observer*, 3 May.

Crafts, N. (1988), 'The Assessment: British Economic Growth over the Long Run', *Oxford Review of Economic Policy*, 4/1: pp. i–xxi.

—— (1991a), 'Reversing Relative Economic Decline? The 1980s in Historical Perspective', *Oxford Review of Economic Policy*, 7/3: 81–98.

—— (1991b), 'Economic Growth', in N. Crafts and N. Woodward (eds.), *The British Economy since 1945* (Oxford: Oxford University Press).

—— (1992), 'Productivity Growth Reconsidered', *Economic Policy*, 15 (Oct.): 387–426.

—— (1993), *Can Deindustrialisation Seriously Damage Your Wealth?* (London: Institute of Economic Affairs).

—— (1996), 'Deindustrialization and Economic Growth', *Economic Journal*, 106 (Jan.).

Deakin, S. (1992), 'Labour Law and Industrial Relations', in J. Michie (ed.), *The Economic Legacy, 1979–1992* (London: Academic Press).

—— Michie, J., and Wilkinson, F. (1992), *Inflation, Employment, Wage-Bargaining and the Law* (London: Institute of Employment Rights).

De Long, B., and Summers, L. (1991), 'Equipment Investment and Economic Growth', *Quarterly Journal of Economics*, May.

Dixit, A. (1992), 'Investment and Hysteresis', *Journal of Economic Perspectives*, 6/1 (winter): 107–32.

Eatwell, J. (1982), *Whatever Happened to Britain?* (London: BBC Publications and Gerald Duckworth).

Eichengreen, B. (1992), *Golden Fetters: The Gold Standard and the Great Depression 1919–1939* (Oxford: Oxford University Press).

Eltis, W. (1996), 'How Low Profitability and Weak Innovativeness Undermined UK Industrial Growth', *Economic Journal*, 106 (Jan.).

Fine, B., and Harris, L. (1985), *Peculiarities of the British Economy* (London: Laurence & Wishart).

—— and Poletti, C. (1992), 'Industrial Prospects in the Light of Privatisation', in J. Michie (ed.), *The Economic Legacy, 1979–1992* (London: Academic Press).

Fisher, I. (1935), *The Clash of Progress and Security* (New York: Macmillan).

Fuchs, V. (1968), *The Service Economy* (New York: Columbia University Press).

Gershuny, J. (1978), *After Industrial Society* (London: Macmillan).

—— and Miles, I. (1983), *The New Service Economy* (London: Frances Pinter).

Glyn, A. (1992), 'The "Productivity Miracle", Profits and Investment', in J. Michie (ed.), *The Economic Legacy, 1979–1992* (London: Academic Press).

Godley, W. (1986), 'Manufacturing and the Future of the British Economy', paper presented to Manufacturing or Services? A Conference on UK Industry and the Economy, Robinson College, Cambridge.

Halimi, S., Michie, J., and Milne, S. (1994), 'The Mitterrand Experience', ch. 6 of J. Michie and J. Grieve Smith (eds.), *Unemployment in Europe* (London: Academic Press).

Hutton, W. (1995), *The State We're In* (London: Jonathan Cape).

Kaldor, N. (1957), 'A Model of Economic Growth', *Economic Journal*, 67 (Dec.).

—— (1961), 'Capital Accumulation and Economic Growth', in F. Lutz and D. Hague (eds.), *The Theory of Capital* (New York: Macmillan).

—— (1966), *Causes of the Slow Rate of Growth in the United Kingdom* (Cambridge: Cambridge University Press).

—— (1972), 'The Irrelevance of Equilibrium Economics', *Economic Journal*, 82 (Dec.).

—— (1985), *Economics without Equilibrium* (New York: M. E. Sharpe).

Kitson, M. (1994), 'Seedcorn or Chaff? Unemployment and Small Firm Performance', ESRC Centre for Business Research, Working Paper 2, University of Cambridge.

—— and Michie, J. (1994), 'Fixed Exchange Rates and Deflation: The ERM and the Gold Standard', *Economics and Business Education*, 2 pt 1/5 (spring): 11–16. Repr. in N. Healey (ed.), *The Economics of the New Europe: From Community to Union* (Routledge: 1995), 68–81.

—— —— (1995a), 'Trade and Growth: A Historical Perspective', ch. 1 of J. Michie and J. Grieve Smith (eds.), *Managing The Global Economy* (Oxford: Oxford University Press).

—— —— (1995b), 'Conflict, Cooperation and Change: The Political Economy of Trade and Trade Policy', *Review of International Political Economy*, 2/4 (winter).

—— —— (1996), 'Britain's Industrial Performance since 1960: Underinvestment and Relative Decline', *Economic Journal*, 106 (Jan.).

Kuznets, S. (1966), *Modern Economic Growth: Rate, Structure and Spread* (New Haven: Yale University Press).

Lawson, N. (1992), *The View From No. 11* (London: Bantam Press).

Lewis, W. A. (1954), 'Economic Development with Unlimited Supplies of Labour', *Manchester School*, 22: 139–91.

Lucas, R. (1988), 'On the Mechanisms of Economic Development', *Journal of Monetary Economics*, 22 (July).

McCombie, J., and Thirlwall, T. (1992), 'The Re-emergence of the Balance of Payments Constraint', in J. Michie (ed.), *The Economic Legacy, 1979–1992* (London: Academic Press).

Marquand, J. (1979), 'The Service Sector and Regional Policy in the United Kingdom', mimeo, Centre for Environmental Studies, London.

Marsden, D., and Ryan, P. (1991), 'Initial Training, Labour Market Structure and Public Policy: Intermediate Skills in British and German Industry', in P. Ryan (ed.), *International Comparisons of Vocational Training for Intermediate Skills* (Lewes: Falmer Press).

Mayes, D., and Young, G. (1994), 'Improving the Estimates of the UK Capital Stock', *National Institute Economic Review* (Feb.): 84–96.

Metcalf, D. (1989), 'Water Notes Dry up: The Impact of the Donovan Reform Proposal and Thatcherism at Work on Labour Productivity in British Manufacturing Industry', *British Journal of Industrial Relations*, 27: 1–31.

Michie, J. (1992), 'Introduction', in J. Michie (ed.), *The Economic Legacy, 1979–1992* (London: Academic Press).

—— and Wilkinson, F. (1995), 'Wages, Government Policy and Unemployment', *Review of Political Economy*, 7/2 (Apr.): 133–49.

Myrdal, G. (1957), *Economic Theory and Underdeveloped Regions* (London: Duckworth).

Nolan, P. (1989), 'Walking on Water? Performance and Industrial Relations under Thatcher', *Industrial Relations Journal*, 20/2: 81–92.

—— (1994), 'Labour Market Institutions, Industrial Restructuring and Unemployment in Europe', ch. 4 of J. Michie and J. Grieve Smith (eds.), *Unemployment in Europe* (London: Academic Press).

—— and Marginson, P. (1990), 'Skating on Thin Ice? David Metcalf on Trade Unions and Productivity', *British Journal of Industrial Relations*, 28/2: 227–47.

—— and O'Donnell, K. (1995), 'The Political Economy of Productivity: Britain 1945–1994', mimeo, University of Leeds.

OECD (1994), *The OECD Jobs Study: Evidence and Explanations* (part I and part II) (OECD: Paris).

O'Mahony, M. (1993a), 'Capital Stocks and Productivity in Industrial Nations', *National Institute Economic Review* (Aug.): 108–17.

—— (1993b), 'International Measures of Fixed Capital Stocks: A Five-Country Study', National Institute of Economic and Social Research, Discussion Paper 51, Sept.

Oulton, N., and O'Mahony, M. (1994), *Productivity and Growth: A Disaggregated Study of British Industry, 1954–1986* (Cambridge: Cambridge University Press).

Petit, P. (1986), *Slow Growth and the Service Economy* (London: Frances Pinter).

Raphael, A. (1992), 'Beware the Siren Devaluers who Lure us to Ruin', *Observer*, 26 Apr.

Romer, P. (1986), 'Increasing Returns and Long-Run Growth', *Journal of Political Economy*, 94 (Oct.): 1002–37.

—— (1990), 'Endogenous Technical Change', *Journal of Political Economy*, 98 (Oct.): S71–S102.

Rostow, W. W. (1960), *The Stages of Economic Growth* (Cambridge: Cambridge University Press).

Rowthorn, R. E. (1995), 'Capital Formation and Unemployment', *Oxford Review of Economic Policy*, 11/1: 26–39.

—— and Wells, J. (1987), *Deindustrialisation and Foreign Trade* (Cambridge: Cambridge University Press).

Sawyer, M. (1994), 'Industrial Strategy and Employment in Europe', ch. 11 of J. Michie and J. Grieve Smith (eds.), *Unemployment in Europe* (London: Academic Press).

Saxenhouse, G. (1985), 'Services in the Japanese Economy', in R. E. Inman (ed.), *Managing the Service Economy: Prospects and Problems* (Cambridge: Cambridge University Press).

Scott, M. F. G. (1989), *A New View of Economic Growth* (Oxford: Clarendon Press).

—— (1992), 'Policy Implications of "A New View of Economic Growth"', *Economic Journal*, 102: 622–32.

Singh, A. (1977), 'UK Industry and the World Economy: A Case of De-industrialisation?', *Cambridge Journal of Economics*, 1/2 (June).

—— (1987), 'Deindustrialisation', in J. Eatwell, M. Milgate, and P. Newman (eds.), *The New Palgrave Dictionary of Economics* (London: Macmillan).

Small Business Research Centre (1992), *The State of British Enterprise: Growth, Innovation and Competitive Advantage in Small and Medium Sized Enterprises* (Cambridge: Small Business Research Centre, University of Cambridge).

Solow, R. M. (1970), *Growth Theory: An Exposition* (Oxford: Oxford University Press).

Stoneman, P., and Francis, N. (1992), 'Double Deflation and the Measurement of Output and Productivity in UK Manufacturing 1979–1989', Warwick Business School Discussion Paper.

Summers, R. (1985), 'Services in the International Economy', in R. E. Inman (ed.), *Managing the Service Economy: Prospects and Problems* (Cambridge: Cambridge University Press).

Tiratsoo, N., and Tomlinson, J. (1994), 'Restrictive Practices on the Shopfloor in Britain, 1945–60: Myth and Reality', *Business History*, 36/2 (Apr.): 65–82.

Van Ark, Bart (1993), 'International Comparisons of Output and Productivity: Manufacturing Productivity Performance of Ten Countries from 1950 to 1990', unpublished Ph.D. thesis.

Wells, J. (1993a), 'The UK Record since 1979 (A Reply to Crafts)', University of Cambridge, mimeo.

—— (1993b), 'The Trouble with Thatcher', *New Economy* (autumn): 52–6.

Wilkinson, F. (1992), *Why Britain Needs a Minimum Wage* (London: Institute for Public Policy Research).

You, J.-I. (1994), 'Macroeconomic Structure, Endogenous Technical Change and Growth', *Cambridge Journal of Economics*, 18/2 (Apr.): 213–33.

Young, A. (1928), 'Increasing Returns and Economic Progress', *Economic Journal*, 38 (Dec.): 527–40.

3. Manufacturing, the Balance of Payments, and Capacity

Andy Cosh, Ken Coutts, and Alan Hughes

INTRODUCTION

This chapter examines the contribution manufacturing industry must make if Britain is to restore full employment within the foreseeable future and estimates the investment in capacity required if that contribution is to come about. It must be emphasized from the outset that the *direct* contribution of manufacturing in terms of more jobs is likely to be small. The manufacturing sector has been shedding jobs since the 1960s: over 3.5 million jobs went between 1971 and the mid-1990s, mostly during the 1980s. The result was that manufacturing accounted for about 20 per cent of GDP whilst employing about 15 per cent of the work-force. But Britain's small manufacturing sector is highly integrated into international trade. Manufactured exports are over 80 per cent of Britain's total exports of goods, and account for 60 per cent of trade in goods and services. The primary contribution of manufacturing will be *indirect*; by creating a more favourable trade-off between growth and external deficits, it will raise the overall level of activity and employment which it is possible to sustain. By increasing domestic and export sales, it will also generate jobs in industries which supply manufacturing with inputs and services.

The scale of job generation required is very large. To restore full employment by 2000 or 2005—even in the limited sense of reducing unemployment to the levels experienced in the 1970s—will require the creation of around 3 million jobs. This is what is required if jobs are going to be available for those currently unemployed, to provide for a rising labour force and provide jobs for the disguised unemployed who would become economically active if more jobs were available (Coutts and Rowthorn 1995). A necessary condition for this to happen is a sustained growth of output, avoiding the kind of short-lived boom which leads within two years to enormous balance of payments deficits or rising inflation.

We assess the possibility of achieving such a sustained growth by using a model of the UK economy to explore the consequences of alternative

The authors are grateful to the ESRC for financial support of the project underlying this chapter. It forms part of the Technical Change, Manufacturing Strategy and Industrial Policy programme of the ESRC Centre for Business Research at the University of Cambridge.

scenarios. This enables us to quantify both the outcome of projections based upon the continuation of existing trends and the magnitude of the changes to these trends which would be required in order to achieve a sustained improvement.

The model is used to show that, if existing medium-term trends continued, unemployment could only be reduced at the expense of an unsustainable rise in international indebtedness. On the other hand, growth which is compatible with an acceptable external position brings an unacceptably slow reduction in unemployment. We conclude that an expansion of capacity in manufacturing is essential if the economy is to achieve a sustained recovery without running up against a balance of payments constraint. The chapter begins by setting out the historical context for the assessment of these changes.

MANUFACTURING OUTPUT, INVESTMENT, AND CAPACITY UTILIZATION

The manufacturing sector has an impact on the balance of payments which is far more dominant than its importance in terms of national production. The well-known changes of fortune of the manufacturing sector since 1948 are summarized in Figure 3.1. Up until the first oil crisis at the end of 1973, output increased at an annual trend rate of about 3.2 per cent. Between 1973 and 1979 output increased slowly. The great 'shake-out' occurred between 1979 and 1982 when output fell by 16 per cent and 1.4 million jobs were shed. This was followed by a slow recovery in output but a further loss of jobs. During the Lawson boom output grew rapidly, reaching by 1988 the level of production last achieved in 1979. After the recession of 1990–2 output began to recover and by the first quarter of 1995 was just back to the level last reached in 1990.

Figure 3.1 shows two alternative trends. One is a linear proportional trend (that is, a trend expressed as a constant rate of growth in percentage terms) estimated from 1948 until the second quarter of 1973 (the last period before the oil shock) and extrapolated to 1995. It shows what growth of manufacturing output might have been expected on the basis of the average growth rate achieved during the 'golden age' of post-war economic history if the various structural changes and shocks to the manufacturing sector had not occurred. The second is a stochastic trend in which large shocks to manufacturing output have a permanent impact by changing the trend.[1] Both trends are entirely descriptive statistical summaries of the historical data for manufacturing production. The stochastic trend can be

---

[1] The trend is estimated using the Beveridge and Nelson (1981) decomposition of a time series into a random walk component and a cyclical component, using a low-order ARIMA representation.

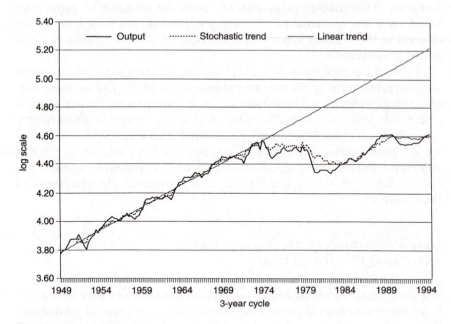

Fig. 3.1. Manufacturing output and trend

interpreted as having an upward component of about 3.2 per cent annually, with 'random' shocks to output modifying this trend. After the shake-
out of the early 1980s manufacturing output recovered towards a lower and
more slowly growing trend of output. In the Lawson boom output and
trend were close together. The recent recovery in output once again brings
output close to this trend.

The underlying position of 'full-capacity' output for manufacturing may
lie somewhere between these two trends but is likely to be nearer the lower
line. Figure 3.2 suggests that since 1980 manufacturing investment has been
no higher on average than during the previous decade in absolute terms—
in each decade investment spending at 1990 prices averaged £11.8 billion.
There is also substantial evidence of the loss of industrial capacity during
this period through capital scrapping. The CBI indices of capacity utilisation in Figure 3.3 suggest, despite the low level of output from which production recovered after 1982, that 'normal' rates of capacity utilization
were restored by the mid 1980s.[2] The boom of 1987–9 raised capacity utilization rates to abnormally high levels. This is consistent with the rapid
growth of manufactured imports during this period.

[2] Figure 2.3 plots the % of manufacturing firms in the CBI Survey reporting that they are
not working below capacity, i.e. a rise indicates that output is increasingly being constrained
by capacity limitations.

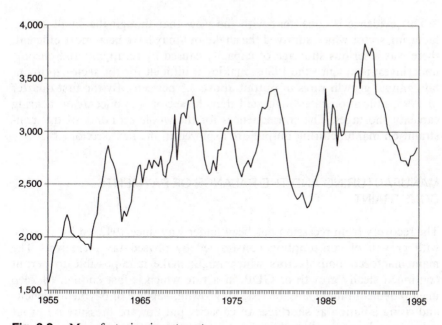

Fig. 3.2. Manufacturing investment

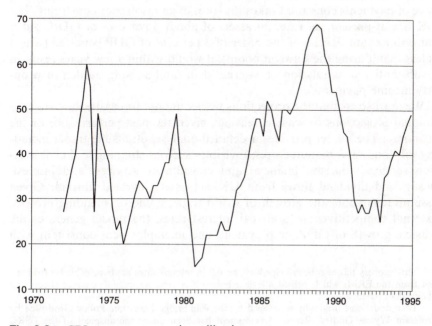

Fig. 3.3. CBI percentage capacity utilization

This evidence is consistent with the view that though the small manufacturing sector which survived the shake-out may have been more efficient,
there was a serious shortage of capacity caused by scrapping and chronic
underinvestment since the 1980s, making it difficult for the sector to maintain annual growth rates of output above 3.5 per cent. By the first quarter
of 1995, utilization rates suggested that the sector was once again nearing
capacity shortages. The consequences for the whole economy of this constraint on manufacturing output are explored in the next section.

MANUFACTURING AND THE BALANCE OF PAYMENTS CONSTRAINT

The recovery from recession has been under way since 1992 led by exports,
with growth of consumption constrained by phased tax increases.[3] The
main macroeconomic factors which might make it impossible to permit
continued steady growth of GDP, at a rate which is fast enough to keep
unemployment falling, are the risks of growing balance of payments deficits
and rising inflation as shortages of capacity put upward pressure on profit
margins and wage settlements respond to anticipated rising prices.

To gain some idea of the extent to which the balance of payments might
limit future growth of the UK economy we use a small macroeconomic
model.[4] In a regime of internationally mobile capital flows, the external balance of payments constraint takes the form of an insolvency constraint. The
UK has at present net external assets of about 5 per cent of GDP, but if
current-account deficits of the order of 3 per cent of GDP persisted (which
is less than during the Lawson boom), it would within a few years result in
a substantial accumulation of external debt (and a rising burden of property income payments).

We must stress that the projections we use are not forecasts: they are conditional projections of what is feasible, given the past performance of the
economy. The model provides a detailed analysis of: visible trade, including oil, food, and manufactures; invisibles such as shipping and civil avia-
tion services, tourism, financial and consultancy services; and interest,
profit, and dividend flows from UK net assets invested abroad. Given
assumptions about the growth of world trade, domestic spending growth,
external competitiveness, and real interest rates, the model generates the
feasible growth of GDP, employment, and unemployment consistent with

---

[3] The recovery has also been helped by the fall in interest rates made possible by Britain's
exit from the ERM, which helped alleviate households' and companies' balance sheets and
reduce debt payments.

[4] This model was originally developed by the Cambridge Economic Policy Group led by
Professor Wynne Godley. Recent development has been under the auspices of the ESRC
Centre for Business Research.

Table 3.1. Base projection: principal assumptions

	1996–2000(%)
World trade: growth rate	5.5
Cost competitiveness: constant from 1995	
Domestic spending: growth rate	2.5
Work-force: growth rate	0.5
Real interest rates	2.5

these assumptions. It also generates the implications for the current-account balance and net external wealth or debt.

The model is first used to provide a base projection by assuming that the behaviour of the key parameters will be in line with the past medium-term performance of the UK economy. Table 3.1 sets out the main assumptions of the base projection from 1996 until 2005. World trade is projected over a ten-year period to grow at about the average rate achieved during the 1980s. Relative cost competitiveness is maintained from 1995 and domestic spending is allowed to grow at 2.5 per cent annually.

Table 3.2 and Figures 3.4–9 summarize the main features of the base projection. On these assumptions GDP can grow at an annual average of 2.4 per cent over the ten-year period. This is consistent with an increase in employment of 2.2 million over ten years, and, given the assumption about the growth of the work-force shown in Table 3.1, implies a reduction in unemployment of about 1 million. However, Figure 3.5 shows that the projected current account balance deteriorates at a rate which is not sustainable in the medium term and we need to analyse this further.

Table 3.2. Base projection: summary

	1996–2005
Average growth of GDP (%)	2.4
Increase in employment (millions)	+2.2
Fall in unemployment from 1995 (millions)	−1.0
Growth rate of exports: manufactures (%)	4.8
End period current-account balance (% GDP)	−3.8

There is considerable uncertainty surrounding these calculations. They are based on macroeconomic data which are themselves estimated with significant error, and the model employs the standard methodology of estimating structural econometric relationships with all their pitfalls. Whether the projected growth does turn out to be inconsistent with medium-term

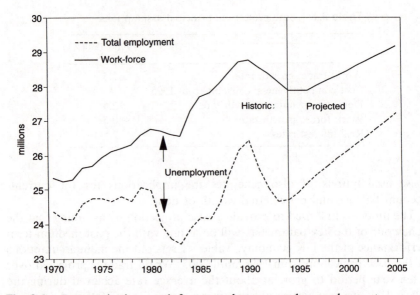

Fig. 3.4. Base projection: work-force, employment, and unemployment

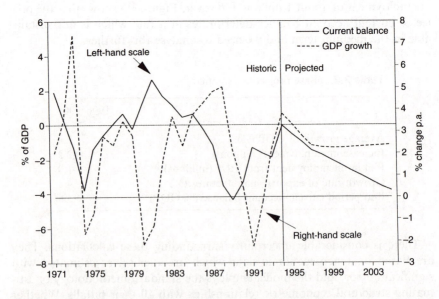

Fig. 3.5. Base projection: current balance and GDP growth

external balance will depend mainly on trade in manufactures, financial services, and net property income, these being the components of the current-account balance with the greatest potential for improved performance. The division of the current account balance between manufactures and other sectors is shown in Figure 3.6 for both the historic and projected period. It shows a worsening of the balance for both manufactures and for non-manufactures components of the current account over the decade to 2005.

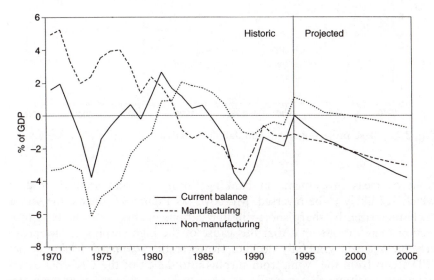

Fig. 3.6. Base projection: current balance, manufacturing balance, and non-manufacturing balance

A more detailed analysis of these other components is shown in Figure 3.7. The projection for financial services takes account of the abnormally low earnings from insurance underwriting from which the industry is just emerging. The projection assumes that financial service earnings will continue to be a buoyant and dynamic part of invisible earnings, increasing as a share of GDP at a faster rate than recently.

The disaggregation shows that the overall upturn in 1994 was dominated by net property income which increased sharply that year. This appears to be an exceptional change with most of the improvement arising from net earnings from direct investment. If this heralded a permanent increase in the share of net interest, profit, and dividends (IPD) income in GDP, it would relax the balance of payments constraint for at least the next five years and would make possible a more rapid creation of jobs. Part of the improvement, however, arises from unusually low outward income flows

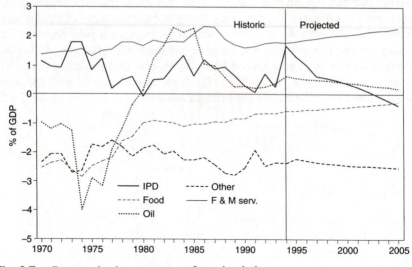

Fig. 3.7. Base projection: non-manufacturing balance

from overseas investments in banking, insurance, and security trading which are likely to be reversed. Moreover as Figure 3.7 shows, the sector is characterized by sharp short-run fluctuations of this sort. The base projection therefore assumes that this cause of the high surplus on net property income will gradually decline. However the *continued* decline in net IPD stems from the swing from surplus into deficit of the UK's net external assets position, shown in Figure 3.8, which is itself a result of the worsening manufactures trade position. Therefore, even if the exceptional features of the 1994 IPD position were assumed to be maintained, this would merely delay by about five years the time at which the net IPD balance would become negative.

It is therefore evident that the performance of the current account in this base case is critically dependent on the performance of trade in manufactures. An earlier study using this model has shown that the alternative of the spectacular transformation of the other sectors' trade performance required to alleviate the balance of payments constraint is beyond what could reasonably be expected (Cosh, Hughes, and Rowthorn 1993). Therefore we must look carefully at the conditional predictions for the trade in manufactures shown in Figure 3.9, which assume that the long-term trends towards slower growth of exports compared with imports will reassert themselves.

Although the base case increase in jobs would represent a substantial step towards restoring full employment, it takes no account of the likely change in participation rates of the labour force as the increased availability of jobs

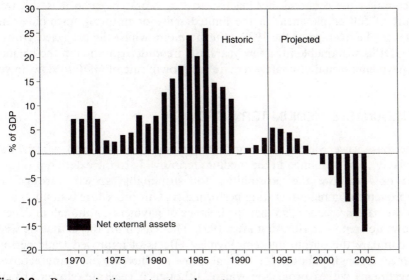

Fig. 3.8. Base projection: net external assets

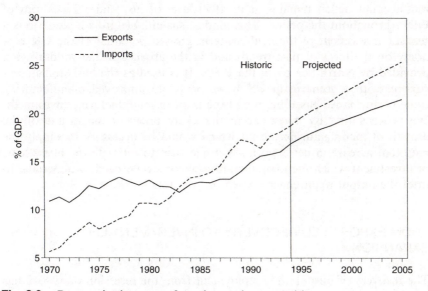

Fig. 3.9. Base projection: manufacturing trade propensities

encourages the economically inactive to seek work. Even so it is still well short of full employment in the limited sense of restoring unemployment rates to the average of the 1970s. Furthermore, whilst the projected growth of GDP is sustainable for a few years, the trend deterioration in the balance of payments would ultimately require the growth rate of GDP to slow down.

SUSTAINABLE MEDIUM-TERM GROWTH

The base case yielded an improvement in unemployment which was unlikely to be sustained in the medium term owing to the external position. We now explore the possibilities for sustainable growth through an improvement in manufacturing performance. Our procedure is first to modify the base projection, so that the balance of payments, although in deficit, shows no trend deterioration after 1997. The reason for this is that we wish to compare the output and employment effects of improved trade performance (brought about, for instance, by an increase in manufacturing investment) with a projection which, although it generates slower growth than in the base case, is sustainable in the medium term with a supportable balance of payments position. This slow-growth scenario is achieved by domestic spending growth being cut to 2 per cent annually compared with 2.5 per cent in the base projection. The other assumptions identified in Table 3.1 remain unchanged and the consequences of the slower growth are shown in Table 3.3. This reveals that the growth of GDP at 2.2 per cent leaves unemployment at over 2 million at the end of the decade and the current-account deficit remains at its 1997 level of just under 2 per cent of GDP throughout the period. This modest sustainable-growth scenario is a realistic assessment of the medium-term growth potential of the UK economy on the basis of past trends and in the absence of the windfall gain provided by North Sea oil in the 1980s. It is used as the basis for a comparison with a scenario in which we postulate improved manufacturing trade performance based upon an expansion of manufacturing investment. We proceed first by investigating the likely order of magnitude of the growth of manufacturing output which would be necessary to supply the required increase in net exports. We then turn to estimate the likely scale of investment which the manufacturing sector would need to undertake to meet the output requirement, based on past relationships.

FROM EXPORT-LED RECOVERY TO INVESTMENT-LED EXPANSION

The recovery of output and employment from the recession of 1990–2 has by 1995 not been matched by much rise in investment. As Figure 3.2 shows, investment in manufacturing only just began to increase in 1994, with a long way to go to before reaching the previous peak of 1990. However, several factors favoured prospects for a rise in investment. The first is that the balanced recovery of aggregate demand provides a reasonable basis on which to expect continued growth, so that investment projects begun in the mid-1990s could expect to be profitable when completed. By 1995 profits of industrial and commercial companies had begun to rise sharply, and companies' balance sheets and financial surpluses were much improved compared with 1990. Firms had larger sources of funds from which to finance a major investment programme. Although monetary policy began to tighten from the second half of 1994, interest rates were lower than during the 1990–2 period. So long as interest rates are not increased sharply, the prospects for investment are good. The CBI intentions survey for the first quarter of 1995 suggested that investment in manufacturing industry would increase strongly during the course of 1995 (CBI 1995). The pressure on capacity, reported by the CBI, would also provide an incentive to invest, not only for replacement or to incorporate technical innovation into the existing capital stock, but to add to production capacity.

One feature which caused the prolonged high unemployment of the 1980s was the loss of capacity which turned Keynesian unemployment (caused by the restrictive fiscal and monetary stance of governments to control inflation in their economies after the second oil shock) into structural unemployment.[5] This is an example of hysteresis where sustained low demand gradually brings capacity utilization back to normal rates through adjustment to lower capital stock and loss of jobs.

Loss of capacity through the closure of plants or entire firms is not quickly reversed. But when firms become confident of conditions in which to reinvest in capacity one may expect several beneficial effects on productivity and trade performance to follow. It is reasonable, for example, to expect that investment in new capacity will introduce best-practice technology and raise average productivity. In addition, in manufacturing markets dominated by trade in differentiated products, an expansion of capacity associated with product, as well as process innovation, may generate more export sales *at given levels of world demand* by increasing the variety of products on offer. Firms with more capacity may thus expect to capture more export orders as a result of improvements in non-price competitiveness. Investment in capacity will also have a direct effect on employment as labour is recruited to work with new plant and equipment (unless extreme assumptions are made about the short-run elasticity of substitution of capital for labour).

These factors are plausible as microeconomic hypotheses at the level of the firm and industry, but it is notoriously difficult to find econometric

---

[5] See Rowthorn (1977; 1995).

evidence of their effects on trade and employment at the macroeconomic level. (For a review of the relevant macroeconomic evidence see Rowthorn 1995). It is also notoriously difficult to quantify the additional potential supply of output generated by a given amount of investment in increased capacity. We can, however, make some progress in assessing the magnitude of investment that would be associated with significant changes in employment prospects in the medium term. We can do this by using our model to work backwards from the trade improvements necessary for sustained expansion in the medium term, to the employment and output changes with which they would be associated, and then to the investment programme that would be implied.

Suppose that from 1995 the manufacturing sector begins a programme of investment to expand the capital stock. Then as a result of a combination of improved non-price competition and increased product variety, suppose that the competitive position of UK manufacturing gradually increases over the next ten years. We can model this by modifying our slow-growth scenario to generate a great enough improvement in the UK's manufactured trade performance to bring the current account deficit into approximate balance by the end of the period. Let us call this the 'investment in capacity' scenario.[6] The improvement in the current balance which this produces is illustrated in Figure 3.10. It is important to remember that the slow growth and investment scenarios share common assumptions on the projected growth of world trade, domestic spending, and relative cost competitiveness of internationally traded goods and services. They differ, as we have seen, because the equations for the volume of manufactured exports and imports are modified in the 'investment in capacity' scenario to accelerate the growth rate of exports and diminish the growth rate of imports on a scale which is sufficient to hit the target of a zero balance in the current account of the balance of payments by 2005. The effect on the trends in the manufactured export and import volumes is gradual, as shown in Figure 3.11, where the improvement in favourable trends is greater after 2000. This is consistent with the assumption that the trade benefits of an investment programme would be small in the short term. The current account initially moves into deficit by about 1–1.5 per cent of GDP, but the improved manufactured net export growth gradually restores the current account to zero balance by 2005. Better net export growth, compared with

---

[6] The assumption of the investment in capacity scenario is that export volume growth will increase relative to world *demand* for manufactures (compared with the slow-growth scenario) and that import volumes will grow more slowly relative to domestic *demand* for manufactures. Neither of these effects can easily be included in the equations for exports or imports on which the projections are based because we lack direct historical evidence of the size of the effects. In principle the improved trade performance should have a symmetrical impact on higher domestic sales by UK producers, causing import substitution to rise. The improvements are therefore simulated as an *exogenous* acceleration of the growth rate of exports and some diminution in the growth of imports.

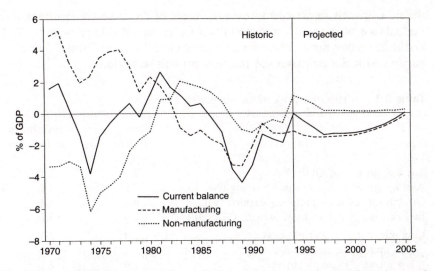

Fig. 3.10. Investment in capacity scenario: current account, manufacturing, and non-manufacturing balances

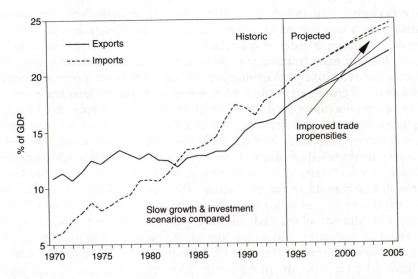

Fig. 3.11. Investment in capacity scenario: manufacturing trade propensities

the slow-growth scenario, improves the trade-off between GDP growth and the balance of payments and permits a faster sustainable growth of GDP and total employment. These improvements are shown in Table 3.3 in comparison with the estimates for the slow growth scenario.

Table 3.3. Alternative projections: summary, 1995–2005

	Slow growth	Investment in capacity
Average growth of GDP (%)	2.2	2.4
Average growth of domestic spending (%)	2.0	2.0
Growth rate of manufacturing exports (%)	4.8	5.4
End period current-account balance (% GDP)	–1.9	+0.1
Unemployment: 1995 (millions)	2.4	2.4
plus increase in work-force	1.2	1.2
less increase in employment	1.6	2.1
Unemployment: 2005 (millions)	2.0	1.5

FROM IMPROVED TRADE PERFORMANCE TO OUTPUT AND INVESTMENT

The next step is to calculate the likely increase in manufacturing output which would be required to supply the additional exports and to displace imports in domestic sales of manufactures. Figure 3.12 shows the ratio of the volume of manufactured exports to the volume of manufacturing production since 1970, scaled so that the ratio in 1990 is the value of exports as a share of gross output (derived from input–output tables). The proportion of manufacturing production which is exported has risen steadily and approximately doubled between 1970 and 1995. For comparison, the trend in the export propensity between 1970 and 1980 is extrapolated to 1995. The export share fell relative to trend between 1980 and 1983, following the decline in world trade after the second oil shock. This was despite the large drop in UK manufacturing production which occurred during this period. An important feature of the collapse of the manufacturing sector was the high overvaluation of the exchange rate, which would have reduced export demand in particular. Thereafter, the share resumed its upward path and by 1994 had returned to the long-term trend. For the projection period in Figure 3.12 we make the heroic assumption that the share of exports in manufacturing production will continue to rise on trend as the economy

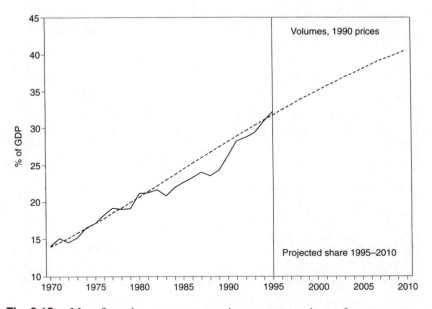

Fig. 3.12. Manufacturing export propensity: exports as share of gross output

becomes further integrated into European and World markets.[7] From the projected growth of export volumes and the projected rise in the export–production ratio we can derive a path for the annual growth of manufacturing output in the decade to 2005 which is about 3.7 per cent.

An alternative approach is to use the ratio of imports to domestic expenditure to provide an estimate of domestic expenditure on manufactures. Figure 3.13 shows the ratio of the volume of imports to domestic sales of manufactures (supplied from domestic production and imports). We assume that this import propensity will increase at a slower rate than under the slow-growth scenario as imports are displaced in domestic sales because of better non-price competition and increased product variety.[8] From the projected growth of import volumes and the projected rise in the import–demand ratio we calculate a path for the projected growth of manufactured sales. From this and our projected trade balance for manufactures we derive an alternative path for the growth of manufacturing production which averages about 2.9 per cent from 1995 to 2005.

If the export–output ratio were to increase more slowly than we have

[7] The trend line is constrained to have an upper limit of 50% in the projection. The trend line increases but at a slightly decelerating rate described by a logistic curve.

[8] This is achieved by constraining the trend line to an upper limit of 60% and extrapolating a logistic trend from 1995.

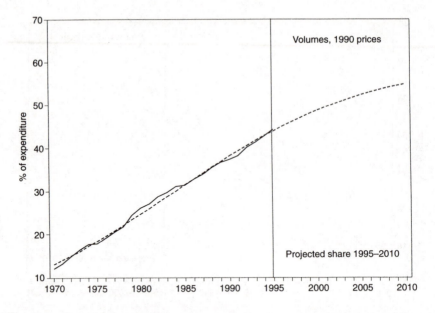

Fig. 3.13. Manufacturing import propensity: imports as share of demand

assumed, the required annual growth in output would be higher than 3.7 per cent. Similarly if the import–demand ratio increased by more than we have assumed, the resulting annual growth in output would be less than 2.9 per cent. The tentative conclusion we draw from these calculations is that the likely range of output growth consistent with achieving the required improvement in net exports is about 3–4 per cent annually.

The central projection for manufacturing output of a 3.5 per cent average annual growth rate between 1995 and 2005, derived from these two estimation procedures, is shown in Figure 3.14, which plots annual manufacturing output between 1948 and 1995. For comparison the postwar average trend rate of annual growth up to 1973 of 3.2 per cent is extrapolated to 2005. This shows that the required growth of manufacturing output would have to be only a little faster than the 'golden age' average growth rate, although considerably better than the miserable annual growth rate of 0.8 per cent achieved between 1979 and 1995. From this middle estimate we calculate the growth rate of investment, given the growth rate of output, based on the past statistical relationship between the two over the period 1956–94.[9] The final calculation is the annual investment expenditure (at constant prices) implied by the growth in manufacturing output. This is shown in Figure 3.15.

[9] We assume that skilled labour will not pose a constraint on this expansion—for a discussion of this issue see Robinson (Ch. 5, this volume).

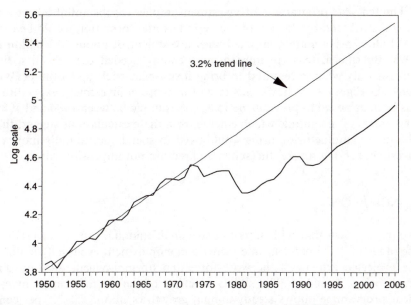

Fig. 3.14. Manufacturing output: growth in capacity, 1995–2005

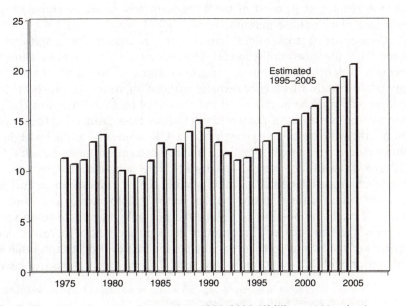

Fig. 3.15. Manufacturing investment, 1975–2005 (£billion, 1990 prices)

The ten-year programme of investment implies a substantial increase in capital stock and by the end of the period capital formation would be over £20 billion per annum compared with investment of about £12 billion in 1995. But the increase in investment spending needed over the first five years is only what is required to bring investment back up to the peak of 1989. As Figure 3.15 shows, this rate of increase in investment expenditure has been achieved in previous periods, for example between 1984 and 1989. The orders of magnitude which emerge from these calculations suggest that although manufacturing firms would need to spend substantially more on investment in the future, the sums required are not impossibly large.

CONCLUSIONS

We have shown that with slow but sustainable annual growth of GDP in the range of 2–2.3 per cent, the increase in employment eventually matches the projected growth of the work-force and unemployment does not fall much below 2 million. The simulated effect of the manufacturing investment programme allows steady annual growth of about 2.3–2.5 per cent, with sufficient improvement in manufactured trade to alleviate the balance of payments constraint.[10] The increase in employment might allow unemployment to fall to about 1.4 million. The annual growth rate of manufacturing output consistent with this simulation would be about 3.5 per cent. While growth at this rate might be fast enough to reverse the thirty-year decline in employment, most of the increase in private sector employment would take place outside manufacturing.

A number of factors might improve the prospects for employment beyond those identified in the model. The current balance might be allowed to remain in deficit with some expansion of domestic spending. If the economy could sustain this higher demand without inflation, the prospects for employment would be improved. If the growth of trade in European Union economies or in the rest of the world were better than assumed in these projections, then the sustained growth of the UK economy could be higher, with attendant greater job creation. If the job creation made possible by GDP growth without external constraints were supplemented by special employment measures such as more young people staying on in further education and training, more public sector employment, and shorter hours,[11] it might be possible to reduce the unemployment rate to about 3 per cent of the work-force. This estimate takes no account of increased participation of the labour force as employment increases. But it shows that in combination with 2.2 million jobs and special employment measures creat-

[10] In practice the investment in increased capacity would be widespread across most sectors of the economy and not confined to manufacturing industry.

[11] An estimate of the impact of these measures is discussed in Coutts and Rowthorn (1995).

ing another 0.8 million jobs, a target of 3 million could be achieved. This would probably reduce recorded unemployment to under 1 million people. Even if this can be achieved in the next five years, by the end of the twentieth century, the British people will have lived through a quarter-century with unemployment continuously over 1 million.

To achieve the kind of sustained investment and improved competitive performance which even this would imply will require a major and credible policy commitment. The extent of the investment expansion will be strongly influenced by the specific macro- and fiscal-policy environment within which manufacturing firms must make their investment decisions. In addition to maintaining a tight control on consumption, it will be necessary via interest rate and fiscal policy to create and maintain attractive conditions for manufacturing investment. In this context consideration should be given to fiscal incentives to encourage longer-term investment in innovation enhancing activities such as R&D expenditure, as well as to raise the relative expected return on manufacturing investment generally. A more focused approach here could be built on the various technology foresight exercises currently under way or completed in a variety of manufacturing and related sectors. These could form an important input into an industrial policy oriented towards enhancing capacity and efficiency in manufacturing. Important too will be policies aimed at the longer-run improvement of the nation's stock of human capital through the reform of education and training systems and policies directed towards the enhancement of corporate and personal saving. Here too fiscal policy has a role to play in the encouragement of retentions in large and small firms and the expansion of venture capital provision. These issues and the related questions of institutional and political reform with which they may be associated are taken up in the remaining chapters of this book.

REFERENCES

Beveridge, S., and Nelson, C. (1981), 'A New Approach to Decomposition of Economic Time Series into Permanent and Transitory Components with Particular Attention to Measurement of the "Business Cycle"', *Journal of Monetary Economics*, 7: 151–74.

Cosh, A., Hughes, A., and Rowthorn, R., (1993), 'The Competitive Role of UK Manufacturing Industry: 1979–2003', in K. Hughes (ed.), *The Future of UK Competitiveness and the Role of Industrial Policy* (London: Policy Studies Institute).

Coutts, K., and Rowthorn, R. (1995), 'Employment in the United Kingdom: Trends and Prospects', *Political Quarterly: Special Issue* (Oxford: Blackwell).

CBI (1995), *Industrial Trends Survey* (London: Confederation of British Industry), April.

Rowthorn, R. (1977), 'Conflict, Inflation and Money', *Cambridge Journal of Economics*, 1/3 (Sept.): 215–39.

—— (1995), 'Capital Formation and Unemployment', *Oxford Review of Economic Policy*, 11/1 (spring).

Part II
Industrial Problems and Policies

4. Tightening the Reins: The Capacity Stance of UK Manufacturing Firms 1976–1995

Ciaran Driver

> If firms do not have the confidence that macro policies will succeed and growth trajectories will be maintained, they are afraid to invest, but if they do not invest, macro policies are indeed doomed to fail.
>
> (Robert Pindyck and Andres Solimano, 1993)

> Companies are investing far less than their US counterparts at the equivalent point in the economic cycle . . . Insofar as this adds to the inflationary pressures in the UK economy, it will provoke higher interest rates.
>
> (Lex column, *Financial Times*, 24 April 1995)

Corporate culture in the present climate is focused on cost-cutting. One way of implementing this programme is to rein in capital spending and to contain expansionary plans. On the assumption that this is what your competitor is doing anyway, cost-cutting plans are consistent and, in a narrow sense, rational. What corporation wants to shoulder the burden of kick-starting whole economies?

In this chapter we will examine the statistical evidence suggesting that firms have become more cautious in respect of investment in new capacity, despite the pro-business policies pursued in the early 1990s. We will establish that the reasons for this caution have less to do with inflationary expectations than with the prospects for sustainable demand growth. Finally we will argue that high levels of liquidity characterizing firms and financial institutions are inappropriate and should be viewed as a form of market failure: corrective policies will be suggested.

I am grateful to David Shepherd, Paul Temple and participants at the Robinson Conference and a seminar at the University of Hertfordshire for comments on a previous draft. Author's address for correspondence: Economics Section, Imperial College Management School, University of London, 53 Princes' Gate, Exhibition Road, London SW7 2PG, UK. e-mail: c.driver@ic.ac.uk.

THE DESIRED CAPACITY STANCE

Investment is a prime mover of growth because it is an autonomous or unexplained component of demand. Assuming the economy to be demand-constrained, higher demand expectations can be self-fulfilling.[1] Of course these expectations have to be generalized, that is, consistent and credible: otherwise disproportional growth results in excess capacity. The success of the post-war boom is often attributed to the success of institutional arrangements which underpinned general confidence. Demand was strong partly because it was understood that co-ordinated attempts would be made to ensure this: furthermore the promise was credible because firms generally had access to a supply of labour that was adequately prepared for the production demands of the time.

A break in economic conditions occurred at the end of the 1960s: the demand and profitability conditions were no longer assured. New forms of technology and social relations made incremental change ineffective, but deeper changes implied social and economic disruption. In the mid-1990s the pace of structural change accelerated and brought in its wake greater competition and the eclipse of whole sets of functions and hierarchies within firms. Less job security for middle-class workers has been paralleled by tighter rules on social security provision and higher manual unemployment. Inevitably this affects the floor for consumption demand. Although the bargaining power of workers has been much reduced, the resulting profit windfall is perceived not to be stable. The memories of firms encompass the historical experience of profit squeeze in the 1960s and 1970s and the heightened volatility of market demands that has accompanied the restoration of profitability in the mid-1990s. The resulting caution keeps investment low.

It would be wrong, however, to identify only the *demand* effects of low investment as a chief cause of slow growth.[2] The demand deficiency could easily be resolved, especially in conditions of restored profitability, by a compensating boost to one of the other final-expenditure categories such as consumption or public spending. The true position is different; the current climate is one in which the trend growth of demand is held back by *supply* constraints. These supply constraints arise because firms have adjusted up their preferred utilization rates. The rate of growth of the capital stock,

---

[1] For a formal argument to this effect, see Kiyotaki (1988).

[2] There have been a number of unsuccessful attempts to explain slow growth as a problem of insufficient demand: most of these rely on implausibly rigid savings patterns. Steindl (1952) suggests that investment is held back by an overhang of excess capacity with market power of firms holding consumption in check. The theory falls in the face of empirical evidence that most industries do not maintain excess capacity for decades on end. In his mature works, Steindl considers an alternative that slow growth is imposed by exogenous influences (e.g. environmental) but that mark-ups will not adjust downward. This is at variance with the entire period of the profit squeeze.

which decelerated from the 1960s in OECD countries, has not bounced back in response to the profit recovery of the 1980s and 1990s. Companies have become more cautious in building expansionary capacity, preferring to remain liquid or to invest in cost-saving, less risky forms of outlay (Driver 1994). The result of this is that incipient recoveries are choked off by a shortage of capacity (plant and skilled labour) before the economy has managed to reabsorb the workers displaced by the preceding downturn. In short, companies have adopted a tighter *capacity stance*, the explanation of which is the object of this chapter.

Before going on to investigate the question empirically, we may usefully draw attention to a related literature which deals with 'short-termism' and the allegedly excessive hurdle rates of return which are said to characterize British firms. This issue is directly related to that of capacity stance in that a tight capacity stance coincides with a caution in respect of capital commitment and a high rate of required return. Critics of industrial firms argue that these high hurdle rates have been inherited from past inflationary periods and should be adjusted down to reflect the prevailing low inflation climate (Wardlow 1994). It is not clear, however, that firms are being entirely irrational in failing to do this since inflation is but one component of required nominal return. Risk is another important factor and there may well be a trade-off between low inflation and greater demand instability and risk. Later in the chapter we will investigate these issues formally and explain why the required return, far from falling, may well have increased in recent years. The policy implications of this will be explored at the end of the chapter.

THE CAPACITY STANCE OF UK MANUFACTURING FIRMS 1976–1995

We aim to show in what follows that utilization rates have increased because firms have tended to display increased caution in respect of capital investment. We define the capacity stance formally as a measure of the ratio of capacity to expected demand.[3] A loose capacity stance implies that the firm is planning or expecting to hold excess capacity.[4] Theoretical work suggests that this ratio, or capacity stance, depends positively on unit

---

[3] Expected demand is the mean of conceptualised future demand outcomes.

[4] The economic rationale for a tighter capital stance is relatively simple. Firms aim to equalize at the margin the expected cost of carrying unused capacity and the expected cost of stockout. Unless the profit mark-up is exceptionally high, it is in the interest of firms not to plan to meet all expected demand. This is intuitively clear in the case of the inventory Newsboy model where the unit profit is the price less the cost c. Unless $(p-c)>c$, the cost of stockout is less than the carrying cost of a paper and the Newsboy should not aim to meet demand in full. Furthermore as the spread of the demand distribution increases, i.e. as risk increases, the downward bias to the capital stock is accentuated (Driver and Moreton 1992; Aiginger 1987).

profitability: at higher rates of profit there is a greater loss of profit occasioned by inadequate capacity. Theory also predicts that higher risk decreases the ratio, that is, tightens the capacity stance; there is a large variety of models giving more specific results.[5] Empirical testing of these ideas has been minimal, perhaps because the capacity stance itself can only be inferred rather than directly observed. Measures of deficient or excess capacity, that is, capacity utilization, reflect only the ex-post realization rather than the planned capacity stance.

DATA AND MEASUREMENT

In the UK, a reliable (if possibly non-linear) measure of capacity utilization is the Confederation of British Industry (CBI) *Industrial Trends Survey* question, eliciting a yes/no response, as to whether firms are working below a satisfactory full rate of capacity utilization—Appendix 1 lists the exact question.[6] In Figure 4.1 we show a five-quarter moving average of capacity

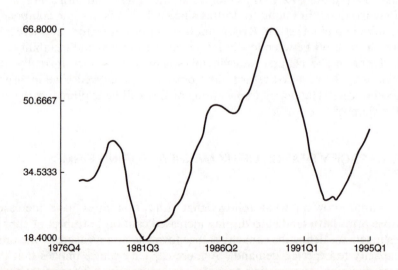

Fig. 4.1. Percentage at or above satisfactory utilization: 5-quarter moving average

[5] This is explicitly shown in the models of Nickell (1978, sect. 5a); Malinvaud (1983); Lambert and Mulkay (1987), and Driver, Lambert, and Vial (1993). Models which impose full capacity utilization tend to generate the opposite result, but are hardly credible.

[6] The CBI survey, established in the 1950s, has been carried out quarterly on nearly 2,000 firms since the mid-1970s and is the major such survey for Britain (CBI 1983; Junankar 1989). It has a good response rate and the replies are weighted before aggregation. The same question cited here (CBI question 4) is asked in business surveys in a number of other European countries and in Australia. It is possible to construct a measure of capacity utilization from the reply if assumptions are made regarding the statistical distribution of firms and the utilisation level that corresponds to satisfactory working (Driver 1986).

utilization in the period 1976–95. Although the graph shows an upward trend, this is not necessarily suggestive of a tightening capacity stance since the responses to the survey will differ depending on the length and pattern of the cycle.

Fortunately, the CBI question referred to above is complemented in the Survey by another question (14) asking respondents to cite the main expected constraint on future output, including the category plant capacity. This additional question will be used in conjunction with the one on utilization to form a proxy for the capacity stance in UK manufacturing.[7]

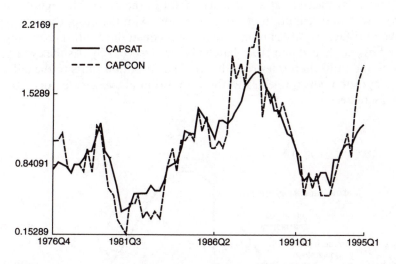

Fig. 4.2. Capacity satisfaction and capacity constraint indices: series scaled by own means

Figure 4.2 shows the behaviour of two indices. The first index (shown as 'Capacity Satisfaction', or CAPSAT) is the proportion of firms at or above satisfactory capacity, those answering 'no' to CBI question 4. The second index (shown as 'Capacity Constraint', or CAPCON) is the percentage of firms expecting to face a plant capacity constraint (question 14). In the graph both indices have been scaled by their time averages for comparability. It appears that the indices move largely in tandem though marked discrepancies occurred during the recoveries of the late 1980s and mid-1990s as the constraint figure rose more sharply than the measure of satisfactory utilization.

[7] It is sometimes argued that the two questions are not comparable since the utilization series refers to general capacity while the constraint question refers to plant capacity. It is shown in App. 2 that this is not a serious concern.

One possible explanation for the high level of constraint in these periods is that firms were uncertain of the durability of these expansion phases and deemed temporary constraint to be 'satisfactory'. While the utilization series is purely cyclical, the constraint series reflects, at least in part, the capacity stance of firms: the divergence between the series can thus be used as a measure of the capacity stance. Put differently, the same rate of satisfactory utilization as perceived by firms may be associated with differing rates of capacity constraint. When the constraint incidence is high in relation to satisfactory utilization, it may be inferred that firms have chosen a tight capacity stance.

Figure 4.3 illustrates the difference between the utilization measure and the constraint measure at a particular point in the cycle. The figure shows a cross-section distribution of utilization rates with the proportion of firms above satisfactory utilization, and above constrained utilization, represented by the shaded and cross-hatched areas respectively. As the cycle progresses and utilization rates rise, the whole distribution shifts to the left and the proportion constrained, and the proportion above satisfactory utilization, increase.

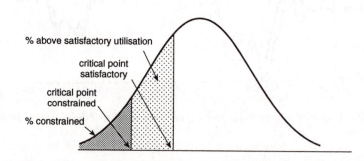

Fig. 4.3. Critical points for satisfactory and constrained utilization, showing distribution of spare capacity across firms shifting to left in expansion

There are at least two difficulties with using the above framework to obtain a measure of the capacity stance. First, as is clear from the diagram, the relationship between the 'satisfactory' and the 'constrained' series is inherently non-linear. This implies that the simple difference between the series cannot be taken as a direct measure of the capacity stance. Secondly, the shape of the distribution in Figure 4.3 is likely to change over the cycle and/or when the degree of structural change in the economy varies, as in the recovery in the early 1980s when considerable excess capacity coexisted with capacity constraints. In Appendix 2 we take account of these problems

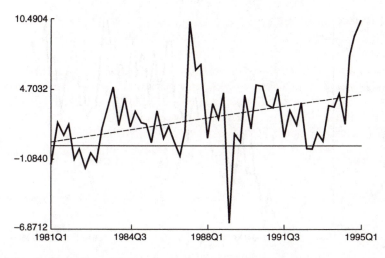

Fig. 4.4. Estimated capacity stance and corresponding trend

Note: See text for explanation of the vertical axis measure of capacity stance.

and construct a measure of the capacity stance as shown in Figure 4.4. A high positive number indicates a tight capacity stance.

MODELLING THE CAPACITY STANCE

Some insight into why firms have adopted a more cautious approach to capital investment over the 1980s is given in Figure 4.5. This shows the percentage of firms in the CBI Survey (Question 16c) reporting that investment was constrained by inadequate expected returns. It is apparent that the proportion of firms believing investment to be constrained by profitability rather than demand, financial availability, or other factors, rose sharply over the sample period.[8] The variable shown in Figure 4.5 is, in fact, a hybrid variable capturing expected profitability and required profitability: a rise in this proportion could mean either a rise in the required rate or a fall in expected returns. Some may argue that the recession of the early 1980s reduced profit expectations and that the trend in Figure 4.5 reflects this pessimism. However, such an interpretation sits uneasily with the observed trend in profitability, as the actual rate of return was rising strongly during the period in question. The pre-tax rate of return for Industrial and Commercial Companies trended from 4.1 per cent in 1980

[8] It might be argued that the initial figures are suspect owing to the question being introduced as a new question in the last quarter of 1979. However, an examination of the series of alternative replies to the same question dispels this worry in that at most the four quarters seem to display a learning process with the number of all responses rising—but only slightly.

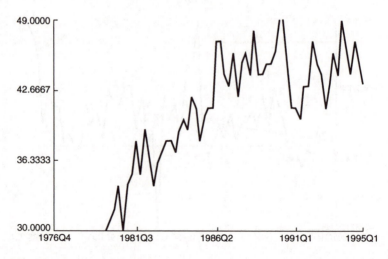

Fig. 4.5.   Percentage citing inadequate return to explain non-investment (INADR)

to 8.3 in 1993 (Bank of England *Quarterly Bulletin*, Aug. 1994). Furthermore the burden of corporate taxation was reduced during the period. It is stretching credulity to argue that this profit growth coexisted with pessimistic profit expectations over such a lengthy period. Thus the trend in Figure 4.5 can only reflect underlying forces raising the *required* rate of return. Among these may be numbered the rate of return on other assets and the perception of relative risk of investing in UK industry as opposed to holding liquid or foreign assets.

It should also be noted that any rise in the required rate is not likely to reflect movement in the cost of capital as this is recorded in the survey as an alternative reason for non-investing.[9] This is an important point, for some commentators such as Rowthorn (1995) have lain great stress on higher real interest rates in the 1980s as an explanation for lower investment. The level of interest rates is in turn related to lender risk. This, however, is at most half of the story as borrower risk is not reflected in the level of interest rates. Yet CBI sources show that the single most important determinant of real hurdle rates—more serious than the cost of finance—is the level of project risk (CBI 1994).

Appendix 2 offers statistical evidence that the percentage citing inadequate return as a reason for non-investment is important in explaining the capacity stance of firms. It is possible to quantify the magnitude of the effect on the capital constraint. The appendix shows that a 50 per cent increase in the percentage answering 'inadequate return' to CBI question 16 would raise the percentage constrained by plant capacity by over 5 per-

---

[9] Econometric evidence on this is also cited in App. 2.

centage points. This is a sizeable increase and would imply a considerable amount of lost sales, much of it perhaps permanent. It is of interest to note that the required return variable did indeed increase by 50 per cent over the sample period.

POLICY MEASURES TO STIMULATE INVESTMENT

The statistical analysis in Appendix 2 suggests that the required rate of return variable—a proxy for reluctance to take on risk—explains the cautious capacity stance of firms despite rising profitability. It is possible that this is rational from the point of view of firms themselves. Put differently, if the downside from over-optimistic capital programmes tends to outweigh the losses incurred from a wait-and-see approach, it is hard to criticize firms for exercising caution. If there are no market failures or externalities, it is not clear that any intervention is justified to change the capacity stance: government also needs to consider the balance of risks involved in promoting capital expenditure (Dixit and Pindyck 1994).

These arguments, while theoretically valid, tend to distract attention from what should be obvious through introspection and common sense. Firms do not benefit fully from the validation of an optimistic view and do not suffer unduly from refusing to be bullish about uncertain prospects. We may characterize their position by a stylized regret matrix where the first number is the regret ranking of a private firm and the second number in parenthesis is the regret ranking of a social planner. The highest rank (1) means least regret in respect of the decision stance: regret is measured relative to the alternative decision. We abstract from the possibility of self-fulfilling prophecy and assume that the outcomes are simply states of nature.

	Good out-turn	Poor out-turn
Bullish	2(1)	4(3)
Bearish	3(4)	1(2)

The reason for the reversal of private and social rankings in the top left and bottom right boxes is that part of private profits are appropriated in taxation but losses cannot be fully set off against tax.

The different rankings in the top right box arise for similar reasons. The private firm regrets more than the social planner a bullish stance in the face of a poor out-turn if capital markets are imperfect so that over-optimism results in distress selling. The worst outcome for the firm is to be overexposed. For the economy as a whole, however the bottom left box represents the maximum regret because there are external costs such as unemployment benefit, increased crime, and macroeconomic repercussions which are not all paid for by the firm or do not at any rate enter its private calculation.

PROPOSED POLICY CHANGE

In theory there are a number of ways to reform the investment climate to overcome the problem of excessive caution uncovered in this chapter. It is possible to make the macroeconomic climate more stable or to compensate for heightened risk through the incentive system.

The business of stabilizing the economic climate is one that policy-makers frequently champion. The goal is elusive, however, because the process of stabilization makes other variables (instruments and their correlates) more *unstable*. Without knowing which variables are most important to stabilize (demand; exchange rate; interest rate or prices) the danger is that perceived risk to firms will rise. On the evidence offered here and in Driver and Moreton (1991; 1992) it is demand variability that is most important to minimize. One route through which this would be possible would be to insure the consumer against large swings in personal disposable income net of committed expenditure such as mortgages. Recent evidence (Treasury 1993) has confirmed that both firms and households in the UK are more exposed to short-term interest rate fluctuations than in other countries. This is particularly serious in a world of quasi-fixed exchange rates where short-run interest rates are correspondingly volatile. Policy-makers might usefully consider whether incentives should be offered to encourage individuals to stabilize their non-discretionary outlays by converting to fixed-rate loans. The problem of income and demand instability is not, however, confined to the UK: capital investment in much of Europe has suffered a trend decline. It seems likely that income instability is a structural feature of the present phase of world development (Driver 1996). Nevertheless, recent evidence from the Bank of England suggests that aggregate demand is particularly volatile in the UK as compared with Germany and Japan, where supply shocks appear to dominate output movements (Sterne and Bayoumi 1993).

Policy to neutralize the adverse effects of risk should work at several levels. Not only should incomes be stabilized, but industry should be encouraged to be less risk-averse: private calculation is inadequate where firms are able to avoid the full cost of non-investment. In the remainder of this chapter I want to resurrect a classic argument that has largely been forgotten. This is the stabilizing influence of taxation. Recent reductions in the corporate tax rate have aimed to make the investment climate attractive. Paradoxically, however, the effect may have been to make the climate relatively more risky. Taxation is a form of risk-sharing in which losses are relatively less severe in relation to gains, the higher the rate of tax. Of course a high marginal tax rate could encourage profit-taking rather than reinvestment. But that effect can be offset by compensating capital allowances. Under some conditions a higher tax rate actually encourages investment. This was pointed out in a lucid piece by Eltis (1971) where he studied the effect of free depreciation, that is, where companies can write off the costs of investment against taxation immediately. As Eltis noted, this regime amounts to the 'strongest discrimination in favour of reinvestment and against dividends of any system' (1971: 21). Something approximating this system was in place before the UK corporation tax reforms of the mid-1980s. A feature of free depreciation is that the rate of return is always the same after tax as before tax: this happens because the incidence of taxation reduces the effective cost of the capital asset in the same proportion as the income streams are reduced. Thus it would appear quite possible to combine an increase in corporate taxation without affecting the incentive to invest.[10] Indeed Eltis goes even further, arguing that since interest relief is tax-deductible, 'the inducement to invest would be greater, the higher the rate of tax' (1971: 23).

The arguments above do not necessarily point to a simple return to the old system of allowances and tax that existed in the 1970s. That system paid out large sums to firms which did not change their investment behaviour; also, it could be argued it favoured quantity over quality of investment. It may be more appropriate to institute a system of discretionary grants, financed by a higher tax rate on most categories of business.[11] Such a system, based on the idea of an investment reserve scheme which releases discretionary funds during a downturn, was proposed in Driver (1994), based on the Swedish system that prevailed up to the 1980s.

Discretionary systems are sometimes unpopular with industrialists because of their reliance on regulators: they certainly necessitate an informed and competent agency. An alternative approach would involve the automatic triggering of retrospective accelerated capital allowances once an industry has exceeded a given degree of capital utilization. These allowances could be claimed by firms if they had achieved a critical capacity growth in the preceding period such as the industry mean capacity growth. Such a system would enhance the upside for the more expansionist firms in any industry. Just as importantly, it would increase the penalty for non-investment since any loss in market share and goodwill due to capital constraint would be more durable if rival firms were not capital-constrained. An advantage of the scheme would be that the subsidy element would be incurred only where the capital investment was justified as evidenced by industry capacity pressure.

[10] This may be preferable to the alternative proposed by Pitt-Watson (1991), who in a perceptive analysis of short-termism proposed an increase in VAT to finance subsidies for investment growth.

[11] Some classes of business—e.g. below a certain size threshold—may be characterized by risk-loving behaviour in which case the argument in the text for risk minimization through a higher rate of corporate tax would be inappropriate.

CONCLUSIONS

This chapter has discussed the factors determining the capacity stance of firms. We have measured changes in this capacity stance by examining the relationship between the proportion of firms constrained by plant capacity and the proportion of firms above satisfactory utilization. Although highly correlated, the series have diverged significantly in the 1980s and 1990s. The capacity stance of firms has become noticeably tighter as firms have adjusted their required rates of return upwards: uncertainty as to the sustainability of demand has been one important influence here. Policy measures are needed to reverse these changes in capital stance and to ensure that private parsimony does not create public penury.

APPENDIX 1

The exact wording of the survey questions extracted from the CBI *Industrial Trends Survey* is given below for those questions referred to in the text.

QUESTION 4   Is your present level of output below capacity (i.e., are you working below a satisfactory full rate of operation)?

QUESTION 8   Excluding seasonal variation what has been the trend over the past four months and what are the expected trends over the next four months with regard to the volume of output—up/same/down?

QUESTION 11   As question 8 with regard to: average cost per unit of output—up/same/down?

QUESTION 12a   As question 8 with regard to: average prices at which domestic orders are booked—up/same/down?

QUESTION 14   What factors are likely to limit your output over the next four months? Please tick the most important factor or factors—orders or sales/skilled labour/other labour/plant capacity/credit or finance/materials or components/other.

QUESTION 16c   What factors are likely to limit (wholly or partly) your capital expenditure authorizations over the next twelve months—inadequate return on proposed investment/shortage of internal finance/inability to raise external finance/cost of finance/uncertainty about demand/shortage of labour including managerial and technical staff/other?

APPENDIX 2.   The econometrics of the Capacity Stance

We define CAPSAT and CAPCON as the proportions in the CBI Survey responding 'no' to questions 4 and 14 respectively. We model the responses CAPSAT and CAPCON as a function of the (unknown) level of spare capacity in the economy (ESC). At time t, the percentage of firms above satisfactory utilization (CAPSAT) and the percentage constrained (CAPCON) are given by:

$$CAPSAT(t) = f1(ESC(t)) + u1 \tag{1}$$
$$CAPCON(t) = f2(ESC(t); Z(t)) + u2 \tag{2}$$

where u1, u2 are error terms; f1, f2 are monotonic but possibly non-linear, time-varying functions; and Z is the capacity stance, the ratio of capacity to expected demand, $K/(E(Y))$.

Equation (1) models CAPSAT simply as a cyclical term i.e. the proportion above satisfactory, adjusted for the cycle, is simply a random error term. Put differently there is no *planned* deviation by the firm from the satisfactory level. In equation (2), on the other hand, the $Z(t)$ term indicates that the proportion of firms constrained is affected by the capacity stance. Combining (1) and (2) we obtain:

$$CAPCON(t) = f4(CAPSAT(t); ESC(t); Z(t)) + u3 \tag{3}$$

As ESC and Z are unobserved, we initially absorbed them into the error term and carried out exploratory linear and log-linear regressions on (3). Not surprisingly, the error-term diagnostics were not acceptable, so we proceeded to specify more carefully the form of the relationship between CAPCON and CAPSAT.

Consider the case in Figure 4.3 in the text where firm-level utilization—more correctly its converse, spare capacity—at a point in time is distributed across firms according to the Sech-squared distribution which may, for convenience, be taken as an approximation to the Normal distribution. For this point in time and a given capacity stance, one critical point will correspond to satisfactory working and another critical point to the left of this will correspond to a capacity constraint. As the economy expands, the distribution will shift to the left. An increasing proportion of firms will find themselves working above satisfactory utilization and the same will apply to the proportion that is capital-constrained. The relationship between these proportions will be given by the relationship between two distribution functions obtained by integrating the Sech-square density functions. Assuming now a *constant level difference* (**d**) between satisfactory and constrained utilization, these distribution functions are logistic.

The logistic functions are expressed by:

$$CAPSAT = 1/(1 + \exp(c1{-}bESC)) \tag{4}$$
$$CAPCON = 1/(1 + \exp(c2{-}bESC)) \tag{5}$$

where b, c1, c2 are (negative) constants with c2 = c1 + **b**d.

From the above we may specify transformed linear regressions as:

$$TCAPCON = a1\ TCAPSAT + a2\ UPXOUT + u4 \tag{6}$$

where

$$TCAPCON = \log(CAPCON/(1 - CAPCON)) \tag{7}$$

and

$$TCAPSAT = \log(CAPSAT/(1 - CAPSAT)) \tag{8}$$

UPXOUT is the percentage of firms which expect output to rise over the next four months (question 8). This is included as CAPCON refers to an expected constraint (over the next four months) while CAPSAT refers to the current position.

In equation (6), a1 is expected to be close to unity; a2 > 0; and u4, the error term, depends on assumptions made in respect of the non-specified error terms that have been omitted from (4) and (5).

Equation (6) is derived on the assumption that **d** is constant. This is unrealistic because **d** may be cyclical. Cyclicality in **d** arises because the distribution in Figure 4.3 may change over time with smaller dispersion at cyclical peaks. The dispersion may not merely be cyclical, however. Periods of high structural change should also imply a higher dispersion of spare capacity with the economy characterized by excess demand in some sectors and excess supply in others. To capture these effects we first approximate the inter-firm dispersion by the standard deviation of CAPSAT across the nine major industrial groups in the CBI survey (SD9CBI), calculated for each quarter. We then model the **d** parameter in equation (6) to be a positive function of this dispersion. If the function is linear, dispersion may be entered in equation (6) in linear form.

Preliminary tests (DF and ADF) confirm that, at the 5 per cent level, TCAPCON and TCAPSAT are integrated of order one, while dispersion (SD9CBI) and its log (LSD9CBI) are either I(1) or stationary. The results for cointegration are mixed with the DF, ADF(2) and CRDW tests rejecting non-cointegration between the I(1) variables but other ADF tests failing to reject. Using the Johansen method with the I(1) variables and the first difference of LSD9CBI included as a stationary variable, non-cointegration was rejected at the 5 per cent level in both the eigen-value and trace tests: a single cointegrated vector was supported. Similar results were obtained when a (stationary) profitability variable (MARKUP) was included as theoretical reasoning might suggest.[12] In view of these results we initially use the dynamic specification below where the D prefix indicates a first difference; lags are indicated in parentheses; L is the lag operator; and RES1 is the residual from the cointegrating regression:

$$DTCAPCON = h_0 + h_1(L)DTCAPSAT + h_2DUPXOUT + h_3(L)DDLSD9CBI + h_4(L)DMARKUP + h_5RES1 + e \tag{9}$$

It is suggested in the text that the hurdle rate of firms is proxied by the percentage citing inadequate return as a reason for non-investment. This variable (INADR) is only available for a limited sample from the last quarter of 1979. Tests show the

---

[12] The profitability variable was constructed as a measure of the difference between the % expecting price rises and those expecting cost rises with a log of 2 on the price variable to capture trade credit. It is possible to argue that this is a liquidity rather than a profitability term.

log level LINADR variable to be I(1). Once again, a single cointegrating vector was significant at the 5 per cent level, relating TCAPCON, TCAPSAT, and LINADR, with MARKUP and DLSD9CBI included as conditioning stationary variables. The restriction of a zero coefficient on LINADR is rejected at the 5 per cent level. The cointegrating vector is:

$$TCAPCON = -5.84 + 0.86TCAPSAT + 1.12LINADR$$

The residual RES2 replaces RES1 in equation (9) for this sample. The long-run elasticity is high, suggesting that each 10 per cent rise in INADR would add a percentage point to CAPCON. As the change in INADR over the sample period is

Table 4.1. Dependent variable DTCAPCON

Regressor/sample	1978Q3–1995Q1 (1) OLS	1981Q1–1995Q1 (2) OLS	1981Q1–1995Q1 (3) OLS
CONSTANT	0.017 (0.65)	0.014 (0.50)	0.013 (0.47)
DTCAPSAT	0.923 (5.95)	0.789 (4.21)	0.785 (4.30)
DDTCAPSAT(–1)	0.336 (3.00)	0.276 (2.19)	0.294 (2.39)
DUPXOUT	0.022 (3.79)	0.017 (2.60)	0.018 (2.79)
D4MARKUP(–1)	—	—	–0.005 (1.90)
DDLINADR(–1)	—	0.807 (3.18)	0.732 (2.52)
DDLSD9CBI	–0.172 (2.39)	–0.161 (2.04)	–0.161 (2.10)
RES(–1)	–0.469 (4.17)	–0.478 (3.71)	–0.539 (4.16)
R^2	0.61	0.64	0.66
DW	2.25	1.97	1.86
$X^2(4)$SC	8.34(0.08)	3.83(0.43)	2.41(0.66)
$X^2(1)$FF	0.57(0.45)	0.46(0.50)	0.07(0.79)
$X^2(2)$N	6.40(0.04)	0.32(0.85)	1.20(0.55)
$X^2(1)$H	0.33(0.56)	1.26(0.26)	1.55(0.21)

Notes: RES1 for column 1 and RES2 for columns 2 and 3.

For mnemonics see Appendix 3.

Diagnostics are *microfit* standard X^2 tests:

X^2 SC: Lagrange multiplier test for fourth-order autocorrelation
X^2FF: Ramsey RESET test using squared fitted values
X^2N: Jarque–Bera test for normality of residuals
X^2H: Heteroscedasticity test

large, we prefer to simulate what CAPCON would have been had INADR remained at the level it attained after the initial recovery in the 1980s (about 35 per cent). The divergence between this simulated value and the actual constraint is then taken as a measure of the tightening capacity stance and shown in Figure 4.4 of the text.

The results of the dynamic regressions are shown in Table 1. Column 1 shows the results of a basic regression based on equation (9) but without either the MARKUP or the LINADR variables. Columns 2 and 3 show how the results are affected by the inclusion of the LINADR and MARKUP variables. The data support entering these in double-differenced and lagged four-quarter difference form respectively. Clearly these variables influence the capacity stance, especially the former. The equations are stable, as indicated by predictive failure tests for six and eight quarters ahead. The significance of LINADR contrasts with no significance for the variable recording cost of finance as the reason for non-investment (question 14). This suggests that non-pecuniary factors such as risk and confidence are dominating the investment decision.[13]

APPENDIX 3.   VARIABLE LISTING

Variable	Definition and Source
TCAPSAT	Logit of % answering NO to Q. 4
TCAPCON	Logit of % response to Q. 14 (plant capacity)
TLABCON	Logit of % response to Q. 14 (skilled labour)
UPXOUT	% answering UP to Q. 8
LSD9CBI	Log of S.D. across the 9 Major Industries of % answering NO to Q. 4
MARKUP	% answering UP to Q. 12a, lagged twice, less % answering UP to Q. 11, unlagged
LINADR	Log of % responding INADEQUATE RETURN to Q. 16c

[13] There was no support either for the inclusion in (9) of a variable representing skilled labour shortages, analogously to TCAPSAT. This was included because special CBI surveys (CBI 1983; Junankar 1989) have reported that the CAPSAT variable captures a wider concept of capacity than plant capital: this could affect the relationship between CAPCON and CAPSAT. We conclude that although some firms may interpret Q. 4 broadly, the responses are dominated by considerations of plant capacity.

REFERENCES

Aiginger, K. (1987), *Production and Decision Theory under Uncertainty* (Oxford: Blackwell).

CBI (1983), *Twenty five years of 'ups and downs'* (London: Confederation of British Industry).

—— (1994), 'Realistic Returns: How do Manufacturers Assess New Investment?' (London: Confederation of British Industry), July.

Dixit, A., and Pindyck, R. (1994) *Investment under Uncertainty* (Princeton: Princeton University Press).

Driver, C. (1986), 'Transformation of the CBI Capacity Utilisation Series: Theory and Evidence', *Oxford Bulletin of Economics and Statistics*, 48/4: 339–52.

—— (1994), 'The Case of Fixed Investment', in T. Buxton, P. Chapman, and P. Temple, *Britain's Economic Performance* (London: Routledge).

—— (1996), 'Stagnation as a Process of Transition', *Cambridge Journal of Economics*, 20.

—— and Meade, N. (1994), 'Why does Capital Shortage Persist?', Working paper, *Imperial College Management School*, Dec.

—— and Moreton, D. (1991), 'The Influence of Uncertainty on UK Manufacturing Investment', *Economic Journal*, 101: 1452–9.

—— (1992), *Investment, Expectations and Uncertainty* (Oxford: Blackwell).

—— Lambert, P., and Vial, S. (1993), 'Risky Production with *ex-ante* Prices under Monopoly: Analytical and Simulation Results', *Bulletin of Economic Research* 45/1: 59–68.

Eltis, W. (1971), 'Taxation and Investment', in R. Shone (ed.), *Problems of Investment* (Oxford: Blackwell).

Junankar, S. N. (1989), 'How do Companies Respond to the Industrial Trends Survey?', CBI Conference, Centre Point, London, 6 Nov.

Kiyotaki, N. (1988), 'Multiple Expectational Equilibria under Monopolistic Competition', *Quarterly Journal of Economics*, 103: 695–713.

Lambert, J. P., and Mulkay, B. (1987), 'Investment in a Disequilibrium Context or Does Profitability Really Matter?', *Cahier du Cerac*, 870, Brussels.

Malinvaud, E. (1983), 'Profitability and Investment Facing Uncertain Demand', Working Paper 8303, INSEE.

Nickell, S. (1978), *The Investment Decision of Firms* (Cambridge: Cambridge University Press).

Pindyck, R., and Solimano, A. (1993), 'Economic Instability and Aggregate Investment', in National Bureau for Economic Research, *NBER Macroeconomic Annual* (Cambridge, Mass.: MIT Press).

Pitt-Watson, D. (1991), 'Economic Short-Termism: A Cure for the British Disease', *Fabian Pamphlet 547* (London: Fabian Society).

Rowthorn, R. (1995), 'Capital Formation and Unemployment', *Oxford Review of Economic Policy*, 11/1: 26–39.

Steindl, J. (1952), *Maturity and Stagnation in American Capitalism* (Oxford: Oxford University Press).

Sterne, G., and Bayoumi, T. (1993), 'Temporary Cycles or Volatile Trends? Economic Fluctuations in 21 OECD Countries', Bank of England Working Paper Series, 13.

Treasury Bulletin (1993), summer 1993 (London: HM Treasury).
Wardlow, A. (1994), 'Investment Appraisal Criteria and the Impact of Low
   Inflation', *Bank of England Quarterly Bulletin*, 34/3 (Aug.): 250–4.

5. Skill Shortages and Full Employment: How Serious a Constraint?

Peter Robinson

Our estimates suggest that skill shortages are not, currently, a major cause of manufacturing wage inflation though they have contributed to the rate of increase edging up since the early 1980s.

(Sentance and Williams 1989)

Skill shortages are a perennial concern in the British economy. Rarely a month passes without the publication of some survey pointing towards the existence of a problem with respect to the skills base of the British economy. Anecdotal evidence of the existence of skill shortages at organization or industry level gains even more frequent exposure. And yet—as this chapter will show—skill shortages are a slippery concept, ill-defined, and measured in a variety of ways. Moreover, there is a reluctance to go behind the headlines proclaiming that x per cent of firms are complaining about skill shortages according to the latest survey, to ask exactly what are the implications, for economic performance and most critically for unemployment, of the existence of any given level of reported skill shortages.

One aspect of the debate needs clarifying immediately. A shortage of skills throughout the British work-force may contribute towards a lower level of productivity, and a lower rate of productivity growth, in the British economy when compared with other advanced industrial countries. The research of the National Institute of Economic and Social Research in the 1980s placed heavy emphasis on the under-skilling of the British work-force in explaining the lag in productivity levels in a number of British industries when compared with their German counterparts (Prais 1990). However, the National Institute's study of the chemical industries in the two countries in the early 1990s (Mason and Wagner 1994) found the same skills gap as in industries previously studied, but without this gap having the same adverse impact on relative British productivity. This cast considerable doubt upon how far the Institute's earlier findings could be generalized to other industries.

This debate—over the impact of skills upon productivity and living standards—is separate from the debate over the impact of skill shortages on inflation and unemployment. The two debates are frequently confused in practice, just as the economic objective of increasing the underlying rate of economic growth, and the economic objective of full employment (without inflation), are confused. This chapter is concerned solely with the possible impact of skill shortages on inflation and unemployment, and the way this is phrased immediately points out the main transmission mechanism whereby skill shortages might lead to unemployment. If skill shortages cause upward pressure on pay and therefore price inflation, the monetary authorities will react to this by tightening monetary policy and this will cause unemployment to be higher than it would otherwise have been. Whether skill shortages do lead to any significant upward pressure on wage inflation is one of the empirical matters which this chapter will attempt to address.

In the first section the chapter tries to define precisely what is meant by a 'skill shortage' and how this concept differs from the more general notions of 'recruitment difficulties' or 'hard-to-fill vacancies'. The second section looks at three of the better-known surveys which purport to measure the incidence of recruitment difficulties, hard-to-fill vacancies, or skill shortages, and compares the reliability of these surveys. The trend in recruitment difficulties or skill shortages over time is discussed, with particular reference to the results of the CBI Quarterly Industrial Trends Survey, which is the only survey which refers specifically to skill shortages, and measures the incidence of skill shortages over a long period of time (over thirty years). The relationship between skill shortages and the economic cycle is outlined. The third section looks at the evidence linking skill shortages and wage inflation and unemployment. The fourth section goes back to the question of what exactly a skill shortage is, where such shortages exist, and therefore what can be done in policy terms about the existence of such shortages.

The chapter does not address the issue of the relative importance of skill shortages in Britain when compared with other European countries because to do so would require an extensive evaluation of the sources of data on skill shortages in these other countries. As will be shown, judging exactly how much reliability to give to the different British surveys is difficult enough.

The chapter concludes by returning to the question of just how serious a constraint skill shortages are on the attainment of full employment. The overall conclusion is a sanguine one—that the current and prospective level of skill shortages in the British economy is low by historical standards, that these shortages have minimal implications for wage inflation, and that a steady and modest year-by-year reduction in unemployment need not be brought to a halt by any inflationary pressure associated with skill shortages.

WHAT ARE SKILL SHORTAGES?

Skill shortages can be said to exist when firms are facing difficulty in recruiting to fill vacancies because of a shortage of suitably qualified or skilled labour. Skill shortages overlap with, but are not the same thing as, recruitment difficulties or hard-to-fill vacancies. And skill shortages only matter if they seem likely to have a significant impact on firms with the consequence that they may therefore be causing upward pressure on pay.

Firms may face recruitment difficulties or may have hard-to-fill vacancies for a variety of reasons:

1. There may not be enough labour with the necessary formal skills or qualifications to fill the jobs available. These are the 'true' skill shortages. Obvious examples would be schools unable to recruit teachers with maths or science qualifications, manufacturing firms unable to recruit qualified engineers or technicians, or clerical employers unable to recruit individuals with basic literacy and numeracy.

2. There is another type of 'skill' shortage which is not related to formal skills and qualifications. Many firms often complain that even when individuals present themselves with the required formal qualifications, they are sometimes seen to lack the 'personal transferable skills' necessary to secure recruitment, that is, they are perceived to lack motivation or interpersonal communication skills or some other personal characteristic, which renders them unsuitable for the job. An example might be a newly qualified engineer with the requisite formal qualifications for an appointment, but perceived by the prospective employer as lacking the skills to communicate effectively with colleagues, customers, or suppliers or lacking real motivation for the job.

3. Individuals may have the requisite formal qualifications to fill a job, but not the necessary recent experience. Evidence is presented below that, other than for professional and associate professional and technical occupations, experience is more highly rated in recruitment to most types of jobs than formal qualifications. A bricklayer applying for a job, for example, might find that his formal qualifications count for little if he cannot quote recent relevant experience.

4. Some jobs may be relatively unattractive, for example because of unsocial hours or poor pay, so that firms' recruitment difficulties reflect these features of the jobs on offer rather than a shortage of suitably qualified or skilled labour. An example might be employment as a night security guard.

5. Finally some employers have lengthy recruitment procedures or unrealistic recruitment standards so that their recruitment problems are 'homegrown'. An example might be recruitment to a university lectureship.

The distinction between these types of recruitment difficulties is very important because many of the surveys commonly quoted in the media actually refer to the incidence of recruitment difficulties as reported by firms, but are sometimes mis-represented as referring to the incidence of skill shortages, as if recruitment difficulties and skill shortages were one and the same thing. Clearly they are not. There are several reasons other than a shortage of suitably qualified labour for why firms might experience recruitment difficulties.

TRENDS IN SKILL SHORTAGES, RECRUITMENT DIFFICULTIES, AND HARD-TO-FILL VACANCIES

There are now a number of surveys which at regular intervals report on the incidence of skill shortages, recruitment difficulties, or hard-to-fill vacancies in the British economy. Table 5.1 and Figure 5.1 report the most recent results for three of these surveys, the CBI Quarterly Industrial Trends Survey, the British Chamber of Commerce Quarterly Economic Survey, and the annual Skill Needs Survey carried out on behalf of the Department of Employment.

Each survey has its strengths and weaknesses. The Skill Needs Surveys, carried out annually since 1990, ask a structured sample of firms with over twenty-five employees whether they have currently, or have had in the past

Table 5.1 Incidence of hard-to-fill vacancies, recruitment difficulties, and skill shortages (% of all employers)

	1990	1991	1992	1993	1994
(a) EMPLOYERS WITH HARD-TO-FILL VACANCIES					
Skill Needs Surveys, spring					
All employers	22	7	5	6	11
Manufacturing employers	23	6	5	7	11
(b) MANUFACTURING EMPLOYERS REPORTING SKILL SHORTAGES					
CBI Survey, April–June	14	6	5	6	8
(c) EMPLOYERS RECRUITING REPORTING RECRUITMENT DIFFICULTIES					
BCC Survey, June					
Manufacturing	73	34	23	32	45
Services	60	29	23	28	44

Sources: 1. Skill Needs in Britain Surveys, 1990–4: 6,000 establishments in manufacturing and services surveyed (by phone); 75–77% overall response rate. *c*.1,650 manufacturing employers reached. 2. CBI Quarterly Industrial Trends Survey: 2,500 manufacturing firms surveyed (by post); 44–54% response rate. *c*.1,300 manufacturing employers reached. 3. British Chamber of Commerce Quarterly Economic Survey: 8,000 member firms in manufacturing and services surveyed (by post); 30% average response rate. *c*.1,100 manufacturing employers reached.

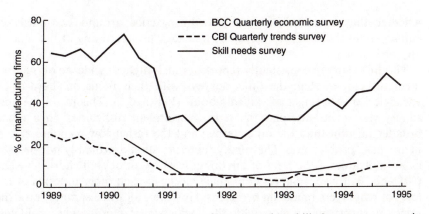

Fig. 5.1. Percentage of manufacturing firms reporting skill shortages or recruitment difficulties, 1989–1995

Sources: See Table 5.1.

twelve months, any vacancies that are proving, or have proved, hard to fill. The vacancies may be hard to fill for any of the reasons outlined above and not just because of skill shortages. The survey covers manufacturing and services and as a telephone survey has a good response rate (Table 5.1).

The CBI Quarterly Industrial Trends Survey asks a sample of manufacturing firms 'What factors are likely to limit your output over the next four months?', to which one of the seven answers can be 'a shortage of skilled labour'. The overall response rate averages around 50 per cent, but each industry and firm size receives a weighting in the results which corresponds to total manufacturing output. It is the only survey of the three which focuses specifically on shortages of skilled labour and, through the wording of the question, on the impact which those shortages may be having on firms. The survey also allows one to compare this constraint on output with the other constraints, such as a shortage of orders or sales, or of capacity. Indeed it is clear that firms themselves are comparing these constraints when responding to the question. Most critically it is the only survey which gives information over a long span of time, back in fact to 1960.

The British Chamber of Commerce (BCC) Quarterly Economic Survey covers both manufacturing and service sector firms of all sizes, but has a low—30 per cent—average response rate. It asks whether firms are experiencing 'recruitment difficulties' which can exist for any of the reasons discussed above. It does not therefore measure the incidence of skill shortages. Its achieved sample of manufacturing firms is below the numbers achieved in the CBI survey and well below the numbers achieved in the Skill Needs Surveys (Table 5.1). The reported 'headline' figure refers to the proportion of employers who are recruiting who face recruitment difficulties, whereas the denominator for the other surveys is all employers, regardless of whether they are recruiting or not. In practice around two-thirds of employers in the BCC survey report that they are recruiting at the time of any one survey.

The BCC survey consistently reports a much higher incidence of 'recruitment difficulties' than the other surveys with their focus on 'hard-to-fill vacancies' or 'shortages of skilled labour' (Figure 5.1). This raises the possibility that firms interpret the term 'recruitment difficulties' in a much broader fashion than the other terms, and the rather low response rate is in any case problematic. The survey therefore should probably not be used as an indicator of the *level* of anything, least of all of skill shortages. The CBI and Skill Needs Surveys are much closer to each other in terms of the level of employers reporting problems. However, all three surveys show the same, unsurprising, *trends*, with the incidence of recruitment problems, however defined, declining sharply in the early 1990s recession and creeping up a little between 1993 and 1994 as the economy recovered (Table 5.1 and Figure 5.1).

The Skill Needs Surveys show that the proportion of manufacturing firms reporting hard-to-fill vacancies is almost identical to the proportion of all establishments reporting hard-to-fill vacancies (Table 5.1). Similarly the differences in responses to the BCC survey from manufacturing and service sector firms is small, although manufacturing firms have registered a slightly higher incidence of recruitment difficulties in all but one of the quarterly surveys since 1989. These comments are of significance because they suggest that the incidence of problems as reported by manufacturing firms can be taken as a reasonable proxy for problems being experienced by all employers. It is of importance to show that this is true in recent data, because the only survey which goes back over a long period of time—the CBI survey—refers solely to manufacturing firms. It is being suggested here that it is not unreasonable to take the results of the CBI survey, referring to manufacturing firms, as a proxy for the trend in 'skill shortage' problems for the economy as a whole.

If this assumption is valid then Figure 5.2, showing the response to the question on factors limiting output in the CBI survey over thirty years, might have even more important implications than merely making it clear that the current incidence of reported skill shortages in manufacturing is low by historical standards. If manufacturing can proxy the whole economy, then the current incidence of skill shortages in the whole economy is low by historical standards.

In April 1995 only 11 per cent of manufacturing firms in the CBI Survey reported that a shortage of skilled labour would be likely to limit output in the coming four months. During the whole period from 1960 to 1979 an average of 24 per cent of firms reported skill shortages as a constraint, with peaks of 42 per cent in June 1966, 32 per cent in October 1969, and 51 per cent in October 1973. This last peak was the only time when skill shortages

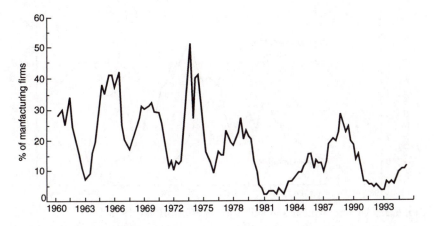

Fig. 5.2. Proportion of manufacturing firms citing shortage of skilled labour as constraint, 1960–1995

Source: CBI Quarterly Industrial Trends Survey.

were rated as a more important factor limiting output than orders or sales; otherwise this latter measure of 'deficient demand' as a constraint dominates the responses to the question, especially since the mid-1970s.

Up until 1980, firms tended to rate skill shortages as a more important constraint than shortages of physical capacity. Since 1980 capacity constraints have been reported as more important, and indeed by April 1995, while one in ten manufacturing firms were reporting skill shortages as a constraint, one in four were reporting capacity constraints.

The late 1980s peak in the proportion of firms reporting skill shortages as a constraint (28 per cent in October 1988) caused much renewed concern over the nature and consequences of possible skill deficiencies for Britain's economic performance. However, this peak was almost identical to the peak in the late 1970s (27 per cent in October 1978) and well below the peaks in the 1960s and early 1970s referred to in the last paragraph. What is striking about Figure 5.2 is how sharp the cyclical swings can be.

The pattern in the reported incidence of skill shortages in the early to mid-1990s looks remarkably similar to the pattern of the early to mid-1980s. In itself this is significant. As Figure 5.3 shows, in early 1995 unemployment in Britain stood at around 8.5 per cent of the work-force, having fallen gradually for two years. The last time unemployment had declined to this level was at the start of 1988, at which point 20 per cent of manufacturing firms were reporting skill shortages as a constraint. So the reported incidence of skill shortages in the mid-1990s was running at only half the level reported in the late 1980s when unemployment had last declined to around 8.5 per cent of the work-force.

However, one critical feature of Figure 5.3 is that it illustrates that the

Fig. 5.3. Unemployment and skill shortages in Britain, 1981–1995

Sources: Employment Department (claimant count) and CBI Quarterly Industrial Trends Survey.

fall in unemployment in the period 1993–4 was at a more steady pace than in 1987–8. During the Lawson boom the unemployment rate was falling at an annual rate of around 2 percentage points a year. Between 1993 and 1994 unemployment in Britain was falling at an annual rate of only 1 percentage point a year.

Figure 5.4 shows the relationship between output growth and skill shortages in Britain since the late 1970s. In the late 1980s the peak in reported skill shortages only occurred after annual rates of output growth of over 4 per cent were sustained over several quarters.

When considered alongside the picture in Figure 5.3 showing the pace of

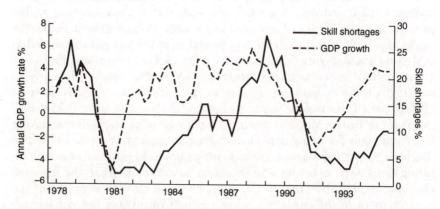

Fig. 5.4. Growth in output and skill shortages in Britain, 1978–1995

Sources: Economic Trends and CBI Quarterly Industrial Trends Survey.

change in unemployment, this suggests strongly that reported skill shortages only increased sharply in the late 1980s when the economy was going through a period of very rapid output growth and sharply falling unemployment. But this leaves open the possibility that a more sedate pace of output growth and a more gradual reduction in unemployment might not have caused serious skill shortage problems.

Another feature of the Lawson boom is that in 1987–8 the pace of the expansion was such that manufacturing employment was actually increasing, in contrast to the quite rapid fall in manufacturing employment over the rest of the period since 1979. So only when manufacturing output was rising so rapidly that manufacturing employment was also rising did skill shortages in manufacturing increase sharply. This again points to the pace of expansion as being a critical variable in determining whether or not skill shortages become a significant problem.

SKILL SHORTAGES, WAGE INFLATION, AND UNEMPLOYMENT

To what extent is a higher reported incidence of skill shortages associated with an increase in the underlying rate of growth of average earnings? As noted earlier this must be the main transmission mechanism by which skill shortages and unemployment are linked. If skill shortages generate wage inflation, the monetary authorities will respond by raising interest rates and unemployment will be higher than would otherwise be the case.

This section tries to explore the evidence for a link between skill shortages and wage inflation by looking at the experience of the 1980s. It does so in two ways, by describing in simple terms the trends in the data, and by referring to two econometric studies which tried to assess the impact which skill shortages could have had on wage inflation. These studies, which exploit the CBI data, refer to the impact of skill shortages in manufacturing firms on manufacturing wage inflation. In the discussion which follows the trend in skill shortages in manufacturing is taken as a proxy for the trend in the whole economy. The trends in wage inflation in manufacturing in the 1980s quite closely matched the trends in the whole economy, so that it does not seem unreasonable to generalize from the experience of manufacturing to the economy as a whole.

Following the onset of the early 1980s recession the reported incidence of skill shortages in manufacturing fell rapidly in the British economy. The underlying rate of average earnings growth also fell rapidly (Figure 5.5), as did wage inflation in manufacturing. Between 1983 and 1987 the underlying rate of average earnings growth in the whole economy remained remarkably stable at 7.5 per cent a year, despite the upward creep in reported skill shortages from a low of 2 per cent of manufacturing firms reporting skill shortages as a limit on output in January 1983, to 15 per cent

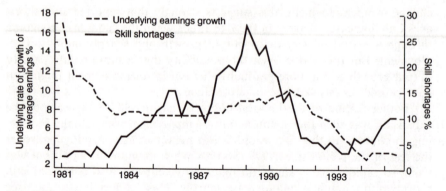

Fig. 5.5. Average earnings growth and skill shortages in Britain, 1981–1995

Sources: Department of Employment average earnings series and CBI Quarterly Industrial Trends Survey.

of firms in July–October 1985, with skill shortages easing again in 1986. So a steady increase in the reported incidence of skill shortages in the mid-1980s had no apparent impact on wage inflation.

The underlying rate of growth in average earnings began to increase modestly in 1987, rising from an annual rate of 7.5 per cent to 9 per cent over the eighteen-month period from early 1987 to late 1988. Reported skill shortages also rose quickly from 12 per cent of manufacturing firms in April 1987 to 28 per cent in October 1988. This was the period of rapid expansion of output and employment across the whole economy and of growth in employment, even in the manufacturing sector. The critical value as far as skill shortages are concerned seemed to lie in the range of about 15–20 per cent; that is, only when the reported incidence of skill shortages in manufacturing rose well above 15–20 per cent for a period of time was this associated with an increase in the underlying rate of growth of average earnings.

In 1989 the growth in average earnings plateaued out again at around 9 per cent. Meanwhile the rate of growth in the economy was falling (Figure 5.4) and, after a lag, the reported incidence of skill shortages also began to fall, and by October 1989 was back down to 19 per cent. In the first half of 1990 the underlying rate of growth of average earnings increased again from around 9 per cent to peak at around 10 per cent in July, despite a continued drop in the reported incidence of skill shortages.

It might be noted that the above description of the trends consciously avoided using the term 'acceleration' of average earnings growth, for the 'upward creep' in the underlying rate of growth in average earnings from 7.5 per cent to 10 per cent seems a more appropriate use of language. However, this simple description does give us some idea of what contribution skill shortages might have made to this 'upward creep'. Clearly a part of the increase in average earnings growth between 1987 and 1989 might be attributable to the increased incidence of reported skill shortages, but then only 1.5 percentage points were added to the underlying rate of growth of average earnings over this period. Skill shortages might have been responsible for some fraction of this. The further increase in average earnings in 1990 took place some fifteen months after the peak in skill shortages, which, even assuming some lag in the effect of skill shortages on wage inflation, suggests that this increase was associated more with the rise in headline price inflation brought about by an increase in mortgage rates and the poll tax, rather than it being anything much to do with skill shortages.

In 1989 the CBI published a paper by two of its economists from which the quotation at the beginning of this chapter is taken (Sentance and Williams 1989). They estimated a very simple model to see what influence skill shortages might have had on wage inflation in the 1980s using information from the Quarterly Industrial Trends Survey and the CBI's Pay Databank. They concluded that the rise in reported skill shortages after 1983 might have increased the rate of manufacturing wage inflation by around 2 per cent per annum over the period 1983–9.

However, their model would have predicted a fall in wage inflation in 1990 as the reported incidence of skill shortages fell back. The fact that this did not happen suggests that their 2 per cent figure was itself an overestimate of the impact of skill shortages on wage inflation in the 1980s. Moreover, their skill shortages variable was acting as a proxy for all the demand-led variables, and especially growing profit levels, which would have been pushing up wage inflation. Yet Sentance and Williams were still able to conclude in 1989 that skill shortages and other demand-led variables had not been the major cause of manufacturing wage inflation, which had after all averaged 8 per cent over the period 1983–9. This conclusion proved embarrassing to the CBI, which had been making a great deal of fuss about skill shortages at the time.

Sentance and Williams also pointed out there was only a very weak relationship at an industry level between output and employment growth on the one hand, and skill shortages on the other. In other words those industries which were growing rapidly did not tend to experience above average increases in reported skill shortages. It was only when the manufacturing sector (and the economy) as a whole was growing strongly that skill shortages began to emerge. This fits well with earlier observations about the relationship between output growth and skill shortages. Sentance and Williams also noted that this suggested that the skills which were in high demand must be quite mobile across industries.

These observations are backed up by the results of the other econometric work in this field by Haskel and Martin (1993). They also used the CBI data on skill shortages along with matched Census of Production data for

81 industries for the period 1980–89. They found that variations in skill shortages across industries had little effect on wages across industries, but that aggregate skill shortages across the whole economy had an effect on aggregate wage inflation. So just as the Sentance and Williams paper had found no link between output and employment growth in particular industries and skill shortages in those industries, so Haskel and Martins found no link between skill shortages in particular industries and wages in those industries.

Skill shortages only began to emerge and only affected wages if the manufacturing sector as a whole was growing strongly.

Haskel and Martins noted that firms had good reason not to adjust wages to firm-specific skill shortages as reversing any wage rise might prove very difficult when skill shortage problems abated again, and they emphasized that skill shortages were highly cyclical. Moreover, as Sentance and Williams had inferred, the skills in short supply did seem to be highly mobile across industries, so that the possible emergence of skill shortages in any one sector was not going to cause problems.

Haskel and Martins estimated that skill shortages raised the rate of growth in manufacturing earnings over the period 1980–9 by about 1 percentage point per annum, as against average earnings growth of 7 per cent over this period.

The results of these two econometric investigations are consistent with each other and with a straightforward look at the data in Figure 5.5. Skill shortages made only a marginal contribution to the upward creep in wage inflation in the late 1980s. At most, perhaps 1 percentage point of the modest increase in the underlying rate of growth in average earnings in the late 1980s can be attributed to the increase in the reported incidence of skill shortages from an average of around 9 per cent of manufacturing firms in 1983–6 to an average of around 20 per cent between 1987 and 1989. Moreover, this average of around 20 per cent for the late 1980s should be contrasted with an average level of response of over 25 per cent through the 1960s, which was not a decade which witnessed continuously accelerating wage and price inflation.

WHAT CAN AND SHOULD BE DONE ABOUT SKILL SHORTAGES?

In order to establish the appropriate policy response to the existence of skill shortages it is first necessary to establish where these shortages exist. What type of labour might be in short supply? To answer this question the CBI Quarterly Industrial Trends Survey is of less use. Although it might usefully proxy the *trend* in skill shortages across the economy, as its sample is restricted to manufacturing which covers less than 20 per cent of the workforce, it cannot give us a well-rounded picture of where the recruitment difficulties and/or skill shortages actually are across the whole economy.

For this picture we can turn back to the Skill Needs in Britain Surveys. These surveys ask employers about their 'hard-to-fill vacancies', a measure of recruitment difficulties which will include skill shortages, but which will also cover the other reasons—lack of experience amongst applicants, poor working conditions and so on—which might make recruitment problematic.

If recruitment difficulties were primarily due to skill shortages, we might expect to see a heavy preponderance of hard-to-fill vacancies in the high skill occupations which often demand higher or intermediate qualifications. If, however, recruitment difficulties appear in the lower occupations, it seems likely that they may be more a consequence of those other factors which can make recruitment problematic. Also one would expect to find recruitment difficulties to be most acute in those occupations with lower unemployment rates. It might seem strange to find a heavy incidence of recruitment difficulties in occupations with high levels of unemployment.

Table 5.2 reports the results from the 1992 and 1994 Skill Needs Surveys. It shows the proportion of employers employing each occupational group

Table 5.2 Unemployment rates by previous occupation and employers reporting hard-to-fill vacancies by occupation, 1993–1994 (%)

Occupation	Unemployment rate[a]		Employers with hard-to-fill vacancies over previous 12 months[b]	
	1991–92	1993–94	1992	1994
Managers and administrators	3.9	4.9	2	2
Professional	2.4	3.2	5	6
Associate professional and technical	4.4	5.0	6	7
Clerical and secretarial	5.8	6.7	2	3
Personal and protective services	6.9	8.0	9	11
Sales	7.3	8.6	3	5
Craft and related	10.8	13.1	6	8
Plant and machine operatives	11.5	12.9	4	7
Other occupations	11.9	13.4	–	–
ALL OCCUPATIONS	9.0	10.0	16	21

Sources: a. Labour Force Survey, average spring 1991 and spring 1992; and summer 1993—spring 1994.
b. Skill Needs in Britain Surveys, 1992 and 1994—all employers employing each occupational group.

Table 5.3. Relative importance of qualifications and experience in recruitment

	Manag. & admin.	Prof.	Ass. Prof. & tech.	Clerical & sec.	Personal services	Sales	Craft	Operatives	Other
Experience sought	89	90	86	73	65	68	91	66	48
Qualifications sought	73	98	94	79	31	46	74	25	5
If qualifications sought:									
other qualities more important	27	22	19	36	20	31	24	14	3
qualifications more important	3	20	16	4	0	1	8	4	0

Note: Other qualities looked for included, for all occupational groups, personal transferable skills such as honesty, motivation, and interpersonal skills; for clerical, sales, and operatives jobs literacy and numeracy skills; and for managers business awareness.

Source: Employers' Manpower and Skills Practices Survey; Dench 1993.

reporting that they had experienced hard-to-fill vacancies over the previous twelve months. Alongside this the table presents data on unemployment rates by previous occupation derived from the Labour Force Survey (LFS), with the LFS data matched to the time periods which the Skill Needs Surveys cover. Contrary to what one might expect to find, the proportion of employers having difficulties recruiting to the top professional and associate professional and technical occupations is similar to the proportion of employers having difficulty recruiting to the manual occupations. This is in spite of the fact that unemployment rates for the manual occupations are three to four times as high as for the professional and technical occupations. Recruitment difficulties are least prevalent for managers and administrators, and for clerical and secretarial staff. In both 1992 and 1994 the heaviest incidence of recruitment difficulties occurred in the personal and protective services occupations. In other words it is *not* true that recruitment difficulties were disproportionately concentrated in the higher occupations and in those occupations where unemployment rates were the lowest.

If the analysis focuses on more closely defined occupational groups, then consistently the same groups emerge year after year in response to the question on hard-to-fill vacancies in the Skill Needs Surveys. They include some high-skill groups—health associate professionals (mainly nurses), engineers and technologists, teaching professionals; some 'intermediate' skill groups—textile and garments and related trades, sales representatives; and some relatively low-skill groups—sales assistants, catering occupations. It is this last occupational group which consistently comes at or near the top of the list of occupations where recruitment difficulties are located. Apparently some employers face consistent problems in recruiting people to fill posts as chefs, waiters, and waitresses.

To what extent are these recruitment difficulties to be equated with skill shortages as opposed to the other factors which can lead to difficulties in recruitment?

Table 5.3 offers some further clues. It reports results from the Employers' Manpower and Skill Practices Survey, carried out for the Department of Employment, involving interviews conducted between 1991 and 1992 in 1,693 workplaces with twenty-five or more employees (Dench 1993). It looked at the kind of qualities employers were looking for when recruiting for jobs in different occupations. In common with the Skill Needs Surveys it shows the greater weight given to experience rather than qualifications in recruitment to the lower occupations. Unsurprisingly it is only in the professional and associate professional and technical occupations that qualifications are seen as being of critical importance, though even here experience and so-called 'personal transferable skills', such as motivation and the ability to communicate, are also seen as relevant. Qualifications are sought after in three-quarters of craft-level jobs, but experience was sought in over nine out of ten of these jobs and again such qualities as motivation were rated highly. In the personal service occupations—which includes catering—qualifications were sought for only one in three jobs, but experience was sought for in two-thirds of jobs, and for no jobs were qualifications thought to be more important than the employer's judgement about individuals' personal qualities such as their motivation, honesty, and ability to get along with others.

If Table 5.3 is considered alongside Table 5.2, it is possible to begin making some sense of the 'recruitment difficulties' reported by British employers.

1. Firms or organizations which have difficulties recruiting health associate professionals, teachers, or engineers and technologists are looking for individuals who must possess the requisite qualifications, but who should also ideally have relevant experience. Individuals' 'personal transferable skills' are also of importance. These recruitment difficulties can be interpreted as 'true' skill shortages, that is, firms and organizations face a genuine shortage of suitable qualified labour.

2. Firms which have difficulties recruiting craft workers in occupational areas such as the textile and garments trades may be having problems recruiting labour with the right qualifications, but in the light of the high level of unemployment in the craft occupations reported in Table 5.2 (and especially high unemployment in the textile occupations) it seems likely that these difficulties are more to do with finding people with relevant and very specific experience of working in particular kinds of enterprises.

3. For such relatively low-skill jobs as in the catering occupations it is hard to believe that what these surveys of employers are registering is a skills shortage with the implication that FE colleges should be greatly expanding courses to train cooks, waiters, and waitresses. Rather the recruitment difficulties in these high-turnover occupations are more likely to be a function of relatively poorer working conditions, and the desire of employers to recruit staff with specific recent relevant experience and/or staff with high levels of motivation, honesty, and other personal qualities.

Once it has proved possible to sketch in this way the nature of the recruitment difficulties faced by firms, it becomes feasible to think about the appropriate response in terms of public policy. The 'real' skill shortages seem to lie primarily in the professional and technical occupations—shortages of certain kinds of teachers, nurses, engineers, and technicians, for example. This type of labour can only be supplied, of course, through the higher education system. The significant increase in higher education enrolment in Britain since 1988 augers well for the general supply of highly qualified labour in Britain in the 1990s, but the pay and status of some professions is such that it would not be surprising to find shortages re-emerging with much fanfare in certain parts of the public and private sectors. Nevertheless, the unprecedented increase in the rate of staying on in full-time further and higher education since 1988 ought to inform any debate about the nature of Britain's 'skills problem'.

There are also probably some genuine skill shortage problems in certain craft and other intermediate-skill occupations, although how many of the recruitment problems faced by employers are to do with individuals lacking appropriate qualifications, as opposed to appropriate experience or personal skills, remains unclear.

To the extent that the problem does lie with a lack of vocational qualifications, then this is the area where the conventional training programmes aimed at the unemployed—such as Training for Work—might be expected to make a contribution. But in 1992–3 only 13 per cent of participants on Employment Training—the precursor to Training for Work—gained a full qualification at NVQ level 2 or above, approaching craft status.

Clearly there is a well-recognized problem with regard to the *quality* of state training schemes in Britain, and it is a problem which extends across the OECD. However, there is no obvious problem with the *quantity* of provision. It is hard to conclude from the evidence that British employers are reporting that they face shortages of many tens of thousands of craft workers, so that it is not clear that the authorities need to sponsor vast training schemes. This in itself would be a useful conclusion to reach, as the overwhelming evidence from around the OECD is that large-scale training programmes aimed at the unemployed cannot be shown to boost the employment and earnings prospects of participants significantly (OECD 1993; Robinson 1995a). Small-scale, well-targeted, high-quality programmes might have modest significantly positive effects, and the scale of the problem in Britain might argue for just such a small high-quality scheme. This would look much like the old Training Opportunities Programme (TOPs), which at its peak in the mid-1980s provided some 80,000 places a year. This is only one-third of the size of the Training for Work programme as it was running in 1995. Such a reasonably high quality but small training programme needs to be clearly distinguished from work-based schemes whose aims are primarily social in nature.

Finally there are the recruitment difficulties faced by firms employing people in the lower occupations. It seems unlikely that the recruitment difficulties which occur in areas such as the catering occupations are much to do with a lack of formally certified skills in the work-force. These recruitment difficulties are probably to do with a lack of relevant experience amongst job-seekers, employers' perceptions of applicants' poor motivation or other deficiencies in their personal transferable skills, and the relatively poorer working conditions prevalent in such sectors of the labour market. They are not 'skill shortages'.

The same research from across the OECD which casts doubt on the efficacy of large-scale training programmes does, however, suggest that simple programmes run by the Employment Service, designed to enhance the effectiveness of job search or to improve job placement or matching services, can have modestly significant positive effects on participants' job and earnings prospects (OECD 1993; Robinson, 1995*a*). These programmes, such as Restart in the UK, are best described as cheap but surprisingly effective. It is worth pondering why.

Surveys of employers constantly pick up concerns about the 'personal transferable skills' of job applicants, that is, their motivation, ability to communicate, and so on. Generally the existence or not of those skills is a more important factor than possession of formal qualifications in determining recruitment, especially for the lower-skill occupations (see Table 5.3). Apparently simple interventions which have the effect of raising individuals' outward signs of motivation, or helping them to improve the way they compile a CV or handle an interview, which are the means by which an individual can best signal their possession of some of the 'personal transferable skills', might thus have a more significant effect on participants' job prospects than 'training' programmes.

In recent years the British Government has been moving resources into Employment Service programmes and away from training programmes (Robinson 1995*b*). It needs to be stressed that research from across the OECD points precisely in this direction and suggests that the Government's re-ordering of priorities has been exactly right.

CONCLUSIONS: ARE SKILL SHORTAGES A SERIOUS CONSTRAINT ON FULL EMPLOYMENT?

In April 1995 only 11 per cent of manufacturing firms in Britain said that shortages of skilled labour were likely to limit output over the coming four months. The unemployment rate in that month stood at around 8.5 per cent of the work-force and the last time unemployment had declined to such a level, early in 1988, 20 per cent of manufacturing firms were reporting skill shortages. The late 1980s peak in reported skill shortages was similar to the late 1970s peak but well below the peaks reached in the early 1970s and 1960s. The current incidence of reported skill shortages in the British economy is low by historical standards.

At most the increase in reported skill shortages in the late 1980s in Britain probably added no more than about 1 percentage point to the underlying rate of growth of average earnings. This was in the context of several quarters of output growth at well above 4 per cent on an annual basis, with unemployment falling at the rate of 2 percentage points on an annual basis, with manufacturing employment actually rising, and with the whole process being driven by a credit-financed consumer boom.

The critical question to ask is whether a more gradual and sustained recovery in output with annual growth rates of 3–4 per cent, sufficient to allow unemployment to fall by 1 percentage point a year, with net exports and investment driving the process, would lead to skill shortages of a magnitude which might generate significant additional wage inflation. There is good reason to believe that the answer is no. If the circumstances which produced the skill shortages of the late 1980s generated only a 1 percentage point increase in the underlying rate of growth of average earnings, then a modest but sustained recovery in the mid-1990s will generate only a fraction of this small number. On the basis of 1980s experience, only if the incidence of reported skill shortages rose above 15–20 per cent for a period of time could it be expected that average earnings growth might creep upwards under the impact of economy-wide skill shortages. Specific sectors may suffer more acute shortages but the evidence is strong that such sector-specific shortages do not put significant upward pressure on pay, in part because the skills in demand do seem quite highly mobile across sectors.

The debate over skill shortages is in many ways a microcosm of the whole debate over unemployment in the 1990s, and the lessons to be learned from the late 1980s. Did the Lawson boom come unstuck because there exists some 'natural' rate of unemployment such that any attempt to go below that level would inevitably generate accelerating wage and price inflation, which would have to be brought to a halt by a tightening of monetary policy? Or did it become unstuck because the nature and above all the *pace* of that boom, with output growing too quickly and unemployment coming down too rapidly, was faster than the economy could sustain without inevitable problems leading to some upward pressure on wage and price inflation?

Even the wage and price inflation of the Lawson boom looks more like an 'upward creep' than an acceleration, and the distinction is more than a matter of semantics. A gradual but sustained increase in output and reduction in unemployment in Britain in the mid-1990s may well lead to some modest 'upward creep' in wage and price inflation. Perhaps the underlying rate of growth in average earnings would creep up from 3.5 to 4.5 per cent and underlying price inflation from 2.5 to 3.5 per cent. But this does not look like 'acceleration', but rather a modest movement north-west up a short-run Phillips Curve with a very shallow slope. Renewed wage and price inflation may well threaten in the event of another external shock to the economy, but skill shortages in the 1990s do not pose a major threat to a sustained gradual economic recovery.

REFERENCES

Dench, S. (1993), 'What Types of People are Employers Seeking to Employ? Some Evidence from the Employers' Manpower and Skills Practices Survey', mimeo (London: Department of Employment).

Haskel, J., and Martin, C. (1993), 'Skill Shortages, Productivity Growth and Wage Inflation in UK Manufacturing', Discussion Paper 859, Centre for Economic Policy Research.

Mason, G., and Wagner, K. (1994), 'Innovation and the Skill Mix: Chemicals and Engineering in Britain and Germany', *National Institute Economic Review*, 148 (May): 61–72.

OECD (1993), 'Active Labour Market Policies: Assessing Macroeconomic and Microeconomic Effects', in *Employment Outlook*, ch. 2.

Prais, S., (1990) (ed.), 'Productivity, Education and Training: Britain and Other Countries Compared', National Institute of Economic and Social Research, London.

Robinson, P. (1995a), 'The Decline of the Swedish Model and the Limits to Active Labour Market Policy', Working Paper 667, Centre for Economic Performance, London School of Economics.

—— (1995b), 'Jobs and Skills: The Programmes of the Employment Department', in A. Gillie, (ed.), *The Big Spenders, 1995–96* (London: Public Finance Foundation).

Sentance, A., and Williams, N. (1989), 'Skill Shortages and the CBI Industrial Trends Survey', mimeo, Confederation of British Industry.

6 Finance for Industry

Simon Lee

INTRODUCTION

The role of the financial system in any national economy is to 'transform savings into investment and to allocate those funds among competing users' (Zysman 1983: 57). The relationship between finance and industry is as a consequence of central importance to the prospects for rebuilding industrial capacity and creating full employment in the UK. Capacity cannot expand nor output increase unless the financial system generates savings and allocates a sufficient proportion of them on favourable terms to companies to enable them to invest. The central problem identified in this chapter is the fact that UK industrial companies have not invested sufficiently either to expand capacity or to maintain even a semblance of full employment since 1980. UK financial institutions have made capital available to industry only at such a prohibitively high cost and for repayment over such a punitively short period of time that industrial companies have been confronted with one of the highest costs of capital in the world. This is directly attributable to the domination of the UK's financial system by the interests of the City of London which allocate finance on the basis of prices established in competitive capital markets, dominated by the desire for liquidity, that is, 'the ability to be able to reverse a lending or investment decision and return to the status quo ante of holding cash' (Hutton 1995: 132). This desire for liquidity has therefore given the UK's financial system an essentially short-term orientation characterized by a preoccupation with immediate profitability, an aversion to risk-taking, and a lack of interest in—and financial commitment to—longer-term domestic industrial investment.

To examine the degree to which the UK's industrial development has been constrained by the operation of its financial system, a number of key themes are introduced and explored in this chapter. First, the importance of a central distinction that has been drawn in the political economy of finance–industry relations between national economies, most notably those of Germany and Japan, whose industrial development has been financed primarily by loans from banks, and national economies, most notably those of the UK and the USA, whose development has been more reliant on finance raised from equity markets. Secondly, the fact that bank-financed industrial development is generally recognized to have been more success-ful is illustrated by reference to the manner in which the UK's recent industrial investment and output performance has been damaged by the absence of supportive banking and other financial structures. Thirdly, in order to demonstrate that both the historical and modern debates about finance and industry in the UK remain unresolved, contending explanations for the causes of the ineffective relationship between finance and industry in the UK are documented. The manner in which a succession of inquiries by committees sponsored by Parliament, and representatives of both industry and finance, have failed to agree on and deliver either the nature or the necessity of introducing policies to remedy the deficiencies in the relationship between finance and industry in the UK is then set out. Fourthly, a brief analysis of the contemporary debate concerning finance–industry relations in the UK is provided in order to demonstrate the variety of limited initiatives being undertaken by the Treasury, the Bank of England, and the City of London to improve finance–industry relations, and the fact that the Major Government's policies have reflected a reluctance to contemplate even the idea of a state-funded development bank. Fifthly, the chapter concludes with an analysis of the prospects for reform of the relationship between finance and industry. Attention is drawn to the conservatism of the Labour Party's policies for finance and industry. The chapter concludes that in the absence of constitutional reform to replace the overly centralized political and financial structures of the unitary state in the UK, the prospects for rebuilding industrial capacity and moving towards full employment remain remote.

THE TRIUMPH OF THE RHINE

Although there is by no means unanimity about the appropriate roles for the state and the market in the political economy of finance–industry relations, there is a consensus that the UK has failed to develop a relationship between finance and industry conducive to successful long-term industrial development. The central argument of Zysman's analysis of finance–industry relations in leading industrial economies is that 'discretion in the provision of industrial finance—in the selective allocation of credit—is necessary for the state to enter continuously into the industrial life of private companies and to influence their strategies in the way that a rival or partner would' (Zysman 1983: 76). In the specific case of the UK, Zysman asserts that although the state has been forced to play a more proactive role in promoting economic growth because of the onset of relative economic decline, its attempts to develop an effective industrial policy have been undermined by the fact that the state 'has never controlled the channels of borrowing and lending that would facilitate the selective manipulation of credit allocation by the state' (1983: 197).

Zysman's analysis is founded upon the identification of three distinct types of financial systems, namely a system based on capital markets with resources allocated by prices established in competitive markets, a credit-based system with prices administered by government, and a credit-based system dominated by financial institutions (1983: 55). More recently, Albert has argued that, following the collapse of communism, the principal global rivalry is now between two forms of capitalism. On the one hand is the 'neo-American model' of capitalism, characteristic of the US and the UK, where the emphasis is on short-term profit, the speculator enjoys primacy over the entrepreneur, and the operating principle is 'the profitable management, through speculation, of individual risk' (Albert 1993: 65). On the other hand is the 'Rhine model' of capitalism, practised in Germany but also partly in Japan, where the emphasis is on the long term, primacy is accorded to the company as 'an expression of the partnership of capital and labour', and the operating principle is 'the community of interests, both within the company as well as between company and consumer' (Albert 1993: 86–8). Both models are indisputably capitalist in that they are based on the principles of the market economy, private property, and free enterprise, but Albert asserts that the Rhine model is economically and socially superior not least because it incorporates an interpenetration rather than a separation of finance and industry that increases the supply of long-term investment capital.

The community of interests in Rhine capitalism extends to the provision of finance to industry where banks and not stock markets 'are the principal guardians of the capitalist flame'. In the case of German banks, for example, they have been able to develop as 'universal' institutions because regulations do not exist to restrict their role to a single activity or sector. They do deal in stocks and bonds but, unlike their American and British competitors, neither primarily nor exclusively. They also play a variety of roles as commercial and industrial banks, which means that a special relationship has developed between bankers and customers 'in which mutual cooperation is constantly reinforced' (Albert 1993: 106–7). Albert contends that this symbiosis of banking and industry is even more pronounced in Japan, where the relationship is so intertwined that it is not entirely clear whether it is the industrial groups that own the banks or vice versa. Above all, the interpenetration of finance and industry in Germany and Japan has provided at least three benefits for long-term industrial development. First, unlike their American or British rivals, for whom short-term profits are the sole criterion of operation, German banks 'tend to have the long-term interests of business at heart', 'see their stake in a company as an enduring commitment', and 'accept that risks must be taken, involving large sums over long periods of time, as the price for backing a difficult but potentially rewarding venture'. Secondly, banks operating within Rhine capitalism 'make for stable shareholders' whose basic loyalty gives management the freedom to develop the business rather than be preoccupied in the unproductive anti-takeover strategies characteristic of Anglo-American capitalism. Thirdly, 'the sheer density of the web of mutual interests' between finance and industry' means that they 'cannot be easily penetrated by outside forces'. Not only does this reduce the opportunities for destabilizing take-over activity but it also means that the industrial development of Rhine capitalism companies is driven by consensus 'involving a relatively small group of people, who all know one another well and travel in the same social circles' (Albert 1993: 108–9).

When to this interpenetration of finance and industry is added the German co-responsibility system of industrial democracy or the Japanese large-company practices of lifetime employment, seniority-based pay, and in-house, enterprise-based trade unionism, it is evident that German and Japanese companies possess an institutional structure that facilitates the engendering of a collective sense of belonging. Unlike the neo-American 'stockholder' model of corporate organization, where only those who own shares (stock) enjoy the possibility of consultation, Rhine capitalism's 'stakeholder' model of organization 'treats everyone as a partner with a personal interest (stake) in the company's fortune'. Albert suggests that 'Stability at home is all the more valuable when uncertainty and instability are abroad; far from stifling change and adaptability, domestic harmony can be turned to competitive advantage' (Albert 1993: 112–13). Whether measured in terms of market share, or investment in R&D, work-force skills or any other measure of competitiveness, Albert concludes that Rhine capitalism provides a more economically effective and socially stable framework of institutions for industrial development than does the neo-American model. The lesson that he draws from Reaganomics in the US and Thatcherism in the UK is that the pursuit of profit can weaken free enterprise, be damaging to the economy and hinder industrial development when 'the tyranny of finance' threatens the spirit of free enterprise (1993: 76, 79).

THE TYRANNY OF FINANCE

Albert's assertion of the superiority of Rhine capitalism for building industrial capacity, and the threat posed to industrial development in the UK by 'the tyranny of finance' has been given vigorous support in Hutton's *The State We're In* (1995). Hutton's analysis is particularly important for the question of building capacity and creating full employment for two reasons. First, it recognizes that questions of economics and economic performance cannot be divorced from the wider operation of British society and its political system. Secondly, it provides an important critique of some of the tenets of New Right thinking that have dominated the political economy of the UK since the late 1970s. Hutton (1995: 285) asserts that 'the market economy is not an act of nature. It is socially produced and politically governed. Free markets do not of themselves produce the "best" institutions and outcomes; they must be carefully sustained by social and public action.' Hutton thereby demonstrates the viability of the project of rebuilding capacity and creating full employment provided that any action to transform the relationship between finance and industry is not detached from a broader agenda of political and social change.

Hutton's central economic argument is that the weakness of the British economy originates in the financial system, with targets for profit too high and time horizons too short: 'The story of British capitalism is at heart the peculiar history of the destructive relationship between British finance and industry' (1995: 112). Hutton contends that the private sector in the UK has always demanded too high a return on its investment, not least because finance for industry has been supplied by a stock market-based financial system and clearing banks characterized by an aversion to risk, and disengagement from and lack of commitment to industrial investment and innovation. At the same time, the UK's system of corporate governance has been organized so as to emphasize the pursuit of short-term profit as companies' sole operational goal. The stock market's desire for liquidity and instant gratification has generated a permanent bias in the British system; the stock market and clearing bank system has provided the UK's capital markets with a culture that delivers innovative financial instruments and a willingness to trade in them but simultaneously fails the corporate sector, affecting companies negatively at all stages of their life cycle.

Because British finance has not grown up in a vacuum but has instead been supported and sustained by a history, a class, a set of values, and a political system which has placed the City of London, Westminster, and Whitehall in a symbiotic relationship, Hutton's central economic argument is joined to a political argument, namely that 'the semi-modern nature of the British state is a fundamental cause of Britain's economic and social problems' (pp. xi–xii). The failure of the UK financial system to deliver effective long-term support to industry is traced by Hutton to a unique structure of values and institutions. In terms of the financial system's values, Hutton draws upon Cain and Hopkins' thesis of 'gentlemanly capitalism' to argue that the state has developed a *rentier* culture that complements 'gentlemanly capitalism', in which the state stresses the financial virtues of balanced budgets and financial targets over investment and production. In terms of the financial system's institutional structure, Hutton focuses upon the role played by the Bank of England in asserting that liquidity in the UK is provided by an unspoken but explicit deal between the Bank and the financial markets, which is the first of many impulses driving the system's short-termism; this particular bargain is unique to the UK because the central bank has chosen to execute the bargain through a system of markets (Hutton 1995: 146). Unlike the rest of the world, where every other central bank requires its financial system to lodge a certain amount of cash with it, in Britain such minimum reserve requirements were abolished in 1980 with the consequence that the Bank of England has been reduced to manipulating the financial system wholly through shifts in interest rates, possessing neither direct leverage over the banks' balance sheets nor the right to use changes in reserve requirements to supplement interest-rate movements in altering the banks' ability to lend. The UK's financial system has become a free for all in which the only constraint is the price of money (1995: 148–9).

Hutton claims that this institutional structure has had far-reaching implications for industrial development in the UK because when banks themselves have to borrow large amounts of cash in the short-term money markets, it is not very attractive for them to lend long-term to industry at fixed rates of interest. Other countries possess long-term development banks: for example, Japan has its Industrial Bank of Japan; Germany its Kreditanstalt für Wiederaufbau (K.f.W.) or reconstruction bank; Korea a state development bank; France the Credit National and various *credit mobiliers* and so on. British companies have no long-term development bank; nor is there a private industrial banking system, as in Europe and Japan, ready to provide longer-term loans. Whilst banks have not made investment capital available at affordable rates, not least because of the need to satisfy their own investors' desire for high returns, another key constraint on industrial development in the UK has been the London stock market's absence of commitment to manufacturing. Hutton contends that the 'fundamental weakness of the British system' is the fact that the high cost of capital and fears of an inadequate return in the UK have acted as the most effective deterrent to long-term industrial investment. Companies in the UK therefore 'not only suffer one of the highest costs of capital in the world, but the febrile stock market compels them to earn a very big mark-up over even that cost of capital to fend off the threat of takeover and keep their shareholder base stable' (1995: 157).

The particular effectiveness of and importance for long-term industrial development of the German system for supplying finance to industry has been also been emphasized in an Anglo-German Foundation study. Mullineux (1994: 7) notes how government support for Germany's vigorous structure of SMEs (known as the *Mittelstand*) has been primarily channelled through 'the funding of loan guarantees and the provision of implicitly subsidised medium- to long-term bank loans'. This task has been undertaken by a network of specialized loan-guarantee banks (*Burgschafts-banken*) and development banks, principally the K.f.W. and Deutsche Ausgleichsbank. The *Burgschaftsbanken* provide a network of twenty-five regionally oriented loan-guarantee associations, five of which have been created in the new *Länder* of the former German Democratic Republic. These non-profit-making banks, which are owned by local commercial, trading, and financial institutions, provide 'guarantees of 80 per cent of the

credit risk which banks and savings bear on loans to Mittelstand companies and self-employed professional people' (Mullineux 1994: 7). Because
82.5 per cent of the loan guarantee is counter-guaranteed by *Länder* governments, the federal *Länder* and the Economic Recovery Programme fund
managed by the K.f.W., the burden of risk borne by the *Burgschaftsbanken*
is effectively reduced to only 17.5 per cent of the loan.

For its part, the K.f.W. is the largest of the German development banks.
When a borrower is referred to the K.f.W. by a bank, that bank is expected
to bear all the risk of the loan concerned, with the K.f.W. serving to
refinance the bank partly. Moreover, because the finance provided by the
K.f.W. is cheaper than bank finance, the *Mittelstand* actively seek funding
from the K.f.W. The largest single conduit for K.f.W. lending is provided
by the Deutsche .Industriekreditbank (I.k.B.), a private sector
industrial/merchant bank, which focuses primarily on loans to medium-
sized companies turning over more than DM20 million. Mullineux also
notes that the subsidized lending at the fixed (up to 1 per cent) margins and
the loan guarantees are often mutually reinforcing, since the guarantees are
often essential to induce the banks to participate in co-financing with the
K.f.W. Furthermore, because the K.f.W. provides around 20 per cent of
the long-term, fixed-rate loans to the *Mittelstand* and imposes a maximum margin of only 1 per cent over the funding rate on co-financed
lending, it effectively sets a ceiling on margins for such lending. The cost
of capital to SMEs in Germany is therefore markedly lower than in the
UK.

The damaging effect that the absence of an effective relationship between
finance and industry in the UK has had on domestic industrial development
is illustrated by the investment and output performance of manufacturing
in the UK since 1979. From 1979 to 1989, investment in manufacturing
grew by a mere 12.8 per cent, compared with a 108 per cent increase in
investment in the UK services sector as a whole, and a 320.2 per cent
increase in investment in financial services (Glyn 1992: 84). Moreover, bank
lending to manufacturing in the UK increased in constant price terms by
only 49 per cent between 1980 and 1991 and declined, as a percentage of
total bank lending, from 27.7 per cent in 1980 to 10.8 per cent in 1991. This
49 per cent increase in bank lending to manufacturing is put into perspective by the 801 per cent and 648 per cent increases respectively in lending
to the property and personal sectors (CBI 1992: 22). This lack of industrial
investment in the UK has manifested itself most clearly in terms of the relatively slow growth of industrial output. In 1992, UK manufacturing output was less than 1 per cent above its 1973 peak, whereas, during the same
period, output in Germany rose by 25 per cent, in France by 27 per cent,
in Italy by 85 per cent, and in Japan by 119 per cent (House of Commons
1994: 16). In the first quarter of 1993, the index of UK manufacturing output stood at 133.5, compared to 103.9 in the first three months of 1979, the

last full quarter of manufacturing activity under the Callaghan Government. During almost fourteen years of Conservative government, manufacturing output had grown on average by only 0.8 per cent per annum. Even in 1989, at the peak of an economic boom, manufacturing output had grown at no more than 1.2 per cent annually from the peak of the previous cycle. The immediate effect of the failure of capacity to expand has been the rapid deterioration in the UK's balance of trade in manufactures which went into deficit for the first time since the Industrial Revolution during 1983 and reached £26 billion or nearly 5 per cent of GDP in 1989. Between 1979 and 1989, whilst UK exports rose by 18.7 per cent, imports rose by 56.5 per cent.

A HISTORICAL DEBATE

The UK's industrial investment and output performance since 1979 suggests the need for wholesale reform of the UK's system of provision of finance to industry as a prerequisite to any attempt to expand capacity and employment. However, when the debate amongst economic historians concerning the causes of the UK's long-term relative economic decline is considered, the difficulty of implementing such an agenda of industrial and financial reform becomes all too apparent. The failure of UK financial institutions to develop their role from that of financial intermediation via capital markets and the provision of short-term working capital, to one of financial integration via bank ownership and management of manufacturing industries, and the provision of long-term investment capital, has been attributed by economic historians to three factors in particular.

First, the institutional structure of the UK financial system, which has seen its development and profitability divorced from the performance of domestic industry. Secondly, the gentlemanly values that have shaped the development of finance in the UK, which have preferred the civility of 'invisible' income derived from trade and commerce to the 'visible' earnings generated by manufacturing. Thirdly, the timing of the UK's industrialization, with Britain the first industrial nation, and with market forces rather than state intervention the prime agencies of industrialization and social change.

For Ingham, the first of these factors, namely the separation of finance and industry, is attributable to the essentially divided nature of British capitalism and the pivotal role played in its development by the Bank of England, the City of London, and the Treasury, which Ingham depicts as the core institutional nexus of British society (1984: 131–4). The influence of this nexus on the relationship between finance and industry can be traced back to the late seventeenth century, with the establishment of exclusive Treasury control over state spending and revenue in 1668 (Hennessy 1989:

25) and the founding of the London Stock Exchange in 1694. From this era to the present, Ingham contends that the Bank of England and the Treasury have supported policies conducive to the promotion of the City's short-term commercial advantage in the global economy, at the expense of providing long-term finance for domestic industry, because of the dividend that such policies have provided for the maintenance of the Bank of England and Treasury's own institutional power within their respective domains of the UK financial system and Whitehall. By the time that it became the first industrial nation and the 'workshop of the world', the UK had already long established itself as 'the world's major commercial entrepôt' with the City of London possessing an 'essentially commercial (and not simply financial) character' (Ingham 1984: 5). For the past three centuries, the City's commercial interests have been identified 'in the short term gains to be made in the trading of productive assets—in particular through take overs and mergers—and not in the long term profitability of those units of industrial capital whose shares are bought and sold' (Ingham 1984: 62).

In 1994, for example, the London Stock Exchange did provide a record £11.6 billion of new funding for companies, but this pales into insignificance compared to its £607 billion turnover in British and Irish shares and the £717 billion turnover in overseas equities (*Guardian*, 31 Jan. 1994). Indeed, the fact that London held a 93.5 per cent share of the European market in trading of overseas equities in 1992 compared to a paltry 2.3 per cent share for Frankfurt vividly illustrates the different priorities and interests of the UK and German financial systems. As long as the larger part of the City's commercial and financial activity remains dependent on the performance of the international economy and simultaneously divorced from the performance of the domestic economy, the City's commercial interests will provide a major obstacle to any attempts to expand capacity and to move towards full employment.

Ingham's theme of the failure of UK financial institutions to develop a close and long-term working relationship with industry because of the presence of a powerful, pre-industrial institutional nexus is further developed in Cain and Hopkins' thesis of 'gentlemanly capitalism' which focuses upon the role of the City of London in maintaining the pre-industrial gentlemanly values of the landed aristocracy at the expense of providing long-term investment capital to manufacturing. Cain and Hopkins assert that the gentlemanly norms of the English aristocracy had remained fixed points of reference from the time of Chaucer but that by the eighteenth century the power of the aristocracy was in decline. However, the growth of the financial and services sector in the UK proved to be compatible with gentlemanly values because the markets of the City of London 'provided capitalism with an acceptable face by generating income streams that were invisible or indirect' and which did not necessitate the English gentleman having to soil his reputation by investing in the vulgarly visible and culturally inferior activity of manufacturing industry (Cain and Hopkins 1993: 26). The aristocracy was thereby able to replenish both its ranks and its income by assimilating middle-class urban gentlemen 'as a counterpoise to the claims of provincial manufacturing industry, which threatened to elevate the provinces over the centre by means of money made in unacceptable ways' (Cain and Hopkins 1993: 33).

Ingham's emphasis upon its institutional structure and Cain and Hopkins' focus upon its core values as the root causes of the UK financial system's lack of interest in and involvement with the development of domestic industry have, to some extent, been amalgamated in the work of Elbaum and Lazonick. They have asserted that the distinctiveness of the UK's pattern of economic development was derived 'less from the conservatism of its cultural values per se than from a matrix of rigid institutional structures that reinforced these values and obstructed individualistic as well as collective efforts at economic renovation' (Elbaum and Lazonick 1986: 2). Whilst rival economies such as those of the United States, Germany, and France were developing the visible hand of the institutions of corporate capitalism as the dominant mode of economic organization during the late nineteenth century, the UK was consolidating its 'institutions of competitive capitalism' (Elbaum and Lazonick 1986: 4).

Amongst the definitive characteristics of corporate capitalism was the integration of financial and industrial capital, but the UK failed to develop such an integrated structure because the role of finance in domestic industry remained restricted to one of intermediation through the operation of the uncoordinated, invisible hand of its competitive capital markets. Financial institutions 'failed to become involved in the restructuring of industry so as to influence the profitability of enterprise and the demand for long-term industrial capital'; from the late nineteenth century through the inter-war period, this 'adversely affected the volume and allocation of British industrial investment and the long-term competitive performance of British industry compared with its international rivals' (Best and Humphries 1986: 223).

The absence of integration between finance and industry in the UK has been accounted for by Alexander Gerschenkron in terms of a third and alternative explanation to Ingham's thesis of capitalism divided and Cain and Hopkins' emphasis on gentlemanly values. Gerschenkron's thesis of 'relative economic backwardness' focuses on the economic conditions prevalent at the time when various national economies began their 'great spurt' of industrialization. Where industrialization of a national economy was delayed such that it occurred in conditions of economic backwardness relative to its rival nations, Gerschenkron asserts that the likelihood increased of an explosive 'great spurt' and industrialization proceeding 'under some organized direction' with 'ideologies of delayed industrialization' arising to challenge anti-industrial interests (Gerschenkron 1966:

22–6). Most importantly, relative economic backwardness could be surmounted through the creation of 'universal' banks which would combine investment and commercial banking. In Germany, for example, where banks were said to nurture their industrial partners 'from the cradle to the grave, from establishment to liquidation' (Gerschenkron 1966: 14), it was not just the longevity of the relationship between German finance and industry which promoted industrial development. German banks were also prepared to extend their role beyond the provision of long-term finance to a managerial role that was institutionalized by their presence on the supervisory boards of German companies. Decisions about corporate strategy or restructuring would tend not to be taken without their active intervention. Therefore, by the late nineteenth century, a 'complete gulf' had opened up between, on the one hand, 'the paragon of the universal bank' in Germany, which was 'designed to finance the long-run investment needs of the economy', and, on the other, 'the English bank essentially designed to serve as a source of short-term capital' (Gerschenkron 1966: 13).

Gerschenkron's thesis that the UK's failure to develop a tradition of industrial banking can therefore be attributed to the unique degree to which its pattern of industrialization was shaped by institutions and practices based on competitive markets, reflecting its status as the first industrial nation and its domination of early industries. The UK's 'great spurt' of industrialization took place predominantly during the late eighteenth and early nineteenth centuries, but this early start did not lead to the closer integration of the banking system and domestic industry. The latter did not initially suffer from a serious shortage of investment capital because it was able to finance its longer-term investment from retained earnings or the wealth of rich individual investors. Indeed, the capital accumulated from the UK's previous commercial and agricultural development had 'obviated the pressures for developing any special institutional device for provision of long-term capital to industry' (Gerschenkron 1966: 14). However, the lack of integration between finance and industry became more of a constraint on industrial development during the latter half of the nineteenth century, when the increasing technical complexity of innovation in the new, mass-production chemical and electrical industries placed a premium on the availability of large-scale, long-term investment capital to develop both the processes and products of the second industrial revolution (Hobsbawm 1969: 172–7). Whilst its principal competitors' firms were able to draw upon the investment capital provided by universal banks committed to playing an active and supervisory role in industrial development, the absence of such financial structures constrained the capacity of UK firms to make the transition to mass production from their atomized industrial structures.

A SUCCESSION OF INQUIRIES

The failure of the suppliers of finance in the UK to become actively integrated with industry during the second industrial revolution led at the time of the Great Depression to the first of a series of official inquiries into the relationship between finance and industry in the UK which have punctuated the subsequent development of the national economy. The initial inquiry, a parliamentary investigation conducted by the Macmillan Committee, identified an investment 'gap' in the provision of capital by equity markets to medium-sized companies (HMSO 1931). The Committee recommended not only that practice in the City of London should be altered in order that special provision could be made for SMEs but also that bank–industry relations should be created which would enable a process of planned industrial restructuring to be undertaken. The recommendations of the Macmillan Committee for the reform of the UK banking system went largely unheeded. It was not until July 1945 that the Industrial and Commercial Finance Corporation (ICFC) was established to fill the Macmillan 'gap'.

With English and Scottish banks and the Bank of England acting as shareholders, the ICFC's principal objective was to 'provide credit by means of loans or the subscription of loan or share capital or otherwise for industrial and commercial business or enterprises in Great Britain, particularly in cases where the existing facilities provided by banking institutions and the Stock Exchanges are not readily or easily available' (Thomas 1978: 123). However, by 1958 it had developed only five branches. The following year a new inquiry by the Radcliffe Committee was launched into the operation of the monetary system in the UK. It identified an investment 'gap', namely that between the seven-year time limit imposed on lending by clearing banks and the fifteen-year minimum of the finance houses. However, the Committee also reported that the banks were lending on a large scale to finance the medium-term and long-term requirements of industry. It therefore concluded that the clearing banks were not failing to provide finance to industry and did not recommend the creation of any new public or private development banks. At the same time, the Macmillan Government could not manipulate interest rates for the purpose of stimulating industrial development because the Government was already manipulating interest rates for the purpose of financing public debt (Zysman 1983: 199).

During the 1970s, two further official inquiries were undertaken which focused upon the financing of industry in the UK. The first of these, the Bolton Committee inquiry into small firms, reaffirmed the Radcliffe Committee's earlier conclusion that the banks were not failing to supply sufficient finance to industry (HMSO 1971). The second inquiry into the

functioning of financial institutions in the UK, under the chairmanship of
Harold Wilson (HMSO 1980), like its predecessors, largely absolved the
banks and did not recommend the creation of a National Investment Bank.
It did, however, suggest that there was a problem with the finance provided
to small firms and recommended (albeit with a considerable dissenting
minority) that there should be further institutional change to remedy this
deficiency in the form of greater access to equity finance and government-
financed loan guarantees to stimulate bank lending to SMEs. The immediate response of the Thatcher Government was the introduction of the
Business Expansion Scheme and the Loan Guarantee Scheme, the latter
providing a government guarantee of 80 per cent of the value of bank loans
to those small firms unable to provide suitable collateral (Mullineux
1994: 2).

The next significant contribution to the debate about finance and industry in the UK was provided at the height of the stock market boom in 1987
by a report from a joint Confederation of British Industry (CBI)/City of
London task force. This inquiry was largely initiated because of concern
that companies were making extravagantly high dividend payments to persuade their shareholders not to succumb to the attraction of hostile take-
overs from rival companies. Although a survey conducted by the task force
revealed that only 12 per cent of 109 leading chief executives stated that the
threat of take-over was a deterrent to long-term investment, it also discovered that the most effective deterrent to long-term investment was the cost
of capital and/or concern about an inadequate rate of return. But because
it did not examine the operation of the UK financial system as a whole, the
task force failed to identify the major flaws in the relationship between
finance and industry in the UK. It therefore unanimously concluded that
'the City was not seriously inhibiting industrial performance, financial institutions were not overly concerned with the short term, and that the banks
were responsive to the needs of industrial companies' (Collins 1991: 96).
Indeed, the task force suggested that the blame for the UK's poor rate of
economic growth should be laid at the feet of industrialists who had
accorded insufficient importance to long-term investment because of the
general political and economic environment in the UK rather than the
specific influence of the City.

The most comprehensive recent analysis of the finance–industry relationship has been provided by the House of Commons Trade and Industry
Committee inquiry into the competitiveness of UK manufacturing (House
of Commons 1994). The Major Government's response to the Committee's
report confirmed that significant reform of the UK financial system was not
contemplated. The diversity of analyses and prescriptions in the evidence
submitted to the Committee has, however, revealed not only the depth
of concern about the effectiveness of current finance–industry relations in
the UK but also the huge resistance that would confront any future

government attempting to reform the UK financial system. Reflecting the concerns of its witnesses, the Committee devoted more than one-quarter of its report to the question of the relationship between finance and industry in the UK. The Committee identified the relationship between finance and industry in the UK in systemic terms, concluding that 'the problem of short-termism is the result of groups of people responding to a system which requires—indeed insists upon—short-termist behaviour'.

This conclusion was derived from an analysis of the relationship between finance and industry which began with an attempt to account for the relatively poor investment record in UK manufacturing. The Committee had not been convinced when the Department of Trade and Industry (DTI) cited the fact that UK investment in manufacturing as a percentage of value added had been higher for the past thirty years than in the US and similar to that in Germany, because the UK had achieved a low level of value added during this period. For the Committee, the high cost of capital in the UK, a scarcity of investment opportunities offering adequate financial returns, risk aversion to longer-term investment among managers, and a shortage of funds for investment offered four possible explanations for the UK's poor investment record.

The first three of these explanations could be assessed by an evaluation of the internal rate of return on investment required by UK companies. The Committee found that it was these internal rates of return (IRR) which differentiated UK companies most clearly from their competitors. For example, the median required IRR for strategic investments by UK manufacturers was 16 to 20 per cent, and 21 to 25 per cent for relatively low-risk operational investments. Furthermore, the payback period for these investments, that is, how soon a company could expect to secure a return on its investment, was found to be only nineteen to twenty-four months for the median period for operational investments. Indeed, in no less than 56 per cent of manufacturing plants, the payback period was less than two years, and less than three years in 89 per cent of plants. These very high IRR and very short payback periods could be attributed to a number of factors, namely the volatility of exchange rates and the growth rate of the UK economy, the generally higher rate of inflation in the UK which meant that manufacturers could not necessarily raise their prices to compensate for rising costs, shareholders' demands for high and unwavering dividends, and a higher than average failure rate for investments (House of Commons 1994: 56–60).

From its analysis of the evidence submitted to it, the Committee derived four conclusions about investment in UK companies of great importance for capacity building in the UK. First, that high required IRR for UK companies 'have made it difficult to justify longer-term investment, but short payback periods constitute a more specific bias against longer-term investment, especially projects involving structural change, which have heavy initial costs and delayed returns'. Payback periods have been more widely used than IRR which, because of their short-term nature in the UK, has given companies a bias against long-term investment. Secondly, required IRR for strategic investments by UK companies 'appear in many cases to be unrealistic as regards new technologies which may be crucial to the future of the business'. The Committee doubted whether the term 'strategic investment' could have any meaning where the payback period required for such investment was only two years. Thirdly, because operational investments are relatively risk-free in technological terms, required internal rates of return 'far above the cost of capital indicate either that market risks are regarded as high or that there is pressure to maintain a high short-term return on capital'. This may have become a particular problem for companies in the early 1990s when the rate of inflation in the UK fell to relatively low levels historically but, because of their suspicion that such conditions will not endure for the entirety of even their short payback periods, investors and managers have been reluctant to reduce their internal required rates of return. Fourthly, and most importantly for plans for capacity building: 'Low investment can be seen both as a cause and as a result of problems in UK manufacturing—a cause in that it makes it harder to raise competitiveness and output and a result in that it reflects the relatively low returns yielded by UK manufacturing' (House of Commons 1994: 60).

THE MAJOR GOVERNMENTS, FINANCE AND INDUSTRY

The Major Government published its observations on the Trade and Industry Committee's report (HMSO 1994a) to coincide with the publication of its own White Paper on competitiveness (HMSO 1994b). However, neither document addressed the Committee's principal concerns about the relationship between finance and industry in the UK. In its observations on the Committee's report, the Government stated its belief that the best means to encourage businesses to invest 'is through the creation of a stable macroeconomic framework based on low inflation'. It assumed that lower interest rates would automatically lower the cost of capital but, as the Committee report had documented, the IRR for many UK companies had failed to take account of lower inflation, not least because of the Government's previous failure to deliver a stable macroeconomic framework which had led them to doubt the longevity of any period of low inflation.

On the question of the provision of finance for small firms in the UK raised by the Committee, the Government pointed to the review of the supply of finance being undertaken by the Treasury under its Industrial Finance Initiative, which would include the operation of the capital markets, savings, and the flow of funds to business. On the Committee's specific recommendation that 'the Government investigate how a loan guarantee scheme could be established which would provide the UK's smaller firms with similar advantages to those obtained in Germany from the KfW' (House of Commons 1994: 110), the Government confined itself to the observation that any scheme should be 'cost-effective and well-targeted' and, in any case, it already possessed its own, well-established Small Firms Loan Guarantee Scheme. Apparently, the fact that the Loan Guarantee Scheme had guaranteed loans of little more than £1 billion since 1981 compared to the K.f.W.'s £11 billion of loan guarantees in 1992 alone was not regarded as sufficient cause for urgent action.

In its White Paper, *Competitiveness: Helping Business to Win*, the Government readily acknowledged the greater reliance of companies on overdrafts in the UK, pointing to the fact that the Bank of England's report, *Finance for Small Firms*, had found that overdrafts account for 56 per cent of small-firm debt in the UK compared to a mere 14 per cent in Germany (Bank of England 1994: 99). However, the Government defended overdrafts on the grounds that they were often cheaper and quicker to arrange than term loans and businesses would in any event only have to pay interest on the funds that they used under such arrangements. The Government also claimed that whilst overdrafts could be the source of misunderstanding and resentment between companies and banks when the latter chose to reduce their exposure to debt, there was 'evidence that both banks and businesses are now beginning to place greater weight on longer term finance' (HMSO 1994b: 101). None of the sources of this evidence were cited in support of this assertion. The Government chose instead to make clear its belief that long-term relationships between companies and investors are primarily the responsibility of the private sector, and that the Government's own role as 'catalyst' should be restricted to diffusing information about best practice and facilitating private sector-led initiatives.

A fortnight after the simultaneous publication of the White Paper on competitiveness and the Government's observations on its report, the Trade and Industry Committee took further oral evidence from Michael Heseltine, the Secretary of State for Trade and Industry. Heseltine once again rejected the idea of the creation of a publicly owned development bank in the UK to finance SMEs on the grounds that it would 'not of itself create more profitable opportunities' (HMSO 1994a: 2). Emphasizing the importance of sustained low inflation and low interest rates for the development of small and medium-sized companies, Heseltine argued that the strength of this sector of the German economy could be attributed to the pursuit of such policies over half a century. At no stage did Heseltine acknowledge the contribution to the development of small and medium-sized companies made by development banks such as the German K.f.W. and Deutsche Ausgleichs bank. Indeed, in emphasizing the importance of responsible macroeconomic policies as a prerequisite for long-term development, Heseltine failed to recognize that in the German financial system it is the very fact that bankers lend long-term to industry, and therefore along with their industrial clients wish to avoid the possibility of the value of loans being undermined by inflation, that has encouraged stability in the management of the German economy. Thus, in Germany, responsibility in macroeconomic management has been as much a consequence as a cause of long-term investment in industry.

On the question of short-termism governing the relationship between the City of London and industry, Heseltine cited the defence and pharmaceutical industries as evidence that the UK economy could sustain manufacturing companies dedicated to long-term investment. Indeed, he referred to these industries' respective high levels of research expenditure to reject the proposal that the UK's tax regime should be altered to encourage additional investment. At the same time Heseltine, adopting 'a warm blooded British citizen's approach', registered his regret that there was no potential UK purchaser for the Rover Group before its take-over by BMW in February 1994. As with the defence and pharmaceutical industries, the motor vehicle industry demands large-scale, long-term investment, but what neither his select committee inquisitors nor Heseltine acknowledged was the fact that the defence and pharmaceutical industries have enjoyed a continuous long-term subsidy from the taxpayer through state-funded R&D, the procurement of weapons by the Ministry of Defence, and the purchase of drugs by the National Health Service. In stark contrast, the motor vehicle industry in the UK has not enjoyed such subsidies in recent years, with the notable exception of the sale of Rover to British Aerospace (BAe) at a discounted price, which gave BAe an incentive to offload Rover at the earliest permissible opportunity in order to realize a substantial capital gain, and government grants given to Japanese car manufacturers to locate their new manufacturing operations in the UK.

Heseltine also argued that 'the thing that drives the shareowner of the City away from the manager investing in longer-term activities is actually the volatility of the economy' and that therefore there are more profitable short-term opportunities in the money markets, in property, and in speculation than in 'manufacturing longer-term type investment'. At no point did Heseltine acknowledge the contribution the Thatcher Governments' policies of deregulation of the financial-services sector—not least the abolition of minimum reserve requirements—made to such volatility and speculative activity. The Trade and Industry Committee report had pointed to the way in which the UK's tax system actively 'encourages shareholders, especially institutional shareholders, to seek dividend income rather than capital gains (an effect strengthened by tax changes in the 1980s)' by taxing pension fund income on profits retained in the companies whose shares they hold at 33 per cent, compared with only 16.25 per cent tax for their income from dividends (House of Commons 1994: 72).

Indeed, the tax reforms of the 1980s had increased the value to a higher-rate taxpayer of a pre-tax profit of £100, fully distributed as dividend, from £17 in 1982 to £53 in 1992. The White Paper on competitiveness too had conceded that UK companies currently distribute a relatively high proportion of their profits in dividends compared to their French, German, and Japanese competitors, and that such action might not only reduce the flow of funds for investment but also 'reinforce a pressure on management to show good returns in the short term, even though this may be at the expense of long term growth' (HMSO 1994b: 101). The Government, however, was content to comfort itself with the thought that dividends might be recycled for the purpose of investment. It might be thought obvious from the UK's relatively low investment record that the evidence of dividend-recycling for investment purposes is pretty thin at best.

INDUSTRY DIVIDED

One of the trends that the submission of written and oral evidence to parliamentary select committee inquiries has tended to highlight is the division of interests and opinion amongst representatives of industry, both multinationals and SMEs, concerning the nature of relations between finance and industry in the UK. The salience of parliamentary inquiries, such as those furnished by Macmillan, Radcliffe, Bolton, and Wilson, in the political economy of finance–industry relations in the UK serves as testament to the vacuum in analysis and policy that has been created by the weakness of those organizations seeking to represent industrial interests to government and the City of London. Recourse to pleas to government and exhortation to the City has not only demonstrated civil manufacturing's lack of influence and leverage over the state and finance in the UK but also often served as a substitute for more sharply defined recommendations about how the relationship between finance and industry might be altered to the benefit of the latter. For example, when seeking to promote the merits of its industrial strategy, the Engineering Employers' Federation (EEF) exhorted the City and financial institutions to 'review financial investment in industry in the light of achievable future rates of return . . . [and] not demand excessive dividends from companies who could better utilise funds to reinvest for future dividends'. It also pleaded with government to 'extend capital allowances for plant and machinery permanently to 100 per cent' (EEF 1992: 6). In its interim report on the progress of its industrial strategy some six months later, the EEF was unable to specify amongst its achievements a single measure that the City and financial institutions had taken in response to its exhortations (EEF 1993: 5).

Support for the idea of a development bank has come from some industrial and professional organizations, for example, the Institution of

Electrical Engineers and the UK Industrial Group (IEE 1994; UKIG, 1993). However, the Institute of Directors has repeatedly rejected this suggestion in favour of proposals for the reform of the system of corporation, capital gains, and inheritance taxation, and the provision of up-front income tax relief for long-term investment in new shares of UK quoted and unquoted trading companies as the most effective means by which to close any possible equity gap (I.o.D. 1992a: 10–15; I.o.D. 1992b: 89–90).

In a similar vein, in its reports on the competitiveness of industry in the UK, the CBI's National Manufacturing Council has also failed to display any enthusiasm for a development bank. It has merely repeated the recommendation of the 1987 CBI/City of London task force that communications be improved between companies and all their stakeholders, especially their shareholders (CBI 1991: 59; CBI 1992: 32). There has been a similar absence of unanimity about the benefits to competitiveness to be derived from a development bank amongst those representing SMEs. The CBI Smaller Firms Council, for example, has indicated its admiration for the German K.f.W. but does not think that it would be practical to introduce such an institution to the UK financial system 'because of the cost of setting it up, "the difficulties of operating a two-tier interest rate", and the problem of drawing a line between firms which could benefit and those which could not (introducing a disincentive to growth)' (House of Commons 1994: 109).

THE CORE INSTITUTIONAL NEXUS TO THE RESCUE?

In his personal manifesto of non-Thatcherite conservatism, *Where There's a Will*, Michael Heseltine appealed to the City of London's institutional shareholders to create their own machinery 'to consider and express the wider national interest in a stable and productive pattern of investment' (Heseltine 1987: 125). More recently, Heseltine has recognized the futility of such appeals to industrial patriotism and responded to concerns about the impact of short-termism on investment by referring to the Treasury's industrial finance initiative being led by Stephen Dorrell, the then Financial Secretary to the Treasury. However, this initiative, which was examining 'the whole area of the supply of finance', including 'capital markets, savings generally, and the flow of funds to businesses; and implications for taxation and other policies', had merely been reported in the White Paper and had yet to deliver any substantive reforms of the UK financial system (HMSO 1994b: 103).

The prospects for any meaningful reform of the relationship between finance and industry by the Major Government were reduced when the national press received copies of a letter sent to Dorrell by Lord Hanson in which Hanson not only accused Dorrell of 'sounding like a socialist' but also suggested that the question of dividend payments was 'nothing to do with the government' (*Financial Times*, 24 Nov. 1994). As it happened, Hanson had also written to the Prime Minister about the Treasury's review of dividend payments, although whether Hanson's intervention accelerated Dorrell's departure from the Treasury to become Secretary of State for National Heritage in a Cabinet reshuffle is unclear. What Hanson's attack on Dorrell did demonstrate was the extent to which vested interests in the UK financial system would seek to oppose even modest departures from the status quo. Indeed, it has been reported that the Treasury abandoned its review of dividend payments because, according to an unnamed senior Civil Servant, 'The issue became too much of a hot potato after Hanson attacked the review. No one wanted to pick it up' (*Financial Times*, 24 Nov. 1994).

Beyond the abandonment of its review of dividend payments, and as part of its industrial financial initiative, the Treasury engaged in an extensive process of consultation with companies to elicit their views as to what the Government should be doing to improve the supply of finance to businesses. The consultation process entailed discussions with around 1,000 owners and managers of businesses in ten regions during the fifteen-month period. Treasury officials travelled to other European Union countries and North America to investigate the mechanisms for financing small firms deployed there. They received 200 specific recommendations concerning the action that government should take. Of these recommendations, eight-six are already in practice, forty-seven are regarded sympathetically by the Treasury, and the remainder have been rejected as impractical. More than one-quarter of the recommendations related to improving the cash flow of businesses, whilst sources of investment, bank relations with business and greater financial competence in financial skills for businessmen were the next most popular concerns (*Sunday Times*, 12 Feb. 1995).

However, the overall objective and onus of the industrial financial initiative has been about making the market more efficient rather than extending the role of the state by, for example, giving the building societies more freedom to lend to business and thereby increasing their competition with the major UK banks. The possibility of any UK equivalent of the German development and loan guarantee banks has been explicitly ruled out.

The Bank of England also examined the question of the supply of finance to small firms. In a similar vein to the Treasury, it organized a series of discussions with representatives of the banks, small businesses, and academia in an attempt to discover their respective assessment of the current effectiveness of the UK financial system and to identify any suggestions for improvements in the relationship between finance and business. A previous Bank of England report on bank lending to small businesses had identified a trend towards term borrowing and away from their traditional reliance on overdrafts, although such term loans were being taken at rates of interest well above base rates as opposed to the more attractive rates of interest available to small firms in Germany from the K.f.W. (Young, Cleland, and Freebody 1993: 118).

This trend towards longer-term lending and borrowing has been confirmed in two more recent Bank reports, the second of which found that term loans now account for 60 per cent of total lending by UK banks to small firms compared with around 50 per cent at the end of 1992 (Bank of England 1995). However, the same report also discovered that most lending to small firms in the UK was still at between 2 and 4 percentage points over base rate, and that, despite the fact that banks were 'becoming more transparent' in their pricing of fees and charges, there was a movement away from local branches towards business centres which meant that some customers were having to travel 'unrealistic distances' to see a bank manager (*Financial Times*, 25 Jan. 1995). Since the Banking Liaison Group, a group of former bankers which advises businesses on their relationships with banks, had recently reported that as many as 10 per cent of the UK's SMEs may have been overcharged by up to £1.75 billion by their banks, and the Banking Ombudsman's 1994 annual report had indicated around a 20 per cent increase in the number of complaints by businesses, the upbeat message of the Bank of England's reports may not have disclosed the true nature of contemporary relationships between finance and industry in the UK.

Like its partners in Ingham's core institutional nexus, the nature of the City's supply of finance to small firms has been changing. During the 1980s, and in order to promote their objective of restoring an enterprise culture in Britain, in which entrepreneurial initiative would once more become the prime agency of social change, the Thatcher Governments did launch a number of initiatives to facilitate greater access to equity finance for SMEs. In November 1980 the Unlisted Securities Market (USM) was launched for medium-sized businesses. It was supplemented in 1987 by a Third Market for financing smaller businesses. Unfortunately, the launch of the Third Market was overshadowed by the crisis of investor confidence resulting from the October 1987 Stock Market crash which, when later allied to the recession of the early 1990s, acted as a powerful disincentive for investors to provide finance for growing companies. Since its creation, the USM has been more successful than the ill-starred Third Market, raising around £4 billion of finance for the 881 companies that have joined its list of quoted companies. Of these, 253 have subsequently moved on to the Stock Exchange's Official List. Amongst those graduating to the Official List have been Carlton Communications, the Body Shop, and Central Independent Television.

However, the USM has not enjoyed a history of unbroken success, since no fewer than 184 companies have departed the USM since its creation because of reorganization or the cancellation of their quotation. Indeed, compared to the performance of the Financial Times–Stock Exchange Index of 100 leading companies (FT–SE 100) since November 1980, the overall performance of the USM has been abysmal; the FT–SE 100 Index has witnessed a growth of around 450 per cent since the launch of the USM, whereas the Datastream USM index has never risen by more than 50 per cent above its starting-point and is now back at a position similar to where it started (Kay 1994: 3).

The introduction of new directives from the European Union mean that the USM, which has suffered from a shortage of investors and new entrants in recent years, has to cease trading at the end of 1996. The European Commission has recognized the competitive disadvantage that SMEs in the European Union (EU) have experienced on account of the absence in Europe of a second-tier equity market equivalent to the US Nasdaq market, whose success in providing equity to growing companies has led to its being only second to the New York Stock Exchange in terms of shares traded.

In 1994 the EU's Strategic Programme for Innovation and Technology Transfer identified stock markets as a key element in the process of financing innovative growth companies. A number of initiatives have responded to this need for equity finance for SMEs, principally the proposal for a European equivalent of Nasdaq, known as Easdaq and launched at the end of 1995. For its part, the Stock Exchange has launched a new and rival market initiative, the Alternative Investment Market (AIM), in the hope of attracting equity into young dynamic companies. It commenced trading in June 1995. Proponents of Easdaq contend that it will enjoy a major competitive advantage over the AIM because of Easdaq's pan-European element which it is claimed will enable it to attract more market entrants and greater liquidity. However, Michael Lawrence, the chief executive of the Stock Exchange, has argued that Easdaq lacks a common equity culture. At the same time, by departing from its original idea of an unregulated market to replace the USM, the Stock Exchange has to some degree stolen Easdaq's clothes by making the AIM relatively highly regulated and focusing on growth companies (Gourlay 1995: 17).

As with its predecessor, the principal problem that the AIM may confront is the absence of incentives for the Stock Exchange to devote resources to promote the AIM aggressively. The majority of the Exchange's members draw their income from large companies and will not want to divert attention from the Official List. Furthermore, the AIM will have to balance potentially conflicting objectives. On the one hand, the AIM needs to provide sufficiently tight regulation to provide both private individual and institutional investors with the confidence to invest. The absence of such regulation was one of the contributory factors in deterring investors from providing the USM with greater liquidity. On the other hand, the danger of tighter regulation is that it will raise the cost of gaining entry to the

AIM and thereby deter companies from seeking a quotation. In the hope of reconciling these objectives, the Stock Exchange has created a framework of regulation under which the sponsors or 'nominated advisers' backing companies that seek a listing on the AIM will not be required to produce a comprehensive prospectus. This should enable the cost of gaining entrance to the AIM to be kept low. Furthermore, now that the AIM has commenced trading, the ranks of its list of quoted companies should receive a boost not only from former USM members but also from the more than 300 companies which have been trading under the Stock Exchange's Rule 4.2 matched-bargain facility for lightly traded shares, under which no trading record has been required from companies, but there has been an insistence on a prospectus and a member firm promising to support dealing in the shares (Kay 1994: 3). However, like most second-tier markets for raising finance for growing companies, the AIM will face as its biggest problem that its rapidly growing member companies will soon graduate to the Official List. As a corollary, the publicity that is most likely to attract the attention of potential investors will be for the inevitable share of company failures that arises in this high-risk market.

THE PROSPECTS FOR REFORM

There has been no shortage of advice to the Major Government concerning how finance–industry relations in the UK should be reformed. The House of Commons Trade and Industry Committee has recommended changes in the taxation system to encourage reinvestment in smaller firms and the establishment of a loan guarantee scheme with 'similar advantages to those obtained in Germany from KfW' (House of Commons 1994: 128–9). Mullineux has advocated the establishment of a government-backed small business bank to 'take over responsibility for providing loan guarantees, further reduce guarantee premiums charged to borrowers, and disburse implicitly subsidised medium- to long-term, fixed interest rate loans as part of co-financing packages with other lenders to SMEs' (Mullineux 1994: p. iv). The problem with this remedy is that Mullineux's own analysis has demonstrated that a decentralized, federal structure of government is the prerequisite to an equally decentralized structure of industrial development banks. The centralized political and financial power and structures of the unitary state in the UK is clearly incompatible with Mullineux's remedy. Furthermore, the trends in the period since the election of the first Thatcher Government have been for an accentuation of this centralization of political and financial power. The frontiers of the democratically elected state have been rolled back whilst the clearing banks and building societies have been reducing the number of their local branches.

Mullineux does not acknowledge—let alone provide suggestions for surmounting—the incompatibility between his advocacy of a decentralized industrial banking system in the UK and the fact of a centralized political and financial system centred on Westminster, Whitehall, and the City of London. The connection between constitutional reform and improved finance for industry in the UK has been firmly established by Hutton (1995), and the policy prescriptions that flow from his analysis of the relationship between finance and industry in the UK and the obstacle it poses to long-term industrial development are very clear. At the same time, Hutton indicates his belief that there is no cause for optimism concerning the likelihood of their implementation; 'What is now required is a national effort to organise a sustained increase in investment, but the economic institutions and state structures are no more ready to respond to such a call than they ever were' (Hutton 1995: 165, 81). As a consequence, Hutton's remedy is the replacement of this ineffective and deeply damaging financial nexus by an alternative 'stakeholder capitalism', operating through 'a new financial architecture in which private decisions produce a less degenerate capitalism' (1995: 298). Replicating the features of Albert's Rhine capitalism, Hutton's 'stakeholder capitalism' would broaden the ownership of companies and institutions, in order not only to create a greater bias towards longer-term commitment from owners, but also to increase the supply of cheap, long-term debt, and to decentralize decision-making.

For Hutton, this also requires 'A written constitution; the democratisation of civil society; the republicanisation of finance; the recognition that the market economy has to be managed and regulated, both at home and abroad; the upholding of a welfare state that incorporates social citizenship; the construction of a stable international financial order beyond the nation state' (Hutton 1995: 326). Given the UK's unique exposure to and dependence upon the global economy, this last component is particularly important since the well-established capacity of international speculators to undermine national economic management would pose a major threat to any domestic attempts at capacity-building without prior international action to effect some greater degree of stability into global financial markets. The problem with this proposal, as with Hutton's entire agenda for institutional reform of the UK financial and political systems, is that the more he broadens the focus of his attack, the more he multiplies the number of vested interests that would seek to oppose and undermine any concerted attempt to implement his agenda for political reform and industrial modernization.

Whatever the merits of the analyses and policy recommendations put forward by select committees, academics, and journalists, their influence on the actual conduct of policy is likely to be marginal. The greatest prospect for reform lies with the Labour Party, raising the question of what action a Blair-led Government might take to change the relationship between finance and industry in the UK in order to rebuild industrial capacity.

During its years in Opposition, the Labour Party has published a host of strategy documents on industrial policy, most of which have incorporated some form of state-led development bank. For example, in 1986, in his personal manifesto for rebuilding industrial capacity, *Making Our Way: Investing in Britain's Future*, Neil Kinnock envisaged the creation of a British Investment Bank (BIB) to surmount the arm's-length relationship with industry which he claimed was characteristic of UK financial institutions. Kinnock saw the BIB as fulfilling the same developmental role as the Credit National in France and the K.f.W. in Germany, offering not merely finance to SMEs but also a comprehensive package of technical, managerial, and marketing assistance that would enable it to 'act as the financial arm of an aggressive industrial strategy' (Kinnock 1986: 113). The BIB was to be at the heart of a strategy of modernization for both industry in Britain and the institutions of the central British state on a scale with that attempted by the Wilson Governments of the mid- to late 1960s. To complement the role of the BIB, a state holding company, British Enterprise, would be established to assume primary responsibility for industrial restructuring, whilst a rejuvenated DTI and NEDO would assume important strategic planning and co-ordinating roles respectively.

The idea of a development bank reappeared in the form of a National Investment Bank (Labour Party 1990: 15), a commitment that was reiterated in two subsequent policy statements and the 1992 General Election manifesto (Labour Party 1991*a*: 9; 1991*b*: 9; 1992: 12).

During John Smith's brief tenure as Party Leader, Labour published *Making Britain's Future*, a consultative document which deliberately asked as many questions about the relationship between finance and industry as it answered, but marked an important change in Labour's policies away from an emphasis on a national developmental investment bank to 'a full-scale transfer of industrial, financial and political power to the regions' (Labour Party 1993: 13). The language was now one of empowerment and support for industrialists and partnership with, rather than replacement of, private sector financial institutions. In order to further clarify the Party's industrial strategy, Labour's Trade and Industry Team under Robin Cook's leadership duly launched a year-long consultation process with industry in the UK which resulted in the publication of *Winning for Britain: Labour's Strategy for Industrial Success* (Labour Party 1994). Once again, the way forward for the relationship between finance and industry was seen in terms of the creation of an industrial development bank. On this occasion, however, and as a recognition of Labour's desire to redefine its relationship with the private sector, it would be called the Business Development Bank (BDB) and would follow the example of the K.f.W. and similar continental European institutions. The BDB would operate on a profit-making basis and 'build on the experience of 3i and the Small Business Loan Guarantee Scheme and specialise in providing long-term finance for the expansion of small businesses by acting as an intermediary between the short-term demands of financial markets and the longer-term needs of small companies' (Labour Party 1994: 8). The BDB was now no longer seen as the leading element in Labour's attempt to promote a financial system more oriented towards investment in domestic industry, as was indicated by the fact that it was not deemed sufficiently important to merit the italicized highlighting of the proposals for reform of competition policy and the operation of UK pension funds which had preceded its inclusion. This demonstrated the degree to which Labour was now primarily seeking to work with the grain of the UK financial system, placing less emphasis on circumnavigating the markets' failures by establishing a network of state-owned development banks.

CONCLUSION

The Labour Party has either misunderstood or deliberately decided to overlook the fact that the successful operation of the K.f.W. in Germany is inextricably linked to its location within a federal structure of political and financial power. Despite widespread criticism of the quango state created by Conservative Governments since 1979 (e.g. Weir and Hall 1994; Wright 1995), Labour has abandoned plans to establish directly elected regional assemblies in favour of a number of 'shadow regional councils' run by nominated councillors. The sort of synergy and partnership between decentralized political and financial power in a federal structure that Mullineux has identified in his analysis of the financing of the *Mittelstand* in Germany will not be replicated in Britain because the Labour Party, like its Conservative opponents, retains an underlying faith in a unitary rather than a federal structure of government. However, until the connection is made between constitutional reform in Britain and improved economic performance, the prospects for the restoration of anything approaching full employment appear remote.

REFERENCES

Albert, M. (1993), *Capitalism against Capitalism* (London: Whurr).

Bank of England (1994), *Finance for Small Firms* (London: HMSO).

—— (1995), *Finance for Small Firms: A Second Report* (London: HMSO).

Best, M., and Humphries, J. (1986), 'The City and Industrial Decline', in B. Elbaum and W. Lazonick (eds.), *The Decline of the British Economy* (Oxford: Oxford University Press).

Cain, P., and Hopkins, A. (1993), *British Imperialism: Innovation and Expansion 1688–1914* (London: Longman).

CBI (1987), *Investing for Britain's Future: Report of the City/Industry Task Force* (London: Confederation of British Industry).
—— (1991), *Competing with the World's Best: The Report of the CBI Manufacturing Advisory Group* (London: Confederation of British Industry).
—— (1992), *Making it in Britain: Partnership for World Class Manufacturing. The Report of the CBI National Manufacturing Council* (London: Confederation of British Industry).
Collins, M. (1991), *Banks and Industrial Finance in Britain 1800–1939* (London: Macmillan).
EEF (1992), *Industrial Strategy: Proposals for Recovery and Sustained Growth* (London: Engineering Employers Federation).
—— (1993), *Industrial Strategy: Interim Report* (London: Engineering Employers Federation).
Elbaum, B., and Lazonick, W. (1986) (eds.), *The Decline of the British Economy* (Oxford: Oxford University Press).
Gerschenkron, A. (1966), *Economic Backwardness in Historical Perspective: A Book of Essays* (Cambridge, Mass.: Belknap Press).
Glyn, A. (1992), 'The "Productivity Miracle", Profits and Investment', in J. Michie (ed.), *The Economic Legacy: 1979–1992* (London: Academic Press).
Gourlay, R. (1995), 'Nourishment for the Little Ones', *Financial Times*, 17 Feb.: 17.
Hennessy, P. (1989), *Whitehall* (London: Fontana Press).
Heseltine, M. (1987), *Where There's a Will* (London: Hutchinson).
HMSO (1931), *Committee on Finance and Industry*, Report, Cmd 3897 (London: HMSO).
—— (1959), *Committee on the Working of the Monetary System*, Cmnd 827 (London: HMSO).
—— (1971), *Small Firms: Report of the Committee of Inquiry on Small Firms*, Cmnd 4811 (London: HMSO).
—— (1980), *Committee to Review the Functioning of Financial Institutions*, Cmnd 4811 (London: HMSO).
—— (1994a), *Government Observations on the Second Report from the Trade and Industry Committee (Session 1993–94) on the Competitiveness of UK Manufacturing Industry* (London: HMSO).
—— (1994b), *Competitiveness: Helping Business to Win*, Cm 2563 (London: HMSO).
Hobsbawm, E. (1969), *Industry and Empire: From 1750 to the Present Day* (Harmondsworth: Penguin).
House of Commons (1994), *Competitiveness of UK Manufacturing Industry: Second Report from the House of Commons Trade and Industry Committee (Session 1993–94)* (London: HMSO).
Hutton, W. (1995), *The State We're In* (London: Jonathan Cape).
IEE (1994), *UK Manufacturing: Facing International Change* (London: Institution of Electrical Engineers).
Ingham, G. (1984), *Capitalism Divided? The City and Industry in British Social Development* (London: Macmillan).
I.o.D. (1992a), *Forward to Prosperity: A Business Leaders Manifesto for the Next Government* (London: Institute of Directors).

I.o.D. (1992*b*), *Small Firms in the UK Economy: A Business Leader's View* (London: Institute of Directors).

Kay, W. (1994), 'Rough Road Ahead for Junior Market', *Independent on Sunday*, 11 Sept. 3.

Kinnock, N. (1986), *Making our Way: Investing in Britain's Future* (Oxford: Basil Blackwell).

Labour Party (1989), *Meet the Challenge, Make the Change: A New Agenda for Britain* (London: Labour Party).

—— (1990), *Looking to the Future* (London: Labour Party).

—— (1991*a*), *Modern Manufacturing Strength* (London: Labour Party).

—— (1991*b*), *Opportunity Britain: Labour's Better Way for the 1990s* (London: Labour Party).

—— (1992), *It's Time to Get Britain Working Again* (London: Labour Party).

—— (1993), *Making Britain's Future* (London: Labour Party).

—— (1994), *Winning for Britain: Labour's Strategy for Industrial Success* (London: Labour Party).

Mullineux, A. (1994), *Small and Medium-Sized Enterprise (SME) Financing in the UK: Lessons from Germany* (London: Anglo-German Foundation).

Thomas, W. (1978), *The Finance of British Industry 1918–1976* (London: Methuen).

UKIG (1993), *Manufacture or Die: A Policy Statement and Recommendations on the future of the UK's Economy by the UK Industrial Group* (Aldershot: United Kingdom Industrial Group).

Weir, S., and Hall, W. (1994) (eds.), *Ego Trip: Extra-Governmental Organisations in the United Kingdom and their Accountability* (London: Charter 88 Trust).

Wright, T. (1995), *Beyond the Patronage State*, Fabian Pamphlet 569 (London: Fabian Society).

Young, M., Cleland, V., and Freebody, S. (1993), 'Bank Lending to Small Businesses', *Bank of England Quarterly Review* (Feb.): 116–19.

Zysman, J. (1983), *Governments, Markets and Growth: Financial Systems and the Politics of Industrial Change* (Oxford: Martin Robertson).

Part III

International Lessons and Policy

7. Labour Market Mechanisms in Japan

Hidehiro Iwaki

AN OVERVIEW OF EMPLOYMENT PRACTICES IN JAPAN

The notion that the labour market in Japan features several characteristics that are different from those of other industrialized countries is widespread. The following three practices represent those characteristics: lifetime (or long-term) employment, wages based on *nenko* (seniority and contribution), and company-specific (or in-house) labour unions.[1] These special practices have internalized labour markets in Japan by dividing them into markets specific to a company or a corporate group. These internalized labour markets have contributed to the *Gemeinschaft*-like management of a company in Japan.

The term 'lifetime employment' in Japan implies the presence of a common practice by which employers implicitly commit themselves to secure employees' jobs permanently until retirement age. In large companies every employee, except in the case of a temporary worker, expects to be employed until retirement age. This practice generally protects the jobs of not only white-collar but also blue-collar workers. The average length of service for a company has traditionally been long, with a small job turnover ratio for large companies or corporate groups. Thus, one can call it the 'long-time' employment practice. This practice contrasts with small businesses, which sometimes lay off their employees during economic downturns.

Several laws and court cases enhanced this 'lifetime employment' practice during the post-war period. The Employment Promotion Law of 1966 and the Unemployment Benefits Law of 1975 established a public system for job security in Japan. The latter enables the government to subsidize certain employers to avoid lay-offs while restructuring their businesses. The court requires each employer to present 'reasonable background' for the lay-offs, even in the case of a routine restructuring.[2] Since one court case typically places substantial burdens on a company in terms of time and cost, most companies in Japan try to avoid it. As a result, it has become virtually impossible for a company to scale down employment even when profits are declining. In particular, a large company hesitates before cutting

---

[1] OECD (1973) stated these three to be a triad of holy vessels in the labour market in Japan.
[2] See Imai and Komiya (1989: 281).

jobs because it is likely to face social criticism. Rather, overtime work, part-time employment, and out-sourced work would be reduced by forwarding fewer orders to subcontractors and producing more intermediate goods internally with surplus labour. Alternatively, a price cut in subcontracting work might be negotiated. There are therefore both legal and institutional conditions that support the lifetime employment practice within large companies in Japan.

In contrast, most subcontractors are small and medium-sized firms and generally also have to restructure in order to survive. In response to economic difficulties, they typically react by first reducing overtime working hours, which are usually long enough to absorb the cyclical business fluctuations. Secondly, they cut bonuses and then wages; and finally they have no choice but to cut employment or else go out of business. During economic recessions, a large number of small companies do indeed go out of business. It is not the type of work or industry sector but the size of the business that determines job security. Terming the subcontractors the 'shock absorbers' gives meaning to the dual nature of the Japanese economy, which is divided into large companies with strong job security and the rest with much weaker, often even no, job security.

Lower but More Stable Labour Income

The internalized labour market has enhanced the bargaining power of the corporate sector. Two statistics demonstrate that the individual—whether as an employee or a stockholder—is economically less comfortable in Japan: (1) the lower the income share of labour, and (2) the lower the dividend–payout ratio. Despite long working hours, the income share of labour has been about 4–5 per cent lower in Japan than in the United States. The average dividend–payout ratio was about 30 per cent, compared to 60–70 per cent in other major industrialized countries. Thanks to these factors, companies have been able to accumulate large retained earnings and invest them in plant and equipment.

Figure 7.1 depicts the variations in income by type. Corporate profits were far more volatile in Japan, while both employment and wages were more stable. The implicit commitment to lifetime employment has pressured companies to maintain their employment and wage levels by sacrificing higher profits. As a result, corporate profits have become more volatile than would otherwise be the case. Management could survive hard times by realizing the latent capital gains on either stocks or land to window-dress their financial reports. In other words, those unrealized capital gains were also important for lifetime employment.

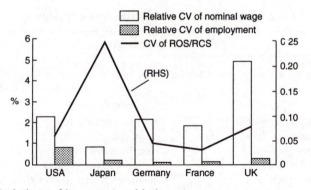

Fig. 7.1. Variations of incomes (total industry)

Notes: CV: Coefficients of Variation   ROS: Real Operating Surpluses
RCS: Real Capital Stock   Relative: Divided by CV of total output (1960–88).

Source: H. Iwaki, *Market Mechanisms in Japan*, Oct. 1992.

FACTORS SUPPORTING THESE EMPLOYMENT PRACTICES

Table 7.1 and Figure 7.2 summarize the economic system in Japan relating to employment practices, their merits and drawbacks. The Japanese economic system has two key distinctive features: stable long-term relationships and teamwork orientation.

Long-term economic relationships include *keiretsu* (corporate groups), lifetime employment, and the main-bank system. The merits to be found here are lower transaction costs, faster information flows, lower learning curves, smaller agent costs, stable employment, and a resulting stable society. These relationships offer job security and give workers an incentive to be loyal and work longer under quite competitive conditions. Workers engaged in multiple tasks, with long meeting hours and incurring large social expenses, have facilitated the teamwork orientation. These elements place emphasis on team responsibility and enable workers to be well informed. The merits are enhanced product quality and competitiveness in world markets.

These two factors have accounted for high economic growth in post-war Japan. In a virtuous cycle, the high growth has in turn supported these two elements as well. In other words, had it not been for high growth, these practices would probably not have resulted. A third important aspect of the Japanese system is 'governmental control and guidance' to support these practices. Although these features helped achieve high growth and keep down unemployment, they also had some significant adverse effects on the

Table 7.1. Long-term relationships and team-work orientation

Merits	Drawbacks
LONG-TERM STABLE ECONOMIC TRANSACTIONS: *keiretsu* transactions; lifetime employment; main-bank system; cross-shareholding	
smaller transactions cost	natural barriers to entry
faster information flow	competition-restrictive
better learning-by-using	discriminatory to outsiders
smaller agency cost	(natural trade barrier)
smaller job-search cost	inefficiency due to imperfect competition
stable employment and society	
facilitates fuzzy contracts	difficult to understand for outsiders
enhances flexibility	time-consuming process
	disadvantage to small firms and individuals
TEAM-WORK ORIENTATION (GROUPISM)	
greater corporate performance	sacrifice of individual freedom
more competitive in the world market	smaller diversity
	less innovative
	less democratic
GOVERNMENTAL CONTROL AND GUIDANCE: political financial support; long-term economic planning; a large number of regulations; weak anti-competition enforcement	
assure long-term economic transactions	smaller role of market mechanisms
clearer economic targets	smaller emphasis on consumer interests

economy. The drawbacks are the resulting minor role of market mechanisms and smaller consideration of consumer interests. Stock dividends are small and individual stockholders' control over management are severely limited due to widespread cross-holding of stocks.

The role of government has been too broad to allow private businesses to act according to market principles. The rights of an individual worker can be exploited in a society oriented towards 'groupism'. From the viewpoint of a democratic market economy, these drawbacks are quite costly. From the perspective that economic prosperity is more dependent on individual freedom, diversity, and innovation, it is time for Japan to reconsider its economic system. However, the fact that most consumers are also workers complicates the picture: people who are conscious of consumers' rights are also conscious of job security. That is why the government that supports industry can also be seen as supporting workers through stable expansion. The adjustment process in Japan's labour market is one example.

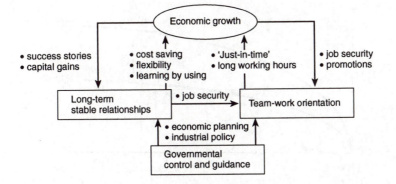

Fig. 7.2.   The 'virtuous cycle' in Japan in the high-growth era

Figure 7.3 depicts the mechanisms of the labour market in Japan in terms of neoclassical modelling. When the real wage does not correspond to the marginal product of labour, profit is not maximized. At Point O, the economy is in equilibrium with the real wage at $(W/P)_0$. As indicated in Figure 7.3, there are three adjustment patterns: (1) to increase or decrease employment (L); (2) to change the real wage; and (3) to shift the production function from f_0 to f_1 and change the marginal product of labour until it equals the real wage. During the high economic growth era, the real wage tended to be suboptimal owing to inflation. Japanese companies expanded production rather than swiftly increasing wages. In the process of moving from O to B, the real wage remained below the marginal product of labour. In contrast, during the stable growth era Japanese firms try to maintain employment and wages while increasing production. In the process of moving from O to B, the real wage remains above the marginal product of labour and suppresses corporate profits.

Thanks to the expansion of exports, this type of adjustment process aiming at a combination of stable employment and stable wages was successful. However, it was widely criticized as the export of unemployment (or a beggar-my-neighbour policy). As long as Japan pursues this kind of adjustment process, there will be endless cyclical trade friction with trade partners. One can no longer expect the kind of high economic growth in Japan witnessed during the post-war era because the population is growing rapidly older and the economic catch-up gap has narrowed. At the same time, the export of economic recession can no longer be allowed because Japan now has a large share of the world market. Therefore, the difficulty in expanding production while maintaining employment levels will gradually alter the orientation of the Japanese labour market.

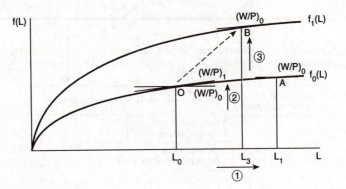

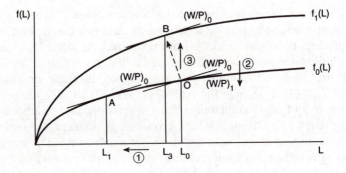

Fig. 7.3. Adjustment process in the labour market

Phase I. High growth
Phase II. Stable growth

DEVELOPMENTS IN THE LABOUR MARKET IN JAPAN

In post-war Japan the rate of unemployment has been lower than in other industrialized countries. This fact itself may account for the extent of the lifetime employment practice. In Japan in 1994 the number of persons who were 'wholly' unemployed (a peculiar but precise translation of the statistical wording in Japanese) stood at 1.8 million, with the *rate* of 'whole' unemployment at 2.9 per cent. When comparing the rate of unemployment internationally, this 'whole' unemployment rate is lower than in other G5 countries. In 1994 the unemployment rate was 6.1 per cent in the USA, 9.2 per cent in Germany, 12.5 per cent in France, and 9.3 per cent in the UK.

One common notion claims that the special economic and employment practices in Japan have produced high economic performance and this low unemployment rate. This point would therefore lead to the argument that, if lifetime employment were to diminish in Japan, unemployment would rise and result in social instability. However, the Japanese rate is based on the definition in the Labour Force Statistics by the Management and Co-ordination Agency of the Japanese government. Since the definition differs from that in other countries, such comparisons tend to be somewhat problematic.

In various statistical sources, Japan's unemployment rate also differs. According to the 'Employment Status Survey in 1992' conducted by the Management and Co-ordination Agency, 3.83 million people were out of work and seeking a job at the time of survey. This survey is conducted every five years and is more comprehensive and reliable than the monthly Labour Force Statistics.[3] More specifically, the survey found that these unemployed job seekers accounted for 5.5 per cent of the total labour force (Table 7.2). The figure implies that the use of more precise measures for

Table 7.2. Rate of unemployed job seekers by age, 1992

| | Employed | | Unemployed job seekers millions | Rate of unemployed job seekers | |
	Total millions	Employees millions		(%)a	(%)b
TOTAL M/F	65.76	52.58	3.83	5.51	6.79
Men	38.78	32.05	1.25	3.13	3.76
15–19	0.91	0.87	0.24	20.54	21.23
20–9	7.53	7.13	0.36	4.57	4.80
30–9	7.84	6.99	0.10	1.30	1.45
40–9	9.66	8.07	0.09	0.89	1.07
50–9	7.70	6.11	0.11	1.40	1.75
60+	5.16	2.87	0.36	6.49	11.09
Women	26.98	20.53	2.58	8.73	11.16
15–19	0.81	0.79	0.25	23.80	24.21
20–9	5.98	5.70	0.61	9.25	9.66
30–9	4.65	3.72	0.56	10.80	13.14
40–9	7.11	5.44	0.57	7.45	9.51
50–9	5.24	3.57	0.38	6.80	9.67
60+	3.20	1.31	0.20	5.86	13.21

Notes a Rate of Unemployed Job Seekers = Unemployed Job Seekers / (Total Employed + Unemployed Job Seekers)
b Employees' Rate of Unemployed Job Seekers = Unemployed Job Seekers / (Employees + Unemployed Job Seekers)

Source: Management and Co-ordination Agency, 'Employment Status Survey', 1992.

[3] The Employment Status Survey is a detailed survey on employment conditions conducted every five years by the Management and Co-ordination Agency of Japan. The survey samples

Table 7.3. Unemployment according to monthly Labour Force Statistics, 1992

| | Employed | | Unemployment | Unemploy-ment rate | Employees' Unemploy-ment rate |
	Total (millions)	Employees (millions)	(millions)	(%)[a]	(%)[b]
TOTAL M/F	64.36	51.19	1.42	2.16	2.70
Men	38.17	31.45	0.82	2.10	2.54
Women	26.79	19.74	0.60	2.19	2.95

Notes: [a] Unemployment rate = Unemployment / (Total employed + Unemployment).
[b] Employees' Unemployment Rate = Unemployment / (Employee + Unemployment).

Source: Management and Co-ordination Agency, 'Annual Report on Labour Force', 1992.

unemployment renders a 'true' rate of unemployment in Japan higher than the 2–3 per cent 'wholly' unemployed rate. Taking the 5.5 per cent jobless-ness rate into account, one could argue that the perception that Japanese-style employment practices have significantly contributed to the better performance of the labour market in Japan has been exaggerated.[4]

Table 7.2 also lists the joblessness by gender and age, defined in the Employment Status Survey 1992 as the share of unemployed job seekers in the total labour force. Except for the age group over 60, the rates for women are higher than those for men. Specifically, the rates for women hover at about the same rate, except for women under 20. In contrast, the rate for men dips at the 30–59 age group to only 1–2 per cent. These age groups typically have significant expenditures for housing and education to support their families. It is important to keep these people employed to ensure social stability, and in Japan some executives even feel they are per-sonally responsible for maintaining these jobs.

approximately 330,000 households consisting of a total of 830,000 people. In the Survey, the employed are defined as those who maintain regular income-earning jobs. The employed include family members who work in family businesses, and secondary workers. The unem-ployed are defined as those who do not have regular jobs (including those working on a tem-porary basis). The unemployment data consist of both those who do and those who do not desire to work. Those who desire to work include both those who are and those who are not seeking jobs at the time of the survey. The Labour Force Report is a monthly survey that sam-ples approximately 40,000 households and 100,000 people. The Report defines the employed as those who work at least one hour for a job that brings compensation during the last week of the month. The unemployed are those who did not work for more than one hour but are eligible for work and searched for a job during the last week of the month.

[4] Alternative unemployment indicators also suggest that Japan's rate of unemployment is understated in the Monthly Labour Force Report. If one uses U-7 as an indicator, which includes discouraged workers in the numerator and denominator, the rate for Japan was 7.2% in Feb. 1990, compared with 7.9% in the USA (Sorrentino 1993: 6). According to the Bureau of Census of the Management and Co-ordination Agency, this unemployment rate (U-7) stood at 8.9% in Japan, surpassing that for the US of 8.8% in Feb. 1994.

Male workers in these age groups comprise the core of the lifetime employment practice. If the jobless rate in these age groups were to rise to the same level as that for other age groups, it would probably mean the end of the lifetime employment system as it is known today. Except for the above-mentioned 'core' groups, the labour force is highly mobile in Japan owing to the fairly high jobless rate for other age groups, which stands at nearly 10 per cent.[5]

The Externalization of the Labour Market in Japan

To fully grasp the fluidity of the labour markets and the true extent of life-time employment, one has to look into job transfer and job-leaving. The Employment Status Survey of 1992 shows that those workers who had been employed by the same employer for more than a year—*continuous employees*—stood at 46.16 million. It also shows that those who had worked for a different employer a year before—*job transfers*—stood at 2.78 million. Those who were working at the time of the survey but had not worked a year before—*new workers*—were 3.56 million. Those who were not working but had been a year before—*job leavers*—were 2.34 million.

The *rate of job transfer* is the ratio of job transfers to the total number of workers a year before, and the *rate of job-leaving* is the ratio of job leavers to the total number of workers a year before. The *number of workers a year* before, which is the sum of continued workers, job transfers, and job leavers less new workers, stood at 47.72 million. In 1992, the rate of job transfer was 5.8 per cent and the rate of job leaving was 4.9 per cent. The sum of the 'annual' job transfer rate and the 'annual' job leaving rate was 10.7 per cent.

This annual rate of job transfer and leaving (ARJTL) of 10.7 per cent may be surprisingly high, if one believes that lifetime employment is a common practice in Japan. This unexpectedly higher ARJTL is partly due to a large increase in part-time workers during the 1980s. In 1987 the rate of job transfer for regular workers was 4.9 per cent, while that for part-timers was 13.0 per cent: a big margin of difference. In 1982 the rate of job transfer was 3.5 per cent and the rate of job-leaving was 5.7 per cent. While job transfers increased sharply, job-leaving declined during the ten years from 1982 to 1992.

It may not be appropriate to assess the long-term unemployment trend based on the above changes because these two ratios are affected by the short-term balance between supply and demand in the labour market. For example, the rate of job transfer may rise owing to better job opportunities during a favourable business environment; the rate of job leaving might decline because workers can easily transfer to a new job. However, when

---

[5] Note that this argument excludes in-house unemployment that will presumably become more problematic during 1995.

business conditions are unfavourable, fewer workers but more employers will seek job transfers or leaving. On average, job-leaving is more sensitive than job transfer to fluctuations in the business cycle: the rate will decline when in a boom, and vice versa. Therefore, the economic conditions in 1992, when the job-leaving ratio declined, were far better than those in 1982. While the job transfer ratio is generally more independent of business conditions, it will rise during a boom because transfers made by employees' choice are typically more sensitive to such economic factors as wages than are transfers initiated by employers during a boom. The latter is all the more the case as the Japanese management style tends to disfavour personnel cuts. As a result, the transfer ratio rose between 1982 and 1992. Thus these two ratios tend to offset each other's reaction to business conditions.

Calculated independently of the business cycle, however, the ARJTL rose from 9.2 per cent to 10.7 per cent during the period 1982–92, with the ARJTL at 11.8 per cent in 1987, out of which the ARJT was 5.6 per cent and the ARJL was 6.3 per cent. The job transfer rate, which is less affected by business conditions, has consistently risen from 3.5 per cent in 1982, to 5.6 per cent in 1987 and to 5.8 per cent in 1992. Therefore one can perhaps spot a gradually increasing mobility in the Japanese labour market.

A closer look at the behaviour of the ARJTL offers an impression about another characteristic of the labour market in Japan (Figures 7.4 and 7.5).

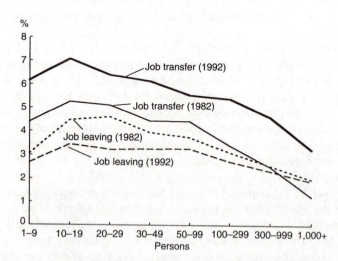

Fig. 7.4.   Rate of job transfer and leaving by company size (men)

Source: Management and Co-ordination Agency, Employment Status Survey; 1982, 1992.

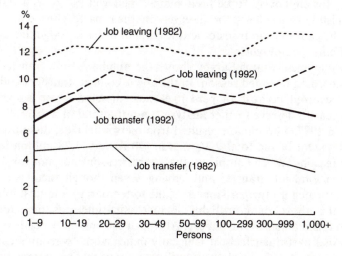

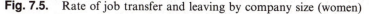

Fig. 7.5.   Rate of job transfer and leaving by company size (women)

Source: Management and Co-ordination Agency, Employment Status Survey; 1982, 1992.

These graphs attempt to determine a long-term trend by depicting the ARJT and ARJL by gender and by company size in 1982 and 1992. Both for transfers and for leaving, the ratios for women are higher than those for men. This is probably because part-timers account for a larger share of the female work-force. Notice also that the leaving ratio for women is particularly high. The ratios for men tend to decline as the company size increases, while such a tendency is clearly not visible for women. Nevertheless between 1982 and 1992 the transfer rate increased while the leaving rate declined, regardless of gender or company size. There was little change in the ARJTL for women because the rise in the transfer ratio almost offset the decrease in the leaving ratio (15.7 per cent in 1982 to 16.3 per cent in 1992 in total). In contrast, the ARJTL for men rose as the transfer ratio increased by much greater than the decline in the leaving ratio (6.0 per cent to 7.4 per cent in total).

   In sum, there was a more swift shift toward increasing mobility of the labour market for men than for women in the 1980s in Japan. This is probably because male rather than female employment *had* in fact been less mobile in Japan.

The Ratio of Lifetime Employment

The practice of 'lifetime' employment is not dictated on any written contract but is a *de facto* permanent job security under which there is little possibility for employees to be fired against their will except as a result of serious mistakes, accidents, or diseases on their part. Thus one should examine the cause of job transfer and leaving in order to judge the validity of this 'lifetime' employment.

The Employment Status Survey shows the number of job transfers and leaving according to stated reason. In the above context, transfers and leaving that occurred because of personnel cuts, dissolution, or bankruptcy would appear to deserve further analysis. Out of a total of 2.78 million job transfers in 1992, 1.86 million resulted from personnel cuts, dissolution, or bankruptcy. Out of the total 2.34 million job leavers, 1.28 million left for the same reasons. When combined, these three reasons account for 6.1 per cent of the total job transfer and leaving. Even though there is a more appropriate category for part-timers—'due to temporary and unstable type of job'—the above data probably include part-timers as they too can answer in this manner to the Survey. Although the answer depends on how an individual part-timer feels, it is usually indicated as 'personnel cut', for the majority of part-timers do not work on an unstable temporary basis in Japan.

Therefore the number of job transfers and leaving due to personnel cuts, dissolution, and bankruptcy has been small even when part-timers are included. Figure 7.6 depicts these data categorized by gender and company

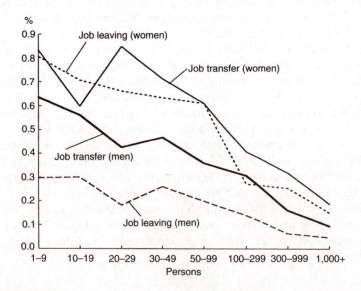

Fig. 7.6. Rate of job transfer and leaving caused by personnel cuts, dissolution, and bankruptcy

Source: Management and Co-ordination Agency, Employment Status Survey; 1992.

size. First, one finds a large gender gap for both transfers and leaving, with lower rates for men—in particular, the job-leaving rate for men was about one-half that for women. Secondly, the larger the company, the lower these rates. The ratio for women dropped sharply when the number of employees exceeded 100; the ratio for men in firms of over 300 workers was only 0.06 per cent. These data suggest that job transfers and leaving due to 'personnel cuts, dissolution, and bankruptcy' are rare occurrences in firms with over 100 workers.

As a result, lifetime employment exists in Japan even without its explicit written provision. In particular, those men who work for companies with over 300 employees were seldom forced to leave as a result of personnel cuts: the ratio of unwilling leavers was below 0.1 per cent. It is then precisely the *de facto* lifetime employment provision that has provided such employees with perfect job security. For firms with over 100 workers, 46.6 per cent of private employees are covered by this *de facto* provision; in contrast, for firms with over 300 workers, this figure for men falls to only 23.0 per cent of private employees in Japan. In other words, the rate of job transfer and leaving is considerably higher for employees in small and medium-sized firms, with 'perfect' lifetime employment generally being a practice only for male employees of large corporations. None the less, this practice was still in effect in 1992 according to the Employment Status Survey.

Facts of the Nenko *Wage*

A typical *nenko* wage system provides a worker with a status and a salary that depend primarily on the length of employment at that company rather than the productivity of the worker. What does *nenko* mean in Japanese? The word itself consists of two parts: *nen* and *ko,* the former meaning age and the latter contribution. *Nen* sometimes means the length of service for a company, instead of the age. Some argue that the *nenko* wage system is not based solely on seniority but also reflects the productivity of each worker because bonuses, salaries, and promotions vary with each worker in accordance with contribution to the company even under the same length of service. In addition, the length of service is an important factor in calculating performance because it enhances a worker's company-specific skills. This in turn gives grounds for the argument that the *nenko* wage system is actually based on performance rather than age and length of service.

To test the extent of the *nenko* wage system, the following sections look into wages according to the duration of work, based on the 'Wage Census'—Basic Survey on the Wage Structure. Figures 7.7 and 7.8 compare the regular monthly income, which does not include overtime, bonus, or other temporary payment, by age group for male workers in manufacturing firms with over 1000 employees.[6] Since most do not change company

---

[6] This enables us to compare wages irrespective of gender, sector, and company size.

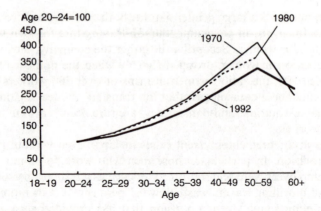

Fig. 7.7. The 'wage curve': white-collar workers by age (manufacturing, with over 1,000 employees, men)

Note: Regular monthly payroll of male college graduates.

Source: Ministry of Labour, Wage Census.

since their employment as college graduates owing to lifetime employment, the age usually corresponds to the length of service, in particular for large companies. In addition, in most cases a transferred worker receives a similar salary to that of workers of the same age in the new company. Thus, age is a better measurement for *nenko* than length of service.

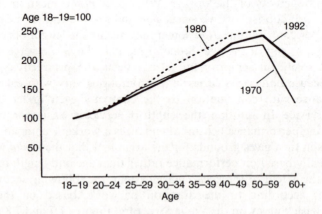

Fig. 7.8. The 'wage curve': blue-collar workers by age (manufacturing, with over 1,000 employees, men)

Note: Regular monthly payroll of male college graduates.

Source: Ministry of Labour, Wage Census.

The curves in Figures 7.7 and 7.8 indicate the relative level of wages for each age group—so-called wage curves. These wage curves show data for 1970, 1980, and 1992 to see the changes over time. The data for white-collar workers—managerial, clerical, and technical jobs—and blue-collar workers—production jobs—are based on wages for each category of worker, namely college graduates and high-school graduates, respectively. The white-collar wage is indexed with that for the 20–24 age group and the blue-collar wage with that for the 18–19 age group.

The wage curve is steeper for white-collar than blue-collar workers; in other words, the age factor accounts for the wage difference more for white-collar than blue-collar workers. The peak wage, which is at age 50–9 for both types, was 3.2 times as high as that for the benchmark for the white-collar worker, while the ratio was only 2.3 times as high for the blue-collar worker in 1992. However, the wage curve has become less steep since 1970, when the peak wage was 4.0 times as high as the benchmark, with the ratio declining to 3.6 in 1980 and further to 3.2 in 1992. In contrast, the wage curve for blue-collar workers was flat in 1970, steeper in 1980, and gradually flattening out again throughout the decade to 1992, similar to the pattern for this latter time period for white-collar workers.

Figure 7.9 depicts the wage curve by company size based on the same

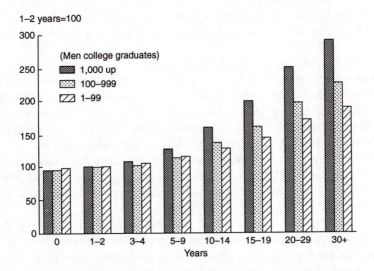

Fig. 7.9. The 'wage curve' by company: length of employment (manufacturing, men)

Note: Regular monthly payroll of male employees in manufacturing.

Source: Ministry of Labour, Wage Census; 1992.

Wage Census. One can observe that the wage curve becomes steeper as the size of company increases. For companies with more than 1,000 employees, manufacturing employees who have worked for over thirty years after college graduation are paid 2.9 times as much as employees with 1–2 years' experience. In contrast, for companies with less than 100 employees, workers with over thirty years of service earned only 1.9 times as much as employees with 1–2 years of service. These data indicate that the larger the company, the stronger the tendency for reliance on the *nenko* wage principle. Since the data in the previous section also indicate that the lifetime employment practice is more pervasive in larger companies, there is a clear complementary relationship between the *nenko* wage and lifetime employment.

MERITS AND DRAWBACKS OF THESE EMPLOYMENT PRACTICES

The lifetime employment practice has produced social stability and safety, with companies absorbing excessive employment internally for a short time. For workers, the 'job security' that is implicitly assured by lifetime employment is highly valued and is acceptable as a substitute for wages. If the managerial objective of a company is explicitly expressed as 'stable employment', the enhanced labour–management relationship stimulates the loyalty of workers and eventually improves the company's labour productivity. Although the lifetime employment has become an inevitable factor for the *Gemeinschaft*-oriented corporate management in Japan, it has several drawbacks.

First, the lifetime employment requires that the management explicitly list job security as one of its top priorities. Clearly, however, this commitment may conflict with other priorities such as maximizing corporate profits. In particular, protecting job security tends to be inconsistent with maximizing the rate of return on equity. Under lifetime employment, a stock company tends to become controlled by its employees and thus the interest of shareholders has often been practically neglected. Since a stock company essentially belongs to its stockholders and not to the employees, these practices would be a violation of the fundamental function of stock companies.

Where lifetime employment is in control, companies have difficulty adjusting swiftly to changes in the managerial environment because the organization has become inflexible as the employment adjustment mechanism is severely limited. Large companies often dispatch workers to smaller group companies both on a temporary and on a permanent basis to secure jobs for those workers. As a result, large companies have to maintain good relations with several small *keiretsu* companies to achieve permanent job security and so the efficiency of management may be sacrificed.

For those smaller companies, accepting workers from the larger companies in turn deprives them of the right of independent management and ability to pursue the most efficient allocation of human resources for the company. In addition, lifetime employment has formed a natural barrier for other domestic or foreign companies because the practice has internalized labour markets within the large corporations. Most foreign companies entering the Japanese market have therefore faced difficulty in recruiting appropriately qualified human resources in Japan because good prospects rarely come out of the closed internalized market of large corporations or corporate groups in Japan. The closed nature of the lifetime employment system, along with geographic and language barriers, might also account for the small share of Japanese workers in many international public organizations. In the face of rapid globalization world-wide, this unique internalized labour market tends to create friction both inside and outside Japan.

Merits and Drawbacks of the Nenko *Wage*

Since the *nenko* wage has been perceived as benefiting both companies and workers, it has been in effect for a long time in Japan. Workers tend to welcome the pattern that under the *nenko* system wages consistently rise until their forties or fifties because their living expenses peak during those years as expenditure for housing and education for their children are also high. It may therefore be desirable for workers to be paid in accordance with their living expenses. In other words, companies undertake savings and spending plans on behalf of each worker that are consistent with each employee's life cycle. The worker does not have to make a precise financial plan because the company largely takes over this function. In addition, a large number of workers do not worry about housing which in most cases the companies provide. Neither do workers have to report their income and pay taxes themselves to the tax bureau, as the company does so on their behalf, with workers receiving their salaries on an after-tax basis. Thus most workers can concentrate on work without worrying about troublesome tax-reporting and a long-term household financial plan. Similarly, the government can save on clerical work and the number of tax collectors because companies pay income taxes directly to the government in advance. As a result, most workers rely heavily on the company, which in fact carries quite a burden in handling tax-reporting and the like for its employees and in saving the government time; this is a substantial cost for companies. However, companies can benefit from the system because they can better ensure that employees do not run into serious financial problems and thereby indirectly damage the company. Society itself benefits from this built-in income stabilizer.

Although there is some competition for promotion and a slight but consistent difference in the speed of promotion, most employees had been provided with a certain position and treatment by the company that is largely consistent with their length of service. This provided employees and their families with some comfort, which led to loyalty and diligence on their part. Since short-term success and high performance do not fully translate into immediate promotion, a time lag between the evaluation of workers' performance and their reward naturally exists. This lengthy time lag leads to long-term competition among workers, which in turn provides the incentive to work hard, as workers know that they are in competition with each other for the top positions over the long term. Moreover, workers can afford to risk doing something unknown because of this longer time lag to allow for their recovery in the company.

Furthermore, this long-term competitive relationship also allows the company to evaluate the potential, capability, consistency, and long-term stability of workers more thoroughly. Even while the efforts by workers are not remarkable in the short term and become so only after several years, those contributions are still likely to be properly evaluated in the long term. Both the companies and Japanese society traditionally esteem such hidden efforts as a truly heroic deed. The long-term competitive relationship is consistent with this cultural aspect.

The merit of the *nenko* wage system for the company, then, is first that it can defer high salary payments and instead utilize these funds at its command. The tax deductibility of special types of internal funds—for example, retirement funds—provides the company (as well as its employees) with the incentive to set these funds aside for future use. So long as the fund is guaranteed to be paid to the worker in the future, workers benefit from this tax-deductible in-house savings fund. Secondly, such lending by the worker to the company would all be cancelled if the worker were to quit the company, therefore making it difficult for workers to quit and abandon the lending before redeeming their right to be paid. Such in-house savings practices have had the effect of workers being trapping by the company. The more efficient the worker, the larger the amount of the savings and in parallel the growing 'power of hostage'. This works as an effective power to keep capable people in the company.[7]

In contrast, the *nenko* wage system has several clear drawbacks for both workers and employers. The deferred wage payment described above can also be viewed as compulsory in-house saving at the expense of the employees, who clearly cannot control the use of such funds. The effectual lending to the company raises the cost of job transfer because workers have to give up redeeming those funds when they quit the company. Further, if employees quit the company before having worked there for twenty years, the employee is in most cases neither entitled to the explicit company-specific pension plan nor the implicit in-house savings.

[7] This 'theory of hostages' is detailed in Williamson (1983).

This mechanism may in effect work as an infringement on the free right to choose one's occupation as assured by the Japanese constitution. For the company, the availability of young workers reduces the burden of the *nenko* wage system by reducing the share of labour falling within the responsibility of *nenko* and thus assures larger retained earnings. As the work-force ages, the share of labour costs rises and payments for retirement benefits exerts downward pressure on retained earnings. The company's financial position, then, largely depends on the demographic character of its work-force. If the retirement age were to rise, for example, as some have recommended, the company would be forced to reform its compensation plans and the companies' profits would probably be squeezed.

These drawbacks of the *nenko* system can be expected to emerge in the face of a rapidly ageing population in Japan. In particular, as the post-war baby boomers approach retirement age, the demerits will become self-evident. The slow-down in corporate growth reduces the hiring of new graduates, thus further raising the average age of employees and aggravating the problem. In addition, companies will be forced to extend the retirement age to 65 because the public pension programme is set to postpone step by step the start of payment from the present age of 60 to the age of 65. The negative impact of the *nenko* wage system is likely to mount.

It has become increasingly difficult for companies to keep the *nenko* system because the underlying conditions have been gradually disappearing: the population pyramid, a steady expansion of markets, and the continuous growth of companies. The *nenko* system creates problems with the globalization of companies: foreign companies in Japan can offer higher compensation for younger workers because they do not accumulate compulsory in-house savings in the form of the *nenko* wage. The Japanese firms face this challenge with the result of an outflow of younger workers who prefer being paid more earlier on in their working lives. Japanese firms operating overseas face similar problems because it is difficult to compete in the market under this inconsistent wage system; the wage structure is so different outside Japan that it is difficult for Japanese companies to globalize and for foreign companies to operate smoothly in Japanese markets.

Furthermore, it is questionable whether highly specialized skilled workers can fit into the Japanese post-war employment system, which was designed to promote general managerial workers who are highly homogenized in skills and who can be easily substituted without the company suffering a decline in its operations. The number of specialized technically skilled workers is likely to increase in the knowledge-based creative industries. The quality of jobs will continue to become more oriented towards knowledge and technology and to diversify in the near future. Under these circumstances the ongoing *nenko* wage system is highly likely to become outdated and dwindle. Inevitably the *nenko* wage system in Japan has been forced to transform itself in the face of an ageing work force, globalization, and a shift in the nature of work toward knowledge-intensive industries.

EMPLOYMENT PRACTICES IN THE FUTURE

The practice of long-term work for the same company has been protected and promoted by both companies and the government in Japan with a variety of social and economic institutional measures. Since these institutional factors, as Figure 7.10 shows, have supported the lifetime employment practice, the future of lifetime employment depends on these factors.

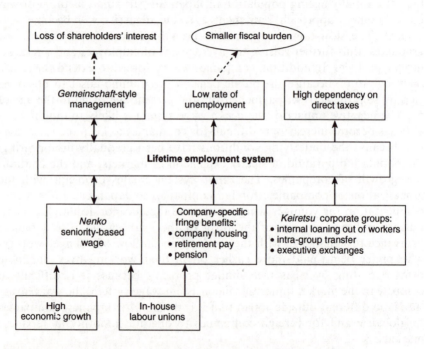

Fig. 7.10. The framework of employment practices in Japan

The *nenko* wage and company-specific fringe benefits have elevated the cost of job transfer for workers and function as a way to hold employees hostage. Most fringe benefits such as company housing, subsidized in-house housing loans, and retirement benefits are linked to the length of employment. As this linkage is often not linear but exponential, those benefits rapidly rise with the length of employment. For example, workers can receive their company pension in most cases only after they work for twenty years. If workers change job, they have to give up all the money they paid for the programme during their employment for that company. Public pension plans and unemployment benefits are also linked to the length of employment. The longer one works for the same company, the more beneficial these benefits become. Therefore, workers would be severely disadvantaged if lifetime employment were to suddenly be dismantled while these subsystems that support it remain intact.

The wage curve has already become less steep with the rapidly ageing population because the *nenko* wage becomes increasingly difficult to maintain as the baby boomers approach retirement age. The *nenko* wage is a supporting factor but not a necessary condition for lifetime employment: a company can maintain lifetime job security with a written long-term contract based on the productivity wage, so that wages are based on the productivity of the worker.[8] In this case, the cost to the worker of changing job is reduced, and, if fringe benefits become independent of seniority, workers will have more flexibility to transfer to other jobs. Since the *nenko* wage and employee benefits have the effect of holding the worker hostage by the company, labour mobility is likely to increase when the *nenko* wage becomes less dominant, even if companies maintain their management policy of lifetime employment.

On the other hand, the *Gemeinschaft*-style of employment that targets permanent job security will become a serious burden to management. In particular, the managerial target will shift towards a more efficient use of capital and a higher return on investment as economic growth diminishes. Under these circumstances Japanese companies will need to review the *keiretsu* relationship that has supported lifetime employment and perhaps establish more efficient methods of corporate management. In addition, a more prominent competition (anti-trust) policy will enforce fairer operation of corporate groups.

Based on the above, lifetime employment is likely to fade as the *nenko* wage shifts towards the productivity wage and as both private and public fringe benefits become more neutral to the length of employment. These shifts would externalize the labour market in Japan, making it more open and more fluid in the near future. This would stimulate the inter-sectoral and international exchange of human resources, which would, first, help private businesses become more creative and innovative, which in turn will stimulate private business to change its management and employment style. Jobs will rapidly diversify because the sectoral structure of the economy has shifted towards knowledge, service, and R&D-related industries, which would in turn force the multiplicity of employment and work in the labour market in Japan.

Secondly, tax revenues largely depend at present on income taxes that are

---

[8] The potential obstacles are Article 626 of the Private Law that prohibits employment contracts from exceeding five years, and Article 14 of the Labour Standards Law that restricts labour contracts from exceeding one year.

paid directly by companies; corporate policies ensuring high employment have supported this system. Once the high-employment policy changes, however, tax revenues will automatically decline while expenses for unemployment benefits will rise. To avoid a drastic deterioration of the fiscal balance, Japan has to modify elements of its tax structure, such as the consumption tax, so that it becomes more neutral to the level of employment.

Thirdly, a more liquid employment system inevitably will cause more frictional unemployment. Thus such programmes as re-educating workers and promoting smooth job transfers would be necessary, in addition to better infrastructure for employment information.

REFERENCES (* DENOTES THAT THE ORIGINAL IS IN JAPANESE)

Abraham, K. G., and Houseman, S. N. (1993), *Job Security in America: Lessons from Germany* (Washington Brookings Institution).

Imai, K., and Komiya, R. (1989) (eds.), *Corporations in Japan* (Tokyo: University of Tokyo Press).*

Inoki, T., and Higuchi, Y. (1995), *The Employment System and Labour Market in Japan*, Contemporary Economic Study Series, 9 (Tokyo: Nikkei).*

Itami, H., Kagono, T., and Itoh, M. (1993) (eds.), *The System of Corporations in Japan* (Tokyo: Yuhikaku).*

Iwaki, H. (1990), 'Facing the Labour Shortage in Japan', *NRI Quarterly Economic Review,* 20: 37–54.

—— (1992), 'Market Mechanisms in Japan (I): Openness and Efficiency of Japanese Corporate Groups', *Tokyo Club Papers,* 6: 166–219.

—— (1994), 'Markets and Corporations: Creative Distractions of Japanese Principles', *Zaikai Kansoku,* 2: 2–33.*

Nomura, M. (1994), *Lifetime Employment* (Iwanami).*

OECD (1973), *Manpower Policy in Japan* (Paris: OECD).

Okazaki, T., and Okuno, M. (1993), *The Roots of the Modern Economic Systems in Japan*, Contemporary Economic Study Series, 6 (Tokyo: Nikkei).*

Sorrentino, C. (1993), 'International Comparisons of Unemployment Indicators', *Monthly Labour Review,* 116: 3–24.

Study Group on the Japanese Employment System (1995), *Facts and Perspectives of the Japanese-Style Employment System*, Mid-Term Report of the Study Group on the Japanese Employment System, March.*

Williamson, O. E. (1983), 'Credible Commitments: Using Hostages to Support Exchange', *American Economic Review,* 83: 519–40.

8. The Death of a Keynesian Europe? Prospects for Expansion and Political Constraints

Grahame F. Thompson

The death of a Keynesian Europe is a story that has yet to be fully told. An intriguing feature of European economic history since the mid-1970s remains the demise of the commitment to full employment as a policy goal by the emerging continental superpower, the European Union (EU), just as its own economies were being swept first into a recession and then on into what has proved to be at most a hesitant recovery. As we shall see, three interconnected features are relevant here: the institution-building associated with an internal market, the advent of Euro-monetarism via the role unwittingly assigned to the Bundesbank as guarantor of a European anti-inflationary policy, and finally the turn towards 'international competitiveness' as the criterion for judging the effectiveness of economic performance.

The effort made by the Commission of the European Communities ('the Commission') first to launch and then to consolidate advances towards an integrated European market undoubtedly diverted attention from the issue of European employment. That project required a supreme political effort, and it remains a testament to the then Commission President Jacques Delors that, at a primitive level at least, the European economies are now so integrated that they are virtually inseparable. Despite the still formidable unresolved problems associated with monetary and full economic union, which threaten to disrupt a full integration, the EU economies will remain to all practical intents and purposes a 'single market'. But such a political project was secured at some cost. This was registered in a lack of attention to the emerging twin problems of unemployment and competitiveness. Since these two features are themselves so intertwined, they will serve to organize the main thrust of the discussion that follows.

However, it should not be thought that a broadly Keynesian approach towards the development of the European economy has been totally absent since the mid-1970s; it was just completely marginalized. Thus the call for a co-ordinated European expansion by Blanchard, Dornbusch, and Layard (1986) fell on deaf ears. They argued that the European employment problem did not have a single cause, and in particular that it was not a real wage problem, so cuts in real wages were not the appropriate centre-piece for policy action. Rather, in most part unemployment was the result of the monetary and fiscal policies designed to fight accelerating inflation, so that the expansion of aggregate demand along with an incomes policy was the correct response in an attempt to render more favourable the trade-off between recovery and disinflation. Under the circumstances of the mid-1980s, they suggested, the fiscal and monetary position of the UK and Germany in particular would have enabled them to have led the co-ordinated recovery.

Similar sentiments pervaded the analysis of Cripps and Ward (1994), reflecting upon the continuing recession in the early 1990s. Stressing the need for monetary as well as fiscal co-ordination, they called for effective employment creation programmes as a central feature of a strategy for European recovery. Cripps and Ward criticized the results of the Edinburgh Summit of December 1992 as representing only a token gesture in pulling the European economy out of recession.

An interesting feature of this relative marginalization of the broad Keynesian framework for tackling unemployment can be seen in an important UK left-of-centre think-tank report: *Social Justice: Strategies for National Renewal* (IPPR, 1994). The authors of this report call for a 'supply-side socialism' emphasizing investment in education and training, and 'social justice' in the provision of welfare service and the conduct of civic duties and responsibilities, but fail to provide for a comprehensive organization of aggregate demand expansion to support these other two features.[1] Thus one of the main planks of an otherwise admirable policy for halting the UK's continued slide down the route of a failing social and economic order is missing. These examples of lost opportunities, lack of political will, and shortcomings in analysis could easily be extended for the European arena more generally.

While accounting for such policy timidity cannot be fully explored here, its main characteristics and implications form the rationale for the following analysis.

THE EDINBURGH SUMMIT INITIATIVES: GROWTH AND EMPLOYMENT

A key moment in the European Commission's rediscovery of unemployment as a problem was the Edinburgh summit of late 1992. This launched the Commission's subsequent refocusing upon employment and growth issues after the initial successful 'completion' of its integration programme.

---

[1] Sustained discussion of the role of aggregate demand gets just four pages (162–5) in a book of over 400 pages.

This summit involved a number of initiatives, including increased public expenditure, promotion of private investment, support for small and medium-sized businesses, additional training, wage moderation, and structural reforms (Commission of the European Communities 1993: 191). The bottom line of these initiatives, however, was an expected ECU30 billion stimulus to EU aggregate demand—via increased public and private investments—spread over a number of years (*European Economy* 1993*a*: 116).[2] The question thus becomes the possible economic consequences of such an expansionary injection.

Here the Commission looked to its QUEST macroeconomic model to simulate the consequences of the proposed initiatives and we concentrate upon that analysis here.[3] Examining the QUEST model is important because of its role in EU policy determination. It embodies the Commission's philosophy on matters macroeconomic (though it would be an exaggeration to say that policy was solely determined by the QUEST framework). As well as being centrally employed in simulating the possible effects of the Edinburgh summit initiatives, the model was used extensively in respect of forecasting the economic benefits to be derived from the single-market programme. The assumptions behind this model are discussed later in the chapter.

There are two main stages to the analysis conducted here. The first part involves investigating combinations of wage moderation and increases in investment. It relates to recommendations made by the Commission to the Council of Ministers at the end of 1993, the full extent of which is reported in *European Economy* (1993*c*). In fact this was part of a restrictive set of policy suggestions based upon budget consolidation, stability-oriented monetary policy, and wage moderation. The three scenarios explored here are: (1) a 'no policy change' option acting as a base-line case; (2) wage moderation plus increased private investment; and (3) the wage moderation and private investment plus the addition of public investment. The results of the analysis are shown in Figure 8.1. The effects of the scenarios on real unit labour costs, on employment, and on real output are computed separately.[4]

Two conclusions follow from this exercise. The first is that the two active

[2] This sum was subsequently pared down by the Copenhagen ECOFIN meeting called to endorse the 1992 'Declaration on Promoting Economic Recovery in Europe', and it is difficult to judge exactly how much real additional expenditure will eventually be involved (Dreze and Malinvaud 1994: 92).

[3] This analysis partly relies upon runs of the QUEST model conducted in Sept. 1994. The results included here are taken from the Open University TV programme 'Modelling in the Long Run' associated with course D216, *Economics and Changing Economies*. The exercise is supplemented by the reports in *European Economy* (1993*b*; 1993*c*).

[4] Note that these are illustrative simulation exercises; they are not meant to show actual forecasts. The wage moderation assumptions for scenario (2) are that a social consensus is voluntarily reached that restricts real wage costs to 1 percentage point below the growth of real labour productivity between 1994 and 2000, but that an increased wage moderation doubles the moderation for the two years 1994 and 1995.

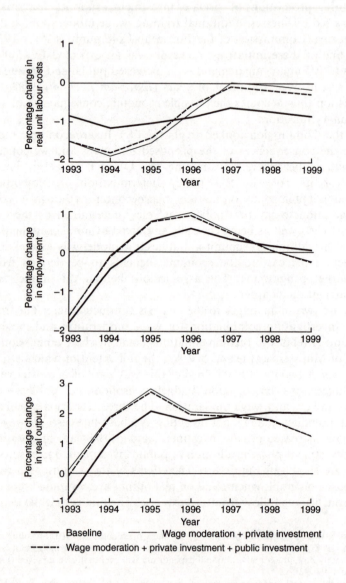

Fig. 8.1.   Investment and wage moderation simulations

Base line
Wage moderation + private investment
Wage moderation + private investment + public investment

Source: Commission Services.

policy moves improve the situation against the do-nothing case, though the effects of these seem to disappear quickly and towards the end of the simulated period a worse situation than the do-nothing case emerges. This is mainly because the initial real wage moderation stimulates a subsequent wage acceleration. The implication is that fresh rounds of wage moderation and investments are needed. Secondly, the 'plus public investment' scenario does not add much to the 'wage moderation plus private investment' option; in fact most of the work (good or bad) is done by the wage moderation effects rather than either of the two investment effects. The levels of new investment envisaged by the Edinburgh summit make some, but not much, difference to the employment position when wage moderation is imposed upon the model.

More favourable results for the Edinburgh investment initiatives were forthcoming from the Commission's earlier simulation exercise, which forms the second strand to this analysis. This recognized the initial dampening effects of wage moderation on the growth of aggregate demand. The growth of disposable income is immediately reduced by real wage moderation, which only after a lag produces favourable growth, inflation, and employment effects. Overall this simulation assumed a number of key favourable developments in the domestic European and international economies; 'voluntary' wage moderation along the lines of that achieved between 1982 and 1989 (that is, very low real wage growth, at 1 per cent below any productivity growth, followed by favourable investment growth from the consequent enhanced profitability—essentially the same as assumed for Figure 8.1); the full ECU30 billion additional investment spread evenly over three years from 1993 to 1995; favourable international developments including the successful completion of the Uruguay Round of trade talks, improved multinational economic co-ordination (producing constant real exchange rates after 1994), and moderate growth in the rest of the OECD economies (*European Economy* 1993*b*: 110–17).

The aggregated impact of these policy initiatives and favourable external outcomes on the EU rate of unemployment is shown in Figure 8.2 (scenario 0 is the no policy change case, scenario 2 sums the aggregate changes). In Table 8.1 the differences between various economic indicators in 1993 and 2000 are shown. Clearly, the impacts here are significant: the unemployment rate falls from 10.6 per cent to as low as 4.3 per cent, the investment share climbs from 19.4 per cent of GDP to 24.2 per cent, and the growth rate climbs from 0.7 per cent to 3.8 per cent.

The differences between these two simulation exercises is revealing, since both were performed with the same underlying model. In fact they produce rather similar results up until the late 1990s. From then on the first set produces a rather rapid tailing off and even reversal of fortunes while for the second set the positive benefits continue. Clearly, it is the rise in the real unit labour costs between 1995 and 1997 that probably adversely affects the

Table 8.1. Growth scenarios for the European Union: 1993 compared to 2000 (%)

	1993	2000
Real GDP growth rate		
Scenario 0	0.7	2.1
Scenario 2	0.9	3.8
Investment share		
Scenario 0	19.4	20.4
Scenario 1	19.6	24.2
Unemployment rate		
Scenario 0	10.6	11.7
Scenario 2	10.5	4.3

Source: Adapted from *European Economy* (1993*b*: 117), table 6.

employment and output growth in the first set shown by Figure 8.1. In addition, the importance of wage moderation to these results indicates the key feature of how the labour market reaction is modelled within the QUEST framework. The Commission has stressed the importance of wage moderation to the whole exercise of simulating the effects of events like the Edinburgh summit.[5]

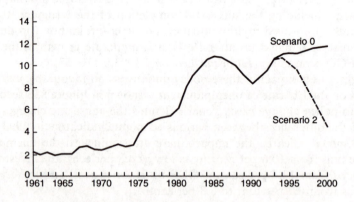

Fig. 8.2. EU unemployment rate, 1961–2000 (% of civilian labour force)
Source: *European Economy* (1993*b*), adapted from fig. 7, p. 112.

[5] Personal discussions. If nothing else these differing results testify to the politically sensitive nature of the Commission's economic policy analysis.

The Commission's QUEST model is described as 'a typical representative of the neoclassical-Keynesian synthesis' (*European Economy*, 1991*a*: 178). The supply side in this model introduces a potential GDP in addition to an actual GDP so that adjustment of supply may not be instantaneous, allowing for possible disequilibrium in the goods market to persist for some time. The production function defines potential output as the maximum technologically feasible output given the capital stock. Potential output is central to the basic dynamic behaviour of supply, since in the short run it relates productive capacity to aggregate demand, the difference between the two being the degree of capacity utilization. At one level capacity utilization plays a very significant role in the model because it acts as an indicator of demand pressure, as a counterpart on the demand side to the role played by the unemployment rate on the supply side. What matters for firms in assessing demand conditions is the utilization of the capital stock; inventory adjustments and investment in equipment are also determined by capacity utilization. When the level of the existing capital stock is not thought to be optimal because of changes in expected demand conditions, capital costs, or profitability, it is adjusted via investment in fixed capital to change potential output to meet these new conditions.

Employment is the other factor of production, with labour supply treated as exogenous in the model so that employment is determined largely by labour demand. Again, it is assumed that the short-run adjustment of employment to changes in actual output is not immediate, so that past employment levels exert an influence on present employment levels (via 'adjustment costs'). Given this proviso, labour demand is determined by a conventional neoclassical demand function where output, real wage costs, and an autonomous technology trend constitute the independent variables. In the longer term, actual employment adjusts to potential employment via the adjustment of actual output to potential output. The underlying production function is of the CES-type.

The demand sector is equally conventional as the supply sector just outlined. It essentially describes a standard neoclassical-Keynesian IS function (European Economy 1991*a*: 192). This demand sector includes an investment in equipment equation which in determining the capital stock provides the link between the supply and demand sides of the model. Furthermore, through the deployment of an accelerator-type mechanism, it explicitly links the supply measures to the volume of GDP. The consumption function is quite conventional, government consumption and investment are modelled together, and private equipment, construction, and inventory investments are separated out as far as is possible. In general these investment functions have a rate of interest term, a demand term, and a profit rate as their main arguments. Net trade is also modelled along traditional lines.

The QUEST model is, then, similar to all standard macroeconomic models of the neoclassical-synthesis type, and thus suffers from all the well-known shortcomings of those models. One of the great conundrums for these models is the effects of fiscal and monetary policy on the price level, and the effects of wages on prices. Here there is nothing unusual to report on the QUEST model or its simulation properties. An increase in public investment, for instance, provides a direct impulse to the demand for goods and services and has indirect effects which depend on the reaction of wages and prices to the change in demand conditions. In the longer term, prices also react to the change in supply conditions, that is, to the addition to the capital stock due to increased investment. Higher utilization rates have an upward effect on prices in the short term, and the reaction of wages to changes in unemployment is also fast, though employment itself is slow to adjust to the rise in demand. Because of this the early-year effects of a rise in government investment have little impact on the price level. Any increase in demand for goods and services prompts an immediate acceleration in investment, causing the first-year impact on demand to be greater than the *ex-ante* increase of the government investment. Whilst consumption also rises (via higher real wages—though wage moderation also dampens this, as mentioned above), this adds little to domestic demand because of the lag in the response of private consumption to changes in real disposable income (which helps explain the moderate effect of the Edinburgh initiatives on the real unit labour costs in the early years of the simulation shown in Figure 8.1).

Of course, part of any increase in demand is directed towards foreign goods and services. The more open the economy, the greater the import leakages. For the larger EU countries, the elasticity of imports with respect to final demand (GDP + imports) is greater than 1, so imports rise even faster than does domestic demand.

One obvious problem with the adjustments properties that form the core of the QUEST model is that they revolve around capacity utilization, the differences between potential and actual demand with a given level of capacity, and the way in which levels of capacity utilization trigger longer-term changes. In fact, the relationship between capacity utilization and employment is a weak one; once a given level of capacity is installed with a particular technological vintage, it can be used more or less intensively without much change in employment levels. In addition, the position facing the EU by the mid-1990s was more one of a lack of capacity, not the existence or otherwise of 'excess capacity'. Capacity has been scrapped, so it is not even 'idle capacity'.[6] Given that firms in the QUEST model are

---

[6] Excess capacity is traditionally defined by the notion that a fixed amount of capital, k^*, is worked less intensively by a reduced amount of labour. Idle capacity, by contrast, arises when capital in use, k', is less than the planned fixed capital stock available k^*, so that idle capacity is measured by $(k^* - k')$, where $k' < k^*$. For the significance of these distinctions to the debate about Keynes's as opposed to neoclassical-synthesis notions of macroeconomic adjustment, see Brown (1991).

assumed to adjust their employment decisions in relation to the differences between actual and potential output/demand, the levels of employment in the model are crucially affected by a mechanism that is now not the main or most important one. Under conditions of an absolute lack of capacity (not excess or idle capacity) firms are presumably potentially less willing to expand employment, since to do so will require new investment and this is likely to be more costly than merely hiring labour to work existing capacity more fully or bringing idle capacity back into activity. The key feature for the medium to longer term, therefore, is the expansion of capacity via new investment. The question is how to provide the right incentives to encourage private investment on the one hand, and to bolster public investment on the other. The emphasis on wage moderation tended to overwhelm the positive effects of private and public investment in the simulations discussed above, but wage moderation may not now constitute the main problem. Indeed, the wage trends shown in Figure 8.1 seem to be slightly perverse. While for the wage moderation scenarios real unit labour cost changes are all less than 0 (or just above it), for the do-nothing scenario these hover around –1 per cent over the entire period.[7] What needs to be borne firmly in mind, therefore, is that investment affects both aggregate demand and aggregate supply (which seems to be in part at least recognized within the QUEST modelling framework). However, it implies that the demand sector and the supply sector should not be modelled autonomously; they are interdependent. A number of important conclusions follow for this.

The first is that concentrating on the role of investment has a key advantage. Any concern about a potential inflationary impact of a demand expansion if it takes the form of investment is misplaced. It can easily be demonstrated that there is no reason for the price level to rise if investment at the same time causes supply to adjust appropriately (Brown 1987). This is so even accepting the conventional framework of a very short-run aggregate supply and demand synthesis-type model (with any change in investment *both* the aggregate demand and the aggregate supply curves move out to the right). Secondly, the emphasis on the equilibrating properties of QUEST-type models (where things tend to revert continually to the initial state) diverts attention from issues of the economic environment necessary to provide a long-term sustainable upturn in the European economy. The results of the simulations imply the requirement of a continual set of similar policy impulses if the positive short-term effects produced are not to fade rapidly. We return to these issues in a moment.

The emphasis on the role of investment in this discussion is deliberate, since it downplays the importance of a purely labour-market adjustment for

---

[7] Clearly, this is based upon quite stringent *assumptions* about wage moderation in the future as expansion ensues, but the Commission stresses that this is no more than that actually *achieved* between 1982 and 1989.

the problem of employment. Conventional economic surveys of European unemployment devote surprisingly little space to investment issues (Bean 1994; CEPR 1995) and the relationship between investment and employment remains under-investigated in macroeconomic analysis. Exceptions are Bean (1989) and Rowthorn (1995). Bean shows how uncertainty is a key issue for the investment decision, easily dominating the cost of capital (these uncertainty issues seem to be rolled into the growth of final demand variable in the QUEST investment modelling framework, and not treated separately). But more importantly he shows how European unemployment rates have increased in relation to capacity utilization since the 1960s (Bean 1989: 22 fig. 3; and Bean 1994: 613 fig. 7), confirming the relative 'independence' of employment from the rate of capacity utilization. Rowthorn (1995) builds on this to press the argument that the unemployment problem in Europe revolves not so much around the utilization of a given capital stock as around the lack of capital stock—the 'capital gap'. Capital formation has declined in Europe since the 'golden age', and there is a strong relationship between capital investment and employment. According to Rowthorn's analysis capital formation has declined because the cost of capital has risen (real interest rates are at a historically high level) and profitability has declined and become more uncertain.

But despite the QUEST model's shortcomings in many respects, the investment simulation results are not unimportant. Indeed the effects shown in the figures and table are impressive, particularly if one takes into account the meagre provisions of the Edinburgh summit policy initiatives (the new investment envisaged, for instance, constituted about 0.5 per cent of EU GDP). The problem was the subsequent loss of momentum behind the original proposals. Thus perhaps more important than the shortcomings of the modelling techniques was the lack of political will to do more on the part of European political leaders. It is thus easy to overestimate the disadvantages of working with a conventional model.

An interesting feature of the period in which the main focus of EU community-building was still the completion of the integration project is that a quite different economic modelling strategy was experimented with. In parallel to the use of the QUEST model, other longer-term approaches to modelling were raised. These explored 'endogenous growth theory' and the 'long-wave approach'. In the Commission's Annual Economic Report for 1990–1 a discussion of new growth theory appears alongside the long-wave approach associated with the Kodratieff cycle. These were presented as constituting the two main ways the Commission was dealing with the possible growth effects of the integration process (*European Economy*, 1990*b*).

The two key documents that embody this emphasis on long-term growth are *One Market, One Money* (*European Economy* 1990*a*) and *The Economics of EMU* (*European Economy* 1991*b*). These explore the use of the new growth models that rely heavily upon the analysis of external economies of scale, which are aggregate economy-wide economies—the spill-overs and intermediate public goods that might emerge from the expansion induced by further integration.

Traditional (neoclassical) growth models of the Solow type assume decreasing or constant returns to scale so that any one-off increase in capital as a factor eventually comes up against decreasing returns to labour and a new steady-state growth rate is achieved. But if the economy displays economy-wide increasing returns this is not necessarily the case. The result will be continued dynamic growth (Winters 1995). It has been suggested that this could greatly increase the potential benefits from the one-off EU 1992 programme. Indeed, Baldwin suggested that the 'static' analysis of the Cecchini Report (*European Economy*, 1988) could have underestimated the beneficial effects by as much as between 300 per cent and 450 per cent (Baldwin 1989: 269).

These results emerge in the context of an endogenous growth model developed from an economy-wide Cobb–Douglas production function, which is 'dynamized' by an additional factor added to the coefficient of the capital variable. This long-term growth factor arises from endogenizing innovations and technical progress (which are otherwise specified as an exogenous time trend—indeed this is how technical progress is handled in the QUEST model equations).

In many ways the long-wave approach is the most unorthodox of the Commission's experiments in modelling, and it is also the most controversial. The controversy refers to the actual existence of such a cycle, though the Commission presentation insists that new statistical filtering techniques have provided conclusive evidence that a long-wave cycle of some fifty-year duration does indeed exist (*European Economy* 1990b: 96). The initiation of these cycles is associated with technological revolutions, clustered around innovations in processes and products. Each cycle is characterized by a new leading sector, the latest one being associated with the technological revolution in computer and information technologies which started in the 1970s. Tracing out the evolution of aggregate value added and profitability, sometimes also in respect to key sectors, for a number of leading European countries, the Commission argues that these add up to a co-ordinated upswing commensurate with a new long wave.

One point about the long-wave theory as described by the Commission is that it does not give any hard and fast empirical estimates of the extent and level of future GDP growth, unlike either the QUEST or external economy/new growth theory models. On the other hand it is a highly aggregated model like that of the new growth theory; it rather abstracts from the detail of comparative industrial structure in those economies included in its assessments. However, both new-growth theory and the long-wave theory produce very optimistic scenarios as far as the immediate growth prospects for Europe are concerned, though neither of them have anything specific to say about the employment implications of growth. In general the Commission is upbeat about the future for European growth in all the documents associated with the single market and economic union. Perhaps that is to be expected from an organization that has led the arguments in favour of ever greater European integration. But in a critical assessment Grahl and Thompson (1995) find these forecasts to be far too optimistic.

INTERNATIONAL 'COMPETITIVENESS'

In part, variations on these approaches to growth theory inform the third leg of this analysis of European employment prospects. Like many other official assessments of the international economy the Commission fully endorsed the notion of 'international competitiveness' as the criterion for the future economic performance of the European economy. Its White Paper *Growth, Competitiveness, Employment* (European Commission 1994) embodies the particular inflection of this adopted by the Commission. It contains a rather rambling analysis that lacks a clear focus. It more or less includes something on everything and something for everyone; the macro-economic framework, technology policy, human capital development, employment prospects, conditions for competitiveness, infrastructure investment, information highways, industrial-policy initiatives, labour-market flexibilities, environmental concerns, new development models, etc. all find a place and all are argued to add up to a 'way forward to the 21st century'. In fact the largest section is devoted to 'competitiveness' issues, though there is also a good deal of soul-searching about employment. Perhaps the key to the employment concerns shown by the document can be illustrated by Figures 8.3 and 8.4—similar to ones included in the White Paper. These data provide a sobering picture which almost speak for themselves; Europe is not providing jobs to the same extent as its main international rivals, and its unemployment levels have increased faster than theirs.

It is useful to contrast the EU's approach to international competitiveness with that of the UK. The title of the UK Government's White Paper issued around the same time as the EU document is *Competitiveness: Helping Business to Win* (HMSO 1994), which neatly illustrated the precise way in which the UK sees the future developing. The UK paper at least has the merit of being focused—it is 'business' that will win the international competitiveness race for Britain. Unemployment hardly gets a mention in the document (just two pages out of 163), where it is set in a congratulatory context of the success of the 'new flexibility' now characterizing the UK labour market.

The issue of 'flexibility' pervades the EU document as well, as it tends to do in all analyses of international competitiveness. Here the issue of com-

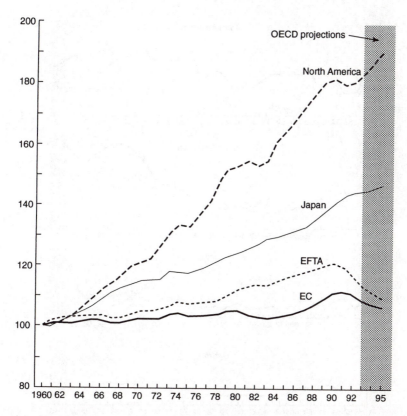

Fig. 8.3. Employment growth in OECD regions, 1960–1995 (Index 1960 = 100)
Source: OECD (1994*a*), adapted from fig. 8, p. 17.

parative real wages provides a key stage in the competitiveness argument, bringing in once again the role of wage moderation. It is trends like that shown in Figure 8.5 which have galvanized European policy makers. And it *is* very difficult to combat the type of argument about real wage moderation that inevitably flows from discussions of these kind of data, and that shown in Figures 8.3 and 8.4.

To do this we must take a brief look at the whole 'international competitiveness' debate. International competitiveness can be defined widely as the ability of a country to realize central economic policy goals, especially the growth of incomes, the growth of employment, and the control of inflation, without running into balance of payment difficulties. When it comes to operationalizing and measuring this, however, it is trends in the labour cost per unit of output relative to other nations (RULC) that

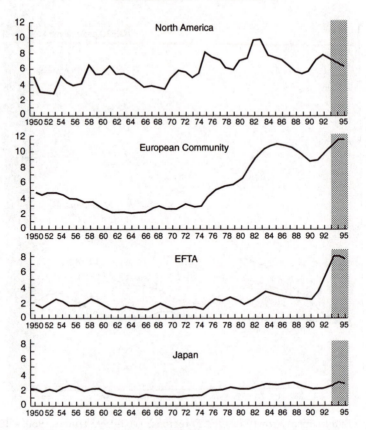

Fig. 8.4. Unemployment rates in OECD regions, 1950–1995 (%)
Source: OECD (1994*a*), adapted from fig. 2, p. 10.

becomes the main measure used to identify international competitiveness, and a variation on this measure is employed by the Commission.[8]

The problem with this measure (which is partly recognized by the Commission's own analysis—see *European Economy* 1994*a*: 116) is, however, that it is those countries with *deteriorating* RULC that have *maintained or increased* their trade surpluses on current account (e.g. Germany and Japan) while those with an *improving* RULC have sustained a continuing balance of trade deficit (e.g. the UK and the USA). This was the case during the 1960s and 1970s (Thompson 1987) and similarly over the period

[8] Unit labour costs in the manufacturing sector (ULCM)—calculated as the ratio of an index of manufacturing unit labour costs in the home country to the indices of trading partners' manufacturing unit labour costs, all expressed in a common currency; thus this latter part is an indicator of the real effective exchange rate, and adjusts the comparative unit labour costs for exchange rate changes (*European Economy* 1994*a*: 115).

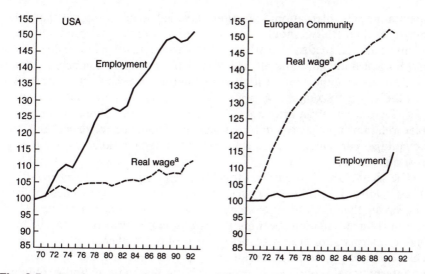

Fig. 8.5. Employment and real wages, USA and European Community (Index 1970 = 100)

Source: OECD (1994*b*), fig. 2.3, p. 64.

since 1983 (Thompson 1995). Thus those countries that were becoming *more* internationally competitive during these periods, measured in these terms, were doing *less well* in terms of their trade accounts than were those countries becoming *less* internationally competitive.[9]

It is evidence of this kind, which seems to be counter-intuitive, that has led to a series of criticisms of the RULC approach to measuring international competitiveness, and indeed to the notion that such competitiveness is of key importance.

The first set of criticisms relates to the idea that it may not be *cost* competitiveness that adequately accounts for a successful national economic performance. With this idea it is *non-price competition* that is thought the most important determinant of international success. Non-price issues involve a host of less tangible factors than hard cost or price factors. With respect to manufacturing, *quality* and *design* matter to purchasers as well as price. For capital and durable goods, *delivery dates* and *after-sales service* will be important; for non-durable goods and services it is *reliability* and *continuity of supply*. Along with *effective marketing*, these items are what drives non-price competitiveness.

The experiences of Japan between 1963 and 1975, with a rise in RULC and yet an expanded world market share and above average growth in national income, and Germany with a similar trend in RULC while broadly

[9] This paradox was first highlighted by Kaldor (1978).

maintaining its international position, have led some to suggest that other measures than RULC should be considered as more appropriate indicators of international success. Fagerberg (1988) argues that various indicators of technological advance and efficiency, and the ability to compete on delivery, are more important to long-term international competitiveness than just the ability to compete on price. Clearly, there is a limit to the way non-price factors can offset price ones, but at least it means there is a more complex relationship between international economic performance and cost advantage, particularly where that cost advantage is taken to mean wage cost advantage.

The second set of criticisms, though related to the first, are more radical. They involve the difference between notions of the competitiveness of firms and saying that a national economy can be assessed in a similar way. There is a fairly unambiguous meaning to firms' competitiveness. It can be measured in terms of productivity, prices, or profits (as where long-run average costs are below prices). It is tempting simply to transfer these measures into an international economic environment by looking at a nation's comparative aggregate productivity, its relative prices of international traded goods, and the balance on its trade account, etc. But Krugman (1994) has pointed out that firms 'export' virtually all of their output beyond the boundaries of their organization, while countries do not export the bulk of their output. The USA, the EU, and Japan, for instance, only export about 10–11 per cent of their respective GDPs, thus around 90 per cent meets a home demand which is not subject to the dictates of 'international competitiveness' (it involves domestic productivity pure and simple). Thus there is a radical difference between the competitiveness of a firm and that of a country, he argues.

But there are many important demonstration and learning effects of international trade for domestically oriented activity, so the two cannot be quite so easily isolated as Krugman would like (Prestowitz 1994). Krugman's argument is really one that wishes to reinstate comparative advantage as the main theoretical underpinning for international trade, against the 'competitive advantage' argument of the likes of Porter (1990) and others. There are currently three approaches towards modelling international trade: comparative advantage, competitive advantage, and new trade theory (the latter two are closely connected).[10] The key feature of the competitive advantage model is that it demotes *factor cost advantage* and international prices in the determination of international trade and national performance, and replaces it with an emphasis on *product-based advantage*. Product-based advantage itself is manifest in product differentiation and the rise of intra-industry trade. The theory of comparative advantage is most relevant for the exploitation of cost-based advantage, depending as it

[10] For a discussion of new trade theory in this context see Krugman (1987). The empirical results from new trade theory modelling are not particularly strong—see CEPR (1994).

does on the underlying social opportunity cost of factors of production. Competitive advantage is more closely associated with the success or otherwise of individual firms, and the exploitation of technologically driven innovations.

Problems begin when economies where the conditions for competitive advantage have matured and consolidated develop a strategy to try to re-exploit simple comparative advantages, which means they focus upon and re-emphasize cost-reduction. Instead of developing their resource base in terms of upgrading human skills, investing in training, infrastructure, communications, transport and public utilities, or promoting new product development and R&D capabilities, they retreat into a low labour-cost, low productivity, low value-added, 'sweatshop'-type flexibility in their production systems. This is to re-emphasize, perhaps unwittingly, the standardized manufacture of low-technology-based products at the expense of a differentiated high-technology product mix. The fact that the EU already 'specializes' in the weak-demand sectors relative to its main international rivals is warning enough of the potential consequences of such a strategy.[11]

Fortunately, the EU competitiveness strategy outlined in *Growth, Competitiveness, Employment* is not totally driven by the downward flexibility in wage cost approach. Generally it argues against an 'American-style' deregulation of the labour market.[12] In addition, there are important calls for investment in 'trans-European networks' involving public infrastructures, new information technologies, biotechnology, and ecotechnologies, with a proposal that these be financed by new bond issues backed by the Union (European Commission 1994: 33). These investments would amount to six years of funding at ECU20 billion a year.

This proposal is similar to the call made by Dreze and Malinvaud (1994) for greater funding for infrastructure and construction investment of up to ECU250 billion over three years. This would be closely targeted and would be accompanied by a subsidy to the labour employed on the designated projects to drive a wedge between the private and public cost of employment. Dreze and Malinvaud argue that sums of this magnitude (eight times the Edinburgh estimated expenditures) would be feasible without compromising other tight economic constraints if there were a combination of public and private funding. Inevitably, however, these proposals come up

---

[11] 'Considering the world market (including intra-EC exports), the EC is the Triad member with the lowest share of strong-demand sectors (23.4%, against 29% in the USA and 33.6% in Japan) . . . but the highest share of weak-demand sectors (30.1%, against 18.3% in the USA and 14.2% in Japan)' (*European Economy* 1994a: 125).

[12] 'American-style' deregulation refers to the rapid removal of all employee protection, the undermining of benefit systems, increasing inequality, etc., amounting to strong downward pressure on real wages—see *European Economy* (1994b). This would be unlikely to be successful anyway, since even the OECD jobs study makes clear that there is no obvious close or consistent relationship between flexibly low wages and labour standards and increased employment and international competitiveness (OECD 1994a; 1994b; 1994c; and 1994d).

against political obstacles and the prevailing macroeconomic climate in Europe, which we briefly explore now.

CONSEQUENCES OF THE INTEGRATIONIST PUSH

The 1990s period of European community-building has been dominated by the effort to secure the internal market first and then to follow this up by continuing the momentum and advancing rapidly towards further monetary and economic union. In the context of this second feature, the general deflationary criteria associated with the Maastricht Treaty have become firmly established as the guiding principles for internal European macroeconomic management (Thompson 1993). In effect this amounts to acceding to the Bundesbank's anti-inflationary monetary and fiscal stance, at least until any new system of European central banks and a complementary fiscal policy regime become established with the advent of full monetary union. The Bundesbank's own policy has been guided by the German unification process in the context of the so-called Emminger letter.[13] The Emminger letter clarifies the obligations of the Bundesbank *vis-à-vis* domestic German economic policy on the one hand, and its obligation to support the EMS and European policy on the other. It reasserts the constitutional priority of the Bundesbank to fulfil what it conceives to be its domestic duties first, even if this be at the expense of German treaty obligations to the wider EMS and European Union. It is well known that the main constitutional duty for the Bundesbank on the domestic front is to maintain the value of the Deutschemark.

The outcome of these constraints is a prevailing deflationary sentiment throughout the EU. The asymmetric nature of the way the Maastricht convergence criteria operate—those countries not meeting the criteria being required to retrench and deflate, with those already meeting them not being required to adopt an opposite stance and expand—means that the overall system is deflationary. Aided and abetted by countries like the UK, which have their own agenda for strongly resisting any expansionary line in Europe, along with the fact that the Commission itself is weak in terms of its taxing and other fiscal powers, the system bodes ill for European employment. While this situation lasts there seems little immediate prospect of a more generous *internal* EU expansionary policy.

The problem is that the EU has great difficulty in harmonizing and co-ordinating its internal policies—this is where the key intra-European disputes are located which threaten to seriously disrupt and constrain the EU in any further integrationist moves. Where the Union is likely to prove

---

[13] After Otmar Emminger, President of the Bundesbank. The significance of this, from which the discussion in the main text is drawn, is signalled by Eichengreen and Wyplosz (1993) and Kenen (1995).

more successful, and perhaps less controversial, is in connection with its *external* relationships. The EU is a proto-superpower in the international arena, large and important enough to do things that its individual member nations cannot do by themselves (the EU accounts for 30 per cent of world GDP and 40 per cent of its trade). It is in this context that a more radical Keynesianism could still have some purpose and purchase—as a 'Euro-Keynesianism' with a clear external embrace (Hirst and Thompson 1995).

The obvious object for this external orientation would be Eastern Europe and the CIS, so it is worth briefly considering the background to the situation here. Figure 8.6 illustrates what has happened to GDP and manufacturing value added in these economies. The general downward trend from 1960 lay behind the economic crisis which exploded in the late 1980s with such devastating effect. The rest of the world should not look upon this with any complacency, however, since the trends here have not been much better. The global economy more generally needs a sustainable upturn in economic activity.

In the European context more specifically, one of the ironies of the recent history of Eastern Europe and the ex-Soviet Union is that despite all the rhetoric of Western commitments and financial assistance with restructuring their economies, the figures show that in aggregate there has been a *net outflow* of financial resources from these economies since their old orders crumbled in the late 1980s (Table 8.2). This has mainly to do with high debt servicing charges on the official loans made to them, but it also indicates

Table 8.2. Net transfer of resources to transitional market economies ($US billion)[a]

	1990	1991	1992	1993
Bulgaria	0.5	0.1	−0.5	n/a
Czechoslovakia	0.6	−0.4	−0.2	2.3[b]
Hungary	−0.7	−0.8	−0.8	3.8
Poland	−3.8	−0.5	−3.0	0.7
Romania	1.7	1.3	0.4	1.3
(ex-) Soviet Union	−6.4	−3.8	−0.9	−13.4[c]
TOTAL	−8.1	−4.1	−5.0	−5.0

Notes: [a] Definitions of 'net transfer of financial resources' differ slightly between years and publications.
[b] Czech Republic only.
[c] Russia only.

Sources: Compiled from *UN World Economic Survey* (1994), fig. IV.7; *UN Economic Survey of Europe* (1992), table 5.2.5; and *UN Economic Survey of Europe* (1994), table 4.1.8.

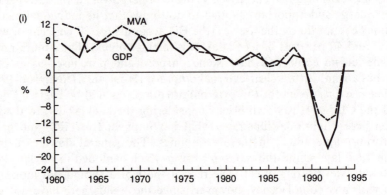

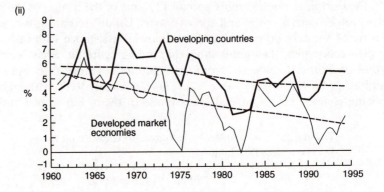

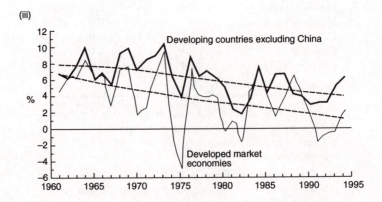

widespread capital flight on the part of those benefiting internally from the restructuring process. Clearly, after 1992 there was a reversal of the net outflow from the main Eastern European economies but not from the (former) Soviet Union.

This situation raises the more general role of Western aid as a whole to the economies in transition. It is difficult to get precise figures here since there are many initiatives from diverse sources. The G7 countries negotiated a US$24 billion aid package with Boris Yeltsin's Government in the early 1990s, though difficulties with Russia meeting the criteria laid down have held up the actual transfer of resources. The World Bank agreed a US$30 million fund for technical assistance to the EE and ex-SU economies. There has been a good deal of humanitarian aid and other technical assistance, though these have tended to be organized on an emergency *ad hoc* basis. Large-scale financial aid clearly needs co-ordination and expansion.

A point to remember is that these aid package are made up of loans not gifts, though most of the technical terms for the loans were 'soft' ones. In addition, the package is predicated upon the recipients meeting required terms for the reform process which push them along a very orthodox route towards a fully marketized economy.

Contrast this, instead, to the situation in respect to Western Europe immediately after the Second World War. The main institutional instrument of US-led reconstruction efforts then centred on the Marshall Plan. The Plan was a specially formed programme with its own separate institutional apparatus. Originally intended to operate for only four years (1947–51), it continued into a second phase to well after the Korean War (which ended in 1953). The Plan involved $US3 billion of official (World Bank) loans and $US17 billion of direct US government gifts (in total reaching some 3 per cent of US GDP in 1948 and 1949). The Marshall Plan significantly contributed to a modernization of Europe's infrastructure and the reconstruction of its productive industries (but also enabling rearmament to take place at the same time).

Fig. 8.6.   Growth rates of GDP and Manufacturing Value Added (MVA) in developed and developing regions, 1961–1994

(i) Growth rates of GDP and MVA in Eastern Europe and former USSR
(ii) Gross domestic product
(iii) Manufacturing value added

Note: Growth rates are computed using GDP and MVA data expressed in national currencies at 1980 prices and aggregated in terms of 1980 US$ exchange rates. The dashed lines show the long-term historical trend.

Source: *Industry and Development Global Report 1993/4* (Vienna: UN Industrial and Development Organization, 1993).

An equivalent amount to these Marshall Plan totals in the early 1990s would have been US$180 billion, and this for a single year only. The USA was in a different economic position in the early 1990s than it was in the late 1940s and early 1950s, so it might be fairer to think in terms of a shared burden of aid from the three leading economies: the USA, the EU and Japan. Aid amounting to 3 per cent of their joint GDP in 1992 would have been US$480 billion, so that only 1 per cent would still have come to US$160 billion. Compared with the amounts actually granted, this shows the limited extent of the aid actually considered in the present period.[14]

The point of this discussion is, first, to contrast the amounts available for restructuring in the two periods; secondly to stress the fact that most of the financial resources made available to Western Europe after the War were outright gifts not loans, and finally to suggest that the EU could well lead now in the organization of a much greater commitment to these economies as part of a co-ordinated Euro-Keynesian programme. If the EU is serious about eventually fully integrating these economies into its community structures (and even the UK Government is committed to this aspect of EU development), then something along these lines would be necessary anyway.

The problem is to provide a 'ladder' onto which candidate member countries can climb as a means for full entry into the EU. If the EU is not to become an exclusive 'rich-nations club' on the one hand, or simply a larger 'free-trade area' on the other, but is to mature into a regulated economic space with a strong commitment to its successful enlargement, then that will require it to provide significant aid and assistance in the restructuring of the candidate economies to the east. At present they are not in an economic position to make a successful entry without destroying the existing EU in the process. Their economies are not strong enough to withstand the competitive pressures within the EU as it is at present constituted, let alone as it develops further towards monetary and economic union possibly by the end of this century.

To join the EU successfully they need long-term assistance mainly in the form of infrastructure investment, technical aid, and directed trade credits. Such a 'Euro-Keynesian' policy package would have the objective of providing funds to the East so that its population could purchase the goods and services from the West: a pump-priming process that would benefit both halves of Europe. At the moment there are 'excess demands' in the East and 'excess supply' potential in the West. While it has become virtually impossible for any single economy to pursue an independent 'national Keynesian' policy, the continent-wide nature of the EU economy allows it

---

[14] A recent estimate puts the aggregate of CIS residents' externally held funds at US$50 billion to 60 billion (Kaser 1995: 49). Such funds would be enough to take over Russian industry in its entirety (p. 50). The rate of capital flight seems to have peaked in 1992/3, however, as the worst excesses of inflation abated in the CIS.

the scope to do things single governments cannot, even strong and important ones like a united Germany.

CONCLUSIONS

But such a policy package, even to appear credible let alone feasible, probably requires a 'deepening' of the EU first. This deepening would require the establishment of a viable independent 'public sphere' around the Commission, with enough powers to exercise a progressive fiscal and monetary policy at the European-wide level involving significant commitments to genuine redistributive objectives. Thus from this perspective, rather paradoxically, the widening of the Community first requires its deepening.

The question is whether such an ambitious programme is likely in the foreseeable future. At present there is little pressure or incentive for EU leaders to do much about this, other than in terms of rhetoric and gesture. In the case of Marshall Aid after the Second Word War US policy towards Europe was dictated by fundamental strategic considerations and the 'Soviet Threat'. There is no such threat to present-day Europe. But even without this there are good economic reasons for providing greater assistance to the Eastern economies to aid their restructuring efforts. One further problem is that unlike the position after the Second World War with Marshall Aid, the Eastern economies are not market economies, and therefore their capacity to absorb large amounts of resources quickly and use them effectively is limited. Thus providing money on its own will not necessarily help, though large amounts of financial resources will be needed in the context of closely targeted technical and trade credit initiatives.

But the Commission—even with an expanded budget—is probably not in itself yet a large enough fiscal actor to provide the stimulus for 'Euro-Keynesian' policies without coincident fiscal and monetary policies in at least the majority of the member states. Assuming that the Community could orchestrate such a policy on the demand side, then it is even more the case that its central institutions could not create the complementary policies to contain money wage growth and prevent inflation. Such income restraint would fall to national governments: some like Germany could deliver because of residual corporatist structures and a relatively disciplined union movement; others like France would probably be able to comply because unions are weak, and some are manifestly incapable of constraining wage growth without highly restrictive macroeconomic policies like Britain's. A European expansionary policy could, therefore, lead to patchy results; those states most able to restrain wage growth would benefit, those unable to do so would lose out through accelerating unemployment or nationally imposed deflations.

At the Union level itself there seems little prospect of a strong 'Euro-corporatism' that brings the social partners together to make binding agreements with Brussels. Business is unlikely to present itself at this level as a single 'social partner'. It remains divided by national and sectoral interests, and it would prefer to lobby for those interests with the Directorates of the Commission on an issue-by-issue basis. Its national collective bodies are divergent in their degree of organization, in their objectives and their willingness to enter into partnership with labour. German industry remains highly organized on the employers' side, with strong sectoral and peak employers' associations, the member firms of which follow collective policy in a disciplined manner. German employers retain strong commitments both to industry-wide bargaining on wages and working hours and to the co-determination system of consultation with labour at enterprise level. British employers' associations are, in contrast, almost exclusively concerned with representing the most general perceived interests of their members to government, and have few powers to discipline their members or get them to take part in co-ordinated consultation with labour. Wage-bargaining has undergone massive decentralization in Britain since the 1970s, with very few industry-wide agreements. British employers are actively hostile to the idea of an extended dialogue with organized labour to build consent for national policies—that is 'corporatism', which has no place in the modern British manager's lexicon. This stark contrast shows that Europe will find it difficult to create institutionalized means of orchestrating consensus for macroeconomic policy at Community level.

European labour, through its federal-level organizations, may well wish to try to enter into a dialogue with the Commission about policy co-ordination and the orchestration of consent across the Community. It will have problems if it alone is interested and the employers refuse to co-operate, but even greater problems on its own side too—for European-level consultations will not be able to deliver disciplined commitments by member unions in the nation-states in such key areas as wages policy and wage restraint.

This tells us that *some* nation-states will remain the crucial actors in constructing a *political* basis of consent for the macroeconomic policies of the Community and for their own fiscal, regulatory, and industrial policies. In either case it involves the commitment of social actors and the organized social interests representing them to a sustainable distribution of national income between consumption and investment, and to a pattern of expenditure that promotes manufacturing performance. For example, a critical mass of the German financial community accepts the priority of investing in German firms at terms and conditions that protect their competitiveness. Parties, organized labour, and employers accept the need for public and private investments in education and training. In other countries such commitments and their orchestration would require explicit government action—the UK is the prime example, and Conservative Governments since 1979 have seen this as no part of their task.

REFERENCES

Baldwin, R. E. (1989), 'The Growth Effect of 1992', *Economic Policy* 9 (Oct.): 248–81.

Bean, C. (1989), 'Capital Shortages and Persistent Unemployment', *Economic Policy*, 8 (Apr.): 12–53.

—— (1994), 'European Unemployment: A Survey', *Journal of Economic Literature*, 32 (June): 572–691.

Blanchard, O., Dornbusch, R., and Layard, R. (1986) (eds.), *Restoring Europe's Prosperity* (Cambridge, Mass.: MIT Press).

Brown, V. (1987), 'Demand Deficient Unemployment', in G. Thompson, V. Brown, and R. Levacic (eds.), *Managing the UK Economy: Current Controversies* (Cambridge: Polity Press).

—— (1991), 'On Keynes's Inverse Relation between Real Wages and Employment: A Debate over Excess Capacity', *Review of Political Economy* 3/4: 439–65.

CEPR (1994), *New Trade Theories: A Look at the Empirical Evidence* (London: CEPR).

—— (1995), *Unemployment: Choices for Europe*, Monitoring European Integration, 5 (London: CEPR).

Commission of the European Communities (1993), *Employment in Europe 1993*, Directorate-General Employment, Industrial Relations and Social Affairs (Luxembourg: Office of Publications of the European Communities).

Cripps, F., and Ward, T. (1994), 'Strategies for Growth and Employment in the European Community', in J. Michie and J. Grieve Smith, (eds.), *Unemployment in Europe* (London: Academic Press).

Dreze, J. H., and Malinvaud, E. (1994), 'Growth and Employment: The Scope for a European Initiative', Reports and Studies, *European Economy*, 1: 77–105.

Eichengreen, B., and Wyplosz, C. (1993), 'The Unstable EMS', *Brookings Papers on Economic Activity*, 1: 51–145.

European Commission (1994), *Growth, Competitiveness, Employment: The Challenges and Ways Forward into the 21st Century* (Luxembourg: Office for Official Publications of the European Communities).

European Economy (1988), 'The Economics of 1992', *European Economy*, 35.

—— (1990a), 'One Market, One Money: An Evaluation of the Potential Benefits and Costs of Forming an Economic and Monetary Union', *European Economy*, 44.

—— (1990b), 'The Outlook and Potential Growth in the Community at the Beginning of the 1990s', Study 1, Annual Economic Report, 1990–1, *European Economy*, 46.

—— (1991a), 'QUEST—A Macroeconomic Model of the European Community as a Part of the World Economy', *European Economy*, 47: 163–236.

—— (1991b), *The Economics of EMU, European Economy*, Special Edition 1.

European Economy (1993*a*), 'Annual Economic Report for 1993', *European Economy*, 54.

—— (1993*b*), 'Potential for Growth and Employment in the Community until 2000: Simulations with the Commission QUEST model', Annual Economic Report, 1993, Analytical Study 1, *European Economy*, 54: 93–120.

—— (1993*c*), 'Technical Annexe: Scenarios to 2000', *European Economy*, 55: 23–42.

—— (1994*a*), 'European Competitiveness in the Triad: Macroeconomic and Structural Aspects', Annual Economic Report, 1994, *European Economy*, 56: 107–37.

—— (1994*b*), 'Towards a Flexible Labour Market in the European Community', Annual Economic Report, Study 4, *European Economy*, 56: 179–209.

Fagerberg, J. (1988), 'International Competitiveness', *Economic Journal*, 98 (June): 355–71.

Grahl, J., and Thompson, G. F. (1995), 'The Prospects for European Economic Integration: Macroeconomics, Development Models and Growth', in P. Arestis and V. Chick (eds.), *Finance, Development and Structural Change: Post-Keynesian Perspectives* (Cheltenham: Edward Elgar).

Hirst, P. Q., and Thompson, G. F. (1995), *Globalisation in Question: The International Economy and the Possibilities of Governance* (Cambridge: Polity Press).

HMSO (1994), *Competitiveness: Helping Business to Win*, Cm 2563 (London: HMSO).

IPPR (Institute for Public Policy Research/Commission on Social Justice) (1994), *Social Justice: Strategies for National Renewal* (London: Vintage).

Kaldor, N. (1978), 'The Effects of Devaluations on Trade in Manufactures', in *Further Essays on Applied Economics* (London: Duckworth), 99–119.

Kaser, M. (1995), *Privatization in the CIS* (London: Royal Institute of International Affairs).

Kenen, P. B. (1995), 'Capital Controls: The EMS and EMU', *Economic Journal*, 105 (Jan.): 181–92.

Krugman, P. (1986) (ed.), *Strategic Trade Policy and the New International Economics* (Cambridge, Mass.: MIT Press).

—— (1994), 'Competitiveness: A Dangerous Obsession', *Foreign Affairs*, 74/2 (Mar./Apr.): 28–44.

OECD (1994*a*), *The OECD Jobs Study: Facts, Analysis, Strategies* (Paris: OECD).

—— (1994*b*), *The OECD Jobs Study: Evidence and Explanations*, Part I. *Labour Market Trends and Underlying Forces of Change* (Paris: OECD).

—— (1994*c*), *The OECD Jobs Study: Evidence and Explanations*, Part II. *The Adjustment Potential of the Labour Market* (Paris: OECD).

—— (1994*d*), 'Labour Standards and Economic Integration', in *OECD Employment Outlook*, July (Paris: OECD).

Porter, M. E. (1990), *The Competitive Advantage of Nations* (New York: Free Press).

Prestowitz, C. V. (1994), 'Playing to Win', *Foreign Affairs*, 73/4 (July/Aug.): 186–9.

Rowthorn, R. (1995), 'Capital Formation and Unemployment', *Oxford Review of Economic Policy*, 11/1: 26–39.

Thompson, G. F. (1987), 'The Supply Side and Industrial Policy', in G. Thompson, V. Brown, and R. Levacic (eds.), *Managing the UK Economy: Current Controversies* (Cambridge: Polity Press).

—— (1993), *The Economic Emergence of a New Europe? The Political Economy of Cooperation and Competition in the 1990s* (Cheltenham: Edward Elgar).

—— (1995), 'Wither the Industrial Nations?', *Competition and Change*, 1/1 (Aug.).

Winters, L. A. (1995), 'European Integration and Economic Growth', in M. Mackintosh, V. Brown, N. Costello, G. Dawson, G. Thompson, and A. Trigg, (eds.), *Economics and Changing Economies* (London: Chapman & Hall).

9. Financial Market Constraints and Business Strategy in the USA

Eileen Appelbaum and Peter Berg

INTRODUCTION

The productivity slow-down in the 1970s together with increased competition from the newly industrializing countries in the manufacture of standardized goods and the deregulation of service industries such as telecommunications and financial services increased the competitive pressures on firms in the industrialized economies. In the USA, deregulated labour markets and declining union membership have permitted a wide range of business responses to increased competition. Firms face a choice between on the one hand cost cutting strategies that are based on outsourcing, contingent work arrangements, and low wages that reduce living standards and employment security of workers, and on the other hand performance-enhancing strategies that are based on the modernization of physical plant, investments in training of front-line workers, and the transformation to more flexible production systems that improve outcomes for workers as well as for firms.

As companies find themselves competing in markets characterized by differentiated products, high standards of product quality, rapid development of new products, and quick delivery of finished goods, improvements in productivity and reductions in costs depend critically on the nature of the production system and on the organization of work. The decision to transform the basic organization of production from a system based on the principles of mass production and Taylorism to a production system with an entirely different organizational logic may be critical to the ability of the USA to maintain a strong presence in manufacturing and producer services, particularly in traditional industries. The capacity to produce goods and services entails much more than just investment in plant and equipment. The relationship between such investments and the growth of productivity is not just a technical relationship between quantities of inputs of various quality and output. Increasingly, a company's market share depends on the capability to meet a wide range of performance criteria

We would like to thank Dean Baker, Rosemary Batt, Jeff Faux, Jeffrey Keefe, William Lazonick, and Jeffrey Pfeffer for comments on an earlier version, and Stephanie Scott for assistance in preparing this chapter.

including, but not limited to, price. In the 1990s, production capacity is as much a matter of investment in work organization and worker skills as it is of additions to the capital stock.

As has been documented elsewhere (Appelbaum and Batt 1994), the 1980s were a decade of experimentation in the US with new, high-performance work systems; and the number of companies undertaking a fundamental transformation of the production process appears to have accelerated. Nevertheless, major changes in work organization and human resource practices have been slow to diffuse. The most optimistic estimates are that core employees in about one-third of workplaces have been affected by such transformations (Osterman 1994); most estimates are much lower. Several barriers to diffusion have been identified (Appelbaum and Batt 1994: ch. 9; Appelbaum and Berg forthcoming). In the US, these include a lack of training institutions; managerial resistance to organizational change; dilemmas for trade unions related to the circumstances surrounding participation and to meeting new demands on their capabilities; and questions of how workers in non-union settings are to be represented in power-sharing activities. Finally, the institutional context in the USA permits firms the option of pursuing the 'low-road' alternative; in the short run, this can undermine firms that are making costly investments in more efficient forms of organization and in the training of workers, before the gains in productivity, quality, delivery time, and other improvements have materialized.

This chapter examines in some detail a dramatic set of developments in corporate finance that emerged in the USA during the 1980s—developments that paralleled, in time at least, the experiments on the production side with high-performance work systems.[1] The resulting change from organizational control by corporations over financial resources to market control of these resources was marked by the development in the 1980s of the market for corporate control, the increased strength of the shareholder revolution, and the new prominence of agency theory within the economics discipline. The thesis of this chapter is that, as a result of these changes, financial markets have played an increasingly active, and detrimental, role since the late 1980s in discouraging companies from making the large investments necessary to transform the production process. With a few notable exceptions, financial market constraints on the diffusion of high-performance work systems in the USA have gone largely unremarked by the labour market economists or management and human resource experts who study changes in the organization of production.[2] This chapter con-

---

[1] Of course, both workplace reforms and the preoccupation with shareholder value have a longer history than this in the USA. Lazonick and O'Sullivan (1995b) date the beginning of changes in financial control to the 1960s. Green and Berry (1985) provide an early, insightful description of these phenomena.

[2] See e.g. Lazonick (1992) and Lazonick and O'Sullivan (1995a). Porter (1992) noted that the rise of the market for corporate control has made the maximization of the current stock

tributes to remedying this deficiency by analysing financial market constraints on business strategy in the USA in the 1990s.

It is by no means certain that performance-enhancing strategies associated with the adoption of high-performance work systems will win out in the USA over strategies focused more narrowly on immediate cost containment and reductions in permanent staff. In contrast to the assumption of neoclassical economics that the most efficient use of technology and organization of the factors of production is both available to firms and easily achieved, a more dynamic theory suggests that firms' choices are affected by management structures, organizational systems, and company strategies (Chandler 1990, 1992; Teece 1993). These structures and strategies are shaped, in turn, by the institutional framework within which the firm operates. Most important are the financial system (which affects the firm's ability to modernize or invest in new technology) and such intangibles as work reorganization and training, and labour market institutions, which govern skill acquisition and the employment relationship (Porter 1992; Wever and Allen 1992; Berg 1994). We are not suggesting that individual firms can never transform their productions systems successfully in the absence of a supportive institutional environment. Clearly, the evidence demonstrates that a large number of firms have made such changes (Appelbaum and Batt 1994; Pfeffer 1994). But, just as clearly, obstacles to change have slowed the diffusion and threatened the sustainability of organizational transformation. As we argue in this chapter, financial market constraints loom larger in the 1990s than they did in the 1980s as a barrier to workplace innovations that may be essential to maintaining the capacity to produce goods and services in the industrialized economies.

The remainder of this chapter is organized as follows. The next section examines the significance of high-performance work systems in maintaining manufacturing capacity. The following section presents evidence that the influence of financial capital on business strategy has increased. The final sections examine the implications for organizational restructuring of the role played by financial markets and offer some concluding remarks.

HIGH-PERFORMANCE WORK SYSTEMS AND MANUFACTURING CAPACITY

In a mass production system, Taylorist work organization and specialized equipment dedicated to producing standardized products are combined to

price one of the chief goals of firms in the USA and has impaired their ability to make financial commitments to other stakeholders or to make investments that pay off over the long run. Current corporate governance structures in US companies make it difficult for top management to offer commitments to long-term employment relations with workers or to stable, collaborative network relationships with suppliers that many researchers have argued are essential characteristics of high-performance production systems. Blair (1995) argues that, precisely for this reason, corporate governance in the USA needs to be rethought.

yield productivity gains via increasing returns to scale.[3] There are two types of economies of scale. Static economies of scale arise from the firm's ability to spread fixed costs over a large volume of output. These remain important, even in transformed production systems. Dynamic economies of scale arise as the firm 'moves down the learning curve'. Production costs in a mass production system decline initially with increases in the cumulative volume produced of a standardized product (Arrow's learning-by-doing); unit costs decline with an increase in the size of the market for a specific commodity. However, the learning that contributes to steady gains in productivity and reductions in costs as cumulative volume increases is of a very special type: 'practice makes perfect'. Learning in this context refers to the accumulation of knowledge by the company as a result of repetitively making a larger volume of the same product in a dedicated production line or facility. Thus, what firms learn in moving down the learning curve is the most efficient method for mass-producing a standardized item. Moreover, improving conformance quality—eliminating defects and meeting specifications within narrow tolerances—increases cost in a mass production system. It is accomplished by increasing testing and final inspections, identifying defective units before they are shipped, and thus results in more rework or waste. In a mass production system, therefore, there will be some 'optimal' defect rate, beyond which the costs of reducing defects outweigh the benefits.

Deviating from the mass production of standardized items by increasing product variety or meeting more rigorous standards for product quality brings an end to the cumulative gains in productivity and increases costs (see Abernathy and Wayne 1974; Hayes and Wheelwright 1984). Companies that have moved down the learning curve are vulnerable to competition from other firms on the basis of quality and product diversity. At the same time, the changes these companies have undergone in perfecting the production of a standardized product at ever lower costs reduce their ability to respond to such non-price competition.

The advantages of the mass production system have been undermined since the mid-1970s by two developments: (1) the ability of the newly industrialized countries and even the less developed countries, with their much lower wages, to compete successfully in price-conscious markets for standardized products; and (2) the increased capacity for customization and diversity inherent in computer- and information-based process technologies. The latter development reduced the cost advantages of mass production, raised quality standards in mass consumption markets, and increased competition in quality-conscious markets. As a result, new kinds of organizational learning became necessary, to make possible simultaneous improvement in conformance quality and reductions in cost. In much of the

---

[3] This analysis is drawn from Appelbaum and Batt (1994).

industrialized world, the 1970s and 1980s were an important period of experimentation with new work systems and new forms of organizational learning. In manufacturing, where these changes originated and where most of them have occurred, innovations were driven in large part by the example of the Japanese car manufacturers, who achieved reductions in cost and improvements in conformance quality that US competitors at first dismissed in disbelief.

Robert Boyer (1988) attributes persistent high rates of unemployment in Europe to the breakdown of the technological paradigm and work organization associated with the system of mass production. The advanced industrial economies, as Boyer observed, are groping for new institutional mechanisms that can achieve and distribute productivity increases and allow a stable accumulation of capital. Work organization and production technology play key roles in this process.

The precise form that the new, high-performance production systems take vary with the industry and its technology, with the market segment, and with the main basis on which the firm competes (price, conformance quality, performance quality, time-to-market of new products, continuous replenishment of customers' stocks, and so on). Common features of transformed production systems include increased authority and responsibility of front-line workers for day-to-day work activities and their involvement, either directly or through representatives, in the operational and strategic decisions of the enterprise; increased trust between management and workers and among co-workers, which generally involves guarantees of employment security; increased opportunities for individual and organizational learning; increased co-ordination and communication within and between departments; stable relationships with networks of suppliers; appropriate pay, training, and other human resource practices that allow employees, as well as shareholders, to benefit from the company's improved performance. Transformed enterprises take a stakeholder view of the firm in which the objective is to maximize the total wealth firms create for all those with a stake in the firm—workers and managers, as well as shareholders.

As experience with transformed work systems has increased, in the USA and elsewhere, it has become apparent that these transformed production processes hold out the greatest promise for enabling plants in high-wage economies to exploit their proximity to the domestic market and compete in their home markets against imports from overseas branch plants of their own or other companies.

More importantly from a social perspective, a country whose firms adopt more innovative work systems can hope to maintain a broad manufacturing capability, though manufacturing employment may continue to shrink. Increasingly, as even some plants in less industrialized economies adopt innovative work systems, world-wide standards are being set for quality and customization that exceed the capability of mass production systems to achieve. Work restructuring may soon be required not for competitive advantage but in order to compete at all.

Even in services, where the adoption of new work systems is a more recent phenomenon and the penetration of these changes is not very great, it appears that the combination of information technology and innovative workplace practices may lead to simultaneous reductions in cost and improvements in quality in industries as diverse as telecommunications, wholesale distribution, financial services, government services, and health care. If productivity growth in services can be improved, the payoffs are likely to be enormous, since this is where the overwhelming majority of new jobs in the industrialized economies have been created in the last two decades (for a discussion of the significance of this, see Appelbaum and Schettkat, 1995).

One of the enduring myths of the total quality movement is that quality is free. The innovations required to transform the production system process, however, entail high fixed costs. The scale of up-front investments in productive resources is generally quite high. Reorganizing the production process generally involves modernization of the physical plant—more equipment, more technologically sophisticated equipment, new logistical design of the work site; in addition, initial investments in training of front-line workers may be several times the 1.5 per cent of payroll typically expended for training in US firms. Firms need access to financial resources in order to undertake the innovations required to move from mass production to more flexible production systems. And, as with innovative investments generally, firms need a commitment of these resources over the long time period until the required returns are generated (see Lazonick and O'Sullivan, 1995b).

A few examples may help to make the point. In apparel, the introduction of self-managed teams of sewing operators (modular production systems) more than doubles the capital equipment required by manufacturers. In the old assembly line system, each worker spends the entire work day performing a single operation on a single machine. The capital-to-labour ratio is one machine per worker. In the modular system, each team of operators requires a full complement of sewing machines. In women's undergarments, teams of two or three workers require five or six machines; in jeans, teams of ten operators may be working with as many as twenty-five machines. In hospitals, the introduction of patient-focused care, in which a patient is cared for by a team of nursing care givers who provide many specialized services in addition to the usual nursing care, substantially raises skill requirements for nurses' aides and places new co-ordination and communication demands on college-educated nurses. Many of the cost savings in this system come from reductions in transport and waiting time for patients that shorten hospital stays without compromising the quality of care. This is accomplished by decentralizing radiation therapy, laboratory tests, and pharmacy functions to every patient floor, which requires investment in the installation of such facilities throughout the hospital. Finally, the new partnership agreements between the steelworkers' union and several large integrated mills in the USA promises to usher in a new, more flexible production system. But the survival of the integrated producers depends on their ability to maintain market share in the production of high-quality sheet steel for the auto and appliance markets in the face of increasing competition from the minimills. For this, fundamental changes in work organization must be linked to investments as high as half a billion dollars in late-generation casting and finishing technologies. Investments in electronic inventory control and data interchange technology to accommodate increased frequency and reduced delivery times to customers are also necessary. As these cases illustrate, modernization and new work organization generally go together. Organizational transformation entails high upfront investments in the capabilities of productive resources—both in modernizing equipment and in training workers in job-related and team-related skills. Access to financial resources for these investments is critical. As we shall argue in the next section, the influence of financial institutions in the USA on managerial decisions about investments in these capabilities and on firms' ability to restructure has increased substantially in the last decade and a half, and may, in fact, pose an important threat to the ability of US companies to produce at world-class standards.

THE INCREASING INFLUENCE OF FINANCIAL MARKETS ON BUSINESS STRATEGY

The decades following the Second World War were an era of inexpensive financing for US corporations. Banks were highly regulated, households were relatively restricted in their investment opportunities, and institutional investors—insurance companies and pension funds—mainly held long-term corporate bonds. Companies financed industrial investment through retained earnings or stable long-term debt instruments (Lazonick 1992).

Since the managerial revolution in the early decades of the twentieth century, companies have been evaluated on how well they meet the managerial agenda (see, for example, Berle and Means 1933; Berle 1954; Marris 1964; Galbraith 1967; Chandler 1977; Herman 1981). Companies that achieved appropriate strategic goals with respect to market segment, mix of products, sales and revenue growth, and return on investment enjoyed access to bond and equity financing as well as to the banks and insurance companies that were their major sources of finance capital. Corporate managers worked their way up to positions at the top of the corporation and, in the process, accumulated a detailed knowledge of the firm's internal operations. They also learned to manage relations with the board of directors, many of whom were inside directors, in such a way as to retain power and control over the company's strategic agenda. Control of strategic goals in large organizations rested not with shareholders, either directly or via the company's board of directors, but with professional managers with little ownership stake in the company. Shareholders were effectively powerless. Large corporations were safe from take-overs, and the rise of oligopolies sheltered the largest companies from product market competition and the blind pursuit of profit maximization to the exclusion of all other goals. As Michael Useem points out (1993: 19), 'unhappy shareholders were left with the sole alternative of exiting. The "Wall Street Rule" of disinvesting, rather than challenging management, became a norm of necessity.'

While managers in these corporations generally enjoyed the perquisites attendant upon employment in firms buffered from intense product market competition and with highly developed internal labour markets, managerial capitalism was frequently anything but benign in its treatment of front-line workers. In non-union companies, the treatment of lower-level workers ranged from paternalism to despotism. In unionized companies, labour–management relations could generally be characterized as adversarial. The hierarchical organization typical of these companies provided numerous opportunities for what Stephen Smith (1991) referred to as 'managerial opportunism'. The history and culture of managerial control of decision-making and of labour–management relations within firms are frequently cited as important obstacles to the transformation to more participatory and flexible production systems. Nevertheless, corporate managers enjoyed a great deal of flexibility in defining their goals, which generally included the growth of sales and revenue and increased control over the firm's market environment in order to secure the survival of the organization (Eichner 1976; Pfeffer and Salancik 1978). And in the decades following the Second World War, in many successful companies, including those that were unionized, workers gained a share of the economic rents the companies garnered.

As long-term company employees, top corporate managers tended to pursue innovative investment strategies aimed at increasing sales and revenue. They were encouraged to pursue this strategic goal by the low cost of financing made possible by regulated financial markets. Shareholders seemed generally content as long as the company was growing. As a result, the strategic goals of top corporate officials and the process-oriented goals of plant and middle managers were in rough alignment. Growth in sales, revenue and market share were important outcomes by which managers at both corporate levels were judged.

Not everyone agrees that this is how firms should function. Davis and Stout (1992) point out that, at the height of the managerial revolution, academic proponents of finance-based theories of the firm were arguing that even oligopolistic firms with substantial power in product markets remained subject to the discipline of profit maximization. Firms that deviated from that standard, no matter how large, would be disciplined by financial markets and become take-over targets (Alchian and Kessel 1962; Manne 1965). Manne argued that the only objective measure of the performance of corporate managers is the company's share price. He developed the idea that mergers could be viewed as transactions in a market for corporate control; and that low share price indicated a poorly managed company with the potential to yield significant capital gains to outsiders who take over the company by buying its shares and then run it more efficiently. But it was not until the late 1970s and early 1980s, when changing competitive conditions and an overvalued dollar undermined the ability of US manufacturing firms to achieve sales and revenue growth and the deregulation of US financial markets provided increased opportunities and incentives for hostile take-overs and shareholder activism, that investors were able to contest the power of professional corporate executives to set the firm's strategic agenda.

A number of changes in US financial markets set the stage for this increase in shareholder influence. Deregulation of financial markets in the 1970s and the growth of mutual funds and uninsured money market accounts to which small savers have access increased competition for these savings. Bank interest rates on deposits rose, as did rates that banks charge borrowers. The largest borrowers, especially well-managed corporations with stellar reputations, ended relationships with banks or other financial intermediaries that previously were a major source of external finance and borrowed directly through the financial markets. The customer base of banks is now primarily made up of smaller or weaker businesses, and much bank financing consists of variable-rate, short-term loans.

The separation of ownership from management control of the corporate agenda in US companies was challenged in the 1980s by the emergence of the market for corporate control. Corporate take-overs were a significant force between 1980 and 1990 for disciplining firms that set strategic goals, designed to ensure the survival of the organization, but that do not lend themselves easily to present-value calculations.[4] Firms that were deemed to have deviated from the principle of maximizing the present value of the firm often became the targets of hostile take-over bids.[5] Hostile take-overs have subsided somewhat in the 1990s as corporate managers developed internal

[4] Jacobs (1991: 35–7) provides an excellent example of how information asymmetries may cause corporate investments in intangibles—training, R&D, or other expenditures that are not capitalized under US accounting practices—to be misconstrued by shareholders as a decline in the company's prospects. This then causes shareholders to adjust their valuation of the stock downward when they calculate present value, and to behave in a myopic fashion even though they have acted on calculations of the firm's long-term profit prospects.

[5] T. Boone Pickens made his first hostile take-over attempt for Cities Services Corporation in 1982. The attempt failed, but it sparked a wave of take-over bids during the rest of the decade by Pickens and others, most of which succeeded (Davis and Stout 1992).

and external (legal) defences against these bids, and as a wave of bankruptcies followed on the heels of the take-overs.

Institutional investors also emerged as a much more important influence in the 1980s. Mutual funds, through which individuals pool resources and purchase stocks, joined pension funds and insurance companies as holders of corporate shares, displacing individual investors. Many institutional investors look to trading as a way to increase returns. This, together with changes in technology that have made it easier and cheaper to trade shares, has increased the volume of stock-trading dramatically since the early 1980s. One result is that institutional investors are able to exert much greater pressure on corporate managers to place shareholder value ahead of the interests of other stakeholders.

Finally, from the mid-1980s the influence of financial institutions on strategic decisions about restructuring were reinforced by changes in the way the compensation of Chief Executive Officers (CEOs) and other top officials is determined. In an effort to align management goals more closely with shareholder value, corporate boards have tied an increasingly large proportion of CEO pay in the USA to the performance of the company's stock. This provides top managers with a strong incentive to consider the effects of organizational restructuring on share price.

We examine these developments in greater detail below. The implication of these developments is that the creation of shareholder value—as measured by rising share price—has become a key performance measure on which corporate executives are judged and on which the firm's access to capital markets is predicated. The success of a firm's efforts at organizational transformation, as evaluated by top corporate officials, is increasingly determined by Wall Street's response to the initiative and by its effect on financial indicators such as share price. Wall Street's influence has increased, not least of all, because of the access to financial resources that is necessary to bring equipment, facilities, and skills up to the requirements of flexible work systems. Unfortunately, Wall Street appears to favour downsizing over other, more uncertain and more difficult to evaluate approaches to restructuring.[6] This has raised questions about the prospects

[6] Corporate executives also engage in a certain amount of 'gaming' the system—what Jeffrey Pfeffer of Stanford University's business school refers to as 'management by denominator'. One example is Kodak's decision in 1988 to transfer its data-processing operation—including $1 billion of computers and other equipment as well as 700 employees—to the books of IBM (Shapiro 1994). With little or no change in efficiency as economists measure it, Kodak succeeded in boosting return on assets and revenue per employee as Wall Street measures it. Analysts applauded Kodak for downsizing and becoming a leaner company. Other companies that have made similar decisions include General Dynamics, McDonnell Douglas, Sears Roebuck, and Bethlehem Steel. Most recently, Xerox signed a ten-year contract with EDS (General Motors' data-processing subsidiary) estimated in 1994 at over $4 billion (Lohr 1994). Of the 6,000 people employed at Coca Cola headquarters in Atlanta, Georgia, 2,000 are leased employees. This includes administrative staff and information systems professionals leased from the Talent Tree company and building maintenance and cafeteria workers leased from other contractors (Manager interview, 30 Mar. 1994).

for the sustainability and further diffusion of innovative production systems that have high upfront costs and deliver payoffs in the future. These questions have become especially urgent as even firms such as Xerox, that were among the earliest US adopters of high-performance work systems, announce mindless downsizings and carry out across-the-board cuts in staffing levels to the applause and approval of institutional investors and Wall Street analysts.[7]

The Market for Corporate Control

The market for corporate control—take-overs, or the threat of take-overs by corporate raiders—emerged in the 1980s as an effective means of holding corporate managers accountable to shareholders and assuring close adherence to the principle of maximizing the present value of the firm. As Davis and Stout observed (1992: 605):

Corporate takeovers became perhaps the most significant events on the organizational landscape during the 1980s. Due to a confluence of factors—including the availability of large supplies of debt financing, innovations in financial instruments, and a climate of relaxed antitrust enforcement—top managers of large corporations previously thought invulnerable to unwanted takeovers abruptly faced a challenge to their control unlike any in the postwar era. Thus, between 1980 and 1990, 144 members of the 1980 *Fortune* 500 (29 percent) were subject to at least one takeover or buyout attempt . . . [and] the vast majority [125] ultimately led to a change in control.

In examining the factors that made organizations most vulnerable to take-overs, Davis and Stout found that corporations that were most successful by the standards of the managerial revolution—companies with high cash flow and low debt or with long-term employment relationships with their workers—were most likely to be taken over. Corporate raiders used junk bonds to finance leveraged buyouts of these companies, earning huge returns on small initial outlays and saddling the take-over targets with substantial debt burdens that often proved unmanageable. Leveraged buyouts appear to have been driven by the desire for quick financial gains, and to have ignored the strategies designed to achieve long-term payoffs to investments in technology or employees which many of the take-over targets had pursued.

---

[7] Xerox's share price rose $5.63 or 7% after its announcement on 9 Dec. 1993 that it would carry out a 10% across-the-board reduction of its work-force, a cut of 10,000 jobs, by early 1996 and close some operations. Xerox CEO Paul Allaire conceded that the downsizing would disturb employee morale, although he expected the effect to be short-lived (Holusha 1993). In contrast, institutional investors, who have pressed Polaroid for quick cost savings to improve the company's profitability, expressed disappointment with the announcement in Feb. 1995 that Polaroid would dismiss up to 5% of its work-force (400 to 600 workers world-wide) and were not pacified by its offer to establish a committee of outside directors to meet with its CEO, I. MacAllister Booth. Polaroid's share price declined slightly on this news (Holusha 1995).

Agency theory provided a 'quasi-scientific justification for an unrestricted takeover market' (Davis and Stout, 1992: 608). According to agency theory, owners (the principals) delegate control to managers (their agents) because ownership is diffused among many shareholders who have no access to information that is held by managers within the organization (see Goldstein 1994 for an analysis of the assumptions underlying agency theory). The agency problem arises out of this informational asymmetry. While managers are aware of the probability distributions attached to particular technology and investment opportunities, they lack the owner's pure profit motive. From the point of view of agency theory, firms exist only as a nexus of contractual relationships among shareholders, managers, employees, and others. As Jeffrey Pfeffer has observed, the theory 'goes so far as to deny the reality of common interests and shared culture and experience that can constitute organizations' (Pfeffer 1994: 111). According to agency theory, the only legitimate goal of the corporation is maximization of the *present value* of the firm as evidenced in its share price. Managers who favour goals that do not maximize shareholder value face a variety of consequences, of which a hostile take-over is the most severe.

The philosophical foundations for asserting the primacy of shareholder value over other corporate goals were provided by academics like John Pound, who heads the New Foundations research group at Harvard and by financial economists like Michael Jensen and his colleagues (see Jensen and Meckling 1976; Fama and Jensen 1983; Jensen and Ruback 1983). Agency theory provides a rationale for shareholder activism as well as for take-overs.

The take-over frenzy of the 1980s appears now to have slowed considerably, although the threat of take-overs persists. Many take-overs ended in bankruptcy. US companies adopted poison-pill and other defences against hostile take-overs, and forty states adopted legislation making take-overs more difficult. But the pressure on corporate managers from financial investors continues as a result of the increasingly active role played by institutional investors.

Institutional Investors and Shareholder Power

Deregulation of the US banking system in the late 1970s increased investment opportunities for households in mutual funds and money market accounts, and put pressure on traditional institutional investors—pension funds and insurance companies—to increase their returns by substituting stock holdings for long-term bond holdings. From 1981 to 1988, the stock holdings of institutional investors grew at an average annual rate of 14 per cent. Pension fund holdings of shares totalled $2.3 trillion by 1988 (Brancato and Gaughan 1990), and nearly $3 trillion by January 1994 (Wayne 1994). In 1989, institutional investors held 52 per cent of General

Electric shares, 59 per cent of Johnson and Johnson, 71 per cent of Digital Equipment, 83 per cent of Intel, and 84 per cent of Dayton Hudson (Useem 1993: 30). Increasingly, these institutional shareholders are exercising their influence to ensure that the rents, which companies like General Motors and AT&T previously shared with suppliers and employees, are appropriated by shareholders. They exert this pressure in two very different ways: by threatening to turn over shares (and depress share prices); and, in companies where they hold large blocks of stock, by directly influencing the actions of corporate managers.

Despite the fact that stock ownership, which has been fragmented in the USA since the early decades of this century, is now becoming more concentrated in the hands of institutional investors, these investors do not behave like their German or Japanese counterparts. Many of these institutional investors engage in short-term trading practices, holding shares for days or weeks. On average, the period for which institutional investors hold stocks is much shorter than for individual investors. Data from the Department of Labor indicate that pension funds turn over more than half the stocks in their portfolios each year (cited in Jacobs 1991: 42). Given the hundreds of stocks in the typical institutional portfolio, and the difficulty of being knowledgeable about all of them, easily available information such as quarterly earnings or announced reductions in staffing levels may carry undue weight in decisions to buy or sell shares. The problem has been well described by Michael Jacobs, who was Director of Corporate Finance in the US Treasury in the Bush administration (1991: 36–7):

Institutional investors are sophisticated enough to understand valuation techniques, and they certainly have the manpower and computers to perform the math properly. But if the assumptions on which their formulas are based are inaccurate, the resulting valuation will misrepresent the true value of a company.

In many cases, current earnings are a poor proxy for the long-run prospects of the company, which is why relying too heavily on them can produce valuations that misrepresent a firm's true economic worth. Obviously, weak earnings can signal problems ahead. But to the extent that the market inappropriately reads weak interim results caused by long-term investments as discouraging news about the future, it will penalize the stocks of companies that are truly investing for the future. And to the extent that corporate officers care about the value of the company, seeing the stock price decline will make them more hesitant to commit resources to strategic initiatives with distant payoffs.

The problem is not that financial markets are naïve, nor that they deliberately take a short-term perspective, nor that they cannot understand the real basis of long-term success. Rather, it is that high-performance work systems incur high upfront costs (that are easy for financial analysts to measure) in order to yield a potential payoff after a period of long, but uncertain, duration (that are difficult for financial analysts to evaluate). A CEO with detailed knowledge of the product markets in which the firm plans to operate together with production and Human Resource (HR) managers who are intimately familiar with the efficiency and quality gains these investments can yield may be able to have reasonable confidence in the pay-offs they estimate. Even the managers, in comparing the rate of return from investment in this project with the cost of capital, may reject the project because the high (and rising) cost of capital in the USA means that many such projects will not have rates of return that exceed this hurdle, and hence will not be undertaken.

The hurdle set by financial analysts or institutional investors may be even more difficult to surmount. The lack of relationships between companies and most institutional investors that is typical of the US financial system creates uncertainty for the investors about the plans of corporate managers (for example, CEOs may be reluctant to share all the details of their competitive strategy). It also increases the risks to investors related to their inability to monitor the project closely and to their desire for liquidity. As a result, the cost of capital as calculated by Wall Street, with appropriate adjustments for the risk premium which financial analysts perceive, may be higher than the cost of capital as calculated by the firm's managers. Firms that retain earnings (or borrow) to invest in projects that do not earn a rate of return at least equal to the cost of capital may find themselves punished by Wall Street through a reduction in share price, and therefore unable to undertake projects they judge to be profitable. Of course, some investments in training and work reorganization will be judged profitable by this criterion and will be undertaken.[8] In particular, this will be true of firms in which these types of organizational changes are already well established, so that payoffs in the form of higher earnings are readily apparent. It is also true of firms in technologically dynamic industries, or firms in other industries with monopoly market positions. But the rate of return required by Wall Street is likely to lead to the rejection of many more projects, and to increase the difficulty of undertaking such investments for firms just beginning the process of change. Moreover, the higher the cost of capital the sooner it will be necessary for investments in innovative work practices to yield returns in order for them to be judged economically viable. So, while financial markets may be willing to take the long view, and value *all* future returns in calculating the present value of the firm, a high cost of capital will still dictate rejecting any investment that does not begin to pay off in a relatively short period of time.[9]

[8] Pfeffer (1994) documents many highly profitable companies that adopted innovative workplace practices and invested heavily in their work-forces. As he points out, the five firms with the highest returns over the twenty-year period 1972 to 1992 were firms that, for the most part, adopted high-commitment work practices.

[9] The differences between the view that firms should operate to maximize the wealth of all stakeholders, including shareholders, and the view that firms exist solely in order to maximize shareholder value, extends beyond this discussion of differences in the calculation of share-holder value. Fundamentally, it is about a difference in values with respect to the social

Furthermore, given the institutional structure of financial markets in the USA, even institutional investors with large holdings in particular companies are unable either to accept lower returns or to provide more patient capital. In the 1980s, these large shareholders—motivated by the goal of maximizing shareholder value—began to exert their influence directly on corporate management. These investors had accumulated the power to be heard by management, and no longer found it necessary or feasible to express dissatisfaction with the actions of corporate managers by selling their shares. It should not be surprising, however, that this did not lead these institutional investors to act as owners and provide capital for investments in productive resources that pay off over longer time horizons; instead, large shareholders have exercised their clout to pressure these companies to maximize shareholder value. The College Retirement and Equities Fund (CREF), one of the largest US pension funds, described the limitation facing all large funds with large positions in particular companies (cited in Useem 1993: 28):

[CREF] is not in a position to divest itself of a company's stock when it disagrees with the action of that company's management. Furthermore, CREF's obligations to its participants preclude it from making speculative investments. Accordingly, CREF believes that it has a responsibility to use its rights as shareholder to protect shareholder values.

Led by institutional investors such as CREF, shareholders began to demand more accountability from their agents, the top managers of companies.[10] Poor stock price performance was seen as the result of bad management that had become entrenched and unaccountable to shareholders. In January 1985 Jesse Unruh, the state treasurer of California, formed the Council of Institutional Investors to promote shareholder interests. In the same year, the chief pension fund regulator at the Department of Labor, the millionaire businessman Robert A. G. Monks, encouraged pension fund managers 'to view their corporate proxies as assets and vote them on behalf of shareholders rather than siding blindly with management' (Wayne 1994). Changes in the rules of the Securities and Exchange Commission in

function which firms play. Does society have an interest in maintaining the domestic capability to produce a wide variety of manufactured goods and producer services? Or is the production of profits and financial wealth the overriding goal? Should wages be driven down to market-clearing levels, or do higher wages result in higher productivity as efficiency wage theory suggests? Should firms develop long-term supplier relationships, or award contracts to the lowest bidders? As Hutton (1995: 303) observes, 'Much of the so-called "shareholder value" that is "unlocked" by takeover amounts to no more than unravelling co-operative and committed relationships, which are priced above market-clearing levels, and reorganising them in a strictly price-mediated relationship.'

[10] The first attacks by institutional investors on corporate managers accused of not pursuing higher stock prices aggressively enough were directed at Lockheed Corporation in 1990 and Sears Roebuck & Co. in 1991. In late 1992 and early 1993 institutional shareholders caused the ousting of CEOs at IBM, Westinghouse, American Express, Kodak, and GM (Wayne 1994). The lesson was not lost on corporate leaders.

October 1992 allowed large shareholders to take collective action against corporations and required greater disclosure of executive pay packages.

In many corporations, the shareholder challenge to managerial power has gradually succeeded in altering the goals and behaviour of top managers. In his study of the restructuring of US business, Michael Useem (1993: 11) noted that managers 'of the companies observed in this study generally chose to define shareholder value as a combination of stock dividends and share appreciation, accumulated over a period of years. Equally important, it was understood that it was distinct from traditional accounting measures of corporate achievement such as revenue growth or return on equity.' In an increasing number of companies, shareholder value became the overriding goal of strategic company decisions. Growing institutional share ownership has meant that, increasingly, firms' investment strategies are driven by the financial demands of these shareholders. In addition, more outside directors were appointed to corporate boards. By the end of 1993, 86 per cent of manufacturing companies and 91 per cent of financial companies had a majority of outside directors (Wayne 1994).

Perhaps the clearest indicator of the increase in shareholder power in the 1980s can be seen in the change in the price-to-earnings ratios (p/e). Corporate managers following a strategy of using retained earnings to enhance the innovative potential of their enterprises prefer a low p/e ratio for the common stock of their companies. The relatively low dividend payout rate that results when corporate profits are allocated to retained earnings lead, nevertheless, to acceptable stock yields (that is, dividend-to-price ratios) when the p/e ratio is low.

Most shareholders, however, are interested in a high p/e ratio. A rising price, however, puts upward pressure on dividends in order to maintain stock yields.[11] Thus, as shareholders became more powerful and sought to exert greater control over their companies, the share of profits distributed as dividends increased. In the 1960s, the proportion of after-tax corporate profits distributed as dividends was 44 per cent. In the 1970s, this figure was 45 per cent. It increased to 60 per cent in the 1980s, and rose to 72 per cent in the recession year 1990 (Lazonick 1992: 459), before falling to 63 per cent in 1994. This left fewer resources for management to use for investment in innovative equipment, training, or work organization.

---

[11] This argument is most applicable to the large majority of firms found in traditional industries. Specialized companies in some high-technology industries or companies serving specialized niche markets have opportunities to earn levels of monopoly rents not available to most individual investors. High-technology firms such as Cisco Systems, Microsoft, or Genentech, as well as many pharmaceutical companies are rewarded by Wall Street when they pursue growth strategies that require them to retain earnings for internal investments, and would probably see their share price fall if they curtailed such investments in order to increase dividends. The situation is much different, however, for an IBM, AT&T, Polaroid, or Chrysler.

CEO Pay

The view of the corporation as no more than a nexus of contracts, and not as an organization with a legitimate interest in its own growth and survival, provides an obvious means to align the goals of agents with those of principals and reduce any incongruence: simply construct a series of explicit or implicit contracts to bring manager interests into line with shareholder interests. One important example of such a contract is the structuring of management compensation to include company stocks as an incentive for managers to pursue value-maximizing decisions.[12] Rather than relying solely on the board of directors to represent shareholders' interests, agency theory points to a more activist approach to aligning the interests of owners and managers.

Changes in the structure of compensation of top executives at large corporations are a clear manifestation of this activist approach. Throughout the 1980s the composition of executive pay shifted from a more fixed to a more variable structure. The structure of the variable component also shifted from traditional measures of company performance, such as return on equity, to measures linked more closely with shareholder value. An examination of the compensation of the top seven executives of forty-five large companies from 1982 to 1993 found the compensation divided into a fixed portion of salary and benefits and two variable portions: short-term annual bonuses and long-term stock options and other stock-based incentive schemes. In 1982, 37 per cent of top managements' total compensation was in the variable portion; in 1993, 54 per cent had become variable. The reduction in the fixed portion of the compensation package was offset by an increase in long-term incentive pay, which increased from 17 to 38 per cent of the total compensation package. For chief executive officers, the increase in the variable portion of pay was even greater. In 1982, 41 per cent of the CEO's total compensation was variable; by 1993, almost 65 per cent was variable (Useem 1994).

This shift in the compensation structure of top executives has resulted in a fundamental change from the salaried top manager to the owner-manager. Lazonick (1992: 463-4), argues that this change has a negative effect on the ability of companies to invest in continuous innovation. The old salary package was designed to reward managers who remained with the company and moved up the organizational hierarchy. Successful career managers had industry-specific knowledge and could evaluate the payoffs to pursuing alternative innovative projects. The long-run returns to managers depended on the growth of the organization as a whole, which depended on controlling retained earnings and pursuing innovative investment strategies. As managers have become owners, however, their incentive

---

[12] For a discussion of agency theory and its relationship to total quality management practices see Goldstein (1994).

to pursue innovative responses to changing market conditions has weakened. Now they have individualistic alternatives for achieving personal financial success. Lazonick (1992: 464) also points out that in so far as high stock prices put upward pressure on dividends, corporate executives face a conflict of interest in allocating corporate profit between dividends (thus raising the value of their personal portfolios) and retained earnings in order to make investments that could ensure the future success of the company. The most egregious case was Charles Wyly, the Chairman of both Michaels Stores and Sterling Software, arranging a deal with the Wall Street brokerage firm Lehman Brothers that will result in his making millions if either company's share price plummets between 23 February 1995 and 23 February 1998 or his losing millions should the share price of either company soar during this period (Norris 1995).

Thus, in many US corporations in the 1990s, the interest of shareholders in a high share price now takes precedence over the traditional interest of managers (and employees, suppliers, and communities) in the survival of the company. This new focus of corporate strategic goals has important implications for corporate restructuring, for the adoption of innovative workplace and human resource practices in individual firms and, more broadly, for the ability of the USA to maintain and build its productive capacity.

IMPLICATIONS FOR ORGANIZATIONAL RESTRUCTURING

The pressures of pursuing shareholder value as the primary measure of organizational success have made it more difficult for companies to introduce innovative work systems. Many managers, under managerial capitalism, erected obstacles and barriers to the adoption of transformed production systems. But the commitment of both top and middle managers to the long-term survival of the organization and the greater flexibility of top managers in setting growth and profit targets under this regime was less hostile to the stakeholder view of the firm that is central to high-performance work systems than is the agency theory view that the firm exists solely to maximize shareholder value.

In the 1990s, the exercise of power by institutional shareholders has provided much of the impetus for corporate restructuring in the USA as corporate executives have attempted to bring the 'organization's architecture' into conformance with shareholder goals. 'Corporate realignment around ownership-defined [shareholder] objectives became an enduring axis of corporate reorganization during the late 1980s and early 1990s' (Useem 1993: 1). This restructuring around the interests of shareholders may, and often does, conflict with the requirements of high-performance work systems, especially with respect to building trust and high commitment in the workplace.

One result of the recent organizational alignment around the goals of financial markets has been the decentralization of authority through the ranks of management. Companies are reducing levels of management hierarchy, creating flatter organizational structures, and giving managers and operating units more discretion to make decisions. As Useem (1993: 84) points out, however, within the companies he studied this is not done with the desire to create a high-performance work system:

As the traditional Weberian pyramid gave way to a leaner and flatter organizational chart, in no case was the acknowledged motive to empower the workforce, to give managers greater control over decisions, or to improve the quality of work life. To some managers these were of course laudable by-products of the decentralization. But the organizational alignment was result driven, not process driven. The actions were not taken because management believed in decentralization for its own sake . . . The steps were instead simply a derivative of management's commitment to increase shareholder return.

The reduction in management levels and personnel was undertaken to cut waste, reduce bureaucracy, and hold managers accountable for specific financial results. In Useem's case studies (1993: ch. 3), companies had often maintained elaborate rules and procedures governing the procurement of supplies and small investments. Approval for purchases over a certain amount, usually rather small, had to work through several layers of management before final approval could be obtained and then communicated back to the production facility. This cost the company time and money. In response to this problem, central management began requiring less information from its operating units, and reviewed their decisions less frequently. Central management functions, such as strategic planning, human resources, finance, and purchasing, were streamlined and their responsibilities moved into operating units.

In making these changes, however, top managers reduced their ability to monitor and control the decisions of managers lower in the hierarchy. To overcome this, corporations established a new system of control that linked managerial success at all levels of the organization to financial performance results. Companies have begun operationalizing shareholder value with internal performance measures that form the basis of all strategic decisions within operating units. When operating units function as individual profit centres, each decision about investments, acquisitions, shutting plants down, shifting products, and cutting employment must be evaluated against its effects on the bottom line and whether it will add value to the company. In this environment, making long-term innovative investments in workforce training, in reorganizing the production process, and in expanding the job tasks of shop-floor workers becomes more difficult. Although plant and operating unit managers may have more authority to make decisions, they are constrained by the strict financial performance criteria they are required to meet, often on a quarterly basis.

Requiring company units to function as profit centres, often through a reorganization of the company into strategic business units, is viewed by many top executives as an effective means of bringing the goals of middle managers at the plant or department level into alignment with the corporation's new goal of increasing shareholder value. The special appeal of this approach is that by holding business unit, plant, manufacturing, or department managers to the standard of short-run profit maximization, corporate officials can shrink headquarters staff and push authority and responsibility to lower levels of the company without sacrificing their ability to manage the managers. The performance of profit centre managers can be evaluated against a financial standard, easily and frequently, without the necessity of a large corporate staff to administer the company's strategic goals.

This type of results-driven restructuring leaves little room to incorporate the interests of other company stakeholders, such as local trade unions and employees. Whereas in the past plant managers may have been able to justify innovative investments or changes that over time improved the organizational environment of a facility, this is more difficult when top executives hold these managers accountable to a narrow set of value measures. This is particularly detrimental for strategies designed to achieve what Pfeffer (1994) describes as 'competitive advantage through people', which tend to work best when local stakeholders have been involved in the planning, design, and implementation of the restructuring.

Within a company, therefore, different strategies for restructuring the organization are likely to be advanced or embraced with different degrees of enthusiasm at different levels of management. In some companies, the goals of improving product quality and responsiveness to customers now compete head-to-head with the goal of increasing shareholder value.[13] Moreover, the strategies required to achieve these goals are likely to conflict. More flexible forms of work organization based on participatory

[13] In the longer term, of course, there is no conflict between performance improvement and profitability. Companies like Motorola, with a long history of investment in training workers and commitment to quality improvement are now reaping the rewards of those investments in higher earnings. Other companies may be able to escape some of the pressures for immediate returns and adopt a longer time horizon. In a recent study of work organization in the apparel industry in which the present authors participated, the three firms in the study, all of which were in the process of implementing modular production systems, are privately held. In discussing the factors that determine an organization's time horizons, Pfeffer (1994: 54) notes that in general, 'there is some evidence that family ownership, employee ownership, or other forms of organization that lessen the immediate pressures for quick earnings to please the securities market are probably helpful.' Citing companies that have invested heavily in their work-forces, he goes on to point out that 'Lincoln Electric is closely held, and the Nordstrom family retains a substantial fraction of the ownership of that retailer. NUMMI has Toyota as one of the joint venture partners, and Toyota's own plans for the facility virtually dictate that it take a long-term view, which is consistent with its culture and tradition. Again, the Walton family's ownership position in Wal-Mart helps ensure that the organization takes a long view of its business processes. It is almost inconceivable that a firm facing immediate short-term pressure would embark on activities . . . that provide productivity and profit advantages, but only after a longer, and unknown, period of time.'

management and joint decision-making do not immediately enhance share-holder value and require managerial power to be shared with those lower down in the company hierarchy. Decentralizing operating decisions related to purchasing, inventory control, and shipping to improve performance poses serious challenges for achieving tighter financial control over costs and profits. Judging each plant or department solely on its performance in each quarter as a profit centre limits resources available for training, team-work, or quality improvement. It also eliminates opportunities for co-ordination among profit centres. Moreover, a work-force demoralized by downsizing is not likely to share the latent knowledge it possesses in problem-solving or continuous improvement activities.

Conflicting strategies within the corporation reflect the different incen-tives and constraints facing managers at different levels within the organi-zation. Managers at the top of the organization are constrained in their choice of restructuring strategy by Wall Street's influence on investors' per-ceptions of the company. Below the top level, managers may be tied more tightly to specific domestic locations and may be more concerned about the efficiency of the production process as well as with quality and customer service. They are, therefore, more likely to favour strategies that enhance product quality and increase the market share of domestically produced goods and services. Unfortunately, the new requirement which many mid-dle managers face, to function as a profit centre, while nominally a devo-lution of authority and decision-making responsibility to lower levels of the organization, places these managers on a short leash and further constrains their ability to implement performance-enhancing strategies.[14]

These dichotomies in goals within the organization persist because a global market-place sets standards of price, quality, and customer service which, as research on autos, steel, semiconductors, and other industries suggests, can best be met by high-performance work systems. At the same time, however, companies have difficulty in finding measurable effects of Total Quality Management (TQM), training, or other workplace practices on financial performance.[15] It is not difficult to understand why: invest-

[14] A recent survey of senior line and human resource executives at mid-sized and large com-panies in industry, banking, utilities, and insurance by a management consulting firm found the following: 98% of respondents agreed that improving employee performance would significantly improve business results, 91% agreed their peoples' skills and talents were among the company's top issues, and 73% said that their company's most important investment was in people. None the less, when asked to rank a number of business priorities, the respondents put performance of people and investment in people near the end of the list, well below cus-tomer satisfaction and financial performance (Towers Perrin 1995).

[15] Thus, in *Fortune* magazine's annual survey of corporate reputations, analysts, outside directors, and senior managers are asked to rank how well firms in their industry are managed on the basis of eight attributes, only three of which are financial measures. In commenting on the survey results, *Fortune*'s editors observed that the 'impact of Motorola's much-publicized success at total quality management on its financial statement is hard to isolate, but it does explain why the company comes in second when measured by the quality of products and ser-vices' (*Fortune* 1995: 64).

ments in training and work reorganization raise corporate earnings in the long term but, in the short term, they reduce earnings and dividends and, hence, stock yields for many firms, especially those in traditional industries. This in turn encourages a sell-off of the stock and tends to reduce share appreciation. The rub, of course, is that operating units generally cannot adopt high-performance work systems without extensive investments by the parent company in modernizing their facilities, including both more, and more technologically sophisticated, capital; and companies cannot undertake such modernization of their facilities without access to capital markets.

Given the pressures to cut costs and add value to companies, it is not surprising that downsizing has been the central outcome of corporate restructuring since the late 1980s. Reducing the number of employees immediately lowers costs and increases the value of the company. There are examples of share prices rising just on the announcement of downsizing.[16] Several studies provide data that verify the breadth of downsizing.[17] In the 1991 Louis Harris and Associates' *Laborforce 2000* survey of 406 large companies, 64.3 per cent of the managers reported that during the previous five years their organizations had shut down some operations and 47.3 reported that they had laid off a substantial number of workers. In addition, the annual surveys of the American Management Association (AMA) found that downsizing has remained steady during the 1990s despite an economic recovery. In 1990, 36 per cent of the AMA's 7,000 member firms reported reductions in personnel. This figure rose to 56 per cent in 1991, and remained constant at around 47 per cent from 1992 to 1994. The AMA surveys also show the average size of work-force reduction to be 9.9 per cent for each year from 1990 to 1994 (Pearlstein 1994).

The effects of downsizing reported by managers seems to be mixed. In the 1991 Louis Harris and Associates' *Laborforce 2000* survey, 79 per cent of managers reported that they were 'very' or 'somewhat' satisfied with the downsizing that had taken place at their organizations. In contrast, Wyatt's 1993 survey on Corporate Restructuring found that most of the companies engaged in downsizing did not accomplish their objectives and experienced more negative side-effects than expected, such as declines in employee morale and commitment to the company. Moreover, the 1993 AMA survey on downsizing found that 80 per cent of managers reported that employee morale declined after downsizing (reported in Katz 1994). In a recent study of the US telecommunications industry, Batt (1995) finds that reduced job security had a strong negative effect on the overall satisfaction of middle managers, first-line supervisors, and workers in her sample.

[16] e.g. the share price of Xerox common stock rose 7% after the announcement in 1993 that it would cut 10,000 jobs by 1996 (Holusha 1993). When Boeing notified 5,000 workers that they would be laid off after sixty days, its shares rose 62.5 cents to $49.75 on the New York Stock Exchange composite trading (Cole 1995).

[17] For a review of the literature on downsizing and its effects on employees and company performance see Katz (1994).

Understaffing also had a significant negative effect on overall satisfaction for all employees, as well as middle managers and workers. Moreover, she finds that understaffing negatively affects the organizational commitment of all employees in her study.[18]

It is often assumed that downsizing is an effective way to raise productivity. However, a recent study by Baily, Bartelsman, and Haltiwanger (1994) contradicts this assumption. Using plant-level data from the Longitudinal Research Database, they examined the relationship between productivity growth during the 1980s in manufacturing and plant-level employment changes. They found that 55 per cent of the productivity gains came from plants where the work-force fell over the ten years studied, while the remaining 45 per cent of the gains came from plants with growing employment and large increases in total output (Baily *et al.* 1994). They also found that, as measured by productivity gains, there were many unsuccessful downsizers. Their research shows that productivity growth is affected more by plant-specific factors, such as management and worker skills than by simply cutting employment.

While the performance effects of downsizing are mixed, the effects of downsizing on innovative work systems and the implementation of performance-enhancing strategies is clearly negative. Large cuts in personnel not only demoralize a work-force but can also restrict the communication among employees who feel their resources and jobs are threatened. Employees may hunker down and try to protect their department or area against further cuts. Rather than sharing ideas across departments and taking risks, employees become overly cautious and reticent. In the process of downsizing, the company may also lose employees with extensive firm-specific knowledge (Biewener 1994). None of these factors are consistent with performance-enhancing strategies that rely on open communication and trust, and on highly skilled and organizationally committed workers. While downsizing can be conducted in such a way as to mitigate these negative effects on the work-force, Cameron (1993) finds that most companies do not take the necessary steps to do so.

A company that is responsive to the concerns of financial markets and shareholder value is not well suited to the adoption of performance-enhancing strategies or innovative work systems. These two strategic approaches rest on different principles and emphasize different performance priorities. While financial markets view shareholder wealth as the only valid measure of performance, performance-enhancing strategies are designed to affect a broader list of performance measures. These include product quality, market share, revenue, and time-to-market—all of which are related to the long-term survival of the company. Moreover, to be effec-

---

[18] In contrast, Batt finds that organizational strategies designed to enhance performance by increasing the autonomy of the work group and the significance of the work group's tasks increased satisfaction.

tive, performance-enhancing strategies require the participation of other company stakeholders (employees and/or local trade unions) who are most interested in wages, working conditions, employment security, and the survival of the company.

Strategies for maximizing shareholder value and those for adopting innovative work systems both focus on the elimination of waste within the organization as a means to increase performance; however, the two approaches emphasize different methods. Advocates of shareholder value encourage the reduction of management hierarchy and the expansion of the decision-making authority of lower-level managers, circumscribed, however, by the need to meet quarterly financial targets. They also advocate the reduction of cash reserves and retained earnings which are often used for investment purposes, as well as immediate reductions in staffing to industry benchmark levels. In contrast, innovative work systems are structured to eliminate waste among managers and employees by empowering workers to make more decisions and by developing the mutual trust and high commitment necessary if workers are to participate in continuously improving the production process. This process-oriented approach places high strategic value on the development of human resources. Innovative work systems treat human resources as a special resource that can deliver increases in productivity and process efficiency by increasing the breadth and depth of their skills, reorganizing their jobs, and increasing their responsibility. Performance-enhancing strategies recognize the benefits to companies of employees who are encouraged to be creative and who have a sense of commitment to the organization. Moreover, companies pursuing these strategies may adopt a profit 'satisficing' rather than a profit-maximizing view of optimal employment levels in order to achieve a high-commitment workplace.

Financial markets, in contrast, tend to view human resources as one input among many. Labour is essentially a cost to be minimized through downsizing or holding down wages. A recent study of 136 non-financial companies that initiated an initial public offer (IPO) in 1988 found that the price premium (stock price set at the time of the offering minus the book value of the company) was positively affected by such variables as the existence of an executive of human resources, an employee-training programme, or good employee relations, but the premium price was negatively affected by the presence of employee reward systems such as a stock plan for all employees, profit-sharing, or full benefit plans (Welbourne and Andrews). The authors conclude that investors react positively to firms that value their employees, but they react negatively if firms directly compensate non-managerial employees. Wall Street investors do not value the role that employee reward systems can play in increasing worker commitment and job satisfaction or in motivating workers to be more productive. Interestingly, Welbourne and Andrews also found that the use of employee rewards was the single significant factor that predicted the company's survival over five years, even after controlling for human resource value measures and the use of management rewards.

CONCLUSION

Financial markets are putting increasing pressure on companies to concentrate single-mindedly on maximizing shareholder value—to the exclusion of all other performance goals, even including survival of the firm. Economists provide the philosophical underpinnings for this behaviour. The advocates of agency theory reject the idea that a corporation has any interest in its own survival or that managers have any legitimate goals apart from their obligation to maximize the wealth of the company's shareholders, whose agents they are.

In a competitive economy, the product market will in theory discipline companies to ensure that they pursue the goal of short-run profit maximization relentlessly. But the development of large corporations early this century allowed companies to develop buffers against the short-run vicissitudes of the market and the business cycle and provided managers with room to set and pursue strategic goals aimed at enhancing the long-run survival of the organization (managerial capitalism). In agency theory, the financial market replaces the product market as the enforcer of short-run profit maximization. With the emergence in the late 1980s of a full-fledged 'market for corporate control', in which even the largest US firms could be bought and sold against the desires of their managers, theory began to turn into reality.

In the 1980s, the goal of enhancing shareholder value was used to justify hostile take-overs that frequently damaged the target companies and their employees, suppliers, and community. The take-over mania of the 1980s burdened well-managed companies with debt that led to a wave of bankruptcies in the 1990s. Although the pace of take-overs has subsided, the practice remains, as witnessed in 1995 by the hostile bid for Chrysler by Kirk Kekorian and Lee Iacocca. They wanted to tap into the buffer (more than $7 billion) that the company put away to finance new product development and quality improvement during the next downturn of the automobile cycle. But this attempt to increase shareholder value in the short run directly undermines the commitment that Chrysler has made to increasing the company's long-term value by increasing its market share—through integrating design and manufacturing, shortening new product development, negotiating modern operating agreements with the United Autoworkers (UAW), and so on.

In the 1990s, it is the institutional investors—mostly pension funds and mutual funds—who are demanding that companies cut costs to enhance shareholder value, to the exclusion of all other goals. Typical of this is the pressure that Mutual Series funds, which owns a large portion (6 per cent) of Chase Manhattan shares, is currently putting on Chase to increase returns for its shareholders. As one Wall Street observer put it (Sloan 1995):

At Chase, there's no cash hoard to tap for a big quick gain. Instead, you eviscerate Chase's labor force by selling the bank at a premium price to a buyer that tries to pay for the deal by keeping most of Chase's business while firing many of its workers. Chase has cut its workforce sharply in recent years to increase its profits. To preempt Price, Chase may well fire its own workers faster, its public denials not withstanding.

This increasing emphasis on shareholder value is behind the downsizings affecting white-collar as well as blue-collar workers, and contributes to the fact that wages have continued to fall even as productivity and profits have risen, that families face a more severe time squeeze and a rise in economic insecurity, and that communities face increasing instability.

A more charitable view of the shareholder revolution is that companies tend to become complacent or set in their ways, and that managerial resistance make it difficult for firms to undertake the high upfront investments necessary to implement more efficient, high-performance work systems. Firms require external pressure in order for managers to implement workplace reforms that often result in a loss of both power and managerial jobs. In automobiles, for example, it was product market competition from the Japanese that prompted US automakers to pursue employee involvement and other elements of lean production. The market for corporate control may simply impose another form of external pressure on firms to make the fundamental changes necessary to transform work systems, and may provide the necessary impetus for change.

A dramatic increase in product market competition usually has been the main impetus for change in US companies. As Appelbaum and Batt (1994: 150) observed, 'work systems have tended to be transformed when three conditions are occurring: a crisis threatens the product line or market share, the company has the resources to gamble on a high-risk strategy, and top management is willing to take that risk.' But, as these authors go on to observe: 'such crisis conditions, however, often have the opposite effect—they can cause a company to downsize or outsource production and to renege on the commitments it has made to its hourly workers and middle managers on gainsharing or employment security.'

The lack of patient capital in the USA is often identified as one of the weaknesses in the institutional infrastructure. Burton Malkiel (1990, cited in Jacobs 1991: 41) reports that a survey of the 300 largest manufacturing companies in both the USA and Japan found that 67 per cent of equity securities are owned by purely investment return-oriented investors in the USA compared with 22 per cent in Japan. In contrast, 33 per cent of equity securities are owned by relationship-oriented investors in the USA compared with 78 per cent in Japan. As we have argued in this chapter, the emergence of the market for corporate control and the shareholder revolution in the 1980s has, if anything, made capital less patient. Yet, as Pfeffer (1994: 54) points out:

the bad news about achieving competitive advantage through the work force is that it inevitably takes time to accomplish. . . . The good news, however, is that once achieved, competitive advantage obtained through employment practices is likely to be substantially more enduring and more difficult to duplicate. Nevertheless, the time required to implement these practices and start seeing results means that a long-term perspective is needed.

While external pressures from financial markets may occasionally shake up the status quo and provide the impetus for change, it seems more likely that the short time horizons usually associated in practice (if not in theory) with the pursuit of shareholder value will increase the barriers to diffusion of more efficient systems based on investments in people, and may stifle the kinds of workplace transformation that many companies require for their long-term survival. Ultimately, the fear that investments in people may depress earnings in the short term, and may trigger a decline in share price in the traditional manufacturing industries where these changes are most needed, may threaten the diffusion of high-performance work systems and may limit the expansion of industrial capacity in the USA.

REFERENCES

Abernathy, William J., and Wayne, Kenneth (1974), 'Limits of the Learning Curve', *Harvard Business Review*, 52.

Alchian, Armen A., and Kessel, R. A. (1962), 'Competition, Monopoly, and the Pursuit of Pecuniary Gain', in *Aspects of Labor Economics* (Princeton: National Bureau of Economic Research).

Appelbaum, Eileen, and Batt, Rosemary (1994), *The New American Workplace* (Ithaca, NY: ILP Press).

—— and Berg, Peter (forthcoming), 'Work Reorganization and Flexibility in Job Design', in David Lewin, Daniel J. B. Mitchell, and Mahmood A. Zaidi (eds.), *The Human Resource Management Handbook* (Greenwich, Conn.: JAI Press).

—— and Schettkat, Ronald (1995), 'Economic Development in the Industrialized Countries and the prospects for Full Employment', in P. Arestis and M. Marshall (eds.), *The Political Economy of Full Employment* (Aldershot: Edward Elgar).

Baily, Martin, Bartelsman, Eric, and Haltiwanger, John (1994), 'Downsizing and Productivity Growth: Myth or Reality?', National Bureau for Economic Research Working Paper 4741.

Batt, Rosemary (1995), 'Organizational Restructuring in Telephone Services', diss., MIT Sloan School of Management.

Berg, Peter (1994), 'Strategic Adjustments in Training: A Comparative Analysis of the United States and German Automobile Industries', in Lisa M. Lynch (ed.), *Training and the Private Sector* (Chicago: University of Chicago Press).

Berle, Adolph A. (1954), *The Twentieth Century Capitalist Revolution* (New York: Harcourt Brace).

—— (1933), and Means, Gardiner C. *The Modern Corporation and Private Property* (New York: Macmillan).

Biewener, Judith (1994), 'Contradiction or Compatibility? Participation and Downsizing in the High-Performance Workplace', manuscript, University of California, Berkeley, Dept. of Sociology.

Blair, Margaret M. (1995), *Ownership and Control: Rethinking Corporate Governance for the Twenty-First Century* (Washington: Brookings Institution).

Boyer, Robert (1988), 'New Technologies and Employment in the 1980s: From Science and Technology to Macroeconomic Modelling', in J. A. Kregel, E. Matzner, and A. Roncaglia (eds.), *Barriers to Full Employment* (New York: St Martin's Press).

Brancato, Carolyn, and Gaughan Patrick A. (1990), *The Growth of Institutional Investors in US Capital Markets* (New York: Columbia University Institutional Investor Project).

Cameron, Kim (1993), 'Strategies for Successful Organizational Downsizing', *Human Resource Management Journal*, 33.

Cappelli, Peter (1994), 'The Effect of Restructuring on Employees', National Planning Association, *Looking Ahead*, 16: 41–43.

Chandler, Alfred D. (1977), *The Visible Hand* (Cambridge, Mass.: Harvard University Press).

—— (1990), *Scale and Scope: The Dynamics of Industrial Capitalism* (Cambridge, Mass.: Harvard University Press/Belknap Press).

—— (1992), 'Organizational Capabilities and the Economic History of the Industrial Enterprise', *Journal of Economic Perspectives* (summer): 79–100.

Cole, Jeff (1995), 'Boeing's Retirement Incentive Plan Stirs Concern about Number of Jobs to be Cut', *Wall Street Journal*, 27 Mar.

Davis, Gerald F., and Stout, Suzanne K. (1992), 'Organization Theory and the Market for Corporate Control: A Dynamic Analysis of the Characteristics of Large Takeover Targets, 1980–1990', *Administrative Science Quarterly*, 37: 606–33.

Eichner, Alfred S. (1976), *The Megacorp and Oligopoly* (Cambridge: Cambridge University Press).

Fama, Eugene F., and Jensen, Michael C. (1983), 'Separation of Ownership and Control', *Journal of Law and Economics*, 26.

Fortune (1995), 'It's More than Sex Appeal', *Fortune*, 6 Mar. 64.

Galbraith, John Kenneth (1967), *The New Industrial State* (Boston: Houghton Mifflin).

Goldstein, Don (1994), 'Clashing Paradigms: Total Quality, Financial Restructuring, and Theories of the Firm', draft, Allegheny College.

Green, Mark, and Berry, John S. (1985), *The Challenge of Hidden Profits: Reducing Corporate Bureaucracy and Waste* (New York: Morrow).

Hayes, Robert H., and Wheelwright, Steven C. (1984), *Restoring our Competitive Edge: Competing through Manufacturing* (New York: Wiley).

Herman, Edward S. (1981), *Corporate Control, Corporate Power* (Cambridge: Cambridge University Press).

Holusha, John (1993), 'A Profitable Xerox Plans to Cut Staff by 10,000', *New York Times*, 9 Dec.

Holusha, John (1995), 'Up to 600 Jobs may be Cut at Polaroid', *New York Times*, 4 Mar.

Hutton, Will (1995), *The State We're In* (London: Jonathan Cape).

Jacobs, Michael T. (1991), *Short-Term America: The Causes and Cures of our Business Myopia* (Boston: Harvard Business School Press).

Jensen, Michael C., and Meckling, William H. (1976), 'Theory of the Firm: Management Behaviour, Agency Costs and Ownership Structure', *Journal of Financial Economics*, 3.

—— and Ruback, Richard (1983), 'The Market for Corporate Control: The Scientific Evidence', *Journal of Financial Economics*, 11.

Katz, Harry (1994), 'Downsizing and Employment Insecurity', National Planning Association, *Looking Ahead*, 16: 15–19.

—— (forthcoming), 'Downsizing and Employment Insecurity', in a volume edited by Peter Cappelli to be published by Oxford University Press.

Lazonick, William (1992), 'Controlling the Market for Corporate Control: The Historical Significance of Managerial Capitalism', *Industrial and Corporate Change*, 1: 445–88.

—— and O'Sullivan, Mary (1995*a*), 'Big Business and Corporate Control', MSS, University of Massachusetts at Lowell.

—— —— (1995*b*), 'Organization, Finance, and International Competition', MSS, University of Massachusetts at Lowell.

Lohr, Steve (1994), 'Xerox Choice Near on Data Contract', *New York Times*, 14 Mar.

Louis Harris and Associates (1991), *Laborforce 2000 Survey* (New York: Louis Harris Associates).

Manne, Henry G. (1965), 'Mergers and the Market for Corporate Control', *Journal of Political Economy*, 73.

Marris, Robin (1964), *The Economic Theory of 'Managerial' Capitalism* (New York: Free Press).

Norris, Floyd (1995), 'If these Stocks Soar, the Boss May Regret it', *New York Times*, 13 Mar., first business page.

Osterman, Paul (1994), 'How Common is Workplace Transformation and How can We Explain Who Adopts It?', *Industrial and Labor Relations Review*, 47: 173–88.

Pearlstein, Steve (1994), 'Large US Companies Continue Downsizing', *Washington Post*, 27 Sept.

Pfeffer, Jeffrey (1994), *Competitive Advantage through People* (Cambridge, Mass.: Harvard Business School Press).

Pfeffer, Jeffrey, and Salancik, Gerald R. (1978), *The External Control of Organizations: A Resource Dependence Perspective* (New York: Harper and Row).

Porter, Michael (1992), 'Capital Choices: Changing the Way America Invests in Industry', Research report presented to the Council on Competitiveness and co-sponsored by the Harvard Business School.

Shapiro, Joshua (1994), 'An Unusual Climb at Kodak Wins Her a Place at the Top', *New York Times*, 30 Jan.

Sloan, Allan (1995), 'A Golden Oldie from the 1980s May Mean Riches for Dealmakers of '90s', *Washington Post*, 25 Apr.

Smith, Stephen (1991), 'On the Economic Rationale for Codetermination Law', *Journal of Economic Behaviour and Organization*, 16: 261–81.

Teece, David J. (1993), 'The Dynamics of Industrial Capitalism: Perspectives on Alfred Chandler's Scale and Scope', *Journal of Economic Literature*, 31 (Mar.): 199–225.

Towers Perrin (1995), 'Executives Rank People-Related Issues far below Other Business Priorities', Summary of Results, Towers Perrin, New York.

Useem, Michael (1993), *Executive Defense: Shareholder Power and Corporate Reorganization* (Cambridge, Mass.: Harvard University Press).

—— (1994), 'Corporate Restructuring and the Restructured World of Senior Management', draft, University of Pennsylvania.

Wayne, Leslie (1994), 'Have Shareholder Activists Lost their Edge?', *New York Times*, 30 Jan.

Welbourne, Theresa M., and Andrews, Alice O. (undated), 'Predicting Performance of Initial Public Offering (IPO) Firms: Should Human Resource Management (HRM) be in the Equation?', draft, Cornell University.

Wever, Kirsten S., and Allen, Christopher S. (1992), 'Is Germany a Model for Managers?', *Harvard Business Review*, 70 (Sept.–Oct.): 36–43.

Wyatt Company (1993), *Best Practices in Corporate Restructuring* (New York: Wyatt Company).

Part IV

Directions for Policy

10. Creating Industrial Capacity: Pentagon-Led versus Production-Led Industrial Policies

Michael H. Best and Robert Forrant

POST-WAR AMERICAN INDUSTRIAL POLICY

In the aftermath of the Second World War, the United States government developed a vast science/technology infrastructure which linked government agencies; industrial, university, and government laboratories; and business enterprises. The publicly stated purpose was national security. The Manhattan Project and the atom bomb seared into the body politic the role that science and scientists could play in defence and war.

The leading government agencies were the Department of Defense, the Department of Energy (previously named the Atomic Energy Commission), NASA, the National Institute of Health, and the National Science Foundation. Two hundred universities of the 3,500 institutions of higher learning became research universities with laboratories which competed for federal government funding. Engineering education, in particular, was transformed into applied science as federal funding enabled engineering departments and associated laboratories to pursue federal contracts and grants on equal footing with their pure science colleagues. The corporate laboratory system, which had mushroomed from a handful at the turn of the century to over 2,000 labs by mid-century, also turned to federal sponsoring agencies to fund R&D. Finally, the 700 federal laboratories themselves employed one-sixth of US scientists and technologists with a $20 billion annual budget in the late 1980s (Shapira 1990: 50).

Roughly half of total US R&D is funded by the federal government and roughly two-thirds of this is defence R&D. In 1988, total US defence R&D was $40.1 billion contrasted to $1.1 billion in the Federal Republic of Germany and $0.4 billion in Japan. Government-financed R&D in Germany is roughly one-third of total R&D and about one-fifth in Japan (Ziegler 1992: 211).

An earlier version of this chapter is being published as the 1995 Sir Charles Carter Lecture, Northern Ireland Economic Council. We wish to thank Denise Martucci, Project Manager, Centre for Industrial Competitiveness.

In the name of enhancing national security, the federal government sponsored an expansion in the technology base of the nation. But it was a dual-use policy: government-funded R&D for defence purposes could generate new product and process ideas that could be put to commercial use as well as that of national security.

In effect, the dual-use technology policy was also industrial policy. But it was a *de facto* industrial policy. It escaped becoming the object of public debate because, in part, it was an 'invisible' industrial policy that did not involve the government in 'picking winners'. The expanded technology base was made available to the entire business sector to convert freely into commercial products. As a by-product of national security policy, industrial policy escaped public scrutiny and the label of industrial policy, for two reasons. First, it was consistent with the political myth of the separation of public and private spheres. It was an invisible industrial policy in that it did not seem to be managed; it was like a natural process that just happened. Secondly, as technology policy, it worked. The USA was the undisputed world leader in technological innovation. Besides the technological capabilities built up in the Department of Defense prime contractors and their supplier networks, technologically driven spin-offs from university and government laboratories generated whole new high-tech industries. MIT alone is credited with being the seedbed of over 150 business spin-offs of which DEC, a *Fortune* 500 company, is the most illustrious example.

The reality behind the appearance of public and private separation was one of pervasive government involvement in industry both as a major funder of corporate R&D and as a major purchaser of high-technology products. It is widely appreciated that the federal government funded 85 per cent of the R&D for the emerging electronics industry in the 1960s. Less appreciated is the market-creating role of government technology policy (Markusen and Yudken 1992; Alic *et al.* 1992). As late as the mid-1980s the government purchased over two-thirds of the output of the aircraft industry. In the critical early phases of the semi-conductor industry, the government purchased an even greater proportion. In fact, the major export industries of the USA in the post-war period all received both substantial government R&D and purchasing support in their formative, low-productivity years. This includes aircraft, computers, electronics, telecommunications, and instruments.[1] The major US foreign-exchange earner, agriculture, was the recipient of an extensive industrial policy infrastructure centred around the agricultural extension service programme beginning in the early years of the century.

---

[1] In 1987, the Department of Defense purchased 17% of the shipments of the fifty largest defence-related sectors (at the 4-digit SIC level). See Alic *et al.* (1992), table 6-B-1.

COMPETING TECHNOLOGY PARADIGMS

United States industrial policy as dual-use technology policy seemed to be an enormous success. The rapidly expanding technology base was replenished by technological breakthroughs at an unprecedented rate; rapidly growing MIT-inspired spin-off firms around Route 128 and Stanford equivalents in Silicon Valley spawned world-leading high-tech industrial districts that served as models for a series of emerging high-tech 'hotspots' around the USA.[2] What went wrong?

The USA first lost international market share to Japan in the steel industry. This was attributed to a lack of investment in new continuous casting technologies by lethargic US steel companies, long-time members of a cosy cartel. But market share declines in complex production industries such as cameras, cars, and motorcycles soon followed. There was little cause for concern as various interpretations of the causes of decline in 'traditional' industries all agreed that the USA's strength in high-tech industries was unassailed. But suddenly, in the early 1980s, the pattern was repeating itself in semiconductors followed by semiconductor equipment makers and downstream industries such as advanced consumer electronics, computers, and telecommunications. In the late 1980s, the Japanese machine tool companies mounted a vigorous and successful attack on the USA's machine tool industry with devastating effects.

With hindsight, the roots of the problem are clear. The USA's technological strength became its weakness. The Pentagon-sponsored, science-push technological paradigm came into competition with a production-based technological paradigm that engendered an erosion of the USA's industrial leadership. Three implicit assumptions of the US technology paradigm have since been exposed:

Assumption One: Technological innovation follows a linear path.

The first assumption was that technological innovation travels along a one-way sequence of activities proceeding from basic science to applied science, to engineering science to engineering design and development, to production. The presupposition was that scientific pre-eminence generates technological pre-eminence which, in turn, assures product pre-eminence. US technology policy was, in effect, a science/technology-based theory of comparative advantage. The presumption was that since Japan lacked a basic science base, an applied science base, even an engineering science base, the USA could always lead the product development cycle.

---

[2] *Business Week* identified fifteen 'hotspots' or imitations of Route 128 and Silicon Valley which are regionally specialized groups of firms closely linked to a research university and a vigorous local government.

Assumption Two: Technological diffusion follows a twenty-five to fifty-year cycle.

By the time that Japan and other countries were able to capitalize on the commodity production stage of the product 'life' cycle, US firms would have moved into leadership in the development of new products.

Assumption Three: Organizational capabilities are not important in explaining competitive advantage.

In conventional economic theory, while low wages may give a nation comparative advantage in labour-intensive products or in the commodity phase of the product 'life' cycle, organizational capabilities in production are ignored. The Pentagon was also largely unconcerned with process capabilities and process R&D. Product performance, not production process improvements, drove the design and development of military systems. Alic *et al.* estimate that 98 per cent of federal R&D goes to product-related work (1992: 341, 349).

The new technology paradigm, on the other hand, is about shifting the technological base from the science end of the spectrum to the production end. Technological innovation is driven as much by competitive dynamics as by science-push. Research in fundamental science is less important than cultivating the already existing technology base which can be harvested for new technological combinations and permutations as part of the product development process. Fundamental science, according to this view, is as likely to follow technological innovation as to be a driver. But this is just one of many feedbacks in the production-pull, innovation paradigm.

Stephen Kline (1991) presents a long list of industries that were formed without direct linkage to science, at least new science developed in R&D laboratories: jet engines, sewing machines, weaving machinery, machine tools, most construction methods, space shuttles, turbomachinery, combined cycle power plants, vertical and slant take-off and landing aircraft, and integrated circuits.

They all involve the creation of *new* technological knowledge. Knowledge is certainly crucial to new product development. But knowledge is not research; knowledge is the accumulated stock of wisdom that can be reinterpreted, combined, and recombined in new ways. Technological knowledge, unlike scientific knowledge, is not always codified or even explicit. Polanyi, Penrose, and others have stressed the role of technological and experimental knowledge as tacit or informal knowledge—often built into collective organizational practices, much as craft skills are inseparable from muscle memory of machinists and technicians who have learned by doing.

MANUFACTURING MODERNIZATION PROGRAMMES

Beginning in the mid-1980s a variety of programmes and organizations sponsored by the federal government, state governments, private foundations, industry associations, and labour organizations sprang up to address the problem of declining competitiveness. Small and medium-size industrial enterprises (SMEs) have been the focus of attention. (In the US the generally agreed definition of SMEs is fewer than 500 employees.)

State government manufacturing modernization programmes preceded the federal programmes. Between 1985 and 1988, Michigan, Maryland, Minnesota, New York, and Pennsylvania launched industrial extension programmes. Most of these state programmes provide direct services to individual manufacturers through regional offices and a cadre of field agents who assess firm operations and develop assistance plans. Typically, programmes provide a series of direct subsidies to individual firms to reorganize their quality systems, improve their utilization of a piece of high-tech equipment, or conduct market research. At the beginning of the 1990s, an estimated forty-two industrial modernization programmes existed in twenty-eight states.

Some of these states—as well as many others, such as Arkansas, Oregon, and Massachusetts—have provided seed money to stimulate manufacturing networks and consortia in well-defined industrial sectors like apparel, furniture, injection moulding, and precision machining. The concept of these networks is for groups of firms in the same industrial sector to come together, often with the assistance of a third-party intermediary and to address issues of common concern and reach economies of scale in areas such as product development, marketing, financing, and education and training. One estimate is that by 1994 twenty-seven states hosted approximately 140 networks involving 2,600 firms (Shapira 1995a: 16).

These experiments sought to develop new institutions or strengthen existing institutions to help SMEs utilize technology more effectively and upgrade the skills of managers and front-line and entry-level workers. A great deal of this experimentation was inspired by the examples of European programmes made popular in the USA by academics and economic development practitioners impressed by public–private partnerships in support of inter-firm and intra-firm learning in Italy, Germany, and Denmark. These programmes were seen to be consistent with the US agricultural extension service programme and the Morrill Land Grant Act which set up the extensive public university system in the USA.

The first programmatic response of the US Government to production problems in US industry was the passage of the Omnibus Trade and Competition Act of 1988. This Act gave the Department of Commerce a role in manufacturing technology. It led to the redefinition of the National

Institute of Standards and Technology (NIST), the old Bureau of Standards, with two new programmes: the Advanced Technology Programs and the Manufacturing Extension Program (MEP).[3] NIST also sponsors the Baldrige Quality Award.

NIST began funding manufacturing extension centres in 1988. By late 1994, the MEP was overseeing thirty-five manufacturing extension service centres in twenty-six states with nine more designated. The Clinton Administration had proposed that 100 centres be established by 1997, although the programme's budget has recently been cut back in 1995. Manufacturing extension centres are non-profit organizations that 'serve as the focal point for delivering services to smaller manufacturers' (NIST 1994). Each centre must be sponsored by a non-profit organization which can include state governments and educational institutions. The local sponsor must provide approximately 50 per cent of the centre's budget.

Manufacturing extension centres are designed to 'bridge a technology gap between sources of improved manufacturing technology and the small and mid-sized companies that need it' (NIST 1994, June). While each centre tailors its services to the needs of firms in the region, most provide assessments of firms regarding technology needs and competitive position, and help firm owners and managers define and implement company-specific technology projects. All centres rely on field agents who provide on-site advice and assistance to companies. The extension centres vary considerably in size and scope.

The largest extension programmes are the first seven that were created; they were called Manufacturing Technology Centres, with an annual budget of $18 million. The manufacturing extension centres are smaller. In 1993, the Department of Defense announced the Technology Reinvestment Program (TRP), an interagency effort to help US manufacturers become less dependent on defence markets and better equipped to compete in commercial markets. TRP funds supplement the NIST budget for the MEP programme. Philip Shapira (1995) estimates total federal and state funding for manufacturing extension partnerships to have been $80 million in 1992; the projected funding is $250 million annually from 1995 (roughly one-quarter of Japan's $1 billion funding for the related 'kohsetsushi' centres in 1993–4, described below).

All of these efforts, state and federal, are usually referred to under the rubric of industrial modernization programmes (Flynn and Forrant 1995).[4] While it is too early to judge, the manufacturing extension programmes have not lived up to the expectations at least of the most optimistic early

[3] The Advanced Technology Program will not be examined here. Its charter is to help develop technologies for which the benefits cannot be captured by the investors or which cannot attract venture capital. ATPs budget grew from $10 million in 1991 to $430 million in 1995.

[4] The rest of this section draws heavily on Flynn and Forrant's survey.

supporters. But, while the problems facing firms have been fairly well documented, it remains unclear whether or not these organizations can in fact assist firms in making the changes required to become problem-solving organizations, maintain their profitability, and discover new market opportunities.

Consequently, it also remains unclear what kinds of industrial modernization activities warrant government support. Much of the consternation stems from the fact that policy formulators and implementers are bereft of an agreed perspective on how companies change and grow, and lack insight on the industries they are supposed to be assisting.[5] While those engaged in debates over industrial modernization strategies generally agree that to compete successfully in the current economic environment a company must sooner or later undertake a thoroughgoing reformation of the factory floor, what contributes to successful transformation and how outside organizations can facilitate this change process remains an open question.

This lack of knowledge resulted in the initial thrust of industrial modernization efforts towards helping firms acquire sophisticated manufacturing technology. This emphasis stemmed from the widespread and still accurate perception that compared to their foreign counterparts, particularly in Japan and Germany, US small firms lagged behind in their utilization of advanced technologies such as computer-aided design, computer-numerically controlled machines, and industrial robots. Given this one-dimensional problem definition, it was not surprising that the stated goal of industrial modernization programmes was to make the latest technology available to small firms: 'Hardware would get us there'. Islands of advanced technology sprang up as firms suffering from limited worker skill levels, poor work flow, long set-ups, limited product development capability, and shrinking markets sought to side-step their organizational shortcomings with technology.

These well-intentioned but misguided efforts, while boosting the flagging sales of machine tool builders for a brief period, did little to help firms improve their overall competitive position. Such hardware technology-oriented programmes fell short in this way because they lacked a more integrated, systematic approach to organizational change.

However, a significant stumbling-block remains to implementing effective modernization programmes in the USA. The continued confusion as to

---

[5] Economic theory—whether free-market or Keynesian—offers little insight into competitive dynamics, since production or business organization concepts are entirely ignored. The problem is that economic theory seeks to define the firm in terms that are consistent with a theory of markets (as efficient allocators of resources). In so doing, concepts required to give substance to production and organizational capabilities required by a theory of the firm are squeezed out by the test of inconsistency with the assumptions required for an equilibrium theory of markets. The approach in this chapter is to invert the theoretical priority and define markets in terms of firms. From this view, markets are seen as objects of strategic reconstitution. These issues are elaborated in Best (1990: ch.4).

what does and does not work in helping firms make the transition to world-class practices persists because most policy-makers, funders, and implementers lack a dynamic economic perspective on how companies change and develop. While those engaged in industrial modernization debates can agree in the abstract that sustained high performance depends upon a company undertaking a thoroughgoing reorganization on their factory floor and in their business offices, exactly what these changes entail and how outside organizations can act as catalysts remain open questions.

REGIONAL MANUFACTURING STRATEGIES: A METHODOLOGICAL FRAMEWORK

Industrial policy must start with a strategic assessment of a region's or nation's basis for competitive advantage in the global market-place. A competitor analysis, commonly used as a framework for formulating a company's strategic orientation, can provide a conceptual schema for strategic reflection at the level of the sector and region. The task is to assess a region or nation's strengths and weaknesses objectively relative to those regions that enjoy global industrial leadership, sector by sector. These assessments must be considered in light of the threats that a region's or nation's enterprises face relative to world best-practice organizational capabilities. Only then can the real opportunities be identified and used to provide strategic direction to business and industrial policy-makers. The claim is not that local enterprises have to match global best-practice capabilities but that, first, a company's strategic orientation and core competencies must be designed to establish a defendable position given the strategies and capabilities of rival enterprises and, secondly, a company's competitive capabilities cannot be examined in isolation from the regional business system in which it operates.

The purpose of a strategic analysis is to develop, first, a consensus on the fundamental threats or challenges facing a region's industry; secondly, an analysis of the performance gaps between world-class production and organizational practices and local practices; thirdly, a strategic vision; and, fourthly, action plans that close the performance gaps and give force to the vision. Visions without the capacity to manage and execute are exercises in futility for both the enterprises and industrial policy agencies.

The idea of a business system is that firms cannot be understood as isolated units, but only as interdependent units within a broader system made up of four institutions: the firm; inter-firm relations along the vertical production chain and across complementary technologies that are potentially synergistic; intermediary organizations that support firms and inter-firm networking; and government–business relations.

While the strengths and weakness of a region's firms and its business system—including inter-firm relations and intermediary agencies that support industrial modernization—are regionally specific, the threats facing industrial enterprises are everywhere the same: the emergence of business systems based on new principles of production and organization that enable firms to achieve entirely new and comprehensive performance criteria, namely, low cost, high quality, short production lead times, flexible product mixes, and short new product development times. The organizational innovations that enable the new performance standards to be realisticly pursued have been pioneered in business systems constituted by SMEs as well as others dominated by big firms.[6]

However, globalization and even the emergence of powerful new industrial regions does not mean the end of opportunities for regional development elsewhere. The dynamic nature of competition and industry means that even the strengths of global leaders eventually turn into weaknesses. For example, the 800,000 SMEs in Japan have been integral to the establishment of a flexible and innovative business system. However, Japan's very success has contributed to the continued increase in the value of the yen and the resulting attractiveness of overseas suppliers to Japanese lead manufacturers. Consequently, SMEs in Japan are being challenged precisely as the business system has established itself as the leading system in the world. The problem for Japanese policy-makers is not simply a decline in SMEs but the interdependencies of networked groups of firms on a critical mass of firms at each link in the commercial chain.

In the USA, SMEs are at a crossroads in the 1990s. SMEs can be more responsive to the new challenges but they also lack the economies of scale in resources that can focus on organizational transformation. Furthermore, rapid new product development requires a set of manufacturing engineering capabilities that are rare in US SMEs, particularly those that operated merely as subcontractors to defence contractors and/or lead manufacturers organized according to the old principles.

The pressures that lead manufacturers put on their suppliers are not all bad. Certainly, lead manufacturers are responding to the new competitive pressures by demanding ever higher performance standards. At the same time they are forming longer-term, consultative relations with fewer suppliers to drive down the design/manufacturing cycle times. Competition over rapid new product development time has a different supplier–buyer logic: as design integrators, lead manufacturers need to treat suppliers more as partners and less as rivals over the division of thin margins. Furthermore, lead manufacturers being forced to focus more on core competencies generate pressures to network with partners to provide complementary inputs and services.

We turn next to a brief outline of some of the new competitive

---

[6] The contrasting cases of the 'third Italy' and Japan are explored in Best (1990).

dynamics which have revolutionized the performance standards for business enterprises. We look first at the level of the firm followed by networking and intermediary agencies. The final section outlines a ten-step methodology for conducting sector-level strategic analyses, and examines briefly an industrial modernization programme that is seeking to apply such a strategic framework.

THE NEW COMPETITIVE DYNAMICS: PRODUCTIVITY AND INNOVATION

The starting-point for distinguishing new from old business systems is the dominant form of competition. The defining feature of the old competition when it emerged, and the reason it successfully put all competitors on notice, was that it drove down the costs and prices of production. The defining feature of the new competition of today is rapid new product development created by the marriage of productivity and innovation, and the redefinition of both. Whereas productivity and innovation were a trade-off in the old competition, they have become a dynamic in the new.

Both the old competition, when it was the new, and the new competition of today generated a change in order of magnitude in business performance. Henry Ford, as the paradigm case of the old competition in its hey-day, drove down the price of the Model T to a fraction of the competition of the time. Today, the leading competitors successfully introduce new products in a fraction of the time of the competition which are mired in the old principles of production and organization. The result is a new manufacturing and innovation dynamic.

The term dynamic is used to capture the transition from a trade-off between two goals to a mutually reinforcing interaction: improved performance in achieving one goal enhances performance in the second and vice versa. In recent years the quality movement exposed the presumed trade-off between quality and cost that was a taken-for-granted in the era of Big Business. Leaders in quality turned the trade-off into a dynamic: higher-quality products generated, in the long run, lower-cost products. Transcending the quality–cost trade-off is not costless in the short run: without a substantial investment to make the transition from the 'scientific management' to the plan–do–check–act (PDCA) paradigm of work organization, quality improvement will remain a futile exercise in exhortation.[7]

Today, however, high quality and low cost does not offer a formula for sustained success. Firms must be able to produce faster and develop new

---

[7] See Ishakawa (1985) for an elaboration of plan–do–check–act. While the technical aspects of quality control were a US import, their integration within the inclusionary practices of the post-war Japanese firm created a vehicle for converting the factory into a learning organization. Goal-setting and problem-solving became constitutive of work on the shop-floor as never before.

products quicker. Producing in less time involves an organizational change that complements PDCA, namely, application of the principle of flow, in this case multi-product flow. The organizational vehicle for applying the principle of multi-product flow is cellular manufacturing or group technology. Like the principle of flow, first applied to discrete product manufacturing processes by Henry Ford, the principle of multi-product flow demands process integration: Production must be organized to connect sequentially the series of activities required to complete the process. A fully developed application of flow is the denial of batch production methods and the achievement of one-piece flow for multiple products.

The principle of flow and the related concept of process embody the idea of system integration; without the principle of flow, production is broken down into a series of local optima which generate system inefficiency.

The ideal of multiple-product, one-piece flow is not limited to the production process. Fully developed new competition is about the reorganization of business enterprises into a series of core processes each organized according to the principle of (one-piece) multi-product flow. In most cases this means extending the idea of process from manufacturing or material production to processes that involve business activities. For example, the order fulfilment process involves the flow of information (previously the flow of paper) as distinct from material. The economics of time, however, demand that both processes be integrated.

The core process most important to this discussion is the new product development process, one that has been most refined in the electronics sectors where product 'life' cycles have been systematically reduced. Anyone with a personal computer is cognizant of the ever shorter product life span of electronic components and products.

While the pace of change is greatest in the electronics industry, the trend is pervasive. The New Competition is product-led. Product-led competition has opened up a new competitive dynamic between innovation and productivity. Driving down manufacturing cycle times is important because it means more rapid response, more reliable delivery dates, higher inventory turns, and better quality. Driving down the design/manufacturing cycle time is equally important: it determines the pace of technological change that a company can sustain. The design/manufacturing cycle is the time it takes to convert a new product design into a scaled-up plant capable of producing at competitive costs.

The extended design/manufacturability cycle includes all of the following activities:

1. concept development
   (*a*) product architecture
   (*b*) conceptual design
   (*c*) target market

2. product planning
   (a) model building
   (b) small-scale testing
   (c) investment/financial
3. product/process engineering
   (a) detailed design of product and tools/equipment
   (b) building/testing prototypes
   (c) setting standards
4. pilot project/scale-up
   (a) volume production prove out
   (b) factory start-up
   (c) volume increases to commercial targets
5. production
   (a) maintaining standards
   (b) continuous improvement

Several abbreviated variants of the design/manufacturing cycle can be distinguished. A job shop, for example, may always be producing new products but will short-circuit the scaling-up activity. A batch producer may respond to new orders with new product specifications that can be run through the existing production system with minimum alterations.

For any one design/manufacturing cycle, product and process ideas are locked into place for the duration of the cycle. To change any part requires new tooling, altering supplier specifications, new testing, changing work tasks, etc. Each new cycle, however, is an opportunity for the introduction of new technological ideas (Gomery 1992).[8]

The shorter the design/manufacturing cycle, the greater the opportunity and capability to introduce technological innovations into production. A company that is capable of reducing the design/manufacturability cycle to one-half that of a competitor can introduce technological innovations at twice the rate. Being first to market with a new technology is important, but having the shortest design/manufacturing cycle time is more important in that technological refinements can be introduced more rapidly.[9]

Over time, the technological gap widens between companies with rapid and slow design/manufacturing cycle times. The technology dynamic is

[8] Ralph Gomery makes this point in distinguishing 'the cyclic process' from a 'ladder' type of innovation. 'Ladder' refers to the step-by-step process on an innovation that descends from science downward 'step by step' into practice. 'The cyclic process' refers to 'repeated, continuous, incremental improvement' built into a series of dynamic design/manufacturing cycles. We are indebted to Gomery's formulation if not his metaphors.

[9] The engineering change orders and other changes required to implement rapid new product development are not conceivable under the Taylorized, specialized organization of work associated with Big Business. The Wagner Act was not set up to deal with quality, productivity, or innovation (Bluestone and Bluestone 1992). The PDCA model of work organization is a prerequisite, as is the development of a quality system. Shorter cycle times demand doing the job right the first time without fallbacks.

reinforced by higher profit margins, which creates funding for increased research, design, and engineering (RD&E) which, in turn, enhances the investment in—and introduction of—new technologies.[10]

The design/manufacturing cycle or new product development process cannot be understood as a one-way flow of material or data, but it can be reorganized into a sequence of activities several of which involve inherently group activities and feedback channels.

If the first dynamic of the new competition is the synchronization of the design/manufacturing and manufacturing cycle times, the second is the integration of both with technology diffusion. Since a firm can only introduce new technologies with the introduction of new products or model changes, technological change must be synchronized with the beginning of a design/manufacturing cycle. In between, the firm can practise continuous improvement but not innovation.

Historical studies of the technology diffusion cycle point to a twenty-five to fifty-year cycle. But these studies have been conducted on innovations embedded in the old organizational dynamics. What is new is the development and management of a technological diffusion infrastructure that begins with the industrial process and thus reinforces the second innovation path. But the power of attraction of new technologies is what drives the speed-up in technology diffusion. The new manufacturing and design/manufacturing dynamics was a prerequisite to driving down the technology diffusion cycle and gave the impetus to establishing non-linear technology diffusion infrastructures.

Industrial policy, to be successful, must be informed by these new competitive dynamics. Too narrow a focus on either one-on-one technical help or an exclusive focus on helping firms acquire state-of-the-art technology does little to help firms improve their manufacturing processes nor does it diffuse technology in ever widening circles. Product-led competition requires a corresponding production-focused industrial policy, one that focuses on building the capacity of firms and sectors to respond to global manufacturing challenges. To summarize this section, product-led competition has engendered new organizational capabilities which involve the redefinition and integration of three processes:

1. manufacturing: the cell is the building block of the whole edifice; without cellular manufacturing the rest of the business system cannot drive product-led competition.

---

[10] The concept of the design/manufacturing cycle is critical to drawing a distinction between two paths to innovation and to understanding the barriers to rapid new product development in the hierarchical enterprise. A rigid, specialized work organization is not the only barrier to new product development. Equally important is the separation of engineering from production; the decline of design engineering with the rise of engineering as applied science; and the taken-for-granted notion that industrial innovation is a by-product of scientific breakthroughs.

2. design/manufacturing cycle: companies need to compete on the basis of rapid new product development or they will fall behind in technology adoption.
3. technology diffusion: this is pulled by the first two processes as distinct from being pushed by autonomous R&D activities.

As noted, only the manufacturing process is linear; the other two involve the management of networks or infrastructures. We turn next to the concept of networking, an integral aspect of the new competitive dynamics.

NETWORKING AND CO-OPERATIVE RESEARCH PROJECTS

Just as the comprehensive performance criteria of product-led competition require a new set of internal organizational capabilities, they do so with inter-firm relations along the commercial chain. The manufacturing and design/manufacturing cycles extend outside the firm to encompass a range of supplier firms for components, parts, tooling, complementary processing and services, and so on. Networking, or long-term consultative relations, replace both the impersonal, inter-firm market relations and the bureaucratic internal co-ordination of the autarkic firm from the age of price-led competition. Chris Freeman (1991: 505) has described the organizational shift as follows:

instead of the rigid hierarchy within groups with great prestigious firms at the top and small weak ones at the bottom, the parent-firm transformed its position into a nucleus within an industrial combine of 'Kogaisha' ('children' or 'daughter' companies).

Lead manufacturers, prime contractors, or parent firms are in a powerful position to influence the transformation of numerous SME supplier firms. Henry Ford sent his engineers into supplier plants to transform their production capabilities; in the case of Firestone Tire it involved building an entire new tyre-producing plant, getting the bugs out, and turning it back over to the owner (Sorensen 1956). Japanese consumer electronic and automobile firms located outside Japan play a similar role today, particularly with the increased value of the yen.

While influencing the organization and management of supplier networks of lead manufacturers has not been part of US industrial policy in the past, it is an activity in which business policy and industrial policy share the same goal: the upgrading of manufacturing capabilities of the SME supplier base of the region or country. Clearly, industrial policy initiatives that partner firms with large supplier networks can generate a leveraged impact on a regional economy.

The concept of networking does not apply only to large and small firm relations. Focusing on networks calls attention to a variety of inter-firm relations: one, along the industrial food chain; two, cross-sector inter-firm relations crucial to product diversification and new product development; and three, between firms and intermediary agencies providing R&D, technical, design, and managerial services. Industrial policy, as currently carried out by most MEPs, fails to recognize this and continues to measure success through measures that emphasize discrete, one-on-one firm-based projects. Sector learning is not stressed, something that differentiates US policy efforts from the Japanese strategies discussed below.

Taken together, the extent and density of inter-firm networks plus the variety of intermediary agencies within a region make up an industrial district—or in Michael Porter's term a cluster of firms (although Porter's diamond does not stress intermediary agencies). For Porter, competitiveness is explained by features external to the firm, including the intensity of rivalry, complementary sectors, the specificity of factors of production, and the sophistication of customers. In so doing, Porter has brought attention to the idea of clusters, but has not explained the competitive success of a cluster of firms in terms either of the internal dynamics of business enterprises or internal/external organizational dynamics. Furthermore, he does not offer a criterion for distinguishing successful from non-successful clusters.[11] Clearly, clusters differ dramatically in terms of the institutions of co-operation, the form of inter-firm competition and the intermediary agencies.

Cluster analysis not anchored in the production dynamics operates at the level of the superstructure; the task is to identify the dynamics between internal and inter-firm organizations. For example, firms that make the transition to cellular manufacturing must first conduct a Pareto analysis of their product offerings to identify the candidates for cells. This exercise inevitably focuses plants on fewer product lines; however, the need to offer a range of products brings pressures from the marketing people to form alliances with specialist producers of complementary products. Hence the network is generated by the logic of production and not by a nebulous desire to co-operate.

A criterion for distinguishing types of clusters is emerging from real-world case studies. For example, two types of clusters of furniture firms,

[11] It is ironic that Porter, who has brought concepts such as strategy, value chain, and cluster to economic analysis and thereby greatly enriched the industrial organization and policy discourse from that of conventional economic paradigms, does not have an analysis of the internal organization of business enterprises. No distinctions can be found between the organizational capabilities or the business practices that are constitutive of what we have termed the old and the new competition. Perhaps this is one reason for the divergence between Porter's conceptual treatment of industrial policy as counter-productive and his active involvement in industrial policy initiatives. From our perspective, the starting-point of industrial policy must be a careful assessment of the internal organizational capabilities of a region's industrial enterprises. Unless groups of companies develop the specific organizational capabilities to achieve the comprehensive performance standards of cheaper, better, faster, more flexible, and newer, no amount of cluster analysis will affect a region's economic performance.

one in North London pursuing price-led competition, and the others in Italy pursuing product-led competition can be found in Best (1990). Once the two regional clusters came into competition, the price-led cluster declined rapidly and no longer exists.

Annalee Saxenian (1994) has compared Route 128 with Silicon Valley and found two distinctive business systems. The proprietary software, closed-system, autarkic firm model pursued by the Route 128 firms left them poorly equipped to compete against the modularized, open-system, networked groups of vertically specialized firms in Silicon Valley. Critics have complained that both American districts have fared poorly against Japanese, diversified consumer electronic giants (Harrison 1994).

However, the critics have not explored the links between the Japanese big companies and the electronics industrial district in the Keihin region of metropolitan Tokyo which collectively supplies all the main companies. The district is composed of roughly 120,000 establishments and 1.7 million manufacturing workers. Nearly 80 per cent of Japanese computers are shipped from the Keihin region, and nearly 50 per cent of both robotics establishments and engineering R&D laboratories are located in the district. Kanagawa, a prefecture located within the district, ranks first in value added per factory and value added per employee of all forty-seven Japanese prefectures (Castells and Hall 1994). The point is simply that, to understand modern competitive dynamics, the unit of analysis cannot be the firm alone.

Japanese industrial policy has given special attention to inter-firm organization as a vehicle for advancing the modernization of industry. In the early post-war years, recession cartels and restructuring cartels were sponsored by MITI to co-ordinate investments across a range of firms in the same product market seeking to downsize or restructure (Best 1990: ch. 6).

The organizational model for government promotion of technological advance has involved the simultaneous promotion of competition and co-operation. Put differently, strategic industrial policy is about shaping the form that competition takes. The following quote from Kenneth Flam's study of the development of the Japanese computer industry illustrates the point:

Japan never handed over the entire domestic market to a favoured company—a 'national champion'. Instead, support was given to a small group of highly competitive firms, and the virtues of competition were preserved even as limits on entry by outsiders were established. At an early date the government tested co-operative research projects as a vehicle for extending financial support for technological development. They proved successful and became the organizational model for subsidies to research and development. (1988: 173)

Flam describes how two organizations, the Electrotechnical Laboratory (ETL) and the University of Tokyo developed computing and calculating machinery before any private enterprises became involved. ETL, founded in 1891 as part of Japan's Communication Ministry, built the first transistorized computer in Japan in 1956. ETL, which in 1952 had been transferred to MITI, collaborated with a number of then small firms, including Fujitsu, in building the early Japanese computers. In 1957 the Electronics Industry Development Provisional Act was passed by the Diet and, when imports of computers expanded in 1957 and 1958, MITI encouraged firms to establish the Japan Electronic Industry Development Association (Flam 1988: 179).

The Japanese Ministry of International Trade and Industry (MITI) gave little direct assistance to individual firms. Again in the words of Flam:

the total subsidy to R&D awarded during the 1957–61 period was under $1 million. Direct technical assistance from government labs or joint development efforts with universities continued to be the chief instrument of support for computer development in private firms until the early 1960s. (1988: 179)

In recent years the concept of fusion has become a guiding principle in the shaping of government-sponsored consortia. In one industry, machine tools, the results were spectacularly successful and redefined MITI's approach to sector strategies. We turn next to the elements that distinguish the 'new consortia'.

THE NEW CONSORTIA: FUSION AND INNOVATION

The idea of inter-firm co-operation to promote innovation is not new. In studies of innovation in Great Britain in the 1950s Charles Carter and B. R. Williams demonstrated a feature of innovation that has been amply rediscovered in Japan, namely, the roles of multiple sources of information and pluralistic patterns of collaboration (cited in Freeman 1991). They noted that the quality of in-house R&D was linked to associations with universities, government laboratories, consultants, research associations, and other firms. Today we would call these networks, often informal, sometimes formal.

Even the active involvement of government in the promotion of inter-firm co-operation for innovation is not new. When in 1961 a law was passed in Japan establishing Engineering Research Associations (ERAs), it was modelled after the Co-operative Research Associations established in the UK shortly after the First World War (Freeman 1991). They had similar functions; Co-operative Research Associations, in the words of Freeman: 'were seen as a means of sharing the costs of acquiring technical information and of testing facilities, pilot plant and prototype development' (1991: 501). While Research Associations died out in the UK, they have proliferated in 1980s Japan.[12] ERAs are but one form of joint project, but they

[12] In Japan the law passed in 1961 to set up 'Engineering Research Associations' (ERAs) 'envisaged cooperation between government labs, especially MITI's Mechanical Engineering

form a key element in Japanese industrial policy. Freeman estimates that, by the late 1980s, 'four-fifths of all government R&D loans were going to joint projects' (1991: 507). But, like other borrowings from the West, the Japanese have refined, upgraded, and advanced the concept. While important, ERAs are but one type of inter-firm co-operation. Quantitatively much more prevalent are 'exchange groups' based on the concept of technological fusion or the blending of technologies. Unlike the recent Engineering Research Associations, exchange groups are constituted by SMEs.

Exchange groups are administered by the Japan Small Business Corporation (JSBC), an 'external' body under the guidance of MITI. Like the Small and Medium Enterprise (SME) Agency of MITI, its policies are formulated under the strategic umbrella of MITI which includes firms of all sizes. JSBC has a network of Small Business Information Centres with one located in each prefecture (Shapira 1995b: 15–16).

Exchange groups differ in four ways from the conventional Western concept of R&D consortia. We will examine the new consortia using the example of the machine tool industry.

Fusion

First, the purpose is not to form groups of companies in the same sector of the economy. The innovation in the concept of consortia was the idea of fusion: new product ideas can be generated by coupling complementary technologies.[13] Hence the task of exchange group consortia is to link firms that have distinctive but potentially complementary technologies. The first major success story is mechatronics or the marriage of mechanical and electronic technologies.

In 1971 a 'mechatronics law' was passed in Japan which called for the 'consolidation of machinery and electronics into one or *systematization* of them' (Kodama 1986: 46). While the concept of mechatronics applies to many Japanese new product innovations including digital clocks and electronic calculators, the machine tool industry is the major success story. The technology diffusion rates are spectacular: amongst numerical control tools from 10 per cent in 1975 to 70 per cent in 1981; amongst industrial robots from 10 per cent in 1975 to 80 per cent in 1983 (Kodama 1986: 45).

Eventually, the entire machine tool industry was impacted but with dra-

Laboratory, and makers of parts and components, particularly for the car industry'. Twelve were established between 1961 and 1965, none from 1965 to 1970. The early ones were in filters, suspensions, and engine parts. Twenty-five, led by big companies, were established between 1981 and 1983. New ones were created in electronics, information technology, materials technology, and biotechnology. Funding was shared between industry and industry associations in collaboration with MITI (Freeman 1991: 506).

[13] The idea of fusion is consistent with Freeman's research on innovation as a 'coupling process' (Freeman 1982: 111–12).

matic consequences. In 1985 the Japanese and American machine tool industries were of roughly the same size but by 1990 the Japanese machine tool industry nearly tripled in size while the US industry stagnated; between 1987 and 1990 productivity growth of the Japanese machine tool industry was 8.5 per cent annually compared to 1.9 per cent in the USA; by 1990, 65 per cent of Japanese machine tools had electronic controls compared to 41 per cent in the USA; by 1990 the Japanese machine tool industry enjoyed a nearly 20 per cent productivity advantage; Fanuc, a spin-off from the electronics giant Fujitsu, enjoyed nearly 50 per cent global market share in numerical controls; and the USA imported nearly half of machine tools purchased (McKinsey 1993: 7, 9).[14]

In Massachusetts, even though numerical-control machine tools were developed a short turnpike drive down the road in MIT laboratories, neither the machine tool nor the metal-fabricating industries have undergone the same organizational transformation. A survey of SME defence subcontractors revealed that many metal-working firms in Massachusetts have CNC equipment but most were using it for purposes of either mass batch production or precision work for prime contractors to the Department of Defense (Cann and Forrant 1993). The potential offered by CNC equipment to produce a range of products, old and new, with short lead times remains largely untapped. According to McKinsey, in the early 1980s, US machine tool company lead times between orders and deliveries were up to two years.

Over recent years a series of governmental initiatives and programmes have sought to promote the fusion and diffusion model exemplified by the mechatronics success story. In 1981 MITI's SME Agency created the Technology Exchange Plaza Project. This called upon local governments and chambers of commerce to establish exchange groups amongst different trades and to use local government laboratories for support. By the early 1990s there were over 2,500 exchange groups in Japan involving about 80,000 small companies (Shapira 1995*b*: 16). Local public authorities were called upon to act as *catalysts* to group enterprises. Exchange groups enjoy subsidies from both local government and central government, grants, and low-interest programmes for joint R&D expenditures.

Sectoral Advance

While fusion is one guiding principle of Japanese consortia and industrial policy, the focus on technological innovation that advance whole sectors as

---

[14] According to the McKinsey report the following factors were responsible for the transformation: the *redesign* of products to be made from standard parts, modules, and components (design for manufacturing); *redesign* of the process from functional to cellular layout; integration of mechanical processes and electronics with *design*; industry *standards* in the electronics controls and machine tool industry; co-operation with customers to stabilize demand; and automation (emphasis added).

distinct from breakthrough innovations and spin-off firms is a second. Japanese machine tool companies, as in the USA, did not tap the potential of the new CNC equipment before a sector-level effort was made to enhance the competitiveness of machine tool companies as a group. MITI pressured Fanuc, which at the time was still a division of Fujitsu, to provide machine tool makers with standard, flexible, multi-purpose controls. In this way industry standards were established in both the electronic controls and machine tool industry. In contrast, US machine tool companies, like Massachusetts computer makers, pursued proprietary software, custom products, and profitability through after-sales support.

In the five-year period during which Japan's market share rose from fourth in the world, behind the USA, Germany, and Russia, to first, there was no substantial change in market share of machine tool manufacturers over the period (Kodama 1986: 46). In contrast, in the USA, technological innovation which engenders a revolutionary reordering of market shares is deemed a 'natural' process. The challenge of shaping competitive forces to promote a rapid and wide diffusion of new technologies is central to strategic industrial policy-making. It is a non-issue for conventional economic thinking and static industrial policy orientations.

American metal-working firms were a major beneficiary of Pentagon-led industrial policy, but it was a programme that was not focused on advancing new product development capabilities. The heavy defence industry heritage in Massachusetts, for example, left many metal-working shops without short manufacturing or design/manufacturing cycle times. Looked at from the sector level, while these suppliers usually have computer-numerical control and other high-technology equipment, they have not enjoyed the benefits of flexible and standardized electronic controls promulgated by MITI or of the new performance standards imposed by buyers that had themselves achieved them.

Joint Product Development and Commercialization

The machine tool story reflects a third major difference between US-type consortia and 'exchange groups' in Japan. In contrasting US consortia and Japanese exchange groups the same split between science-push or technology-pull orientations to innovation is replicated. American consortia focus more on basic research through the sharing of pre-competitive information and equal access, generally via licensing agreements, to the technological innovations of the consortia. Their aim is to achieve scientific breakthroughs. They do not engage in joint product development or commercialization. Japanese exchange groups, on the other hand, are designed to identify innovative products by combining or reconfiguring existing technologies.

Staged Evolution

A fourth difference between typical US consortia and exchange groups is the patient and staged feature of the evolution of exchange groups. Consortia in the USA seek to establish a formal relationship before commencing development of projects. In contrast, for Japanese exchange groups the emphasis during the first phase is to 'deepen mutual understanding and create mutual trust' among members. Professors and outside consultants frequently are called upon to act as advisers. But the pace is slow-moving and usually takes two to three years. Common activities are study groups which focus on management problems and new developments, and on technological developments. Both may involve study tours by members. However, the specific themes that are focused on by the group are usually generated internally (Subramanian and Subramanian 1991: 320).

The second phase is developmental, during which more formal projects are established usually around new product development, new markets, or new technologies. In 1988 the Technology Diffusion Law was passed which created a fund for subsidizing and providing interest-free loans to groups. A requirement is that the groups have enterprises from four different lines of business and be engaged in the development of a new product or technology.

The third and final stage is that of commercialization. In 1988 the Japanese Fusion Promotion Fund was established to facilitate the commercialization process. The Fund also provides marketing specialists to exchange groups. The government also set up a Fusion Network System linking the fusion centres of each local government. Finally, the project must have the approval of the local government.

Fusion has an important implication for the idea of sector strategy. Historically, the idea of sector strategy was to get a group of key players from within a single product market together to develop a shared vision about the future of their industry in the global market-place. The concept of fusion suggests that the key to successful co-operation, in the age of rapid new product development, is to form groups of key players from sectors with different but potentially complementary technologies. In this way exchange groups are more likely to foster an open process whereas consortia constituted by firms from one sector tend to seek confidentiality and secrecy.

We turn next to the role of intermediary agencies established to promote the rapid diffusion of innovations, particularly organizational innovations. These agencies have historically cut across sectors.

INTERMEDIARY AGENCIES: JAPANESE EXAMPLES

Hidden from most of the industrial organization literature as well as business school curricula which focus on enterprise organization are a range of extra-firm institutions or intermediary institutions that are neither business enterprises nor government agencies but which form integral parts of regional and national business systems. These intermediary organizations can be established by industrial policy-makers, by groups of enterprises, or by professional associations. Here again the emergence of product-led competition has been accompanied by organizational innovations in such institutions. We referred above to the role of the Electrotechnical Laboratory as the seed-bed for the development of the Japanese computer industry. Two other examples from Japan follow.

Technical Research Centres: Kosetsushi

The Fraunhofer Institutes of Germany have long provided the model of technical research centres that service SMEs. But today Japan is perhaps the most innovative. Japan, like Germany, has an extensive SME sector with roughly twice the US number of enterprises.

Japan's public technology programme for SMEs is conducted through 178 *kosetsushi* centres or public testing laboratories. The *kosetsushi* centres are sponsored by the Small and Medium Enterprise Agency of MITI but are administered by prefecture governments. The central government provides 10–20 per cent of the estimated $1 billion annual spending on *kosetsushi* centres and prefecture and local governments pay most of the balance (Shapira 1995a: table III). The *kosetsushi* centres offer research services, technology assistance, testing, training, and management assistance to industrial enterprises with 300 or fewer workers. Of the 6,900 people who work at the *kosetsushi* centres about 5,300 are engineers. About half of staff time is spent on research.[15]

The model for the industrial extension programme which influenced the design of the *kosetsushi* centres is the American agricultural extension programme established early in the twentieth century. The American agricultural extension programme diffused technologies and new practices through

---

[15] A powerful stimulus for co-operation has been the lack of engineering and technical capabilities within individual SMEs. In a 1988 survey asking firms to prioritize their major problems associated with technical development, 69% cited a shortage of engineers and researchers (Subramanian and Subramanian 1991: 316). During this stage, engineering intensity of the projects leads to shortages. In a survey in 1988, over 80% of the enterprises cited shortages of engineers as a bottleneck. This is in spite of the difference in engineering graduation rates. A recent *Science* editorial made the following comparison: 'In 1990, six Asian countries (including Japan) produced more than 250,000 first degree engineers. The United States graduated 65,000' (266 (9 Dec. 1994): 1623).

a system that linked small firms with agricultural experimental stations, and university agricultural research departments via extension agents. Lacking an extensive university system, MITI organized the *kosetsushi* centres to conduct research. They also co-operate with the Japan Small Business Corporation, a public corporation established by MITI to implement the whole range of assistance programmes for SMEs across all sectors including the promotion of fusion groups.

Organizational Practices: Japanese Union of Scientists and Engineers

Japan has a remarkable range of intermediary agencies that specialize in the diffusion of specific and innovative management practices. One is the Japanese Union of Scientists and Engineers (JUSE). The title of the agency suggests the production connotation of the terms science and engineering in Japan.

JUSE, established in 1947, promulgates total quality management, administers two journals, and publishes numerous books. PDCA (plan–do–check–act), the basis for team-based, employee-empowered work organization associated with the continuous improvement paradigm, has been diffused across much of Japanese industry by the activities of JUSE. Kaoru Ishakawa, who invented the fishbone quality tool, was a long-term president of JUSE. The JUSE as much as any other single organization has provided Japanese enterprises with a non-Taylorist definition of work organization and industrial engineering (Ishakawa 1985).

INTERMEDIARY AGENCIES: CRITERIA FOR SUCCESS IN THE USA

In keeping with the search for best-practice organizations, Erin Flynn and Robert Forrant (1995) conducted an evaluation of intermediary organizations associated with industrial modernization in the USA. The key success factors are summarized as follows:

1. *Credible*. The intermediary must be credible with employers. Employers will not utilize the services of an organization they do not respect. For this reason, organizations that develop out of existing relationships with firms are most likely to succeed. Credibility is enhanced to the extent that the intermediary offers a strategic analysis of the deep-seated, common problems facing a group of firms.

2. *Connected*. The intermediary organization must be connected to, networked with, a range of regional training institutions, business and trade associations, financial institutions, and technical colleges and universities. Reinventing the technical services wheel is problematic.

3. *Catalytic*. The intermediary organization must have the intimate

knowledge of a region to facilitate group meetings in which the right combination of industry people participate. The task of the intermediary here is to propose a series of speakers, firm visits, and other activities that begin the process of moving through the stages of 'match-making, honeymoon, and child-rearing'.

4. *Collective*. Group activity is important for advancing self-organizing capabilities and to leverage the impact on the regional economy. One-on-one activities are important to establish credibility and to facilitate firm-level change but sustained learning and improvement is a social process which SMEs cannot easily accomplish acting alone.

5. *Continuous*. For firms to have confidence that timely assistance is possible, they must believe that the intermediary organization has staying power. There is no substitute for the establishment of a long-term, continuous relationship.

A METHODOLOGY FOR ADVANCING REGIONAL INDUSTRIAL COMPETITIVENESS

The foregoing analysis of competitiveness dynamics creates the conceptual space for strategic industrial policy activities to advance the competitiveness of a region's industry. Industrial policy is not the preserve of national governments; strategic industrial policy agents can be, for example, regional or state governments, intermediary agencies, or technology-oriented universities working in partnership with industrial enterprises.

In this section a ten-point methodology is outlined for conducting regional, production-led, strategic industrial policy initiatives. The ten points are suggestive of the requisite activities and their order is not a blueprint. Circumstance will demand modification in both activity and ordering.[16]

1. *Develop a sector-strategy agency capability guided by world 'best-practice' methods*. The concept of agency here is the capacity to act strategically and collectively. Industrial policy-making agencies must be guided by an awareness of the competitive dynamics which both drive and confront business enterprises. A sector strategy orientation points to an awareness of challenges and opportunities and a dynamic sectoral approach to advancing competitiveness. At the sectoral level the challenge is to shape the form of competition and thereby act as a catalyst which enables regional enterprises to strategically redefine the sector. At the agency oper-

---

[16] This methodology has been evolving as the author has participated in sector strategy work in a variety of country and regional contexts, particularly in work with Cristian Gillen and Frederic Richard of the United Nations Industrial Development Organization and at the Center for Industrial Competitiveness at the University of Massachusetts at Lowell.

ations level, success depends upon adopting 'best-practice' characteristics which, as is the case with business organization, can now be readily identified.

2. *Conduct a strategic sector analysis.* The starting-point is an outline of a strategic, competitor analysis that accounts for world-class best practices at the enterprise level and sectoral dynamics at the regional level. The task here is to identify and track the best firms and business systems in the world that compete with specific regional enterprises. The strategic analysis starts with existing industrial activities but the craft of successful industrial policy-making is in creatively redefining the concept of the sector itself. For example, the Japanese have tilted the machine-making sector into mechatronics; Italian furniture firms are strategically repositioning the sector into interior design and furnishings. It is important to capture the emerging threats to reconstitute the sector by strategic actors located elsewhere which, in turn, will redefine the requisite production skills and capabilities of the regional enterprises. It is crucial to foster and not stifle imagination about product development possibilities locally as new product designs are incessantly recasting sectoral boundaries.

3. *Conduct an audit of industrial capabilities by sector.* This analysis will bring 'hidden' sectors and nuclei of firms into focus. The audit begins with the manufacturing census data from which historical trends in employment, output, firms, investment, and national market share can be presented. The next activity is to construct enterprise directories using a variety of business information sources. From the directories, geographical density maps can be constructed using geographical information service software. This information is raw material for the construction of input–output, commercial chain charts that facilitate converting the sector analysis into the inter-sector flows of industrial districts. In such input–output charts both the technical processes for subsectors and the intermediary agencies that support the sectors can be shown. Examples of technical processes for the plastics sector would include injection moulding, extrusion, compression moulding, blow moulding, rotational moulding, and thermoforming. To aid in the identification of fusion activities transparencies of density maps for various three-digit sectors can be overlaid. The density maps themselves can be recategorized by process activity type.

4. *Visit companies to generate primary data and develop case studies.* This step will bring the data to life with examples of success stories from the region. Questionnaires can be developed to explore particular issues for which data are not available. Primary research is required to capture the extent to which firms are addressing the challenges of the new competition and the real barriers to change. Companies, like people, have a capacity to define the barriers in terms that do not generate too much discomfort. The task, in part, is to puncture illusions.

5. *Promote technological R&D and rapid diffusion.* The technology-pull

paradigm of innovation suggests the importance of technological research that is informed by the industrial process. For example, the state of Massachusetts has a large plastics industry; if a biodegradable polymer could be substituted for the toxic resins that now supply the plastics industry, the entire industry would be reconfigured. Eleven firms have formed a consortium which jointly with the National Science Foundation funds three researchers and over twenty graduate students at the University of Massachusetts, Lowell, to conduct biodegradable polymer research. The new model of co-operative R&D is one of partnering in that the companies do not themselves carry out research, but instead collectively shape the research projects and share the results. The projects are all designed by the principal investigators but the sub-projects are subject to refinement at semi-annual meetings when results are presented to R&D staff members of participating companies.

6. *Develop a strategic orientation to technical services.* Most regions have public-sector agencies that offer technical services, particularly technologically oriented colleges and universities. The task is to link such services to a sector strategy to have a leveraged impact. For example, as the construction of printed circuit boards has shifted from through-hole technology to surface mount technology (SMT) many small firms are caught in the squeeze. One SMT line in a technical training programme can facilitate the transition of a whole group of firms in an economical way.

7. *Promote discussion amongst industry insiders on the results of the sector analysis.* Emerging hypotheses about the competitive dynamics of the sectors and districts can be tested and reformulated by dialogue with industry insiders. The purpose is to shape a common vision and develop a shared language to establish, ultimately, a plan of action and identify common services that advance the capabilities of the sector as a whole.

8. *Develop performance and transition indicators.* The purpose is to ground a needs assessment in a strategic analysis. The performance indicators of target companies are contrasted with world-class companies and the resulting gaps are used as targets for developing action plans. A set of production-based performance measures includes innovation diffusion rates; cycle times for manufacturing and new product development; work-in-process turns; waste, including set-up times and defect rates; and targeted skill upgrading programmes. An example of a gap analysis framework for transforming the workplace is the twenty-keys approach of Iwao Kobayashi (1988). Kobayashi's system defines excellence by presenting clear criteria for self-assessing five levels of organizational capability for each of twenty areas that have a major impact on cost, quality, and manufacturing cycle time. It involves the people who must make the changes in the activity of measuring organizational capabilities and, in the process, identifying workable action plans. Learning the criteria for each key itself generates an awareness of the connectedness of programmes to improve

quality, and reduce costs and cycle times. Establishing the capability of self-management and developing performance tools are part of the same process. Quality experts Deming and Juran agree that 80–85 per cent of quality problems are management- and not worker-related. Three conditions are required to hold workers responsible for quality: knowledge of the requirements of the job; measures of conformity-fit to requirements; and tools for bringing jobs into conformity. The production based performance indicators provide a metrics and common language within and across firms which highlights production issues that are otherwise obscured and ignored, particularly by personnel far removed from production activities. In this way production issues have a better chance of competing with those highlighted by narrowly financial measures of economic performance. Benchmarking is a methodology for measuring performance and setting stretch targets for process improvement which extends beyond production performance defined in terms of manufacturing activities. Benchmarking depends upon a prior analysis and identification of the core processes as distinct from individual business activities; examples include order fulfilment, new product development, and strategic planning. The goal in each case is to reduce cycle times but the task is inherently more complex as more business activities are integrated with material transformation activities and as the object of flow shifts from first, material, as in manufacturing cycle times; to second, material and information, as in design/manufacturing cycle times; to third, knowledge creation, as in the process integration of R&D and new product development. Nevertheless, system integration and cycle synchronization are aspects of sustaining competitiveness in an era of product-led competition, and benchmarking is a means of addressing these issues.

9. *Establish group implementation plans.* This involves the development of pilot projects in individual companies, establishing workshops for attacking common problems and skill upgrading, and sharing the results of implementing the pilot projects with all involved companies. Peer learning is a powerful tool for communicating new approaches.

10. *Diffuse the practical restructuring ideas widely in the sector.* Videos, workshops, reports, contests, and exhibits which illustrate principles with local examples can facilitate the diffusion of effective production practices. Case studies of successful firms in the region can be elaborated as learning examples. Here the focus is on the comprehensive performance criteria and examples of innovation, particularly examples of fusion because they illustrate the power of stepping outside traditional product definitions.

The actions suggested by the ten-point methodology are interrelated elements of a change process geared to the goal of transforming a regional economy. Sustained high performance of a regional economy will demand the development of a self-regulating but administratively guided process.

Developing the organizational capabilities of self-management at the production level is fundamental to developing such a regional industrial economy.

Focusing on the goal facilitates the synchronizing of work from different project activities. For example, industrial mapping projects will be better targeted if they are informed by, and themselves inform, R&D and technical service projects. Such a combined approach enhances the positive competitive dynamics associated with new product development and technology diffusion. But, as argued above, the prerequisite to both dynamics is the development of production capabilities based on world-class practices including cellular manufacturing, the plan–do–check–act work paradigm, self-directed work teams, and continuous improvement. Manufacturing extension programmes that work in awareness of and in conjunction with technology R&D offer a greater chance of success.

Social inertia, a barrier to organizational change everywhere, can be confronted indirectly by harnessing the organizational dynamic between projects and organizational change. A project approach suggests forming project teams which integrate the activities of a process. This always means combining people in new ways and people doing new things. Informal teams that cut across organizations can work together to generate and carry out projects which, in turn, will break down the departmental boundaries and fiefdoms which shackle organizations. In this way projects, carefully orchestrated, are a transformative agent on the existing organization: they counter the inherent tendency of people to protect existing structures past their usefulness.

Active pursuit of the ten points simultaneously creates a common language within the industrial community and thereby reinforces the social fabric of community that distinguishes an innovative industrial district from atomistic, disconnected competitors. The existence of community provides the social context within which regionally specific intermediary agencies develop and, in turn, reinforce community. Examples of such agencies include marketing or retailing consortia, industrial parks, technology transfer infrastructures, vocational educational programmes, fashion institutes, quality standards enforcement procedures, and specialized consultancies.

The organizational form of intermediary agencies may be private, public, or quasi-public. Their purpose is to manage and nurture co-operation to avoid the famed free-rider effect in which the 'commons' are depleted because individuals pursue their private interest in a setting with substantial interdependencies. Firms acting as free riders will trap them, collectively, in a negative dynamic. They will be ill-equipped to compete against groups of firms located elsewhere which have organized to generate a positive dynamic. This is what networking is all about.

CONCLUSION

We have contrasted the Pentagon-led with production-led industrial policies. A strategic industrial policy starts with an account of the new competitive dynamics which have generated higher and more comprehensive performance standards for business success including cost, quality, flexibility, cycle times, and innovativeness. The new competition is propelled by and engenders new product development and technology diffusion infrastructures. An industrial policy which is not informed by the new competitive dynamics will be likely to fail; but to deny the catalytic role of industrial policy in advancing the new competitive dynamics is to misunderstand the economic challenges and opportunities of today.

REFERENCES

Alic, J., Branscomb, L., Brooks, H., Carter, A., and Epstein, G. (1992), *Beyond Spinoff: Military and Commercial Technologies in a Changing World* (Boston: Harvard Business School Press).

Best, M. (1990), *The New Competition: Institutions of Industrial Restructuring* (Cambridge, Mass.: Harvard University Press).

—— and Forrant, R. (forthcoming), 'Regional Modernization Programs: Two Cases from Massachusetts', in I. Begg and R. Botham (eds.), *Decentralized Industrial Policies in Practice*.

Bluestone, B., and Bluestone, I. (1992), *Negotiating the Future: A Labor Perspective on American Business* (New York: Basic Books).

Business Week (1992), 'Hot Spots: America's New Growth Regions are Blossoming despite the Slump', 19 Oct.: 80–8.

Cann, E., and Forrant, R. (1993), *The Demise of the Massachusetts Defense Connection* (Springfield, Mass.: Machine Action Project).

Castells, M., and Hall, P. (1994), *Technopoles of the World: the Making of 21st Century Industrial Complexes* (London: Routledge).

Flam, K. (1988), *Creating the Computer: Government, Industry, and High Technology* (Washington: Brookings Institution).

Flynn, E., and Forrant, B. (1995), *Facilitating Firm-Level Changes: The Role of Intermediary Organizations in the Manufacturing Modernization Process* (Boston: Jobs for the Future).

Freeman, C. (1982), *The Economics of Industrial Innovation* (London: Frances Pinter; 1st edn., 1974, Harmondsworth: Penguin).

—— (1991), 'Networks of Innovators: A Synthesis of Research Issues', *Research Policy*, 20: 499–514.

Gomery, R. (1992), 'The Technology–Product Relationship: Early and Late Stages', in N. Rosenberg, R. Landau, and D. Mowery, *Technology and the Wealth of Nations* (Stanford, Calif.: Stanford University Press), 383–94.

Harrison, B. (1994), *Lean and Mean: The Changing Landscape of Corporate Power in the Age of Flexibility* (New York: Basic Books).

Ishakawa, K. (1985), *What is Total Quality Control? The Japanese Way* (Englewood Cliffs, NJ: Prentice-Hall).

Kline, S. (1985), 'Innovation is not a Linear Process', *Research Management*, 28 (July–Aug.): 36–45.

—— (1991), 'Styles of Innovation and their Cultural Basis', *ChemTech*, 21/8: 472–80.

Kobayashi, I. (1988), *20 Keys to Workplace Improvement* (Portland, Ore.: Productivity Press).

Kodama, F. (1986), 'Japanese Innovation in Mechatronics Technology', *Science and Public Policy*, 13/1 (Feb.): 44–51.

McKinsey Global Institute (1993), *Manufacturing Productivity* (Washington: McKinsey and Company).

Markusen, A., and Yudken, J. (1992), *Dismantling the Cold War Economy* (New York: Basic Books).

NIST (National Institute of Standards and Technology) (1994), *Manufacturing Extension Partnership* (Washington: US Department of Commerce, Office of Technology Administration).

Porter, M. (1990), *The Competitive Advantage of Nations* (New York: Macmillan).

Saxenian, A. (1994), *Regional Advantage: Culture and Competition in Silicon Valley and Route 128* (Cambridge, Mass.: Harvard University Press).

Shapira, P. (1990), *Modern Manufacturing: New Policies to Build Industrial Extension Services* (Washington: Economic Policy Institute).

—— (1995a), 'Modernizing Small and Mid-Sized Manufacturing Enterprises: US and Japanese Approaches', in M. Teubal, D. Foray, M. Justman, and E. Zuscovitch (eds.), *Technological Infrastructure Policy: An International Perspective* (Amsterdam: Kluwer Academic Publishers).

—— (1995b), 'Report of the 1994 Modernization Forum Study Mission to Japan' (Dearborn, Mich.: Modernization Forum).

Sorensen, C. E. (1956) (with Samuel T. Williamson), *My Forty Years with Ford* (New York: W. W. Norton).

Subramanian, S. K., and Subramanian, Y. (1991), 'Managing Technology Fusion through Synergy Circles in Japan', *Journal of Engineering and Technology Management*, 8: 313–37.

Ziegler, J. N. (1992), 'Cross-National Comparisons', in Alic *et al.*, *Beyond Spinoff*, 209–47.

11. Saving and Finance: Real and Illusory Constraints on Full Employment Policy

Robert Pollin

Are expansionary economic policies, and in particular the pursuit of full employment policies, constrained by an economy's level of saving? An affirmative answer to this question dominated economic analysis in the pre-Keynesian era, reaching its apogee during the 1930s as the British 'Treasury View'. Perhaps the fundamental innovation of Keynes's *General Theory* and the subsequent Keynesian revolution was to overthrow the Treasury View, and to set in its place the argument that, as Joan Robinson put it, 'firms are free, within wide limits, to accumulate as they please, and the rate of saving of the economy as a whole accommodates itself to the rate of investment that they decree' (1962: 82–3).

The policy implications of this Keynesian perspective were profound. Keynesian theory meant that policy aimed at raising the level of output and employment should focus on directly stimulating investment rather than seeking to increase the available pool of saving. In so far as policy needed to focus on financial markets and practices, here again the primary concern was not on saving behaviour *per se*, but rather on how best to encourage the channelling of funds towards productive activity and away from speculation.

Such Keynesian thinking notwithstanding, the idea that an economy's saving rate is the central determinant of an economy's ability to grow was restored fairly quickly within the mainstream literature, in the realms of both theory and policy. In the USA in recent years, a large body of research has emerged which not only affirms the notion of the centrality of saving, but has also been correspondingly disturbed over the perception that the US savings rate has sharply declined. Laurence Summers captures well the flavour of this recent literature:

It is widely recognized that low national saving is the most serious problem facing the US economy. Low saving accounted for the trade deficit and the slow growth

I am grateful for comments on an earlier draft of this chapter to the participants of the 19 May 1995 conference at the University of East London on 'The Relevance of Keynesian Economics Today' and to those at the 24 May 1995 meetings in Robinson College, Cambridge. I especially wish to thank Jonathan Michie and Professor Brian Reddaway for their careful reading of the earlier draft.

in standards of living that continued through the 1980s. Part of the reason for low national saving is the excessive federal deficit. But the low US saving rate is increasingly the result of insufficient personal saving by US households. (1990: 153)

In the view of Summers as well as many others, there are then two parts to the US savings problem: the first is the federal deficit, and the second is the profligacy of US households.

For the past decade, macroeconomic policy discussion in the USA has been dominated by variations on these aspects of the perceived US savings crisis. This includes the policy-making team within the Clinton Administration (of which Summers himself has been a high-level participant since its inception), which was elected in 1992 on a platform of 'putting people first'–that is, job growth, higher wages, and more public investment, but which abandoned this programme immediately after the election in favour of a 'putting deficit reduction first' set of tax and expenditure initiatives.[1]

And yet, despite this ascendancy of what we may call the 'causal saving' perspective, there are, just as in Keynes's time, several fundamental problems with it; indeed, not surprisingly, many of the same fundamental problems have persisted. This chapter discusses some of the most basic fallacies, through which we reach the conclusion that saving rates *per se* are actually an *illusory* constraint on full employment policy, at least with respect to the US economy.

However, in making this argument, I do not mean to suggest that financial forces more broadly do not affect the level of activity or the prospects for successfully implementing full employment policies. Quite the contrary, in several basic ways, the structure of financial markets and institutions in the USA are major barriers to an egalitarian growth path which includes full employment macro policies. This chapter thus considers these *actual financial constraints* on egalitarian growth policies after examining the illusory saving constraint.

The main arguments that I will develop are as follows:

1. On even the most basic evidence, it is not obvious that private saving rates are actually low. Indeed, when one accounts for depreciation of capital assets and changes in the market value of outstanding assets, saving rates are not low at all by historical standards. Indeed, they are higher than during the 1960s, the most rapid period of post-war economic growth in the USA.

2. Saving rates—defined as simply current income minus consumption— exert at best a weak influence on the availability of financial resources for either investment or other purposes. Keynes argued that his 'most fundamental' conclusion in this area of analysis was that 'the investment market

---

[1] See Baker and Schaefer (1993) on the economic consequences of this decision and Woodward (1994) on the backroom machinations which led Clinton to reverse his policy direction even before taking office.

can become congested through a shortage of cash. It can never become congested through a shortage of saving' (1973: 222). This basic insight is supported by evidence in the USA over the post-war period. Thus, for example, considering quantity flows, the extension of credit as a proportion of gross private saving has ranged between 50 and 170 per cent. Considering prices, evidence shows no strong relationship between the ratio of lending and saving and the movements of the real interest rate.

3. Focusing on the relationship between saving and investment, it is true that the growth of domestic net investment has been stagnant since the 1970s. However, this has not been because the corporations faced a shortage of funds available for investment. Indeed, over 1982–90, corporate internal funds were fully sufficient to pay for *all* of the corporations' fixed investment. Corporations did also borrow to an unprecedented degree over this period, but, in the aggregate, all of these funds were channelled towards mergers, take-overs, and related speculative activities.

4. The view that the federal deficit—that is, public dissaving—has contributed to economic decline by 'crowding out' private sector borrowers from financial markets also faces basic problems. But to understand the limitations of the crowding-out perspective, it is necessary to examine the effects of federal government borrowing within a broader context that includes the overall sources and uses of funds within the US financial system, and in particular the relationship between finance, saving and investment.

5. There are three actual financial constraints on full employment policy:
(*a*) Financial forces create a bias towards short-term time horizons and toward speculative take-overs rather than new investments.
(*b*) These same forces encourage a long-term tendency towards increased financial fragility, meaning that expansions are inhibited by speculative financial activity and downturns are more severe than they would be otherwise because of the vulnerability of the financial system.
(*c*) The structure of the financial system has weakened the ability of the primary tools of interventionist policy, that is, deficit spending and loose monetary policy. Moreover, as has been seen clearly with the Clinton Administration, the increased power·of financial market interests within the realm of macro policy formation has created a deflationary bias in the setting of macro policy.

The rest of the chapter will expand on each of these points, then closes by briefly considering some desirable and feasible policy approaches for dealing with the actual constraints on full employment policy.[2]

[2] This chapter is a survey that seeks to synthesize the main policy-relevant arguments of much of my recent research. Throughout the chapter, I provide references to more fully developed versions of the arguments which are often only fleetingly sketched here. Aside from any inflated sense of self-importance, this is the reason for the chapter's heavy dose of self-references.

The focus here is on saving as a *financial* phenomenon; that is, as Michael Boskin put it, as 'providing funds either directly or indirectly to capital markets to channel into productive investments' (1986: 13). I consider only secondarily the *real* side of saving behaviour; that is, the forgoing of consumption which then releases an economy's physical capacity for creating new productive assets. The real and financial sides of saving are, for the most part, separable topics. The real side-issues, such as considering the capacity of the labour force to utilize the existing stock of plant and equipment to create new output–itself contains many analytic pitfalls, such as the appropriate measurement of a 'natural' rate of unemployment. But I note at the outset that the literature in the USA about a perceived shortage of saving has been concerned almost entirely with financial factors, in particular the extent to which low saving rates have created an inadequate supply of financial resources available for capital accumulation.

ARE SAVING RATES REALLY LOW?

Given the fundamental importance assigned to saving as an economic category, it is striking, amid a voluminous literature, how little consensus exists on the way saving is most appropriately defined and measured. The most widely reported measure, taken from the National Income and Product Accounts (NIPA), is the residual income after accounting for personal and capital consumption. This is the measure to which Summers and other mainstream economists refer when they contend that the USA has experienced a saving crisis beginning in the 1980s. But this is not the only measure of saving, nor can it be reasonably claimed that it is necessarily the most illuminating measure for understanding a range of economic issues, including whether a shortage of saving actually exists.

Two basic considerations which are excluded from the standard NIPA saving measure are the role of depreciation and changes in market values of assets and therefore in net worth. When we take account of these factors, we no longer observe anything resembling a saving crisis in the 1980s and 1990s. The relevant figures to which we will refer are reported in Table 11.1, which, as with succeeding tables, reports data over the five full business cycles since 1960.[3]

Net and Gross Saving

The first two rows of Table 11.1 report figures on net and gross saving. With net saving, see that, at 6.0 per cent of GDP, private saving was at its

---

[3] Cycles are based on annualizing NBER quarterly peaks; peak years are those in which NBER quarterly peaks fall within the first two quarters of that year or the last two quarters of the previous year.

Table 11.1. Net, gross, and net worth saving relative to Gross Domestic Product (%)

NBER cycles:	1960–9	1970–3	1974–9	1980–1	1982–90
Net private saving	8.2	8.3	8.0	7.1	6.0
Gross private saving	20.4	21.0	22.6	21.8	23.6
Net worth saving	18.7	32.6	46.8	44.0	21.3

Note: See Appendix for detailed definitions of data categories.

Source: US National Income and Product Accounts.

low point over 1982–90 relative to the other four full cycles reported in the table. However, gross saving, at 23.6 per cent of GDP, was at a high point relative to the four previous cycles. The difference between net and gross measures of saving thus reflect changes in the rate at which the capital stock is depreciating. The underlying (and generally unspoken) assumption among those who argue that a saving crisis exists must therefore be that changes in the rate of depreciation are not significant for understanding national saving behaviour or the relationship between saving and capital accumulation. But is this a reasonable assumption?

Boskin (1986), for example, argues that net saving is the more appropriate saving category because it measures only the funds available to finance economic growth, not the funds needed to replace worn-out capital stock. However, from the perspective of the financial markets, depreciation allowances constitute a substantial source of funds, mainly short-term deposits for financial intermediaries. They therefore contribute to the lending capacity of intermediaries, just as would deposits from any other source. In addition, depreciation allowances are not employed simply to replace worn-out plant and equipment. Rather, they are primarily used to finance investment in capital stock that represents some advance over previous vintages. This is especially the case when, as was certainly true in the 1980s, the pace of technical change accelerates. Therefore, even from the viewpoint of the non-financial firm, depreciation funds contribute to growth, not merely replacement.[4]

Changes in Net Worth

The third row of Table 11.1 measures changes in private net worth relative to GDP. Here we do see a sharp decline in net worth relative to GDP over 1982–90 as compared to the previous three cycles, the ratio for 1982–90 being 21.3 per cent, while those for the three previous cycles range between

---

[4] See the careful discussion of these issues in Baker (1995).

32.6 and 44.0 per cent. However, the figure for 1982–90 is still higher than for the 1960s, when the US economy experienced its most rapid rate of economic growth. Moreover, the surge in private net worth over the 1970s is primarily explained by speculative booms in residential house and land values. In short, by this measure as well, there is no evidence that the USA departed significantly from past patterns of saving behaviour. Considering then the issues of both depreciation and market values of net worth, the notion cannot be supported that the USA experienced a saving shortfall in the 1980s. Such an argument can be made only through observing the net saving category in NIPA, but there is no basis for singling out this measure as more appropriate than the alternatives we have considered.

SAVING, LENDING, AND THE PROVISION OF FINANCIAL RESOURCES

Sources and Uses of Loan Funds

The foregoing discussion raises a broader issue: for what reason might one want to measure saving rates? It is only within the framework of that question that a consideration of any given measure of saving becomes meaningful. In considering the relationship between saving and macroeconomic performance, the basic issue of concern is really how to measure saving appropriately in determining credit supply, that is, in providing the financial provisions for investment and other uses of credit.[5]

Is there any meaningful difference between *saving* and *financial provisioning*, or lending? Again, this depends on how one defines both terms. Let us begin by defining lending as the *creation of a financial asset* (and a corresponding liability). Though this appears straightforward, two important issues emerge from such a definition. The first is that tangible asset creation is excluded from this definition, whereas the net increases in tangible assets are a component of the net worth measure of saving considered above. However, the creation of tangible assets does not directly contribute to the supply of loan funds.[6]

The second issue is to distinguish the creation of financial assets from saving in non-tangible assets as measured in a national income accounting framework. The basic distinction has to do with the role of financial intermediaries. In national income accounting, intermediaries do not save but

---

[5] This section draws from Pollin and Justice (1994) and Pollin (1995).

[6] There is, of course, close comparability between a significant subset of debt and equity instruments, such that drawing a sharp distinction between debt and equity instruments as forms of lending is somewhat arbitrary. In addition, tangible assets do indirectly contribute to the supply of loan funds through providing collateral for loans. For our purposes here, we simply note these ambiguities in our demarcations. However, in previous work I found that adjusting the definition of lending to include net new equity purchases did not change any of the results regarding the relationship between saving and lending.

simply intermediate–that is, they transmit savings between ultimate savers and borrowers. In fact, however, intermediaries play a crucial role in determining the supply of credit. This is because the system of financial intermediation can create flexibility in supplying financial resources by increasing the possibilities of sharing risk and through the more efficient provisioning of liquidity. These effects in turn will affect both the supply and demand curves for credit.

To illustrate these considerations more carefully, it will be helpful briefly to consider Figure 11.1, which shows a range of alternative financial structures, in which the structures become increasingly complex according to both the types of arrangements through which loans are made and the types of loans being contracted. Figure 11.1 is thus a variation on a standard matrix showing 'sources and uses of funds'. The difference between this and the standard sources and uses framework is that we are distinguishing sources according to the structure of intermediation rather than particular sectors providing funds; and similarly we distinguish uses by type of loan category rather than the sector accepting a loan. With the sources of funds along the vertical axis, we move from the most rudimentary system of 'self-finance' to systems of 'complex intermediation' which allow for asset and liability management as well as foreign lending and government policy as exogenous sources of funds. Along the horizontal axis, we distinguish investment, consumption, asset transfer, and government spending as alternative uses of loan funds.

If we begin at the north-west corner of the matrix in Figure 11.1, we have the simplest system in which investment is entirely self-financed, and there are no other uses of funds. Obviously, in this case, an increment of investment would require an equal prior stock of saving by the investing unit; that is, a willingness of the investors themselves to accept a decline in liquidity equal to the size of the investment. Moving down the vertical axis, the possibilities increase for sharing risk and a more efficient provisioning of liquidity. In particular, allowing for asset and liability management implies the development of thick markets for liquidity. This imparts far greater flexibility to the system of intermediation, and thereby weakens the saving constraint on lending. Indeed, the defining characteristic of a successful innovation in asset or liability management is that it reduces the transaction costs of circulating liquid assets, and therefore allows for the provision of funds at lower interest costs to borrowers, that is, either an outward shift or a flattening of the loan supply schedule.[7]

The flexibility of the sources of funds increases further when we allow for

[7] The outward shift of the loan supply curve would signify the creation of a lower interest rate level on average, but that the trade-off between increments of credit supply and rising interest rates has remained stable. A flattening of the loan supply curve would mean that increments of credit supply would be obtainable at lower rates. A classic paper on the topic of financial innovation and the supply of loan funds is Minsky (1957). An excellent historical reference is Wray (1990) and a good textbook treatment is Podolski (1986).

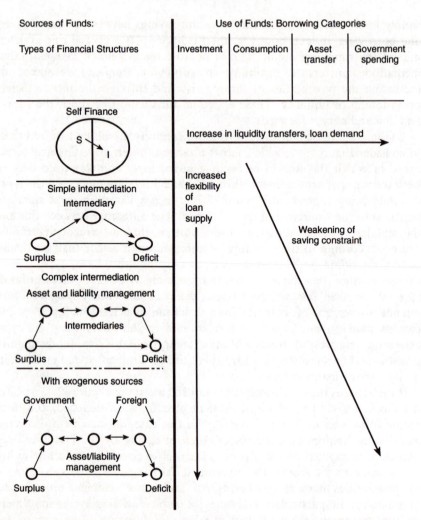

Fig. 11.1. Simple to complex financial systems

exogenous sources, including the foreign sector and government policy. The distinction between these exogenous sources is that a foreign source would have to reduce its own liquidity to provide the domestic economy with loan funds. All else being equal, foreign sources can therefore produce an outward shift of the loan supply schedule. But an increase in foreign sources should not in itself generate a flattening of the loan supply curve unless this increase in foreign sources is associated with innovative asset and liability management practices that reduce the transaction costs of circulating liquid assets.[8]

Government policy however, and in particular central bank policy, can generate a net increase in private liquidity, which, *ceteris paribus*, would flatten the slope of the loan supply curve. Whether the central bank will pursue such a policy outcome will depend on its own goals and constraints. The level of prior domestic saving may be, but need not be, an argument in the central bank's reaction function in considering how it should respond to an autonomous increase in investment financing. It certainly need not be the central bank's only consideration; others might include an aim of encouraging investment, employment, and real incomes.

Let us briefly consider the effects of moving eastward along the 'use of funds' horizontal axis of Figure 11.1. In general, moving eastward will both increase the demand for loan funds—shifting outward the loan demand curve—and create further channels for the efficient transfer of liquid assets, that is, flattening the loan supply curve.

Consumption lending, to begin with, reduces the need for households to carry liquid assets in their portfolios. This will increase the proportion of loanable funds available for a given stock of household saving. It might also increase the relative proportion of consumption to all forms of saving, and thus strengthen the accelerator effects of an autonomous increase in investment.

Asset transfers do not involve the utilization of real resources other than those necessary for effectuating the transactions themselves. Such activities will therefore have a much different impact on the real economy, according to how the real economic variables are affected by changes in capacity utilization. Nevertheless, the direct effect on the liquidity of the financial system of borrowing to finance asset transfers will be the same as that for borrowing for investment (that is, asset creation).[9]

Finally, borrowing by government will shift the loan demand curve outward, just as would borrowing by private sectors. In the government's case, though, this use of funds can also influence its ability to serve as an exogenous source of funds. To the extent that the government borrows to finance its interventions as a lender, it broadens its role as an intermediary in financial markets. This creates further possibilities for the allocation of liquid assets, and thus also for a flattening of the loan supply curve.

---

[8] Of course, the globalization of finance is in fact intimately associated with innovative financial practices. See e.g. Cosh, Hughes, and Singh (1992).

[9] Its indirect impact will differ since, unlike the case where the worker is engaged in building the new machine, no real resources, other than those necessary for arranging the transfer, are being used to effectuate this transfer.

Data on Sources and Uses of Funds

Based on the considerations above, it will now be useful to examine the shifts in both sources and uses of funds over time. This will enable us to gauge the degree to which credit provisioning weakens any possible saving constraint.

Sources In Table 11.2, I report figures on lending sources by sectors. The five sectors shown are three private domestic sectors, depository institutions (banks and thrifts), non-depository institutions (insurance and finance companies), and direct lending from households and nonfinancial businesses (the complete definition of these categories is presented in the Appendix). It also includes the two major exogenous sources, government and foreign lenders.

Table 11.2. Sources of credit supply by lending sector (% of total lending)

NBER cycles	1960–9	1970–3	1974–9	1980–1	1982–90
PRIVATE DOMESTIC SOURCES					
Depository institutions	53.8	58.2	42.8	31.3	23.8
Non-depository					
financial intermediaries	24.9	22.2	24.2	36.8	37.1
Non-intermediated sources	10.1	1.1	12.1	8.5	12.7
GOVERNMENT	10.0	9.9	16.3	16.6	18.7
FOREIGN ENTITIES	1.1	8.5	4.6	6.8	7.6

Note: See Appendix for detailed definitions.
Source: US Flow of Funds Accounts.

The most striking pattern in the table–one, however, that is hardly surprising to observers of contemporary financial market developments–is that the proportion of loans originating with depository institutions has fallen sharply over the full period, from 53.8 per cent of all loans in the first cycle to 23.8 per cent in the most recent full cycle. All the other sectors have increased their relative shares as loan sources. In terms of magnitude, the most significant increase is the rise of loans from non-depository intermediaries. These sources increased sharply beginning in the 1980s, accounting by the time of the last full cycle for 37.1 per cent of all loans. In terms of percentage change over the full period, the largest increase was in foreign sources, rising from 1.1 per cent in the first cycle to 7.6 per cent over the last cycle. However, the increase here began in the second cycle, with the ratio peaking at 8.5 per cent. Since then, cyclical fluctuations of this ratio have been stronger than any trend pattern, as shown by the values for standard deviations for this ratio. Overall, the one clear trend that does emerge is of a movement away from lending sources that are more traditional and constrained to ones that are less so, especially the less constrained domestic sources.

Uses In Table 11.3, lending uses are decomposed by sector in a manner similar to that for sources. It shows the proportion of total borrowing absorbed by three private domestic sectors: households, non-financial businesses, and financial intermediaries. It also shows two exogenous borrowers: government–including state and local as well as federal government–and foreign borrowers. The major pattern that emerges here is the decline in the proportion of borrowing done by private non-financial users–households and non-financial businesses–relative to that of financial businesses and government. Borrowing by foreigners never rises above 5.2 per cent, and over the last cycle declines to 1.4 per cent.

Table 11.3. Sources of credit demand by borrowing sector (% of total borrowing)

NBER cycles	1960–9	1970–3	1974–9	1980–1	1982–90
PRIVATE DOMESTIC USES					
Households	34.0	26.2	30.2	22.4	25.3
Non-financial business	37.5	39.4	29.7	33.1	24.5
Financial business	9.2	13.2	12.5	18.2	21.2
GOVERNMENT	15.4	18.4	22.6	21.1	27.6
FOREIGN ENTITIES	3.9	2.7	5.0	5.2	1.4

Note: See Appendix for detailed definitions.
Source: US Flow of Funds Accounts.

With households and non-financial businesses, the declines in proportions of total borrowing follow a similar pattern. Household borrowing fell from an average of 34.0 to 25.3 per cent between the first and last cycles while business borrowing fell from 37.5 to 24.5 per cent over this same period. Government borrowing rose from 15.4 to 27.6 per cent over the five cycles, and the largest relative increase was for the financial sector, whose share of total borrowing rose from 9.2 to 21.2 per cent.

The growth of borrowing by the financial sector here is a crucial aspect of the overall perspective presented here. It is the liability side of the rise of intermediaries' asset and liability management activities. This growth of liability management within the system of intermediation has generated a thick market for liquidity, including a fall in costs for trading in liquid assets.

The increase in the relative position of government affects financial mar-

kets in several ways. The most straightforward effect is that it has changed
the pattern of government finance itself, with debt financing growing relative to revenue financing. Beyond this, however, lies a range of hotly con-
tested issues, including how the government deficit affects private
investment and consumption patterns and whether, in particular, government borrowing crowds out private investment. Without plunging
specifically into that literature, the framework of analysis presented here
does enable us to raise some basic questions. The fact is that private sector
borrowers have hardly faced significant quantity constraints in credit markets. To the contrary, private borrowing has *increased* along with federal
deficits: the *relative* decline in household and business borrowing that we
observe in Table 11.3 has occurred even while these sectors have increased
their borrowing relative to their incomes and expenditures, and have channelled their borrowed funds towards an increasingly diversified set of uses.
We will return to this question in the next section of the chapter when we
consider the financial patterns of non-financial corporations.[10]

With respect to price constraints, federal deficits have no doubt exerted
some upward pressure on interest rates. But this surely cannot serve as a
full explanation for the rise of real rates. At the very least, we also need to
explain both the factors influencing credit supply (the slope and intercept
of the loan supply curve)–including the goals and constraints governing
Federal Reserve policy–and the factors influencing the private sector's
credit demand. After all, even after the unprecedented increase in the federal government's borrowing requirement over the 1980s, the private sector
still accounted for two-thirds of total domestic borrowing.[11]

In terms of the specific question of lending supply and the saving constraint, the crucial feature of a rise of government borrowing is that, by
increasing the flexibility of government finances, it increases the ability of
the government to operate as an intermediary–that is, to act as a source of
funds through its lending and loan guarantee programmes. Considering this
effect, the rise of government borrowing should then also contribute to
weakening the saving constraint.

Lending, Saving, and Interest Rates

These dramatic shifts in both sources and uses of funds should serve to
weaken the saving constraint, primarily through increasing the lending
capacity for any given level of saving, thereby flattening the loan supply

[10] We will not consider further the change in financial patterns of the household sector. This
topic is covered in Pollin (1990).

[11] See Pollin (1993a) for an extensive critical review of the crowding-out literature and other
perspectives on the macroeconomic effects of the federal deficit. One important if neglected
aspect of the effects of the federal deficit is the extent to which the rise in government borrowing affects financial market stability, given that a rising share of outstanding government
debt by definition means that the proportion of non-defaultable debt also rises.

curve. We now turn to the data on lending and saving to examine the extent to which this has actually occurred.

Figure 11.2 plots the values of the ratio of lending to gross private saving between the second quarter of 1960 and the second quarter of 1990.[12] The vertical lines in the figure divide the period into its constituent NBER business cycles. As can be seen, this relationship is not stable, as the ratio varies both cyclically and over the full period. Some rough decade breakdowns of the ratio provide an interesting initial perspective on the longer-run shifts in the lending–saving relationship, which are of primary interest here. From 1960.2–1969.4, lending averaged 50.0 per cent of saving and the range of values for the ratio was between 19.8 and 69.8 per cent. Over the 1970s, lending rose on average to 72.4 per cent of saving and the ratio ranged between 42.7 and 103.9 per cent. For 1980.1–1990.2, lending averaged 93.2 per cent of saving and the values ranged between 51.2 and 163.4 per cent. In the 1980s, in other words, the flow of lending relative to

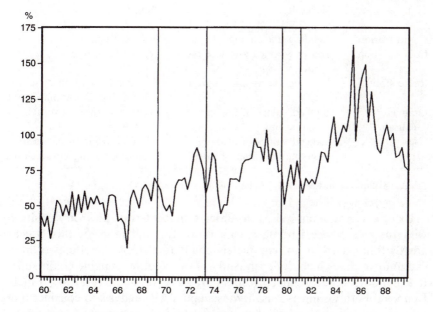

Fig. 11.2. Total domestic lending as a proportion of gross private saving

Sources: US National Income and Product Accounts; Flow of Funds Accounts of Federal Reserve System. See Appendix for detailed definitions.

[12] The data here are reported as quarterly figures, as this time period was used in the formal tests reported below.

gross private saving was roughly double that of the 1960s. At its peak in the 1980s, lending flows were more than 60 per cent greater than that of gross private saving.

Such descriptive evidence on quantity flows between lending and saving clearly needs to be supplemented by more formal tests. I report here the results of three types of time-series and regression analysis. The results of these tests are also summarized in Table 11.4. Through cointegration analysis, lending and saving were found not to be cointegrated, that is, there is no long-term equilibrium relationship between lending and saving. This result was robust across various measures of saving and various lag structures. I also found that the ratio of lending to saving was not cointegrated with the movement of real interest rates. This means that interest rates as well as the quantity flows are, at best, only weakly constrained by the level of saving.

Table 11.4. Summary of time-series tests on lending, saving, and interest rates

Test	Variables	Result
Cointegration	Lending and saving	Not cointegrated
Cointegration	Lending/saving and interest rate	Not cointegrated
Regression	Lending/saving and interest rate	Positive association offset by asset/ liability management
Granger causality	Lagged values of lending and saving	Weak causality from saving to lending
VAR	Lagged values of lending/ saving and interest rates	Weak association between lending/saving interest rates

Sources: Pollin and Justice (1994); Pollin (1995).

Using regression analysis, I do observe that interest rates vary positively with the rise of the lending–saving ratio. But the force of this effect is greatly diminished, if not completely counteracted, by the effects of financial innovations which, independently of saving flows, enable credit supply to expand without forcing corresponding increases in interest rates. Finally, I pursued both Granger-causality tests and VAR analysis to consider more fully the lagged relationship between the lending–saving ratio and interest rates. Here again, I observed at best weak associations between saving and lending, and between the lending/saving ratio and the movements of real interest rates.

In short, the empirical results reported here are supportive of the spirit of Keynes's 'most fundamental conclusion' that 'the banks hold the key position in the transition from a lower to a higher scale of activity,' (1973: 222). Of course, we can no longer refer merely to 'banks', but rather to the entire system of intermediation, and we must also be more explicit than was Keynes in recognizing the central role of government policy in moving 'from lower to higher scales of activity'. But the basic conclusions are nevertheless of clear Keynesian lineage: first, that the behaviour of the standard national income-accounting measure of net saving rates is a far less significant consideration than the attention accorded it would warrant; secondly, that the allocation of credit use and the structural characteristics of financial markets are far more important than their relative neglect would suggest.

FINANCE, INVESTMENT, AND SPECULATION

The concern over inadequate saving rates is not ultimately about saving behaviour *per se*, but rather about the capacity of businesses to invest, and thereby to raise output levels and productivity rates, the benefits of which might then be broadly shared. It is therefore now appropriate to ask the direct question: have there been financial barriers in the USA to capital accumulation, resulting either from low saving rates or other financial variables? In considering this question, it is important to note at the outset that two matters are not in dispute: that the rate of investment growth for US corporations declined over the last two full business cycles; and that spending on mergers, take-overs, and similar asset transfers, financed primarily with borrowed funds, rose correspondingly over the same period. Differences of course emerge in trying to explain these phenomena and their possible connections. To a significant extent, mainstream analysts hold to the view that the primary explanation for these trends is the low saving rate itself. Summers again writes that:

The channel through which low national saving leads to reduced investment is through increases in the *cost of capital*. When low national saving leads to a reduced supply of capital, the cost of capital rises . . . High costs of capital lead investors to set high hurdle rates of return that cheat the future. Consider this comparison: A US investor, given his or her costs of capital, would be willing to invest only 37 cents in return for receiving one dollar six years from now, compared with 66 cents for his or her Japanese counterpart. It is hardly surprising that Japanese managers often appear to take a longer view than their US counterparts do. (1990: 159)

Summers is correct to focus on the problem of short-term time horizons by corporations as a cause of their poor investment performance and their thrust towards speculative finance. The problem with this perspective is that it is so heavily dependent on the assumptions that official NIPA measures of net saving will determine the cost of capital, and that the cost of capital will determine both the rate of fixed investment and the inducements of speculative asset transfers. These assumptions cannot be supported on the basis of either the theoretical or the empirical literature.

We have already considered in some detail the various factors that will cause market-clearing interest rates to change independently of officially measured saving rates, based on changes in the institutional structures through which both sources and uses of funds are channelled as well as through policy interventions. The notion that the cost of capital can itself explain both investment behaviour and a bias towards speculative finance is equally problematic. For one thing, within the contemporary econometric literature, standard neoclassical cost of capital models do not perform well in explaining investment behaviour relative to models focusing on demand influences (that is, variants on an accelerator model) or models focusing on changes in internal funds or profitability (variants of cash flow models).[13]

Building in part on the profitability and demand theories of investment, I would rather propose that there are two basic sources for the short-term bias in the contemporary US financial market. The first is contemporary profitability trends that have rewarded asset transfers over asset creation. The second is an organizational structure that similarly rewards short-term measures to raise equity returns over long-term commitments to productive enterprise. We will consider these in turn, and explore the relationship between these phenomena and the related trend towards increased financial instability. We begin by examining the contemporary finance and investment patterns of non-financial corporations.

Declining Profitability and Rising Interest Rates

Table 11.5 reports data on corporate financial patterns over the past five full business cycles. Beginning with the data on corporate profitability, we see that from a 1960s peak of 12.2 per cent, corporate profitability fell in the early 1970s to 8.1 per cent. The next row presents data on a proxy for Tobin's Q ratio. Tobin's Q measures the market value of firms–including equity and debt valued in financial markets–relative to the value of firms' assets at replacement cost. Because of measurement difficulties, this proxy excludes the value of bonds, and reports the market value of equities relative to firms' net work at replacement cost. This proxy ratio is still a good reflection of the financial market's perception of future corporate profitability. Between the 1960s and early 1970s, we see that this proxy Q ratio fell along with the profit rate, from 0.96 to 0.84 per cent. The growth rate of gross capital expenditures also fell between the first and second cycles, but not by as much as the decline in profitability. Because of this disjuncture

[13] The literature here is of course vast. The most comprehensive econometric 'horse race' between five alternative perspectives—accelerator, cash flow, neoclassical, Tobin's Q, and time-series theories—is that of Kopcke, which in turn is summarized clearly in Berndt (1991). Two recent innovative studies which find support for accelerator and cash flow/profitability perspectives are Fazzari (1993) and Gordon (1995). A lively collection which presents alternative perspectives on investment theory is Davidson (1993).

between profitability–the primary source of corporate internal funds–and capital expenditures, corporate borrowing relative to their capital expenditures rose sharply over this period from 30.2 per cent to 38.7 per cent.

This first upward shift in corporate debt financing is an instance of what we may call *compensatory* credit demand: in the face of declining internal sources, corporations financed capital expenditures increasingly from debt. To a small degree, this tendency may have been promoted by the decline of real interest rates, falling on average from 2.6 to 2.3 per cent. But such a sharp increase in debt-financing cannot be attributed primarily to the small interest rate decline.

In the second half of the 1970s, profit rates fell even further and the proxy Q ratio plunged: the stock market here is valuing the current cost net worth of firms at only 41 cents on the dollar. The growth of capital expenditures again falls, now to 4.1 per cent. In this period, however, corporations as a whole did not increase borrowing to sustain.capital expenditures, even though real interest rates were negative. They primarily cut back capital expenditures, but also relied to a somewhat greater extent on internal funds.

Beginning in 1982, a fundamental shift occurred in corporations' finance and investment strategies. Their commitment to financing capital expenditures remained weak. For the full period, capital expenditures grew by only 2.2 per cent; and *all* of that growth was due to a 35 per cent increase in spending between 1983 and 1984. Otherwise, capital expenditures declined by an average of 1.5 per cent annually.

At the same time, new opportunities opened up in this period for what we will term *speculative* finance–that is, borrowing to purchase existing assets with the expectation of capital gain. With the net worth of corporations for sale at an average of 44 cents on the dollar over 1981–2 (as shown through the proxy Q), firms borrowed to an unprecedented degree to buy up existing assets rather than create new capital stock. The borrowed funds–capital expenditures ratio thus jumped to 37.2 per cent, despite the paltry growth of capital expenditures itself. At the same time, the ratio of internal funds to capital expenditures rose to an average of over 100 per cent. This means that, in the aggregate, *none* of the growth of debt over 1982–90 was necessary to finance new capital expenditures; *all* of it was devoted to mergers and buyouts (as well as current operations). This is the most important sense in which the corporate borrowing patterns of the 1980s were unique. We observe this rise of speculative finance through considering the ratio of net new equity issues/net increase in liabilities. This ratio turns negative in the 1980s, dramatically so, at negative 50 per cent, over the last full cycle. This means that one-half of the increase in corporate liabilities was devoted only to buying back outstanding equities.

This surge in speculative borrowing corresponded with the run-up in real interest rates to an average of 5.8 per cent, a level unprecedented over the past 100 years of US history. The rise of speculative credit demand over 1982–90 was clearly not significantly inhibited by this unprecedented increase in real interest rates.

As to the effects of this investment and finance pattern, profitability did increase somewhat over this period. However, gains in profitability were not nearly adequate to outweigh the growing burden of corporate debt. As Table 11.5 shows, net interest payments absorbed 51 per cent of non-financial corporations pre-tax earnings over the 1980s, a figure more than double the average of 19.8 per cent for the previous two decades.

These descriptive data suggest, then, a fairly straightforward story. US corporations became reluctant to invest in new plant and equipment in the 1980s because of the decline in profitability, beginning in the early 1970s, and the high level of interest rates, sustained through the 1980s. However, firms were not reluctant to borrow, despite the relatively weak profitability performance and high interest rates. But in the aggregate they borrowed predominantly to finance corporate take-overs.[14]

Financial Structure, Corporate Time Horizons, and Instability

Exit and Voice in Financial Markets. The US financial system is organized primarily through arms' length relationships in capital markets. It is, as John Zysman has put it, a 'capital-market' dominated system, similar to that of Great Britain, in which 'financial institutions tend to manage port-folios of stocks, spreading their risks across companies rather than invest-ing in the future of specific companies that they nurture through hard times' (1983: 63). There is now a substantial literature which argues that this insti-tutional structure encourages a short-term focus on dividends and capital returns rather than a long-term focus on nurturing investment projects.[15]

Such an institutional arrangement contrasts sharply with the 'credit market'-based systems which had prevailed in Japan, France, and Germany prior to the 1980s wave of financial innovation and deregulation.[16] In these

[14] The Neo-Marxian literature on the relationship between declining profitability and accu-mulation is enormous. In terms of the present discussion, the most important aspects of that literature are two: the empirical demonstration that such a long-term decline in profitability is observable; and the efforts to test alternative explanations for this observed decline. While there is little dispute by now that such a decline has occurred, beginning in the late 1960s or early 1970s, there is still no consensus as to the predominant explanations. For a range of recent perspectives see Marglin and Schor (1990), Sherman (1991), Moseley and Wolff (1992), and Brenner (1995). There are interesting commonalities between this literature and that of Michael Jensen's 'free cash flow' theory of corporate take-overs. Such parallels become more apparent in the work of those who have tried to operationalize Jensen's approach, in partic-ular Blair and Schary (1994). Pollin (forthcoming *a*) provides a fuller discussion of these par-allels, as well as an extended discussion of the relationship between profitability declines and corporate take-overs.

[15] Pollin (forthcoming *b*) is, in part, a survey of this literature.

[16] The effects of globalization and deregulation on the viability of the credit market-based systems remains an open question. See Goldstein (1994) for some interesting observations on the Japanese case.

Table 11.5. Profitability, investment, and finance for non-financial corporations

NBER cycles:	1960–9	1970–3	1974–9	1980–1	1982–90
Pre-tax profit rate (%)	12.2	8.1	5.9	6.0	8.6
Proxy Q ratio (%)	0.96	0.84	0.41	0.44	0.63
Growth of gross capital expenditures (%)	6.2	4.3	4.1	0.4	2.2
Borrowed funds/capital expenditures (%)	30.2	38.7	28.8	30.1	37.2
Internal funds/ Capital expenditures (%)	93.8	82.8	87.7	82.8	100.7
Net new equities/ net increase in liabilities (%)	4.9	14.0	3.8	–1.2	–50.0
Real interest rate (average of commercial paper and bond rates; %)	2.6	2.3	–0.1	1.8	5.8
Net interest/pre-tax profits (with IVA + CCA; %)	0.9	27.2	29.7	50.7	51.0

Note: See Appendix for detailed definitions.

Sources: US National Income Accounts, Flow of Funds Accounts, and Balance Sheets; Citibank Economic Database.

systems, financial firms interacted closely with non-financial firms and the state in forging commitments to long-term investment projects. The pressures for short-term profitability or capital appreciation were therefore substantially lower. As Zysman again puts it (1983: 64), because Japan, France, and Germany had 'more restricted capital markets and, in particular, a limited secondary capital market, it is harder for financial institutions to treat equity investments simply as a matter of financial portfolio balance'.

The exit/voice analytic framework developed by Hirschmann (1970) is an illuminating tool for understanding these alternative systems. The US/British system is dominated by exit as a means of exercising influence. Thus, dissatisfied shareholders or bondholders will typically express their displeasure through selling their claims to the company. By contrast, the credit-based systems of corporate finance were premised on the exercise of influence by voice. Major financial institutions and state agencies have been actively involved in charting a non-financial firm's long-term plans and then committing themselves to the process of implementing those plans.

The point here is not that credit market systems necessarily encourage voice while the capital market system must rely on exit; rather that in the current US system there is no institutional framework parallel to that which prevailed in Japan, France, and Germany for encouraging the exercise of voice. This absence–embedded within a capital market-based system–has focused the US financial structure towards short-term thinking.

Short-Termism and Financial Instability. The market and institutional interactions associated with bank-based systems induce, among other things, a greater tolerance on the part of the lenders/investors for higher leverage ratios (Grabel 1995, table 10). At the same time, the capital-market-based systems are more susceptible to financial instability than the bank-based systems. Why is this so?

The underlying source of financial instability, at the simplest level of accounting, must be that debt commitments are systematically outstripping the income flows necessary to service them. In turn, the basic explanation for the systematic deviation between debt commitments and income flows is that borrowed funds are used disproportionately to finance speculative and compensatory spending, that is, borrowing to purchase existing assets with the expectation of capital gain and to compensate for declining income streams or other internally generated funds. Put another way, instability results when debt is used insufficiently to finance productive spending, that is, spending that enhances the income-generating capacity of firms and individuals. When credit is extended for speculative and compensatory spending to a disproportionate degree relative to productive spending, the result will be income streams inadequate to finance the growth of debt.

Considered within a cyclical framework, the most influential treatment of this problem has been the work of Minsky.[17] He argues that, as an economy shifts into a growth phase, and, in particular, as full employment is approached, 'euphoric expectations' take hold. The growth rate of debt exceeds that of profits since, for a given distribution of income between wages and profits, profit opportunities are constrained by the growth of productivity, whereas the extension of credit is not so constrained. The financial structure thus becomes increasingly fragile–that is, vulnerable to an interactive debt deflation that induces a generalized depression.

In the absence of government intervention or other administrative arrangements, an economy dominated by free capital markets thus proceeds normally from a cyclical trough to an unsustainable boom characterized by speculative financial behaviour. The cycle culminates in a debt deflation and depression. But the depression itself creates the conditions for a return to financial robustness and recovery. Thus, and here Minsky's position is perfectly consistent with that of Schumpeter and Marx, depressions are functional: they are the destructive but necessary mechanism–the 'slaughtering of capital values' as Marx put it–that returns financial structures to balance.

---

[17] Minsky's position is most fully presented in his *Stabilizing an Unstable Economy* (1986). See Pollin and Dymski (1994) for a fuller treatment of the Minskian argument presented here.

Note here that the basic source of difficulties is not the rise of debt *per se*, or even the rise of debt relative to income or assets. High leverage ratios are therefore sustainable as long as, over time, a return flow of revenue is generated to service them. As a general model, the bank-based systems are better designed to avoid mismatches between debt commitments and income flows. This is because the thrust towards speculative finance is reduced inasmuch as finance is dedicated to a greater degree to long-term productive projects. Moreover, the commitment to long-term projects means that the projects will have a longer grace period before they have to generate returns to their lenders.

Evidence on Short-Termism and Instability. A wide range of research has accumulated in recent years to support the view that the bank-based systems have promoted longer time horizons and greater financial stability. To begin with, survey evidence of corporate Chief Economic Officers (CEOs) in the USA, Japan, and Europe developed by Poterba and Summers (1992) found that US CEOs believe that their time horizons are shorter than those for their counterparts in Europe and Japan. According to the US CEOs, their relatively short horizons derive to a significant extent from the financial market environment in which they operate. These managers contend that US equity markets undervalue long-term investments. Were the firms valued more in accordance with the perceptions of managers, the managers believe that their long-term investments would increase, on average, by perhaps as much as 20 per cent.

The survey also found that, for the US CEOs, the minimum expected rate of return that would induce them to commit to a new investment project–the 'hurdle rate'–is substantially higher than standard cost-of-capital analysis would suggest. On average, US CEOs reported that their hurdle rate was 12.2 per cent. This compares with an average real return over the past fifty years of less than 2 per cent on corporate bonds and around 7 per cent for equities.

Moreover, as Porter (1992) reports, this difference in time frames and hurdle rates is associated with a striking difference in managerial goals: US managers rank return on investment and higher stock prices as their top two corporate objectives, whereas Japanese managers rank improving existing and introducing new products, and increasing market share as their two highest priorities. Higher stock prices is ranked last by Japanese managers among the eight objectives included in the study.

These survey findings are also consistent with evidence from corporations' actual operations. Porter (1992) found that the share of investment going to R&D, intangibles (especially investment in 'corporate training and human resources'), and plant and equipment is lower in the USA than in Germany and Japan. In addition, the proportion of total R&D expenditures going to long-term projects is lower in the USA. In the USA, 22.6 per cent of total R&D budgets were allocated to such projects, while in Japan and Europe the figures were 46.8 and 60.5 per cent respectively.

Studies have also found that, at least over the 1970s and 1980s, the real after-tax cost-of-capital is higher in the USA than in Japan or Germany, and that differences in these countries financial systems are seen as a major contributing factor. McCauley and Zimmer (1989), for example, write that greater integration of industry and finance has permitted higher leverage without raising bankruptcy risks equivalently, and also greatly reduced liquidity risks of non-financial firms. Moreover, according to McCauley and Zimmer, the Japanese and German governments are more actively involved in mitigating the direct costs associated with non-financial firms' periods of financial distress.

ECONOMIC POLICY UNDER ALTERNATIVE SYSTEMS

The McCauley and Zimmer evidence on interventionist policies raises the more general question of policy differences between the bank- and capital market-based systems. Examining such differences involves considering both the constraints on policy imposed by the financial system in place, and the policy options pursued, given such constraints.

Broadly speaking, bank-based systems are structured more suitably than credit market-based systems for achieving favourable results from two primary policy tools–expansionary policy and industrial strategy. The basic source of the advantages inherent in bank-based systems is the greater integration between non-financial and financial firms, which engenders a communality of purpose that is absent in capital market-based systems.

Expansionary Macro Policy

There are basically two macroeconomic policies to achieve growth and employment goals–manipulating government spending relative to tax receipts and thereby the level of an economy's aggregate demand; and central bank policies to adjust both the quantity and price of credit.[18] Here we focus on the limitations, and in particular the diminishing capacities over time, of fiscal and monetary policy as instruments of full employment policies. To try to pre-empt any possible misunderstanding on this point, I will not be suggesting that such policies have become completely ineffectual nor

[18] These policies were accompanied in the post-war period by two types of financial regulatory regimes. The first, of course, was the Bretton Woods international monetary framework, designed to provide administrative procedures for maintaining balance of payments and exchange rate equilibrium between countries. The second was the array of financial regulatory systems developed within domestic economies. These latter are discussed briefly in this chapter's concluding section, and are considered at length from a range of perspectives in Dymski, Epstein, and Pollin (1993).

that they might not become more effective within a restructured institutional environment. The argument is rather that they have become increasingly neutralized within the existing environment.

What are the reasons for the diminished capacities of expansionary policy? To begin with, it will be helpful to return to Minsky's analysis of systemic financial fragility. As Minsky has pointed out–drawing from Kalecki's well-known accounting identity wherein profit equals investment plus the government deficit–the effect of deficit spending is to establish a floor for profits. More favourable profit expectations in turn encourage investors' animal spirits, which should then break the downturn. At the same time, expansionary monetary policy will counteract the liquidity shortages of distressed financial firms.

But what Minsky stresses here is that these interventionist policies will not promote a full employment equilibrium. Rather, the interventionist policies will tend to validate the existing fragile financial structure: problems emerging out of the fragile structure are allowed to continue and even deepen. As a result, the effectiveness of full employment policies will deteriorate over time: government policy is called on increasingly to bale out the fragile system and thereby avoid a depression, but this very policy encourages more fragility and thus increases the burdens placed on future policy interventions.[19]

This analytic framework helps us to explain the extraordinary rise of innovative finance over the second half of the post-war period, including, for example, the rise which we observed above, of asset and liability management within the US financial market.[20] The incentives for innovative finance are a constant, since innovation is essentially a means of lowering the transaction costs of moving funds between surplus and deficit units. Historically however, the collapse of financial markets and subsequent increase in risk aversion by market participants constrained such activities. This constraint has been diminished over the contemporary period. Innovative financial practices, in turn, have weakened the ability of central banks to maintain either price or quantity targets in pursuing expansionary policies.

In bank-based systems, since banks hold equity positions and are active in the management of firms, the banks, along with the non-financial firms, will be more favourably disposed towards expansionary macro policies. In the Anglo-American system, where financial firms are not directly linked to industry, the financial firms are more likely to favour restrictive policies.

[19] Pollin and Dymski (1994) consider these arguments empirically within the US experience between 1875 and 1989, dividing the full period into 'small government' and 'big government' eras. The general finding is that, by several measures, instability had been ameliorated substantially in the post-Second World War 'big government' era through the 1970s. But the 1980s emerge as a unique period, in which government remains large, but the indicators of instability approximate those of the small government era.

[20] This world-wide development is analysed in e.g. De Cecco (1987).

The value of outstanding financial assets is more important to the Anglo-American financial firms than the growth prospects of non-financial firms, so that they are more concerned about the threat of inflation than comparable institutions in bank-based systems.[21]

These attributes are reflected in the central bank policies of different types of countries. In the USA and UK, the central bank has a relatively high degree of independence. Over time that independence has evolved into a close alliance with financial interests. These central banks have therefore tended to favour restrictive policies. In the bank-based systems, where there is a strong link between bank and industry, biases towards restrictiveness tend to be weaker. Germany is a clear exception to this characterization, in that its experiences with hyperinflations created a strong anti-inflation bias and an independent central bank within its bank-based system.

Related to this, in the US/UK model, the independence of the financial system has led to a strong international orientation for the financial sector. In both cases, the domestic currency is used extensively for international transactions, and a formidable industry has developed around international finance. Maintenance of confidence in the currency is therefore given greater priority than in bank-based systems. As Fine and Harris write on the UK:

> Since the beginning of the 1950s, therefore, the City has ensured that (in direct contrast to Japan's post-war policy) interest rates are subordinated to the foreign exchange rather than industrial policy and, by the same token, to short-term factors rather than long-term economic strategy. (1985: 61–2; see also Epstein and Schor 1990).

It also appears that the negative collateral effects of expansionary policy tend to be stronger in the Anglo-American than the bank based systems, though more research is needed to establish this point. This is, first, because capital market systems have a lower tolerance for leverage. Increases in spending, or lower interest rates is more likely to lead firms (and households) to reduce their indebtedness rather than increase expenditures. The relatively greater degree of speculative activity also makes it more difficult in capital market financial systems to affect long-term interest rates. Expansionary policy in these countries are more likely to be met by rising long-term interest rates due to inflationary fears, and this will reduce the effectiveness of monetary policy. The most general problem is that expansionary policy in capital market-based systems is more likely to engender an allocation of credit towards speculative finance, such as mergers, buyouts, and real estate investments.[22]

---

[21] This argument is developed theoretically and empirically in Epstein and Schor (1990).

[22] The bank-based systems have high degrees of speculation as well. But as Goldstein (1994) explains with respect to the Japanese model, at the core of this credit market system is a bifurcation, in which speculative market activity does not exert significant influence over the use of funds for productive proposes. Epstein (1993) discusses what he calls the 'inflation', 'external',

Credit Allocation and Industrial Policy

The advantage of bank-based systems here is that they are more amenable to public credit allocation policies as the centrepiece of industrial strategy. Public credit allocation policies, in turn, can be an effective instrument of an industrial strategy that promotes growth and employment. At the same time, in considering the historical experience, the actual causal relationships between a country's financial structure, its degree of public credit allocation, and its efforts and attainments in the area of industrial policy is not clear-cut. That is, while it may appear that countries with bank-based systems are more successful at implementing credit policies and industrial strategy, this appearance may primarily result from the fact that the same countries are more actively engaged in both credit allocation and industrial strategy. Relatedly, the historical record is not clear on the extent to which countries with capital market systems can deploy credit policies to compensate for the capital market's distortions–that is, engaging credit policies to replicate the desirable features of a bank-based system within the existing capital market institutional framework.

Zysman for one, argues emphatically that public credit allocation policies are necessary–indeed are the one essential tool–for successfully implementing industrial strategies. He says there are two reasons for this. The first is that:

business decisions are hard to control or influence through administrative or regulatory rules. Those same decisions may, however, be influenced by negotiation in which the payment for services rendered is unambiguously calculated in monetary terms. Discretionary influence in industrial finance permits the government to deal within the framework of business decisions and to affect the balance sheet directly (1983: 76–7).

In addition, Zysman argues that public credit allocation is a universally applicable policy instrument. As such, it 'eliminates the need to find specific authority to influence specific decisions or to control an agency that has formal authority over a specific policy instrument'. By comparison, Zysman contends that tax policy is not nearly as effective a policy tool. Taxes tend to operate on gross profits from earnings, and thus are an *ex post* rather than *ex ante* incentive to pursue the priorities of the industrial strategy. Tax policy is also less flexible; it can be used reasonably well to target categories of activity but not specific industrial ends.[23]

and 'domestic financial market' constraints on the pursuit of expansionary monetary policy in the US context. Pollin (1991) presents evidence from Granger causality tests showing interactive causality between central bank- and market-determined interest rates, rather than the predominant one-way causality from the central bank-determined short rates to the market that is needed for expansionary monetary policy to dominate financial market forces.

[23] Working with US data, Karier (1994), for example, finds that tax credits to stimulate private investment are highly inefficient: only 12% of the credits are actually spent on new investment. The other 82% are used to pay higher dividends, buy stocks or bonds, or reduce reliance on external sources of funds.

The US Experience.   Despite its status as the prototypical capital market-based financial system, the US has had considerable experience since the 1930s with public credit allocation policies. Indeed, considering all forms of credit allocation (direct loans, guaranteed loans, and government-sponsored enterprise loans) the federal government is the largest creditor in the US financial market, lending or underwriting on an annual basis about 15–30 per cent of all loans. These figures are reflected in the data in Table 11.2, showing the relative role of the US federal government as a lender. Major recipients of funds have been the housing sector, agriculture, and education. These programmes, moreover, have achieved considerable success relative to their stated goals. For example, they have contributed substantially to the unprecedented access to home ownership enjoyed by a high proportion of the non-wealthy in the USA.[24]

The extent and successes of these programmes demonstrate that credit policies can be implemented effectively within a capital market-based financial system. At the same time, while these policies have been crucial to the development of targeted sectors, they have not been used in the USA to guide an overall industrial strategy. It is therefore difficult to gauge the extent to which a broader-based set of credit/industrial policies might be frustrated by the structure of US financial markets. But the success of these programmes on their own terms suggests, contrary to Zysman, that the ability to implement credit allocation policies successfully may not depend significantly on whether a country's financial system operates as a bank or capital market-based system.

CONCLUSIONS

The financial system in the USA does present formidable obstacles–the tendency towards short time horizons, speculation, and financial instability–to the successful pursuit of national full employment policies. As I have argued, these constraints are diminished in countries using bank-based financial systems. Does this suggest that a viable policy path for the USA would be to appropriate the features of the bank based systems?

There are several reasons why this is neither a viable nor a desirable policy approach for the USA. At the most basic level, it is not realistic to assume that the existing highly developed US financial market could be converted wholesale to a bank-based framework. This is particularly true in light of the trend towards the globalization of financial markets, which widens the opportunities for asset and liability management and innovation, and thereby increases the difficulties of imposing a full break with the existing institutional structure.

[24] Bosworth, Carron, and Rhyne (1987) is a basic reference on the development of federal credit programmes in the USA.

More importantly, despite the many successful features of bank-based systems, these systems also have serious deficiencies, in particular from the perspective of seeking to achieve full employment and other egalitarian ends. The close interlocking relationships between major firms, banks, and government bureaucracies create wide opportunities for clientism in credit allocation and the associated phenomena of industrial collusion and oligopoly. Such an environment obviously limits access to external funds for small and new industrial enterprises, and as a result may diminish opportunity and the prospects for innovation. In addition, as Stiglitz (1993) argues, the credit subsidy programmes associated with bank-based systems face problems because the costs are diffuse and difficult to calculate.

But even more objectionable from the perspective of constructing an egalitarian programme is the fact that bank-based systems have been most successful in East Asian countries such as Japan and South Korea, where government planners were completely independent from democratic decision-making processes. In the US, such policies would be desirable only if they could also extend accountability within the financial system.

The aim of USA policy should therefore be not to emulate the bank-based systems, but rather to reproduce within the US context the elements of these systems that are central for implementing full employment policies. Within this context, policies would be needed to accomplish three things: lengthen time horizons and reduce the tendency towards speculative finance; reduce the conflict of interest between industrial and financial capital; and counteract the factors which weaken the effects of expansionary fiscal and monetary policy.

The policy interventions that would be most important for accomplishing these aims would include the following:

1. A set of financial regulatory policies which 'levelled the playing field upwards' among all financial intermediaries. A substantial inducement towards financial innovation has been simply to exploit differences in how intermediaries are regulated. A consistent regulatory environment would obviously eliminate such opportunities, and would therefore strengthen the impact of any given set of regulations.[25]
2. Credit allocation policies to increase incentives toward productive investment and weaken those for speculative asset transfers. Several instruments could be used here, many of which are already part of existing law.

One instrument would be the existing Community Reinvestment Act (CRA). This law obligates banks to lend for projects among under-served areas of the communities in which they are located. This law has not been seriously enforced by the Federal Reserve, the agency responsible for

---

[25] Discussion on this question began with the innovative work of D'Arista and Schlesinger (1993).

enforcement. But if the CRA were extended to include all intermediaries, not just banks, and were then seriously enforced on a uniform basis, it would have a significant impact on the composition of both lending and investment throughout the country.[26]

A similar approach could be taken with the investment of pension funds. Although pension funds are heavily subsidized by government policy, they are not required to consider the social rate of return on their investments. This is so, despite the fact that such a calculation is fully consistent with what Barber and Ghilarducci describe as fund participants' 'whole identities: as workers who need employment to accumulate retirement income, as citizens whose quality of life depends on the economic health of their communities, [and] as parents who want their children to have as much or more opportunity than their parents had' (1993: 291). It is true that vexing problems stand in the way of implementing such an approach to pension fund investing. For example, how would a single pension fund capture for its own community the social rate of return accruing to that fund's investments? But these problems are becoming less formidable as experience is gained with such investment strategies.

A third instrument of this kind could be Federal Reserve policy itself (see Pollin 1993b). The Federal Reserve could use discount window lending and asset requirements for financial institutions to promote investments with high social rates of return, and discourage short time horizons and speculation. Something like this has already been implemented on a large scale in the USA with, for example, the long-standing asset requirements that were applied to the Savings and Loan industry. Until they were deregulated in 1980, the S&Ls were required to concentrate their lending almost entirely on individual family home mortgages. These policies were extremely successful in promoting home ownership among the non-rich to an unprecedented degree. Comparable policies could be successful in promoting investments with high social rates of return, including high employment multipliers, and to discourage speculative finance.

All of these policies would increase the power of government regulators over the financial system. It would therefore be necessary to increase the accountability of the regulators to the public, which would then also increase the accountability of the financial system more broadly. Several proposals for extending accountability have been formulated, including within the US Congress. One that I have suggested (in Pollin 1993b) calls for direct election of the Presidents of the regional Federal Reserve Banks. Such increased accountability would also address–though never entirely solve–the legitimate concerns that public allocation policies would degenerate into rent-seeking and other hidden costs to the economy.

A securities transaction excise tax would also discourage speculative

---

[26] See Campen (1993) on this question.

finance. Depending on how high the tax were set, one could trade off between discouraging speculative activities on the one hand, or generating substantial taxation revenues on the other. Thus, for example, given existing US financial markets, a transaction tax on equity trades of 0.5 per cent which was then scaled down appropriately by maturity for all bonds and derivative instruments would raise roughly $30 billion a year.[27]

All these policies to channel private investment toward productive activities would have to be complemented by increased public investment. But note that the public investment policies could now be financed, at least to a significant degree, by the securities transaction tax. Taken as a whole, this policy approach would also make conventional expansionary fiscal and monetary policies more effective in promoting full employment. The following effects would be central:

1. The increase in public investment would create a guaranteed domestic outlet for increased government spending policies. This reduces the import leakage of expansionary policies.
2. Investments induced by the accelerator effects of expansionary policies would be channelled increasingly towards investments with high social rates of return, and away from asset transfers that absorb financial resources but do not increase output and income. This would reduce the 'speculative leakage' of expansionary policy.
3. Creating more accountability within the financial system would weaken the power of financial capitalists in the system. This, in turn, would reduce the bias against expansionary policies.

In short, even given the existing conditions in the US financial system, important steps can be taken fairly readily to weaken the financial constraints on full employment policy. To get to that point, however, of course entails overcoming a series of formidable analytical as well as political obstacles. Not least of these is the widespread belief among US economists that raising national saving rates is a first prerequisite for regaining economic prosperity.

[27] The details of designing such a tax are presented in Baker, Pollin, and Schaberg (1995).

DATA APPENDIX

The two basic data sources used here are the National Income and Product Accounts (NIPA) and Flow of Funds Accounts (FFA). I have retrieved NIPA and related data from *Citibase: Citibank Economic Database* and FFA data from the *Flow of Funds Coded Tables*. In the FFA codebook, the prefix 'S' refers to seasonally adjusted flows, 'U' to unadjusted flows, and 'L' to unadjusted levels.

Table 1. Net, gross and net worth saving relative to Gross Domestic Product

'Net private saving' and 'gross private saving' are from NIPA (Table X-5-1 in *Citibase* codebook).
'Net private saving' is 'gross private saving' minus corporate and non-corporate consumption of fixed capital.
Net worth saving is from Table B. 11 (S852090005) in FFA codebook.

Table 2. Sources of credit supply by lending sector

Figures are from FFA codebook, Table F. 6–F. 7.
'Depository institutions' is (S764004005)+(S494004005).
'Non-depository financial intermediaries' is (S694004005)–(S494004005).
'Non-intermediated sources' is (S254004005)–(S314002005).
'Government' is (S314002005)+(S404002005)+(S214002005).
'Foreign entities' is (S264004005).

Table 3. Sources of credit demand by borrowing sector

Figures are from FFA codebook, Table F. 6–F. 7.
'Households' is (S154102005).
'Non-financial business' is (S134102005)+(S114102005)+(S104104005).
'Financial business' is (S794104005).
'Government' is (S314102005)+(S204102005).
'Foreign entities' is (S264104005).

Table 5. Profitability, investment and finance for non-financial corporations

'Pre-tax Profit Rate':

- Numerator is Pre-tax NIPA Profits + Net Interest; raw figures are from Citibase codebook, Page X-1-7; inflation premium is subtracted from net interest payments following the method described in Pollin (1986) pp. 230–231.
- Denominator is net capital stock, defined as current-dollar net reproducible tangible capital stock of nonfinancial corporations, from FFA Balance Sheets for the US Economy, Table B.104, line 3.

'Proxy Q ratio' is from FFA Balance Sheets for the US Economy, Table B. 104, line 50.
'Growth of gross capital expenditures' is from FFA codebook, Table F. 104, (S105050005).
'Borrowed funds' is from FFA codebook, Table F. 104, (S104104005).
'Internal funds' is Internal Funds plus Inventory Valuation Adjustment from FFA codebook, Table F. 104 (S10600105).
'Net new equity' is from FFA codebook, Table F. 104 (S103164003).
'Total liabilities' is from FFA codebook, Table F. 104 (S104190005).
'Real interest rate' is average of six-month Commercial Paper Rate (page I-2-1 in Citibase codebook, FYCP) and Composite Rate on Treasury Bonds over ten years (page I-2-2 in Citibase codebook, FYGL), subtracted by change in contemporaneous GDP deflator.

Figure 11.2

'Total domestic lending' is from FFA codebook, Tables F. 6–7, 'Total net lending' (S894104005)–'Monetary Authority Lending' (S714002105).

REFERENCES

BAKER, DEAN (1995), 'Conceptual and Accounting Issues in the Analysis of Saving, Investment and Macroeconomic Activity', in R. Pollin (ed.), *The Macroeconomics of Finance, Saving and Investment* (Ann Arbor: University of Michigan Press).
—— and SCHAEFER, TODD (1993), 'Putting Deficit Reduction First?', *Challenge* (May–June): 4–10.
—— POLLIN, ROBERT, and SCHABERG, MARC (1995), 'The Case for a Securities Transaction Excise Tax: Taxing the Big Casino', manuscript, Department of Economics, University of California, Riverside.
BARBER, RANDY and GHILARDUCCI, TERESA (1993). 'Pension Funds, Capital Markets, and the Economic Future', in Dymski, Epstein, and Pollin (1993), 287–320.
Berndt, Ernst R. (1991), *The Practice of Econometrics: Classic and Contemporary* (Reading, Mass.: Addison-Wesley).
BLAIR, MARGARET M., and SCHARY MARTHA A. (1994), 'Industry-Level Indicators of Free Cash Flow', in M. Blair (ed.), *The Deal Decade: What Takeovers and Leveraged Buyouts Mean for Corporate Governance* (Washington: Brookings Institution), 99–135.
BOSKIN, MICHAEL J. (1986), 'Theoretical and Empirical Issues in the Measurement, Evaluation, and Interpretation of Postwar US Saving', in G. F. Adams and S. M. Wachter (eds.), *Savings and Capital Formation* (Lexington, Mass.: Lexington Books), 11–44.
BOSWORTH, BARRY P., CARRON ANDREW S., and RHYNE, ELISABETH H. (1987), *The Economics of Federal Credit Programs* (Washington: Brookings Institution).
BRENNER, ROBERT (1995), 'Systemic Crisis and US Decline', *New Left Review*.

CAMPEN, JAMES T. (1993), 'Banks, Communities and Public Policy', in Dymski, Epstein, and Pollin (1993), 221–52.

COSH, ANDREW, HUGHES, ALAN, and SINGH, AJIT (1992), 'Openness, Financial Innovation, Changing Patterns of Ownership and the Structure of Financial Markets', in T. Banuri and J. Schor (eds.), *Financial Openness and National Autonomy* (Oxford: Clarendon Press).

D'ARISTA, JANE and SCHLESINGER, TOM (1993), 'The Parallel Banking System', in Dymski, Epstein, and Pollin (1993), 157–200.

DAVIDSON, PAUL (1993) (ed.), *Can the Free Market Pick Winners: What Determines Investment?* (Armonk, NY: M. E. Sharpe).

DE CECCO, MARCELLO (1987) (ed.), *Changing Money: Financial Innovation in Developed Countries* (Cambridge, Mass.: Basil Blackwell).

DYMSKI, GARY, EPSTEIN, GERALD and POLLIN, ROBERT (1993) (eds), *Transforming the US Financial System: Equity and Efficiency for the 21st Century* (Armonk, NY: M. E. Sharpe).

EPSTEIN, GERALD (1993), 'Monetary Policy in the 1990s: Overcoming the Barriers to Equity and Growth', in Dymski, Epstein, and Pollin (1993), 65–100.

—— and SCHOR, JULIET (1990), 'Macropolicy in the Rise and Fall of the Golden Age', in Marglin and Schor (1990), 126–52.

FAZZARI, STEVEN (1993), 'Monetary Policy, Financial Structure and Investment', in Dymski, Epstein, and Pollin (1993), 35–64.

FINE, BEN, and HARRIS, LAURENCE (1985), *The Peculiarities of the British Economy* (London: Lawrence and Wishart).

GOLDSTEIN, DON (1994), 'The Impact of Financial Structures on Corporate Behavior', manuscript, Department of Economics, Allegheny College.

GORDON, DAVID (1995), 'Must We Save our Way out of Stagnation?', in R. Pollin (ed.), *The Macroeconomics of Finance, Saving and Investment* (Ann Arbor: University of Michigan Press).

GRABEL, ILENE (1995), 'Saving and the Financing of Productive Investment: The Importance of National Financial Complexes', in R. Pollin (ed.), *The Macroeconomics of Finance, Saving and Investment* (Ann Arbor: University of Michigan Press).

HIRSCHMAN, ALBERT O. (1970), *Exit, Voice and Loyalty: Responses to Decline in Firms, Organizations, and States* (Cambridge, Mass.: Harvard University Press).

KARIER, THOMAS (1994), 'Investment Tax Credit Reconsidered: Business Tax Incentives and Investments', Jerome Levy Economics Institute of Bard College, Public Policy Brief, 13.

KEYNES, JOHN MAYNARD (1973), 'The "Ex Ante" Theory of the Rate of Interest' (1938), in *The Collected Writings of John Maynard Keynes*, Vol. 14 (London: Macmillan).

MCCAULEY, ROBERT N. and ZIMMER, STEVEN A. (1989), 'Explaining International Differences in the Cost of Capital', *New York Federal Reserve Bank Quarterly Review* (summer): 7–28.

MARGLIN, STEVEN and SCHOR, JULIET (1990) (eds), *The Golden Age of Capitalism: Reinterpreting the Postwar Experience* (New York: Oxford University Press).

—— (1986), *Stabilizing an Unstable Economy* (New Haven: Yale University Press).

MINSKY, HYMAN P. (1992), 'Central Banking and Money Market Changes' (1957), in *Can 'It' Happen Again? Essays on Instability and Finance* (Armonk, NY: M.E. Sharpe), 162–78.

MOSELEY, FRED and WOLFF, EDWARD (1992) (eds.), *International Perspectives on Profitability and Accumulation* (Brookfield, Vt.: Edward Elgar).

PODOLSKY, T. M. (1986), *Financial Innovation and the Money Supply* (Cambridge, Mass.: Basil Blackwell).

POLLIN, ROBERT (1986), 'Alternative Perspectives on the Rise of Corporate Debt Dependency: The US Postwar Experience', *Review of Radical Political Economics* (spring and summer): 205–35.

—— (1990), *Deeper in Debt: The Changing Financial Conditions of US Households* (Washington: Economic Policy Institute).

—— (1991), 'Two Theories of Money Supply Endogeneity: Some Empirical Tests', *Journal of Post Keynesian Economics*, 13/3: 366–96.

—— (1993*a*), 'Budget Deficits and the US Economy: Considerations in a Heilbronerian Mode', in R. Blackwell, J. Chatha, and E. J. Nell (eds.), *Economics as Worldly Philosophy: Essays in Political and Historical Economics in Honor of Robert L. Heilbroner* (New York: St Martin's Press), 107–44.

—— (1993*b*), 'Public Credit Allocation through the Federal Reserve: Why It Is Needed; How It Should Be Done', in Dymski, Epstein, and Pollin (1993), 321–54.

—— (1995), 'On the Independence of Aggregate Credit Supply from Private Saving', in R. Pollin (ed.), *The Macroeconomics of Finance, Saving and Investment* (Ann Arbor: University of Michigan Press).

—— (forthcoming *a*), 'Borrowing More but Investing Less: Economic Stagnation and the Rise of Corporate Takeovers in the US', *International Review of Applied Economics*.

—— (forthcoming *b*) (1996b), 'Financial Structures and Egalitarian Economic Policy', *International Papers in Political Economy*.

—— and DYMSKI, GARY (1994), 'The Costs and Benefits of Financial Instability: Big Government Capitalism and the Minsky Paradox', in G. Dymski and R. Pollin (eds.), *New Perspectives in Monetary Macroeconomics: Explorations in the Tradition of Hyman P. Minsky* (Ann Arbor: University of Michigan Press), 369–402.

—— and JUSTICE, CRAIG (1994), 'Saving, Finance, and Interest Rates: An Empirical Consideration of Some Basic Keynesian Propositions', in G. Dymski and R. Pollin (eds.), *New Perspectives in Monetary Macroeconomics: Explorations in the Tradition of Hyman P. Minsky* (Ann Arbor: The University of Michigan Press, 279–310).

PORTER, MICHAEL (1992), *Capital Choices: Changing the Way America Invests in Industry* (Washington: Council on Competitiveness).

POTERBA, JAMES and SUMMERS, LAWRENCE (1992), 'Time Horizons of American Firms: New Evidence from a Survey of CEOs', manuscript, Department of Economics, Massachusetts Institute of Technology.

ROBINSON, JOAN (1962), *Essays in the Theory of Economic Growth* (London: Macmillan).

SHERMAN, HOWARD (1991), *Business Cycles* (Princeton: Princeton University Press).

STIGLITZ, JOSEPH (1993), 'The Role of the State in Financial Markets', manuscript, Department of Economics, Stanford University.

SUMMERS, LAURENCE H. (1990), 'Stimulating US Personal Saving', in Charles E. Walker, Mark A. Bloomfield, and Margo Thorning (eds.), *The US Saving Challenge: Policy Options for Productivity and Growth* (Boulder, Colo.: Westview Press), 153–76.

WOODWARD, BOB (1994), *The Agenda* (New York: Simon and Schuster).

WRAY, L. RANDALL (1990), *Money and Credit in Capitalist Economies: The Endogenous Money Approach* (Brookfield, Vt.: Edward Elgar).

ZYSMAN, JOHN (1983), *Government, Markets and Growth: Financial Systems and the Politics of Industrial Change* (Ithaca, NY: Cornell University Press).

12. Capacity, Transnationals, and Industrial Strategy

Keith Cowling and Roger Sugden

A substantial outward shift in the relationship between capacity utilization and unemployment within the European Union has been observed in the early 1990s, with any given level of capacity utilization associated with rising levels of unemployment. This chapter seeks to offer an explanation for this phenomenon in terms of the increasing dominance and changing nature of transnationally organized production. Thus European unemployment is linked to the activities of the transnationals. Whilst demand-side expansion will have a short-term impact it offers no long-term solution. But neither will traditional supply-side policies. To begin to address the issue of European unemployment requires the development of new supply-side strategies which seek to restructure the industrial basis of the European economy.

THE LINKS BETWEEN CAPACITY UTILIZATION AND UNEMPLOYMENT

Whilst capacity utilization poses considerable measurement problems, it would seem clear that a rightward shift in its negative relationship with the level of unemployment has taken place since the 1960s within the countries of the European Union (Bean 1994). Bearing in mind the relationship between capacity utilization and inflationary pressure, and a general desire to avoid inflation, it would appear that capacity is becoming a more and more significant constraint on the achievement of lower levels of unemployment within Europe. This is apparent in the present UK recovery where various commentators and policy-makers appear to have taken the view that the UK is approaching unsafe levels of capacity utilization even while unemployment remains high. Rowthorn (1995a) relates the shifting relationship to the slowdown in the rate of investment since the 1960s (see also the contribution by Kitson and Michie, Ch. 2 in this volume) and in turn relates this to the squeeze on the profit share in the 1970s due to the impact of powerful unions. However, whilst it would seem plausible to offer this as at least part explanation of what happened in the 1970s, it would not appear warranted as a continuing explanation for what remains observable in the 1990s. Rowthorn's explanation appears to rely in part on the deflationary response by governments in the 1970s to the inflationary spiral created by the distributional conflict, which resulted in a profit squeeze as capacity utilization fell. But in so far as the relation between capacity utilization and unemployment has shifted, this source of profit squeeze cannot account for rising unemployment. The trade unions in Britain, and more generally within the European Union, are but a pale reflection of their former selves—certainly not major actors in the elemental forces swirling around the European economy.

As Samuel Brittan observes, 'what is puzzling to a market economist is why it does not pay businesses to extend capacity to take advantage of abundant surplus labour' (*Financial Times*, 6 April 1995). He goes on to remove one explanation commonly offered: 'inadequate domestic savings are not a constraint on investment in a worldwide capital market where any one country can tap the international savings pool'. He finally argues that, 'for reasons that are still not clear—the market clearing price has turned against low skilled, and perhaps other kinds of labour too. In the US the pressure emerges in low wages; in Europe it takes the form of higher unemployment'.

We believe Brittan is right to put investment in its international context, but in restricting himself to the international savings pool he offers an incomplete explanation for what is going on. Not only do the major companies have access to a world-wide capital market for funding their investment, they also have a world-wide choice in their location of that investment, potentially, if not realized at any point in time. The missing element in the discussion of Rowthorn and Brittan is the way in which the whole system of industrial production has taken on a transnational form which is both quantitatively and qualitatively quite different from what it was in the 1960s.

Whilst transnationals' activities have become increasingly important throughout the twentieth century, it is since 1945 and especially since the 1950s that they have grown and spread dramatically, see Dicken (1992), Dunning (1993). Thus by the 1960s they had emerged as important, but it is since then that their growth and spread has continued apace and they have now become what the United Nations (1993) calls 'central actors' in the world economy. The late 1960s, the 1970s, and the late 1980s were periods of dramatic growth in foreign-investment flows. It has been estimated that by 1988 the total value of the (foreign and domestic) capital stock of transnationals was approaching US$5,000 billion, approximately 35 per cent of the combined grossed domestic products of 'industrial market economies' and developing countries (Dunning 1993). (In fact these figures significantly underestimate transnationals' presence because they are based on a narrow view of what is meant by the term 'transnational corporation'; see Cowling and Sugden 1994a.) By the mid-1980s transnationals were responsible for at least 'three-quarters of the world's commodity trade, and four-fifths of the trade in technology and managerial skills' in the world's 'market economies' (Dunning 1993). Moreover since this time there has been an interesting change in international investment flows: in the early 1980s there was a drop in outward direct investment from the 'major investing countries' but by 1986 'capital exports had recovered to a new peak, while between 1987 and 1989 they were more than four times that of the first half of the 1980s' (Dunning 1993). And as further evidence of transnationals' quantitative significance, witness the most recent information on overseas investment by British companies (CSO Bulletin, First Release: *Overseas Direct Investment*, 31 Jan. 1995). At a time when manufacturing investment in the UK was declining, investment in overseas subsidiaries grew by 68 per cent between 1992 and 1993, this representing about one-quarter of private sector investment. The CBI (*Financial Times*, 1 Feb. 1995) attributed the outward investment surge to the UK recovery: apparently the recovery in UK profits was sufficient to generate an interest in investment, but it was not to be in the UK! (See also Driver's contribution to this volume: Ch. 4.) Whilst referring to only one year's observation, this sort of evidence illustrates the potential importance of the decision about the location of production by (British and other) companies currently producing in Britain for the capacity of the British economy to supply jobs.[1] Of course jobs can be supplied by inward investment but for the developed countries there is a growing asymmetry in the two processes leaving a growing deficit in the stock of investment in recent years (see later).

INVESTMENT AND THE TRANSNATIONALS

In offering an explanation for the shift in the capacity utilization–unemployment relationship, Rowthorn assumes profit is the brake on investment, but there are two interpretations: profit as a source of funds or profit as an incentive. The two interpretations tend to coalesce to a substantial degree in the case of a 1960s economy where national, regional, and local firms respond to higher profits by higher domestic investment: locations within the national economy may vary, but, whether as source of funds or incentive, higher profits tended to mean higher levels of domestic investment. Since the 1960s there has been a considerable breakdown in this linkage. Whilst it may be correct to assume that the dominant explanation for the investment decline of the 1970s and early 1980s was the poor levels of profitability achieved within the British economy, it does not follow that as that position is rectified investment rates will return to their former

---

[1] Let it be quite clear that we accept the theoretical and empirical arguments for a strong link between capital accumulation and employment; Rowthorn (1995*a*) offers a recent and compelling review.

levels. Whilst the source of funds argument may remain in place, the incentive explanation now appears in a quite different context. Corporate investment may still be related to corporate profitability, but its location will increasingly be determined by the incentives offered by different locations on a world-wide basis. We now have in place a transnational system of production capable of flexibly adjusting investment flows across nations, and one increasingly capable of exploiting the lowest labour cost sites, wherever they may occur. Of course the corporate economy has not acquired this capacity overnight. It has emerged from an extended process of development of the enabling technologies and organizational forms, coupled with the sweeping away of many barriers to trade and capital movements; see Dicken (1992) for illuminating analysis. The corporate giants have worked long and hard to secure their present position.

Two important qualifications must be made to our argument. First, certain sectors must retain a specific locational presence in production in order to serve a particular market—retailing would be a case in point, but even here there may be transnational relocation possibilities, for example, airline reservation services. And secondly, transnational incentives are only accessible to some organizations—generally small firms do not have access to such opportunities, although there are cases, for example in software. Nevertheless these qualifications do not undermine the basic argument.

The emergence of an international economic system where investment flows are flexibly adjusted to suit transnationals' strategic objectives was foreseen more than twenty years ago by Stephen Hymer (1972). He argued that, if giant transnational corporations dominate the world economy, the structure and organization of such firms would be reflected in the structure and organization of the international economic system. His is a vision which has since been criticized on its details (see, for example, Dicken 1992), but one which we find extremely relevant in its overall thrust and its applicability to the 1990s.

Hymer (1972) focuses on various levels of managerial decision-making in the typical firm, arguing in particular that, whereas some activities in transnationals would be spread throughout the world 'according to the pull of manpower, markets and raw materials', top management would tend to be geographically very concentrated. His basic idea is that firms are characterized by a vertical division of labour, for example, the top level of management being concerned with goal determination and planning whereas the lowest level is concerned with day-to-day events within an established framework. Hymer argues that this lowest level would be widely spread in a giant transnational; thus, for example, it might be supervising unskilled production, which might be carried out in various parts of the world, wherever unskilled labour is cheaply available. By contrast, he suggests that top management in a transnational must be located close to the capital market, the media and the government. Nearly every major corporation in the United States, for example, must have its general office (or a large proportion of its high level personnel) in or near the city of New York, because of the need for face to face contact at higher levels of decision-making.

The crucial implication that Hymer draws from this for the international economic system is that there would be 'a hierarchical division of labour between geographical regions corresponding to the vertical division of labour within the firm'. He concludes:

One would expect to find the highest offices of the [transnational corporations] concentrated in the world's major cities . . . These . . . will be the major centres of high level strategic planning. Lesser cities throughout the world will deal with the day-to-day operations of specific local problems. These in turn will be arranged in a hierarchical fashion: the larger and more important ones will contain regional corporate headquarters while the smaller ones will be confined to lower level activities.

Despite criticisms of Hymer's analysis for over-simplifying a complex reality, it was intended as a characterization and as such his arguments have considerable appeal. As Dicken (1992) concludes from the evidence:

there *are* recognisable hierarchical spatial tendencies in the location of different parts of transnationals. Corporate headquarters do tend to concentrate in a small number of metropolitan centres; regional offices do favour a slightly wider range of cities; production units are more extensively spread both within and between nations, in developed and developing countries.

It seems that there is indeed a correspondence principle relating the structure and organization of transnational corporations to the structure and organization of the international economic system.

What other evidence do we have to support our argument that investment in the advanced industrial countries may be increasingly circumscribed by the transnational activities of the major corporations?[2] Whilst the development of transnational investment within and between the advanced industrial countries can have a major impact on their evolution, resulting in the systemic development of the forces of deindustrialization (see Cowling and Sugden 1994*a*), the recent substantial shift of the flow of foreign direct investment towards the developing countries adds a dramatic new dimension. Where over the period 1987–94 inward investment to the developed countries hardly changed (from $113.4 billion to £117 billion), that to the developing countries rose more than threefold (from $24.1 billion to $80.3 billion): UNCTAD (1995). This is a dramatic shift in the

---

[2] The USA does not reveal the same shifting relationship between capacity utilization and unemployment (Bean 1994). The outcome for the USA has been low wages rather than unemployment. This response undoubtedly relates to the greater flexibility of the US labour market, but whether that flexibility is sufficient for what may be in store in the future is not so clear.

composition of foreign direct investment with possible major consequences for unemployment in the developed world.

Although based on an examination of UK investment within an OECD context, and therefore excluding the phenomenon of rising foreign direct investment to the developing world, recent econometric evidence is strongly supportive of the arguments we have made (Young 1994*a*, 1994*b*). The response of manufacturing investment to costs (labour and capital) in the UK relative to the OECD average was found to be significant and substantial, with a long-run elasticity of 1.62.[3] It is also interesting to note that Young's analysis fails to reveal a significant domestic relative factor price effect (capital/labour) in the presence of the relative international cost effect.

Whilst these results are supportive of our argument, they do not reveal the full story, and increasingly so. The alternative locations for British investment are restricted to the array of OECD countries which of course represent the developed economies. And yet we have argued for the increasing relevance over time of locations within the developing world, and the data support this contention. Correcting for this potential specification error is likely to lead to even more dramatic results than those obtained by Young.

Finally, Young has an interesting comment on the 1970s, the period when the shift of the capacity utilization–unemployment curve appears to begin. He observes the declining OECD investment share in the 1970s and partly explains this in terms of short-run investment demand overshooting the long-run response to the decline in growth of product demand, which he estimates to be unitary elastic. Thus the initial movement in the capacity utilization–unemployment curve may be due to the dynamics of adjustment to a world of slower growth, whereas later movement, we argue, may be more tied up with a world in which the developed economies are losing their share of investment to the developing economies.

To this point we have focused on the locational redirection of investment by the transnationals as an explanation for the shifting relationship between capacity utilization and unemployment. But this is not the only way by which an international transmission of production and jobs is effected within the ambit of the transnational. By simply focusing on the magnitude of investment flows we understate the case. The ambit of the

---

[3] A similar result is obtained for labour demand in Britain, by Barrell, Pain, and Young (1993), which confirms a direct link between unemployment and the international location of production, part of which we might expect to be mediated via the rate of investment. There is also a growing literature relating north–south trade to changing patterns of north–south employment; see e.g. Krugman and Lawrence (1994), Leamer (1994), Sachs and Shatz (1994), Wood (1994), and Rowthorn (1995*b*). Whilst these results are largely supportive of the argument we advance, none of them relate the observed phenomena back to the production and investment decisions of transnational firms and indeed none offer econometric evidence on the underpinning relationships.

transnational should be seen in terms of control rather than ownership. Of course ownership may be seen as a means of effecting control, but control is not uniquely determined by ownership; it is determined by strategic decision-making power. We have argued elsewhere that the concept of strategic decision-making goes to the core of the way in which production is carried out (Cowling and Sugden 1994*b*). This implies that the crucial distinguishing feature of activities within a firm is that they are subject to strategic decision-making from one centre. Thus a firm is the means of co-ordinating production from one centre of strategic decision-making, and a transnational corporation is the means of co-ordinating production from one centre of strategic decision-making when this co-ordination takes a firm across national boundaries. Foreign direct investment (f.d.i.) is one means by which the international co-ordination of production is effected. International subcontracting, franchising, joint-venturing are other means, and they are means which have seen a considerable expansion in their use over time. So long as these alternative means of co-ordination are controlled from a single strategic centre they should be seen as part of a single firm. The transnational's control over the international transmission of production and jobs extends well beyond the legal entity: increasingly the modern corporation, with its transnational capability, incorporates more and more of the market. The market is increasingly subject to the strategic control of the giant firms bestriding it.

DEMAND-SIDE POLICY IS UNDERMINED

The advent of the transnational organization of production and trade would seem a qualitatively distinct process from the arm's length system of production and trade it is more and more displacing. In an increasingly complex world the new system can rapidly and effectively transmit the specification of both product and process characteristics to any production site in the world, and do so within the controlled world of the major corporation. A corporate competence and organization is now present to exploit low labour costs wherever they might occur, subject only to the presence of an adequate infrastructure and an appropriate assessment of political risk. Throughout the world governments are endeavouring to put in place an infrastructure which transnationals will find satisfactory and a welcoming political environment within the context of IMF/World Bank conditionality. As a consequence investment in Britain, and the other advanced industrial countries, does not respond in the same way to the recovery of demand. The lack of capacity in the UK can be made up by capacity elsewhere and at lower cost.

As a result demand-side policy is undermined. Whilst there may be significant short-term response in production, especially following a substantial devaluation, as in the USA and Britain over the recent period, this has failed to deliver the increase in investment previously witnessed at a similar stage of the cycle. Profits rise in the recovery, but are increasingly diverted into investment elsewhere.

'Elsewhere' we have interpreted as alternative international locations. But there is a further qualitative dimension implicit in this process. Clearly not every sector of the economy is equally vulnerable to the international relocation of its activity, although *indirectly* all sectors are vulnerable via multiplier processes. 'Elsewhere' can therefore mean a switch of investment away from manufacturing towards certain areas of service sector activity. Thus we may observe, as a direct consequence of the growing flexibility of international investment, not only a significant deindustrialization of the developed world, but also a retailing revolution within it. Of course retailing itself is increasingly developing a transnational dimension, and can serve to open up domestic markets to a wider range of international products, but in most cases the actual production (delivery) of retail services cannot be dissociated in space from the consumption of these services.

If Western European economies are to be increasingly subject to these processes, and European investment *within Europe* is both to decline and to shift in composition towards non-internationally tradable goods, then the capacity constraint will become a growing balance of payments constraint. But what about the USA? As mentioned earlier, it would appear that the phenomenon of a shifting capacity utilization–unemployment relation has not been present. It seems clear that the USA is characterized by more flexible labour markets than Western Europe (Blinder 1988). Given the same transnational forces, this has led to a very slow growth in real wages for blue-collar workers in the USA since the mid-1970s—indeed many cases of significant money wage cuts have been reported. An enormous relocation of production and jobs has gone on, but it has gone on *within* the USA rather than between the USA and the rest of the world: interregional, from north to south, rather than international. Interestingly, inter-regional econometric analysis within the USA reveals a significant labour cost effect on manufacturing jobs growth (Norton 1986). We can only speculate about the future, but the present and future development of NAFTA may increasingly replace the previous inward migration of people from Latin America with the outward migration of jobs. If this were to happen, and if the flexibility of the US labour market is seen to some extent as the consequence of continuing large-scale immigration, then we may witness a future for the USA more akin to what we have already seen in Western Europe. Capacity may become a binding constraint on employment. Of course Western Europe itself is entering a period with similar tensions. Immigration into Western Europe from Eastern Europe is now clearly on the agenda and there will be increasing pressure to switch production and jobs as a way of alleviating such pressure.

Finally, we need to recognize the likely consequences of these developments for fiscal and monetary policy-making within the developed world. If the existence of transnational corporations serves to reduce the effectiveness of these policies in the context of a nation-state seeking to secure full employment, then the incentive to adopt such policies will be weakened. The decline in Keynesian policy-making, despite the obvious global need for it, may be rooted in the changing industrial structure of the world economy. The growth of transnationalism may then imply a reduction in production and employment in the world economy and not simply their relocation. Indeed we have argued elsewhere that the extension of the transnational organization of production serves more generally to strengthen the forces of economic stagnation (Cowling and Sugden 1995a).

TRADITIONAL SUPPLY-SIDE POLICIES ARE NOT ENOUGH

The processes described are denuding the advanced industrial countries of employment and producing an ever sharper dichotomy within the labour force. The corporate giants became even larger in terms of their control of production, with an ever more tightly defined domestic hierarchical structure, increasingly highly rewarded. With the evolution of the process of job transmission to the developing world, what was originally affecting mainly production operations is increasingly affecting line management. The international competition for jobs, originating within the strategy-making of the giant, transnational companies of the advanced industrial countries, is moving up the production and occupational hierarchy. And it does not stop at line management. More and more, technical and clerical staff see themselves in direct competition with overseas suppliers of similar skills, working through the international putting-out system.[4] Within this context it becomes clear that whilst a supply-side policy is imperative it cannot be simply a skills-enhancing process, organized and financed by the state. This is an important point to establish, given that it has become fashionable, in certain quarters, to offer such a policy as a panacea for the ills of the economy on both sides of the Atlantic (Reich 1991; Brown 1993). It is entirely right to recognize, as these authors have done, the importance of education and skills training for the development of a modern dynamic economy. It is also right to ensure that any bias in government support for industry that favours investment in physical plant at the expense of investment in people should be eliminated. Thus heavy investment in education and training is a *necessary* condition for rapid economic development and a move to full employment and can be effectively supported and encouraged by a

---

[4] Apparently Rolls Royce Aero Engines are putting out an increasing amount of engineering design work to firms in Brazil which can supply the relevant skills at a fraction of the in-house cost (personal correspondence with a Rolls Royce engineer).

modernizing state: but it is not a *sufficient* condition for development in the present context.

We are in danger of overemphasizing the significance of one particular element of a coherent supply-side strategy. Politically this is not very surprising, given that this particular policy is seen generally to be uncontroversial, and even very attractive, by a wide array of different interests. But it is clear that in the world economy we live in today, simply raising the supply of educated and skilled labour does not automatically lead to a higher pace of development within any specific community or nation.[5] A policy of investment in people has to be complemented by other elements of a supply-side strategy through which market forces can be guided or shaped to take up, and offer appropriate opportunities to, such educated and skilled people.

Nevertheless, it is the case that investing in education and training will tend to attract the attention of those organizations capable of supplying jobs on a global basis, the transnational corporations. Instead of seeking to attract investment and jobs by holding down wages and working conditions, for example as Britain has sought to do by opting out of the Social Chapter of the European Union, a country can compete by raising skills—that is, for the transnational corporation, a country can reduce the cost of acquiring skills: a process which might be described as a progressive form of social dumping. This puts the transnationals in the driving seat for a new international game—competing over subsidies for the expansion of a skilled work-force. Under the present rules of such a game, every nation can and will engage in it and we shall observe a competitive escalation of public investment of this sort. This will add a further dimension to the international competition for investment and jobs which is already going on and is resulting in a systemic downward pressure on wages and profits,[6] and a systemic upward pressure on investment subsidies.[7] Adding this further dimension will ultimately undermine the position of skilled workers in general as their relative scarcity is decreased following such public investment.

But it will be argued that whilst in the long term as a result of such policies, skills are removed as an effective constraint on national development, at this point in time they do pose a problem: the growth rate of the economy could be greater if skills availability was enhanced. It was certainly the case that the supply of training by employers collapsed in the 1980s. Margaret Stevens' (1994), econometric analysis was able to explain this in

---

[5] Historically, this has been clear for many smaller, peripheral economies which have sought to follow this route to development. For instance, the benefits of educational investment in Wales, Scotland, and Ireland have, to a considerable extent, been appropriated by England, and more distant economies.

[6] Witness the concerns of the European Commission, which responded by setting up the Ruding Committee in 1990.

[7] Witness the 1995 application by Ford Motor Company (UK) to the British government for substantial support for its proposed investment in a new model of Jaguar car.

the case of engineering apprenticeships by a combination of rising real interest rates and falling recruitment costs, proxied by an index of relative skill shortages. But why no recovery in the boom of the late 1980s? Stevens argues for the same explanation: high real interest rates and low skill shortages, relative to previous booms. Capacity shortages appear much more significant than skill shortages. This probably reflects the unique British experience whereby deindustrialization did not mean simply the contraction of manufacturing employment, but also a contraction in output and capacity. Capacity (in physical terms) was scrapped, but skills were simply unemployed, and available for the recovery when it happened. Stevens' results would suggest that these skills had not become entirely obsolescent—their availability was influencing investment in new skills. Of course, as time elapses and technology develops, and as people grow older, the position changes. It is quite possible that the mid-1990s has seen a reversal of the position, with skills rather than physical capacity being the binding constraint. Certainly Garry Young has argued that the substantial expansion of investment in industrial capacity in the late 1980s may be depressing the present rate of investment (see the interview reported in the *Financial Times*, 9 Mar. 1995, 27).

But one further qualification is necessary before we accept the skill shortage argument. Assuming the existence of monopsonistic or oligopsonistic power in the labour market, particularly likely in the case of specific skills, would imply the general existence of excess demand for skills at the going wage. Just as monopolies and oligopolies are always willing and indeed anxious to sell more product at the going price, and advertise the fact, so employers with some power in the market for skills are always willing and indeed anxious to take on more skilled labour at the going wage, and advertise the fact. Thus we have a perennial 'explanation' for so-called shortages of certain types of labour or skills. It simply reflects a normal state of the economy where employers have achieved certain positions of power. This particular characterization of the economy may have a particular resonance in a world where employers' power has been enhanced by a divide-and-rule strategy operated at an international level (see Cowling and Sugden 1994a).

Nevertheless, let us accept there is a case today for raising investment in skills, even in the absence of other complementary elements of a supply-side strategy, in order to remove an impediment to growth and the attainment of full employment. Paradoxically, gains from such policies can only be short-term. Despite the fact that in isolation such investment is seen as long-term, the nature of the international game means that it has to be evaluated in a short-term context. Since everyone can do it, and most countries see themselves as moving in this direction, gains can only be made by early movers, and they will only be transient.

Of course, the public funding of the acquisition of skills can be seen as socially productive investment, given that problems of appropriation of the benefits of such investment may mean socially sub-optimal investment within the free market economy. But we live in a world where the demand for skills is increasingly sensitive to their price, at any specific location. Measures to increase supply will certainly reduce price, but in this race the gains will be made by those offering the lowest price and the lowest price will be only a fraction of existing wages for skilled workers in the advanced industrial countries. We make the assumption that there is a vast reservoir of people with skills or skilling potential which the new system of transnational production can readily tap. Whilst raising the level of skills will ultimately imply the expansion of output, due to its increasing profitability, for the advanced industrial countries jobs for skilled people increasingly will only be on offer to those willing to work for much diminished real incomes. Within this system, the only people remaining outside this remorseless tendency are the few who control the strategies within which the system evolves. Access to this group is faced by enormous entry barriers. Recent privatizations in the advanced industrial countries and in Central and Eastern Europe, the former Soviet Union and the Third World have witnessed the take-over of substantial private power by those in control of the formerly public assets and offer a particularly dramatic instance of such entry barriers. As Lombardini (1992) predicted for the Soviet Union, 'privatization may provide the historical opportunity for a class of a few, very rich people to emerge'; and so for the countries of Central and Eastern Europe. As an incremental statement, the same observation can be made of the market economies.

For a solution to the problem of unemployment in the world today we have to go much further than traditional policies allow. Demand-side policies, although ameliorative in the short term, are increasingly undermined in the long term. Traditional supply-side policies aimed at attracting investment by acting to reduce business costs are ultimately self-defeating. Holding down wages and reducing taxes on profits may be seen as a logical response to the new situation, but only if it is accepted that the new situation is immutable. This cannot be the case. Rather than accept that investment and jobs will be forthcoming only if wages and profit taxes are significantly reduced, we have to begin to identify a coherent set of policies—a strategy—for moving away from the existing system.

A WAY FORWARD[8]

So how are we to proceed to establish the conditions necessary to secure full employment on a sustainable basis? We have seen that the system

[8] We have set out our thoughts on a way forward in some detail in Cowling and Sugden (1994a). What follows relates that analysis to the specific questions of capacity and full employment.

appears not to be meeting the aims of nations in terms of the provision of employment opportunities and is undermining efforts by nation-states to secure such employment opportunities. We have identified this systemic problem of the present market system as having its roots in powerful transnational organizations, the transnational corporations, outside the control of specific nation-states. The strategies of such organizations, whilst serving the aim of the élite groups (typically senior executives and the representatives of major shareholders) which control them, appear not to be serving the wider interest. Whilst it may be argued that there are winners and losers among nation-states in this process of international competition for jobs, ultimately communities in general will be disadvantaged by the international flexibility of the transnational corporations. A more active pursuit of corporations by communities simply increases the pace of decline in wages and profit taxes in the generally fruitless pursuit of full employment.

However, recognizing the root of the problem, whilst normally being a necessary condition for its alleviation, raises the difficult question of how the present imbalance of power between corporation and community can be rectified. How do we get away from a system where Ford Motor Company can confidently ask the British government for £100 million to secure the location of the production of one model in Britain? One thing is clear—there are no easy answers; but the situation now is becoming so critical that we have to begin to act. Not to act will mean we have effectively given up our right of national autonomy, and this will be true for all nations. To act means that we must challenge the corporate strategies of the major transnationals and, as part of that challenge, we must begin to put in place a set of policies which favour the development of a new system of production more congruent with the needs of the community than the present one. Thus we need to develop an industrial economic strategy reflecting the ambitions of the community, whether local, regional, national, or supra-national. The focus of such a strategy therefore will centre on converting a free market economy to a democratic market economy.

Precisely how we might move in the direction of a more democratic economy needs detailed attention, but four general points warrant some emphasis. First, a key feature is that people take on new roles: strategic decision-making will no longer be the exclusive preserve of an élite. Secondly, we advocate planning: just as the corporation plans for its own future within the market system, so should the community. Thirdly, markets in a democratic economy will become a tool for the community rather than for the élite in a free market system. And fourthly, government at various levels will play a vital, constant role in moving the economy towards a more diffuse, less concentrated structure of decision-making. To provide appropriate illustration of what we have in mind we turn to two important areas of policy which relate directly to the issue of capacity and which serve to identify more precisely the nature and content of the industrial strategy-making we advocate: the two cases are investment policy and technology policy.

Investment Policy

As already discussed, we see international flows of investment as an important determinant of unemployment in a particular economy. When judging the appropriateness of particular investment flows, however, we have first to recognize the simple fact that the strategic decisions resulting in that investment are being taken in the corporate interest and there is no reason why this should be congruent with the general interest. Consider, for example, the case of inward investment, the international pursuit of which has intensified markedly over recent years. The fact that inward investment results from corporate strategies formulated and pursued in the corporate interest does not rule out inward investment as inappropriate for an economy; rather what it means is that inward investment has to be positioned within a broader strategy within which it contributes to the democratic interest of the economy—a positive rather than negative policy, seeking ways in which the strategy of the inward investor can be adapted to the needs of the community.

In this context it is interesting to compare different policy approaches across countries. Whilst many countries do attach conditions to inward investment, some choose not to do so. For instance, the approach of successive British governments puts them in the latter group—a largely unqualified acceptance of the benefits of such investment (Sugden 1989). There has been little monitoring of its consequences, but Scottish experience reveals a lack of connection with the local economy by foreign transnationals (Turok 1993). Electronics plants set up as a result of inward investment were buying only 12 per cent of their components and material inputs from Scottish-based companies. Such observations are repeated in Ireland, which followed a similar policy of unqualified enthusiasm for inward investment: Kennedy *et al.* (1992) conclude that 'the Irish branches were often little more than production platforms which had few linkages with the rest of the economy. They did not therefore go far towards building an indigenous innovative capacity that would be more likely to endure.'

In contrast to the British and Irish position of unqualified enthusiasm, it is instructive to observe how the Japanese approach to inward investment has evolved (Bailey *et al.* 1994). In the earlier post-war period both inward and outward investment was tightly controlled. Since the 1960s there has been a gradual liberalization in response to international pressures, but throughout there has been an explicit awareness of the potential problems involved and barriers have been lowered only when it was felt that the industry in question was strong enough to compete with foreign investment.

Recent policy has taken on a more positive dimension: in certain industries the aim has been to bring in foreign transnationals with certain technological expertise lacking in Japan and to link them into domestic technology complexes. This would seem a particularly important lesson to learn from Japan. Generally the market finds it difficult to handle the innovation and diffusion of new technology, and where the source of that technology is a new foreign entrant there is an even more compelling case for government being an active partner in facilitating the process.

We suggest that policy should seek to expand and develop the various potential connections between inward investment and the domestic economy rather than simply leaving it as an isolated platform of production adding nothing to the underlying vitality of the economy. Whilst some conditions attached to inward investment may serve to curtail it, the contribution of successful industrial strategy-making to the attractiveness of the economy as a site for inward investment, for example in terms of its dynamism and the presence of a modern infrastructure, including a system of supplier firms, will serve to counter such effects. However, the fundamental question is one of creating the conditions for a successful economy rather than creating the conditions for a maximum rate of inward investment. Indeed the issue is not simply to position inward investment; rather it is to influence investment flows more generally, including outward investment; investment flows resulting from corporate strategies formulated and pursued in the corporate interest should be replaced by investment flows formulated and pursued in the democratic interest.

Technology Policy

The conventional view has it that the market should remain as the final arbiter of the direction of investment in new technology, with government simply raising the overall momentum by favouring R&D in general with a variety of policies: a broad-brush approach to the technological capacity of the nation. Obviously favoured areas of scientific activity do emerge, and often disastrously so; nuclear energy and Concorde are often regarded as important British examples. But, essentially, the market remains in control.

We would put the policy emphasis much more on the qualitative dimension. Whether R&D should be raised or not within a particular area of economic activity would be derivative of our overall industrial strategy. The socially incomplete nature of the decision structure within a free market economy means that the pattern of research and development cannot be expected to be socially optimal. For example, a pattern more consonant with the achievement of full employment will generally be sought.

Our view is that, since the development of new technology is so fundamental to the pace, direction, and form of industrial development, it is necessary to consider government involvement within a very broad perspective.

Without such perspective it is all too easy for technology policy to become transmuted into simply subsidizing corporate decisions on R&D. Given that we seek a more diffuse and deconcentrated economy, consistent with our aim to move away from a concentrated structure of decision-making, we need to be circumspect about a policy favouring scale. Automatic grants and tax incentives are then inappropriate, given that they disproportionately favour large firms because they formally account for most R&D, whereas much activity which can accurately be described as R&D goes unrecorded in smaller firms (Geroski 1990). Focusing away from large organizations is also likely to raise the rate of innovation, according to Scherer and Ross (1990). In their survey of innovation research, they conclude: 'very high concentration has a positive effect only in rare cases, and more often it is apt to retard progress by restricting the number of independent sources of initiative'. This concurs with the view that the large, hierarchical firm is, by its very nature, an essentially stifling organization where individual talent is all too often constrained by institutional straightjackets. Promoting an economy of smaller firms is likely to free more and more individuals to pursue their own and their firm's development and thus encourage innovative activity.

But a successful system for encouraging technological progress requires far more than simply shifting the balance of funding for R&D from large to small enterprises; especially important is the design of mutually supportive organizations—developing a collective entrepreneurialism (Best 1990; see also the contribution by Best and Forrant to this volume, Ch. 10) and arrangements to meet the collective needs of smaller firms; that is, public investment in a wider infrastructure rather than state aid in a traditional sense (Geroski 1990). There *are* scale economies associated with the development and use of new techniques, but these economies can be obtained without the need for large, hierarchical organizations—witness the experience of various technology centres in the Third Italy (Best 1990); the USA (Piore and Sabel 1984); Baden-Württemburg (Löhn and Stadelmeier 1990); and Denmark (Kristensen 1990). These represent successful, variegated examples of the non-hierarchical provision of technology to systems of small and medium-sized enterprises. Where current technologies require large-scale production, policy should include efforts to find ways of changing these technologies, having in mind that the original choice may have been dictated as much by power as efficiency considerations. There should be no assumption that existing technologies favouring scale are either optimal or invariant.

Our concern in the above policy discussions has been to identify how to begin to escape the stranglehold on economic capacity imposed by the prevailing transnational system of production and thereby move towards a dynamism capable of restoring full employment. We have looked at two areas, investment flows and technology, and focused on policy as a way of facilitating a process of endogenous development. Inward investment policy aims to fit the transnational to the needs of the community, in contrast to the present position when the community must fit the needs of the transnational. Technology policy aims to create the conditions where a new efficient, indigenous system of small and medium-sized enterprises is capable of evolving into a more significant force in the economy, thus creating one less dependent on the large, typically transnational corporation. But what of the international dimension and the reaction of the transnationals?

The International Dimension

Whereas the major corporations may find much that is advantageous to them in the development of community-based industrial strategies capable of raising the economic dynamism of any particular locality, a dynamism which cannot be achieved within the transnational organization of production, specific features of such industrial strategies will inevitably induce sharp, negative responses, for example disadvantageous changes in subsidy/tax systems. What is to prevent other countries exploiting the situation and undermining the strategy proposed within the crucial transition period before an independent capability is secured? This is clearly a major political issue. We have argued elsewhere that the specific institutional structures within the European Union, and the policy development that has taken place, allows progress to be made along the lines we advocate (Cowling and Sugden 1994a). Community (Union) policy actively seeks 'to avoid . . . monopolisation, excessive concentration and unfair public aids to national companies', and the aim of 'balanced development' of the Single Market identifies as one set of policies public support for the development of small companies through the promotion of a network of innovators (Commission 1990). The ability to move forward with such policies on a broad European front limits the options open to governments to compete for the favours of the transnational.

But as argued earlier the increasing threat to Europe has come from the rising tendency for the transnationals to make north–south moves. And it is interesting to see the present concern of the OECD to establish international rules for foreign direct investment (*Financial Times*, 10 Apr. 1995, 17). The aim appears to be to remove political risk by committing host countries to rules agreed on by the developed world. The focus for such policies is clearly the developing world, with impetus coming from the USA as the major source of this investment. Such policies, if put in place, will undoubtedly speed up the flow of foreign direct investment to the developing countries on terms advantageous to the transnationals. Communities at either end of that flow of investment will find it increasingly difficult to manage it in their own interests.

This would appear not to be the way forward. Rather than rules hatched within the developed countries, favouring the major transnationals with their roots in the developed world, but with their production ambitions within the developing world, we would advocate a co-operative approach between north and south over the process of restructuring world industry. This would involve an organized withdrawal from some activities by the developed world, coupled with an organized expansion in the developing world, with both sets of communities being involved in the process. The UNCTAD model would appear to fit in well with this approach and the experience of Japan and its linkages with developing countries may offer insights into a way forward (UNCTAD 1994). Adopting such an approach will undoubtedly be politically fraught, but ultimately it offers the possibility of sustainable full employment which we see as unattainable under the rules of the existing international competition for jobs.

REFERENCES

BAILEY, D., HARTE, G., and SUGDEN, R. (1994), *Transnationals and Governments: Recent Policies in Japan, France, Germany, the United States and Britain* (London: Routledge).

BARREL, R., PAIN, N., and YOUNG, G. (1993), 'A Cross-Country Comparison of the Demand for Labour in Europe', paper presented at EMRU Labour Economics Study Group.

BEAN, C. R. (1994), 'European Unemployment: A Survey', *Journal of Economic Literature*, 32 (June): 573–619.

BEST, M. (1990), *The New Competition: Institutions of Industrial Restructuring* (Cambridge: Policy Press).

BLINDER, A. (1988), 'The Challenge of Unemployment', *American Economic Press*, 78, 1–15.

BROWN, G. (1993), 'Labour's Economic Approach' (London: Labour Party).

Commission of the European Communities (1990), 'Industrial Policy in an Open and Competitive Environment: Guidelines for a Community Approach', working paper, Brussels.

COWLING, K., and SUGDEN, R. (1994*a*), *Beyond Capitalism: Towards a New World Economic Order* (London: Frances Pinter).

—— —— (1994*b*), 'Behind the Market Facade: A Reassessment of the Theory of the Firm', revised version, November, University of Warwick.

DICKEN, P. (1992), *Global Shift: The Internationalization of Economic Activity* (London, Paul Chapman).

DUNNING, J. H. (1993), *Multinational Enterprises and the Global Economy* (New York: Addison-Wesley).

GEROSKI, P. (1990), 'Encouraging Investment in Science and Technology', in K. Cowling, and R. Sugden (eds.), *A New Economic Policy for Britain: Essays on the Development of Industry* (Manchester, Manchester University Press).

HYMER, S. H. (1972), 'The Multinational Corporation and the Law of Uneven Development', in J. N. Bhagwati (ed.), *Economics and World Order* (London: Macmillan).

KENNEDY, K., GIBLIN, T., and McHUGH, D. (1992), *The Economic Development of Ireland in the Twentieth Century* (London: Routledge).

KRISTENSEN, P. (1990), 'Education, Technical Culture and Regional Prosperity in Denmark', in G. Sweeney, T. Casey, P. Kristensen, and R. Prujai (eds.), *Education, Technical Culture and Regional Prosperity* (Dublin: SICA).

KRUGMAN, P. R., and LAWRENCE, R. Z. (1994), 'Trade, Jobs and Wages', *Scientific American*, April, 44–9.

LEAMER, E. (1994), 'Trade, Wages and Revolving Door Ideas', Working Paper 4716, Cambridge, Mass.: National Bureau of Economic Research, Apr.

LÖHN, J., and STADELMEIER, M. (1990), 'The Baden Württemberg Model of Technology Transfer', in K. Cowling, and H. Tomann (eds.), *Industrial Policy after 1992: An Anglo-German Experience* (London: Anglo-German Foundation).

LOMBARDINI, S. (1992), 'Privatization in Market Economies and for Building a Market Economy', in F. Targetti (ed.), *Privatization in Europe: West and East Experiences* (Aldershot: Dartmouth).

NORTON, R. (1986), 'Industrial Policy and American Renewal', *Journal of Economic Literature*, 24: 1–40.

PIORE, M., and SABEL, C. (1984), *The Second Industrial Divide: Possibility for Prosperity* (New York, Basic Books).

REICH, R. (1991), *The Work of Nations* (New York: Knopf).

ROWTHORN, R. (1995a), 'Capital Formation and Unemployment', *Oxford Review of Economic Policy*, 10/1: 26–39.

—— (1995b), 'A Simulation Model of North–South Trade', ESRC Centre for Business Research, University of Cambridge, Working Paper 9, May.

SACHS, J. D., and SHATZ, H. J. (1994), 'Trade and Jobs in U.S. Manufacturing', *Brookings Papers on Economic Activity*, 1: 1–84.

SCHERER, F. M., and ROSS, D. (1990), *Industrial Market Structure and Economic Performance* (Boston: Houghton Mifflin).

STEVENS, M. (1994), 'An Investment Model for the Supply of Training by Employers', *Economic Journal*, 104 (May): 556–70.

SUGDEN, R. (1989), 'The Warm Welcome for Foreign Owned Transnationals from Recent British Governments', in M. Chick (ed.), *Government–Industry Relations post-1945* (Gloucester: Edward Elgar).

TUROK, I. (1993), 'Loose Connections? Foreign Investment and Local Linkage in Silicon Glen', Strathclyde Papers on Planning, University of Strathclyde.

UNCTAD (1994), 'Trade Policies, Structural Adjustments and Economic Reform: Development Relating to Structural Adjustment Policies in Developed Countries and their Implications', Trade and Development Board.

—— (1995), Database, Division on Transnational Corporations and Investment.

UNITED NATIONS (1993), *World Investment Report 1993. Transnational Corporations and Integrated International Production* (New York, United Nations).

WOOD, A. (1994), *North–South Trade, Employment, and Inequality: Changing Fortunes in a Skill-Driven World* (Oxford: Clarendon Press).

YOUNG, G. (1994a), 'The Influence of Foreign Factor Prices and Industrial Taxation on Fixed Investment in the UK', National Institute Discussion Paper, 66.

—— (1994b), 'International Competitiveness, International Taxation and Domestic Investment', *National Institute Economic Review*, May, 44–8.

INDEX

Note: Most references are to United Kingdom and manufacturing industry unless otherwise specified. Page references with n indicate footnotes.